AF701745

The Limits of Judicialization

Latin America was one of the earliest and most enthusiastic adopters of what has come to be known as the judicialization of politics – the use of law and legal institutions as tools of social contestation to curb the abuse of power in government, resolve policy disputes, and enforce and expand civil, political, and socioeconomic rights. Almost forty years into this experiment, *The Limits of Judicialization* brings together a cross-disciplinary group of scholars to assess the role that law and courts play in Latin American politics. Featuring studies of hot-button topics including abortion, state violence, judicial corruption, and corruption prosecutions, this volume argues that the institutional and cultural changes that empowered courts – the "judicialization superstructure" – often fall short of the promise of greater accountability and rights protection. Illustrative and expansive, this volume offers a truly interdisciplinary analysis of the limits of judicialized politics.

SANDRA BOTERO is Associate Professor at Universidad del Rosario in Bogota. She specializes in studying the relationship between the judiciary and democracy, as well as electoral behavior, with a regional focus on Latin America.

DANIEL BRINKS is Professor of Government and Law at the University of Texas, Austin. He is the author of multiple books, including *The DNA of Constitutional Justice in Latin America* (2018, with Abby Blass), which was awarded APSA's C. Herman Pritchett Prize for Best Book on Law and Courts, and *Understanding Institutional Weakness: Power and Design in Latin American Institutions* (2020, with Steve Levitsky and Maria Victoria Murillo).

EZEQUIEL GONZALEZ-OCANTOS is Associate Professor of Political Science and Professorial Fellow of Nuffield College at the University of Oxford. He is the author of *Shifting Legal Visions: Judicial Change and Human Rights Trials in Latin America* (2016) and *The Politics of Transitional Justice in Latin America: Power Norms and Capacity Building* (2020).

The Limits of Judicialization

From Progress to Backlash in Latin America

Edited by

SANDRA BOTERO

Universidad del Rosario

DANIEL M. BRINKS

University of Texas at Austin

EZEQUIEL A. GONZALEZ-OCANTOS

University of Oxford

CAMBRIDGE
UNIVERSITY PRESS

CAMBRIDGE
UNIVERSITY PRESS

University Printing House, Cambridge CB2 8BS, United Kingdom

One Liberty Plaza, 20th Floor, New York, NY 10006, USA

477 Williamstown Road, Port Melbourne, VIC 3207, Australia

314–321, 3rd Floor, Plot 3, Splendor Forum, Jasola District Centre, New Delhi – 110025, India

103 Penang Road, #05–06/07, Visioncrest Commercial, Singapore 238467

Cambridge University Press is part of the University of Cambridge.

It furthers the University's mission by disseminating knowledge in the pursuit of education, learning, and research at the highest international levels of excellence.

www.cambridge.org
Information on this title: www.cambridge.org/9781009098342
DOI: 10.1017/9781009093859

© Cambridge University Press 2022

This publication is in copyright. Subject to statutory exception and to the provisions of relevant collective licensing agreements, no reproduction of any part may take place without the written permission of Cambridge University Press.

First published 2022

A catalogue record for this publication is available from the British Library.

Library of Congress Cataloging-in-Publication Data
NAMES: Botero Cabrera, Sandra, editor. | Brinks, Daniel M., 1961– editor. | Gonzalez Ocantos, Ezequiel, 1984– editor.
TITLE: The limits of judicialization : from progress to backlash in Latin America / edited by Sandra Botero, Universidad del Rosario; Daniel M. Brinks, University of Texas at Austin; Ezequiel A. Gonzalez-Ocantos, University of Oxford.
DESCRIPTION: Cambridge, United Kingdom ; New York, NY : Cambridge University Press, 2022. | "This book originated at a conference we organized in October 2019 at the Universidad del Rosario, Bogota, Colombia."–ECIP Acknowledgements. | Includes bibliographical references and index.
IDENTIFIERS: LCCN 2022008778 (print) | LCCN 2022008779 (ebook) | ISBN 9781009098342 (hardback) | ISBN 9781009096164 (paperback) | ISBN 9781009093859 (epub)
SUBJECTS: LCSH: Political questions and judicial power–Latin America–Congresses.
CLASSIFICATION: LCC KG608.A6 L56 2022 (print) | LCC KG608.A6 (ebook) | DDC 347.8/012–dc23/eng/20220429
LC record available at https://lccn.loc.gov/2022008778
LC ebook record available at https://lccn.loc.gov/2022008779

ISBN 978-1-009-09834-2 Hardback

Cambridge University Press has no responsibility for the persistence or accuracy of URLs for external or third-party internet websites referred to in this publication and does not guarantee that any content on such websites is, or will remain, accurate or appropriate.

Contents

Figures

Tables

Contributors

Viviana Baraybar, DPhil student, Department of Politics and International Relations, University of Oxford, UK

Santiago Basabe-Serrano, Professor, Department of Political Studies, FLACSO, Ecuador

João Guilherme Bastos dos Santos, Postdoctoral researcher, Brazilian National Institute of Science and Technology for Digital Democracy, Brazil

Laura Bernal-Bermúdez, Assistant Professor, Faculty of Law, Pontificia Universidad Javeriana, Colombia

Sandra Botero, Associate Professor, Faculty of International, Political and Urban Studies, Universidad del Rosario, Colombia

Rachel E. Bowen, Associate Professor, Department of Political Science, Ohio State University, USA

Daniel Brinks, Professor of Government and Law, Department of Government, University of Texas at Austin, USA

Jorge Contesse, Associate Professor, Rutgers Law School, Rutgers University, USA

Luciano Da Ros, Assistant Professor, Department of Sociology and Political Science, Federal University of Santa Catarina, Brazil

Sofía Forero-Alba, Researcher, Center for the Study of Law, Justice and Society – Dejusticia, Colombia

Janice K. Gallagher, Assistant Professor, Department of Political Science, Rutgers University Newark, USA

Camila Gianella, Assistant Professor, Pontificia Universidad Católica del Perú, Peru and Researcher at the Chr. Michelsen Institute, Bergen, Norway

Ezequiel Gonzalez-Ocantos, Associate Professor, Department of Politics and International Relations and Professorial Fellow, Nuffield College, University of Oxford, UK

Mariana Mota Prado, Professor, Faculty of Law, University of Toronto, Canada

Julio Ríos-Figueroa, Professor, Department of Law, ITAM, Mexico

Marta Rodriguez de Assis Machado, Professor of Law, Getúlio Vargas Foundation School of Law, Brazil

Juan Carlos Rodriguez-Raga, Associate Professor, Department of Political Science, Universidad de los Andes, Colombia

Alba Ruibal, Full-Time Researcher, National Scientific and Technological Research Council, Argentina

Esther Solano Gallego, Assistant Professor, Federal University of São Paulo, Brazil

Matthew M. Taylor, Professor, School of International Service, American University, USA

Acknowledgments

This book originated at a conference we organized in October 2019 at the Universidad del Rosario, Bogota, Colombia. As editors, we would like to thank the university's Dirección de Investigación for generously funding the project, as well as the team at the Facultad de Estudios Internacionales, Políticos y Urbanos, for helping us with the organization. At Cambridge University Press, Sara Doskow and Rachel Blaifeder gave us excellent editorial guidance throughout, and Cameron Daddis, Dhivya Elavazhagan, Jadyn Fauconier-Herry, Joan Dale Lace and Joshua Penney helped us get the manuscript across the finish line. Vicky De Negri did a wonderful job with the index.

1

Working in New Political Spaces

The Checkered History of Latin American Judicialization

Sandra Botero, Daniel Brinks and Ezequiel Gonzalez-Ocantos

INTRODUCTION

This book brings together an interdisciplinary group of scholars to take stock of the role that law and courts have played and are playing today in Latin American politics. Beginning in the 1980s, Latin American courts, especially supreme and constitutional courts, left behind decades of subservience and irrelevance to become crucial political actors across the region. In the intervening decades, the law and legal institutions gained prominence as tools for social contestation and change. As never before, judges entered the political maelstrom, serving as arbiters between the branches of government in heated debates over policy and the reach of presidential or legislative prerogatives. Working with prosecutors, courts also investigated corruption – not only, as in the past, the misdeeds of prior administrations but also those of people still in power. In the process, politicians began to realize that laws and constitutions perhaps meant mostly as window dressing were becoming more costly, since courts might actually hold them to the standards they were creating. Motivated by these developments, individuals and social movements turned the courts into battlegrounds for the realization and expansion of civil, political, cultural, and socioeconomic rights.

Latin America was one of the earliest and most enthusiastic adopters of the judicialization of politics. The region saw a wave of changes beginning around 1980 that created what we call the "superstructure" of judicialization: institutional changes including but not limited to the move toward a social rights constitutionalism (see, e.g., Brinks, Gauri, and Shen 2015), and cultural changes that emphasized the transformative power of constitutional law and the political mission of legal actors (see, e.g., Couso, Huneeus, and Sieder 2010). Despite some misgivings about the "government of judges," academics, practitioners, and activists generally saw in the emergence of more powerful courts and more meaningful constitutions a beacon of hope: a new set of actors and institutions that promised to control and punish abuses of power, redress egregious wrongs, and challenge entrenched inequalities in a region in desperate need of progress on all these fronts. But to what extent have Latin American judicial institutions lived up to these expectations? What exactly did these new institutions promise and what did they actually deliver?

Forty years into this experiment, it is clear that expectations have not always been met. The contributions to this volume document the ways in which, despite many successes, the promise of judicialization falls short when the superstructure of judicialization[1] remains unmoored from deeper social and political roots, and when it produces heavy demands that cannot be met by weak states and institutions. As a pioneer in judicialization, Latin America can share lessons and experiences that travel readily to other parts of the world.

Admittedly, the volume focuses on the liabilities side of the balance sheet more than other studies have. But ours is not a critique of judicialization that either regurgitates the well-known counter-majoritarian objection to judicial power (Waldron 2006) or bluntly characterizes courts as "hollow hopes" (Rosenberg 1991). We accept that judicial branches in Latin America have been formally empowered through democratic processes to exercise control over policy decisions and indecisions, and thus promote the enjoyment of a wide range of rights. Expansive judicialization, however counter-majoritarian, now has a clear place in the constitutional order. It is also an unavoidable feature of the political landscape in nearly every democracy on the globe, and even in some countries with questionable democratic credentials.

Moreover, in deeply unequal societies, judicialization definitely plays a role in guaranteeing basic preconditions for the exercise of democratic citizenship (Roa Roa 2019). Indeed, multiple studies have shown that, under certain conditions, judiciaries help advance rights and act as checks on excessive power (see, e.g., Nunes 2010; Rodríguez Raga 2011; Botero 2017; Cano Blandón 2017; Sigal et al. 2017; Antía and Vairo 2019).

[1] See the later section on the judicialization "superstructure" and its limits for a discussion of what we mean by the term.

Latin America is not alone in empowering courts in this way. Some countries in Asia – most notably India – and Africa – most notably South Africa – have seen a similar expansion of the role of constitutional justice in their politics, with nontrivial consequences for the effective enjoyment of rights (see Baxi 1985; Dembowski 2001; Langford et al. 2011; White and Perelman 2011; Bonilla-Maldonado 2013; Kapiszewski, Silverstein, and Kagan 2013). The phenomenon is sufficiently widespread that it has prompted books with titles such as *Constitutionalism of the Global South* (Bonilla-Maldonado 2013) – a phrase that describes a true phenomenon even as it glosses over the wide variety of experiences that can be found in the Global South.

Taking stock, of course, requires a measuring stick. We should not simply cast about for a number of happy stories, and then declare victory. We must also reject unrealistic benchmarks for determining the success or failure of attempts at social progress through judicialization. Following Brinks, Levitsky, and Murillo (2019), who use the statutory goal to evaluate the strength or weakness of institutions, we believe we should measure success or failure with reference to what an institution was meant to achieve. Read naively, many of the new constitutions the courts were working with, and the rights people sought to enforce through the judicialization of politics, promised nothing less than a social, cultural, economic, and political revolution. If one interprets civil rights guarantees as promises of fully realized political agency and inclusion; socioeconomic rights as promises that the government will fulfill everyone's material needs; environmental rights as promises that the government will deliver a clean environment; equality rights as promises that the government will eliminate inequalities of race, ethnicity, and gender, among others; and indigenous rights as promises that indigenous peoples will realize their aspirations for territorial autonomy, full equality, and cultural respect, then anything short of utopia, several decades later, is a broken promise.

But surely this is not the right standard. The realization of a fully democratic society – through the struggle for accountability, the promise of social justice, the enforcement of fundamental rights, and all the other aspirations that can be found in Latin America's constitutions – is bound to be a perpetually unfinished project, one in which goalposts move as governments and societal demands change. It is also a fight that cannot simply be won in court; it requires the activation of multiple institutional levers, and ultimately the transformation of society itself. If a constitutional project is a journey without a fixed final destination, then the benchmark by which we might measure its success is the quality and characteristics of that journey.

On this point, one of us has said elsewhere that "the driving motivation for designers of systems of constitutional justice is to craft political spaces that will reflect their interests, serve their purposes, and secure a role for their successors in governing in the future" (Brinks and Blass 2018: 3–4). Judicialization was driven in large part by the inclusion of social and economic rights, environmental rights, and indigenous rights, together with the creation of mechanisms for their enforcement. Generally, these were elements that the left had sought to include in Latin American constitutions since the 1980s (Brinks and Blass 2018; Brinks and Sandoval Rojas 2019). As a *constitutional* project that relies on rights and courts, one of the core goals was to include or strengthen minority voices in the decision-making around rights-related issues. If this is the objective, then the standard is less whether or to what extent the judicialization of politics has moved us closer to utopia and more whether it has created a new form of politics in which previously suppressed voices are being heard on these issues, and in which previously marginalized groups have a better chance of advancing their agendas.

There were other elements of the judicialization project, also addressed in this book, that were a project from the right (sometimes in cooperation with the left). In particular, this is true of initiatives to strengthen anti-corruption and prosecutorial institutions (Rodríguez-Garavito 2010). As to these innovations, the goal was to improve what has been described as "horizontal accountability" (O'Donnell 1999; Mainwaring and Welna 2003), sometimes in an effort to retrench and restrain the state as countries adopted neoliberal policies (Gathii 2019). The measure of institutional strength, or success, for these institutional innovations will be the degree to which those in power now have to answer for their actions, including those associated with illegal rent-seeking practices.

At the same time, we want to go beyond the extent to which the institutions that underpin the judicialization of politics achieved their own goals. We therefore also consider some of the unintended consequences of strengthening these institutions for counter-majoritarian participation and horizontal accountability, and explore the reasons why things might have gone awry, even as institutions were fulfilling their stated purpose. A few chapters discuss, for instance, the ways in which conservative forces, sometimes reflecting longstanding entrenched interests, have taken advantage of the same counter-majoritarian spaces that were designed to include marginalized groups. Although surely an unexpected outcome from most designers' perspectives, this is, perhaps, a measure of the strength of these institutional spaces. Other chapters look not only at the ways in which prosecutorial institutions have been captured by partisan interests – a clear violation of their institutional purpose – but also at the times when their zeal and success – a measure of institutional strength – have been enormously disruptive of the political system, with clearly deleterious consequences for governance and democracy. Given this complex reality, our conclusions and critiques are necessarily nuanced, as befits the complex and multivalent nature of the institutional innovations we are evaluating, even after considering the fact that there have been many unalloyed successes along the way.

With all this in mind, the book examines the promises and pitfalls of judicialization without failing to recognize that courts have often improved the quality of democracy, effectively expanding the horizons of political possibility for both majorities and minorities. The aim is to call attention to processes and pathologies that the architects of judicialization's institutional superstructure overlooked or failed to anticipate, and that prevent the project from realizing its full potential. In other words, we choose to focus on what is not working properly as an opportunity to shed light on what can be adjusted going forward. Specifically, we demonstrate that deficits in state capacity, variation in the degree of social embeddedness of judicial policy mandates, and pervasive judicial corruption diminish courts' ability and willingness to fulfill their new constitutional role. Furthermore, the book explores instances in which the expectations of the architects of judicialization have been met all too well, especially in terms of strengthening mechanisms of horizontal accountability. At times, the aggressive pursuit of anticorruption is exactly what was contemplated, and in that respect a measure of effective judicialization, but nevertheless does more harm than good due to the broader context in which it takes place.

The various chapters thus evaluate whether the progressive ideals embedded in various constitutional and legal frameworks actually came to fruition, and examine the openness of these systems to a new form of politics that might be more inclusive. In particular, the contributors show that the institutional and cultural changes that empowered courts and put them at the center of policy disputes often fell short of the promised social and political advances for two main reasons. First, courts too often failed to account for persistent state weakness, pushing policies ahead of the bureaucratic infrastructure needed to support them; and, second, courts' and activists' inability to root change in robust structures of social support often led to political and societal backlash that jeopardized reform efforts.

The first shortcoming is neither surprising nor fatal to the project that animated the judicialization of politics – after all, weak states and failing bureaucracies are perennial problems in Latin America, and the failure to accomplish a policy objective may not be especially attributable to the fact that the demand came through legal mobilization rather than more traditional forms of doing politics. A legislative push to fix the public health system in Colombia may have been just as likely to fail as a judicial one; an executive-led attempt to clean up a waterway or address prison conditions may find as many real-world obstacles as a judge-led one. But some of the chapters do show that pushing ahead of what the context could bear and testing the limits of newly minted judicial prerogatives without first fixing other issues can have destructive consequences for the very goals the superstructure of judicialization was meant to advance. The lesson here is not only that courts face enormous challenges when it comes to effecting social and political change but also that courts themselves can pose significant challenges to the democratic regimes they are a part of if they are not sufficiently transparent or if they are excessively empowered relative to other state institutions. Moreover, without proper checks on their own power, courts and prosecutors themselves begin to stretch or even break the rules, contributing to the weakening of democracy.

The second shortcoming, on the other hand, is more aptly a critique of the judicialization model itself – conservative publics and power structures are not exactly new in Latin America, but perhaps the failure was to imagine that simply giving minorities the ability to voice their demands through the courts would be enough to overcome resistance to progressive change. In this regard, some of the chapters can be read to suggest that the creation of robust rights and redress mechanisms may have encouraged social movements to rely on legal strategies as shortcuts, pursuing narrow agendas defined around a particular right, with a limited number of NGO-based supporters and, often, support from abroad. The alternative might have been to embark on the more arduous journey of constructing a broader agenda and building a wider coalition in support of their goals. If this is so, then perhaps the main shortcoming of the judicialization of politics around rights-based claims is that in many cases it has severed – or, perhaps more fairly, not helped to develop – the connection between progressive movements and mass politics.

One group of essays directly explores the limits of institutional change. Studies of Mexico, Colombia, and Guatemala show that the prosecution of complex crimes perpetrated by public officials, including corruption, drug-trafficking, corporate crimes, and human rights violations, can be acutely compromised not only by a backlash orchestrated by powerful political and economic actors but also by deficits in basic investigative capacity. In the case of struggles over gender equality and abortion rights in Argentina, Brazil, Colombia, Mexico, and Peru, backlash and countermovements by conservative forces have been an important limit to the rights-affirming promise of judicialization, especially when judicial interventions are not accompanied by mass-based activism and effective public outreach strategies. Clearly, simply adding a layer of new institutions was not enough to overcome a longstanding and mutually reinforcing topography of state weakness and entrenched social, political, and economic actors.

Another group of essays reveals a microcosm of the same story – institutions too weak to overcome societal resistance – taking place in the interior of the institutions themselves. These chapters look at the informal networks of nepotism and corruption that undermine judicial functioning in Mexico, Ecuador, and Peru. The networks survived processes of formal judicial empowerment, and continue to color the way the courts operate. It is tempting to resurrect the old chestnut about how the judicialization of politics will lead to the politicization of the judiciary, except that these chapters make it clear that the politicization of the judiciary long predated more recent attempts by new groups to pursue their goals through law.

What is new in the story of institutional weakness that runs through these two groups of essays is the nature of the aspirational institutions of the judicialization superstructure (Brinks, Levitsky, and Murillo 2019, 2020). One goal of this institutional change was to alter, in two senses, the way in which politics is done: it was meant to eliminate the old ways of doing law, in favor of more meritocratic, even technocratic approaches; and it was meant to give previously underrepresented groups such as women, gender-nonconforming groups, and other minorities a stronger voice in pursuing equality. To the extent that old ways of doing law endure, and old power structures continue to dominate judicial decision-making, this is a clear failure of the model. The mere presence of contested politics over questions of sexual and reproductive rights or transitional justice, on the other hand, cannot be seen as an institutional failure, since, as we argued earlier, the goal was not to impose a particular solution but to create spaces for a more robust and inclusive politics of constitutional meaning (Brinks and Blass 2018). Backlash and resistance must be seen as merely part of the process by which any society works out the practical application of its constitutional commitments, even if we are not always pleased with the outcomes.

Finally, there is a series of essays on the wholesale criminalization of grand corruption, possibly the ultimate and most recent form of judicial intervention in Latin American politics. These chapters dissect the tension between, on the one hand, a strong form of judicialization that proceeds in line with reformers' aspirations and, on the other, the wider consequences of these prosecutions in a weak institutional context for the construction of the rule of law and good governance more generally. Specifically, studies of the *Lava Jato* operation in Brazil and Peru show clearly empowered prosecution services and courts training their eyes on systemic corruption. These investigations are unprecedented in many ways, and are, at times, exactly what many hoped for in that they address actual corruption and the abuse of power. At the same time, especially because they are targeting widespread practices that affect every corner of the political system, they risk undermining the values they claim to promote. Moreover, they also risk unleashing unproductive clashes with the establishment that compromise judicial integrity, fueling anti-political sentiments and backlash against fundamental rights. In these cases, the weak institutions, at least initially, are not the legal ones but all those that surround the legal complex, particularly the institutions of ordinary politics. Ultimately, however, that surrounding weakness returns to infect the legal complex as well.

WHY ASSESS THE CONSEQUENCES OF JUDICIALIZATION?

In interrogating the promise and ultimate impact of judicialization, we dialogue with three edited collections that defined the contours of the field of Latin American judicial politics: *The Judicialization of Politics in Latin America* (Sieder, Schjolden, and Angell 2005), *Cultures of Legality: Judicialization and Political Activism in Latin America* (Couso, Huneeus, and Sieder 2010), and *Courts in Latin America* (Helmke and Ríos Figueroa 2011). These volumes traced the initial stages in the evolution of courts and law after the third wave of democratization, teaching us that, perhaps irreversibly, the judiciary has established itself as a preeminent site of political contestation.

Sieder, Schjolden, and Angell's book chronicled the journey of courts from dormant institutions into arenas of rights expansion, legal pluralism, and accountability. The editors highlighted the role of independence-enhancing reforms and the transnational diffusion of rights-centered legal discourses via social mobilization, as the factors pushing courts toward greater activism. In this book, we find that these transformative forces often suffer from a lack of domestic support, and that NGO-based legal mobilization can fail to build the necessary social and political base that makes progress sustainable. Their work also asked whether judicialization is indeed an effective tool for sociopolitical change. Written in the thick of this political "awakening," Sieder, Schjolden, and Angell's book offered more and less positive examples, but could not yet hazard an overall assessment. It did, however, call attention to the democratic deficit of policymaking through the courts and the risk of seeing the judicialization of politics morph into the politicization of the judiciary, both issues that are documented in this volume.

Five years later, Couso, Huneeus, and Sieder's (2010) collection sought to make sense of judicialization by looking at the cultural changes it embodied. The editors observed that more aspects of social and political life are now channeled using the language of the law, and that the institutional toolkit available to articulate claims in this way has expanded considerably. But rather than providing a general overview of the phenomenon, or assessing its causes, the book had a more specific goal: to identify the cultural underpinnings of the judicial revolution. As the editors put it, "law exists in the discursive realm and – perhaps more than other political practices – relies on symbolic practices for its legitimacy" (Couso, Huneeus, and Sieder 2010: 4). The book therefore zoomed in on the role of ideas, language, and informal practices in the judicialization of politics. Contributors documented how the shift away from legal formalism in both the courts and related fields (i.e., the academy, the bar) engendered more activist judicial role conceptions. They also explored ideological and organizational changes in civil society, which increased citizens' predisposition to transform political claims into legal battles. Like the previous volume, the focus was not on the consequences or effectiveness of judicialization. But far from being overly optimistic, it suggested that the coexistence of judicialization with weak states that struggle to implement public policies was reason for concern. We too pick up the theme of weak states, now with ten years of additional experience.

Helmke and Ríos-Figueroa's (2011) volume, the most recent of the three but already a decade old, also documented the new place of courts in Latin American politics. This last book went further, investigating the implications of judicialization. Do courts actually behave as arbiters of interbranch conflict? And do they actually protect and expand rights? These questions reflect the two functions of courts that the editors mapped out in their introduction: horizontal and vertical control. A collection of essays then provided evidence that Latin American courts are generally more predisposed to fulfill their horizontal control function than their vertical control function. Building on this observation, we note that excesses of horizontal control can wreak havoc in a weak political system; and show how the weaknesses of social, political, and infrastructural support can undermine the best efforts to impose vertical controls.

In line with the spirit of the times, the three volumes rightly recognized that something fundamental had changed in the character and thus the transformative potential of the region's judicial institutions. While not naively optimistic, all of them exude a newly found sense of possibility, with the law seemingly carving out productive paths to social and political change. They tell compelling stories of disadvantaged groups or aggrieved individuals successfully mounting court challenges against powerful actors, judges making it harder for presidents to govern in a delegative fashion, or courts otherwise shaping the politics of a country. These things simply did not happen, or were extremely rare, before this new era of judicialization.

The broader literature on Latin American judicial politics also offers plenty of examples in which judicialization shifted power inequalities, disrupted policymaking inertia, and moved politics in progressive directions (for reviews, see Kapiszewski and Taylor 2008; Gonzalez-Ocantos 2019). For instance, high courts in the region have handed down rulings that challenged the retrenchment of welfare benefits during periods of neoliberal adjustment (Rodríguez-Garavito 2011; Kapiszewski 2012; Brinks and Forbath 2014; Botero 2017; Brinks and Sandoval Rojas 2019), or recognized the rights of sexual minorities (Wilson 2009, 2011; Albarracín 2011; Díez 2015). Work on Argentina shows that the judiciary in general (Gonzalez-Ocantos 2016), and the Supreme Court in particular (Merlinsky 2009; Herrero 2011; Botero 2018), occasionally provide visibility and relief for citizens in disputes over human rights violations, housing, the environment, and social policy. Others have traced how democratization turned Mexico's Supreme Court into an effective referee in disputes between political parties (Magaloni 2003), branches of the federal government, and federal and state administrations (Domingo 2000; Ríos-Figueroa 2007), and how judges themselves championed reforms to improve judicial quality (Ingram 2015). Furthermore, scholars celebrate the transformative role of Colombia's Constitutional Court in advancing socioeconomic rights, including the rights of millions of internally displaced citizens (Albarracín 2011; Sandoval Rojas 2013; Uprimny and Durán 2014; Rodríguez-Garavito and Rodríguez-Franco 2015), as well as in helping regulate interactions between political and military actors in conflict-related matters (Ríos-Figueroa 2016). Finally, research on Costa Rica describes the crucial role that the Supreme Court's constitutional chamber played in expanding and enforcing health and gay rights, among others (Wilson 2011).

It is clear that Latin American courts now exercise their horizontal and vertical control functions more often and more consequentially than perhaps they ever did, and that these interventions can have a positive impact on politics and on the everyday lives of citizens. Three decades after the onset of this wave of judicialization, however, we find ourselves in a better position to assess the extent to which courts really matter and, especially, when and why they do not, highlighting notable successes alongside notable failures grounded in weak states, resistant politicians, and a lack of social support.

The story that runs through all of our rich case studies indicates that while the judicial revolution successfully built a new institutional framework that significantly and irreversibly disrupted politics and rights enforcement in the region, these institutions and the solutions they propose too often clash with entrenched vested interests, sometimes fail to take root in the social fabric, and occasionally seek to build upon states that are too weak to support the weight. The volume thus draws attention to the precarious political, social, and bureaucratic foundations of the institutional superstructure that inspired judicialization. Many of the chapters trace the ways in which this precarious foundation can lead to limited court impact and sociopolitical backlash, with important implications for judicial legitimacy and stability.

Given this focus, we depart from previous work in important ways. First, we take backlash seriously. In the judicial politics literature, backlash is often understood as what happens when court decisions galvanize and mobilize opposition (Rosenberg 1991; Klarman 1994, 2006; Voeten 2020). Focusing on the United States, some scholars argue that since almost every consequential court (or policy) decision is bound to produce some level of resistance, we shouldn't exaggerate the importance or analytical purchase of the concept (Keck 2009). This back and forth, with policy wins alternating between progressive and conservative forces, is "normal" backlash, in the sense that it is exactly the politics one might expect from any attempt to change society. Indeed, the Latin American experience demonstrates the need to study backlash as an integral part of a dialectical process in which movements and counter-movements turn to legal mobilization (Lehoucq 2021). Consequently, our volume analyzes how the progressive forms of legal mobilization at the heart of the judicialization of politics interact with counter-mobilization, also through judicialization, that seeks to limit the expansion of fundamental rights or horizontal accountability. We further look at how reformism through the courts encounters staunch resistance from actors within the state, including members of the political and judicial establishments. If we accept the premise that judicialization was meant not to impose particular outcomes but to create new arenas for contesting various goals, we should view this as a healthy, albeit judicialized, politics of change. Success for a politics of judicialization might mean the strengthening of previously excluded voices, but it surely cannot mean the imposition of a progressive outcome regardless of social resistance, even if, in our view, this leaves us further from utopia than we might wish.

In contexts of greater institutional weakness and fledgling judicialization, however, backlash has the potential to prove much more consequential. In these contexts, backlash may not just represent a short-term threat to court-mandated policy changes or social movement goals, but an existential threat to the newly created institutions and processes on which judicialization depends. In countries like Guatemala, we have seen backlash take the form of attacks against the courts in an attempt to fully disrupt the institutional playing field, and thus forestall future attempts to use the mechanisms of judicialization against entrenched elites (Braconnier De León 2021). In Brazil and elsewhere, we have also seen backlash by a new right-wing populism that threatens the foundations of everyday politics, let alone the superstructure that enables a judicialized politics. This form of backlash, insofar as it strikes at the heart of the model, can be seen as a failure of judicialization.

Second, we explore the informal practices and networks that govern judicial institutions at all levels to understand the ways in which corruption, nepotism, and other intra-institutional dynamics diminish the transformative potential of courts and prosecutors. In so doing, we document instances in which the judiciary's ability to fulfill the promise of greater accountability and rights effectiveness is not only a function of its interactions with other actors, but also determined from within. Institutional pathologies often lead judicial elites themselves to practice obstructionism when some among their ranks become mavericks. Such pathologies reproduce practices that render independence- or effectiveness-enhancing reforms moot. Furthermore, we show that in an attempt to break the mold and mobilize change, mavericks often stretch the limits of judicial prerogatives one step too far. While some celebrate this, especially when a subordinated minority finds a way to express demands that have long been submerged by mainstream politics, unorthodox judicial behavior can also lend itself to abuses, as implied by the many accusations of "lawfare" lobbed by aggrieved politicians against resolute corruption prosecutors.

Third, because we are concerned with the extent to which judicialization impacts the lives of ordinary citizens, we move beyond high (supreme or constitutional) courts to also explore the actions of prosecution agencies and lower courts, which often deal with the bread-and-butter issues that affect society most directly. Doing so is also important for understanding why high courts sometimes behave in the way they do, as their decisions are often shaped by (or made in reaction to) the actions of prosecutors, public defenders, and lower courts. Our analytical move is in line with Ingram and Kapiszewski's (2019) important call to fill a glaring gap in the literature on law and courts in Latin America, which rarely looks at "low-level" judicial politics. As they put it, "if our ultimate goal is to understand why it has been, and continues to be, so difficult to entrench the rule of law in many parts of the world … then the comparative study of courts must reach [beyond high courts]" (Ingram and Kapiszewski 2019: 4). This volume similarly pays attention to how institutional design affects the behavior of these other actors, but is ultimately more concerned with institutional outcomes, in particular the impact of judges and prosecutors on public policies and the rule of law. To do so, our chapters focus on the interaction between judicial actors at all levels and their nonjudicial interlocutors, including the mass public, the media, politicians, and social movements.

In what follows, we develop our central argument about the shortcomings of the institutional superstructure that enabled judicialization and describe the various themes that run throughout the volume.

THE JUDICIALIZATION SUPERSTRUCTURE AND ITS LIMITS

We use the term "superstructure" to refer to the combination of formal institutional and elite cultural changes largely credited for instigating the judicialization of politics in Latin America. We do not use this term in the Marxist sense at all, or even to invoke some of the many meanings and implications the term has acquired over the years. In fact, although the label is not meant to be pejorative, it is intended to signal some level of potential disconnect between these institutional and cultural changes and the sociopolitical context, and their consequent political precarity.[2] In other words, the notion of a "superstructure" highlights the potential – though not the necessity – for a gap between what happens at the constitutional, supranational, and elite level, and what is happening in the rest of society. Indeed, these changes might even be somewhat remote from political elites with a more direct and more recent electoral connection to the public. We call it the superstructure to distinguish this sphere of institutional change from the space of ordinary politics and public discourse, which might take place in legislatures and political campaigns, or in the media. Moreover, we also mean to distinguish it from what we might consider the "infrastructure" of judicialization, which takes place in low-level courts, in the work of front-line prosecutors and police, and even in grassroots legal mobilization (Brinks and Botero 2014).

Indeed, the key drivers of judicialization have an at times tenuous connection to the mass politics and power structures of a place. For example, many scholars agree that the formal institutional change promoted and enacted during the 1980s and 1990s is one of the main determinants of the judicialization of politics in Latin America (e.g., Gauri and Brinks 2008; Wilson 2009). Academics and practitioners hailed a series of legal and constitutional reforms designed by cosmopolitan elites to strengthen, at least on paper, judicial institutions in their mission to exercise horizontal and vertical control functions and thus behave as checks on government behavior and architects of fundamental rights (Domingo 1999; Schedler 1999; Domingo and Sieder 2001; Nunes 2010). Other authors highlight the role of regional and global human rights instruments and structures in consolidating the bases for greater judicial independence and activism (Von Bogdandy 2015; Huneeus 2016). But it is clear that the institutional changes that supported judicialization, whether they were home-grown or trickled down from abroad, could often take place without a commitment to making them effective (Finkel 2008; Brinks, Levitsky, and Murillo 2020).

[2] See Brinks and Botero (2014) for a discussion of ways in which new rights regimes require extensive support to become effective.

The cultural changes that accompanied the judicialization of politics can also be disconnected from broader social changes. In their book on the emerging "culture of legality" in Latin America, Couso, Huneeus, and Sieder (2010) highlight cultural changes among judicial and other elites, affecting judicial role conceptions on the highest courts, the curricula of law schools, and the interests and careers of law professors. Similarly, many of the NGOs that played a key role in socio-legal mobilization and are part of this cultural change are populated by capital-city civil society elites and supported by external funders, rather than animated by more evenly distributed grassroots domestic forces. Couso, Huneeus, and Sieder argue that one can also find evidence of a culture of legality among publics, and we agree; our claim is, rather, that when the cultural change is limited to elite spaces and not connected to larger-scale cultural changes, it is far less likely to have a meaningful impact.

These changes at the constitutional and supranational levels, and the changes at elite levels in the legal profession, happen in what is, for many ordinary citizens, the stratosphere of politics, a space with which they rarely engage, and of which they may only vaguely be aware. The superstructure is therefore characterized by being not necessarily majoritarian, and certainly not necessarily rooted in mass politics. Changes here – constitutional changes, for example, or the signing of treaties – may arise out of a particular political moment; they may even be the result of a high degree of engagement around an issue or a document at a particular time, and reflect a temporary consensus; but they are difficult to change and are not necessarily sustained by continued support among political elites or the population as a whole.

Superstructural change is, of course, most visible in formal, constitutional changes. After conducting a comprehensive overview of the wave of institutional reengineering that started in the 1980s, Ríos-Figueroa (2011: 29) concludes that "Latin American judges now enjoy considerably greater insulation from political pressure than they have in the past." Importantly, new and reformed constitutions incorporated more rights, thus increasing the textual basis for rights-centered litigation and for a different kind of constitutionalist jurisprudence (Brinks and Blass 2017). Brinks, Gauri, and Shen (2015) detail the increasing tendency to include social and economic rights in constitutions around the world after World War II. Latin America was one of the leaders in this trend, with many countries including lists of individual rights or catalogues of human rights treaties, or both, in their constitutional texts (Figure 1.1).

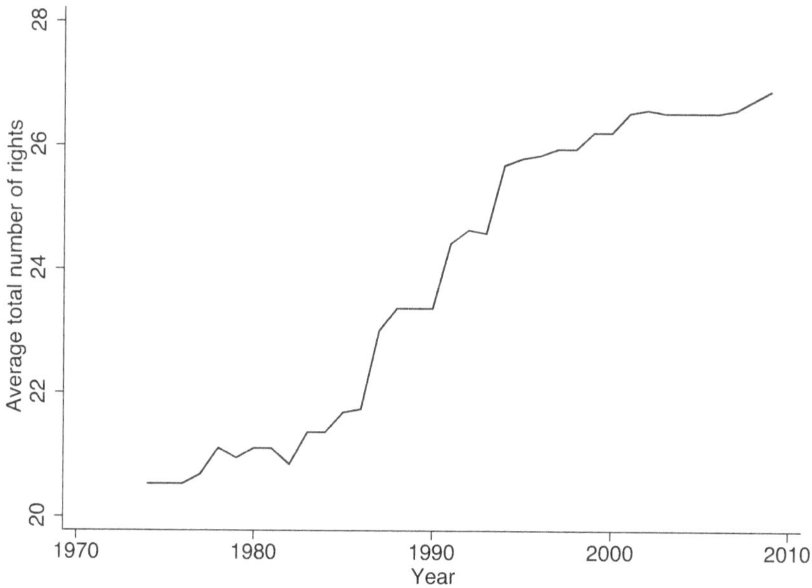

FIGURE 1.1. Average number of rights in Latin American constitutions since 1975

In addition to adding rights, countries created institutional mechanisms to make those rights enforceable, including new constitutional courts or strengthened supreme courts, with more politically insulated appointment and removal mechanisms, new review powers, and new procedural devices for enforcing rights. Brinks and Blass (2017, 2018) explore these changes, showing dramatic increases in courts' formal autonomy and in the scope of their authority, as shown in Figure 1.2. Brinks and Blass's "authority" dimension is in large part based on the number and types of rights included in the constitution, but also includes a measure of the mechanisms included in an attempt to make those rights effective.

Parallel to these domestic constitutional transformations, Latin America saw important supra-constitutional changes. The region is now home to a robust regional system of human rights protections with the American Convention of Human Rights and adjacent treaties at its core (Pasqualucci 2013; Engstrom 2019; Huneeus and Madsen 2019). Since the 1980s, the Inter-American Court and Commission on Human Rights have established themselves as reliable guarantors of fundamental rights, expanding the reach of their jurisprudential tentacles to a variety of issue areas ranging from state repression to indigenous and abortion rights.

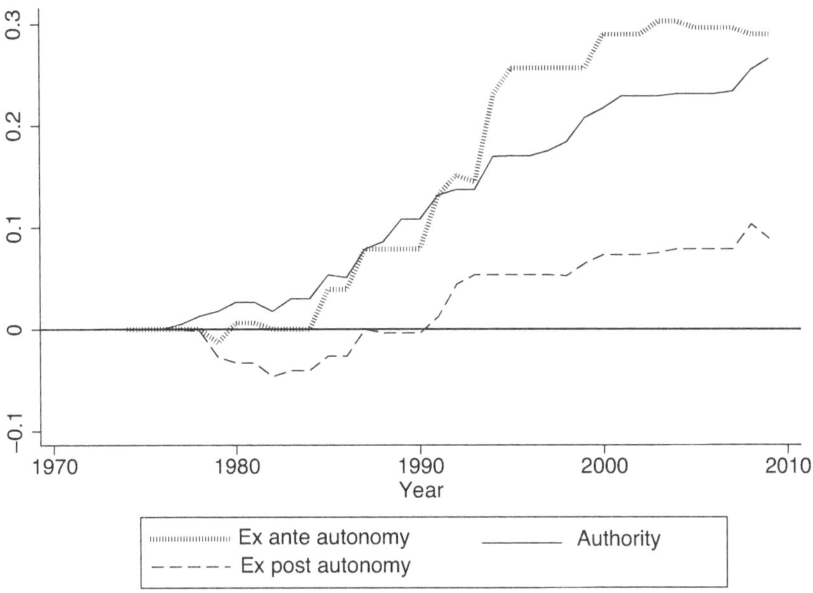

FIGURE 1.2. Regional average levels of *ex ante* autonomy, *ex post* autonomy and authority in Latin America

Importantly, through the development of the conventionality review doctrine, the Inter-American Court of Human Rights has successfully spearheaded a continental judicial dialogue that pushes national supreme and constitutional courts to actively incorporate relatively stringent Inter-American rights-protection standards into their rulings (Dulitzky 2015; Contesse 2018; Gonzalez-Ocantos 2018). As a result, this supra-constitutional structure has embedded itself in most of the countries of the region, and become another tool for rights-claiming and contestation (Gonzalez-Ocantos and Sandholtz 2021).

To support this superstructure, the region's constitutions also included important changes below the level of constitutional or supreme courts. The Brazilian Public Prosecution Service (Ministério Público) is the paradigmatic example. Brazil's 1988 constitution set up the prosecutors as a fourth branch of government, with guarantees of autonomy similar to those that protect the courts, and with a broad mandate to protect the constitutional order from private or public, individual or collective actors (see Da Ros and Taylor, Chapter 10 in this volume). Even more unusual – and unusually removed from a country's politics – was the International Commission against Impunity in Guatemala (the CICIG; see Bowen, Chapter 5 in this volume). This was a hybrid domestic and international commission with a mandate to investigate and work with local prosecutors and courts to root out corruption and impunity in the country. It did not, however, have constitutional status. At both the constitutional and the infra-constitutional level, many countries similarly created anti-corruption commissions, ombudsmen, and auditing offices. These reforms embedded a complex of "mandated horizontal accountability" (O'Donnell 1999) institutions inside the state. The various chapters in this book detail such changes in Mexico (Gallagher and Contesse, Chapter 2), Colombia (Bernal-Bermúdez, Chapter 6), Ecuador (Basabe-Serrano, Chapter 9), and elsewhere. Like the Brazilian Ministério Público and the CICIG, many of these institutions are characterized by quite radical attempts to divorce their behavior from the politics of the country. The goal was "independence," understood as isolation from the surrounding politics; this notion of independence may also be the problem.

Finally, primarily through ordinary legislation, Latin America also underwent a wave of criminal justice reform, focused on promoting a transition from inquisitorial to accusatorial systems (Hammergren 1998, 2002; Langer 2007). The goal was to improve efficiency and expertise, especially in the battle against various forms of macro-criminality, as well as to guarantee respect for due process during criminal investigations. By separating control over the investigation from oversight of its legality (giving the former to prosecutors and the latter to judges), adopting oral proceedings, specializing cohorts of prosecutors in specific types of criminal behavior, and incorporating novel prosecutorial tools such as plea bargains, coupled with the changes in the superstructure we have just described, these reforms empowered prosecutors and injected investigative zeal into prosecutorial agencies across the region (Langer 2004). These changes also transformed the culture of advocacy by turning lawyers into an active party during criminal proceedings (Michel 2018).

Scholars and practitioners expected that judicial institutions anchored in this new superstructure would be able to unleash their horizontal and vertical accountability potential. As we discussed, and as many of our contributors point out, on occasion judicial institutions in fact behave in line with these expectations. This is especially true for newly created or empowered high-level courts, including supreme and constitutional courts. But if we scratch below the surface, as our contributors also do, we sometimes see a failure to build an infrastructure in the state, politics, and society on which this superstructure can rest safely in order to function properly.

In particular, the process of constitutional and institutional change has suffered from two notable deficits: first, the absence of strong states capable of upholding the rule of law and steering the implementation of complex public policies; and second, the absence of solid layers of social support that legitimize court-promoted changes and which judicial institutions can rely on to fend off political attacks or monitor compliance. For all the popularity of constitutional changes such as Brazil's 1988 "citizens' constitution," it is clear that many of the specific outcomes from the superstructure were not solidly rooted in state structures, or in social and political support. In the next paragraphs, we elaborate on these two shortcomings.

The first problem has been a failure to build state capacity and thus enable the judiciary and prosecution services to live up to the expectations embedded in formal institutional changes and new elite norms. Following Yashar (2018: 108), we think of state capacity as "the organizational ability to implement governing projects – separate from the political will to deploy it." Building state capacity is both a political decision and a medium- to long-term endeavor; in most cases, then, state capacity will be built with a degree of urgency determined in large part by the politics of the governing project in question. In many cases, the state capacity to implement the governing projects created by a judicialized demand structure was not there, and has not been created.

In some countries, for example, reforms created autonomous prosecution and criminal investigation services, or mandated existing ones with the enforcement of ambitious international human rights standards. But the lack of funding or basic expertise means that even the most public-spirited law enforcement agents are often incapable of fulfilling their institutional mission. Some prosecution services are so weak that they cannot perform basic forensic tests and must rely on international cooperation to carry out such routine tasks (Michel 2018). Gallagher and Contesse's chapter in this volume (Chapter 2) shows that even though Mexico has formally come to embrace sophisticated human rights legal standards as part of the institutional superstructure, local-level judges and prosecutors lack the know-how and incentives to translate international norms and constitutional provisions into actionable bureaucratic templates. Similarly, Bowen's chapter (Chapter 5) chronicles the organizational barriers and capability deficits encountered by the CICIG when it attempted to trigger productive synergies with Guatemalan law enforcement actors. In both cases, the expansion of networks of macro-criminality that invest heavily in state capture and the surge in criminal violence further compromised the integrity and operational capacity of the prosecution services and the courts.

In other cases, problems of state capacity affect the courts themselves. State capacity can also be understood as the ability of a state to impose its order not only across the territory but within its own organizational structure (Brinks 2012). Our case studies show that Latin American judicial organizations are far from approximating this Weberian ideal. Instead, in some courts, informal practices, deeply entrenched bureaucratic pathologies, and corruption, interact with formal institutional façades to stunt the goals of superstructural reforms.

Superstructural reforms too often depend on actors to abide by the rule of law and behave in line with the guidelines enshrined in formal institutions. In his chapter on Mexico, Ríos-Figueroa (Chapter 8) finds high rates of nepotism in the appointment process for the federal judiciary, which undermine efficiency and breed corruption. These practices, which persist despite ambitious reform efforts, are partly a legacy of hegemonic party rule under the Partido Revolucionario Institucional (PRI). Similarly, in his chapter on Ecuador, Basabe-Serrano (Chapter 9) relies on unprecedented access to legal elites to show that the concentration of power in the Executive during Rafael Correa's administration led to soaring levels of judicial corruption in the Constitutional Court and a crippling of horizontal accountability despite formal empowerment. Basabe-Serrano shows that hegemonic executives strike mutual protection pacts with top judges, creating the space for collusion between private litigants and the court. Finally, Baraybar and Gonzalez-Ocantos's chapter (Chapter 13) suggests that networks of clientelism connecting the political and judicial establishments are also pervasive in Peru, with serious implications for the ability of courts and prosecutors to check abuses of power.

The second problem is that there has been a general failure to build a social base of support for judicialization. Any political project, especially one with ambitious goals such as controlling the exercise of political authority and expanding fundamental rights, must have deep roots in society if it is to become sustainable over time (Brinks, Levitsky, and Murillo 2019, 2020). In this sense, Epp's (2009) work shows that the implementation of rights requires sustained pressure from organized civil society but also reformist ideas being advocated by the bureaucracy charged with compliance. Progressive mobilization seeking the enforcement of rights was and is important in many Latin American countries, but our case studies suggest that all three levels – mass publics, civil society organizations, and the bureaucracy – are crucial when it comes to court-inspired reformism taking hold or not in a given country.

This failure to root change in society manifests in at least four ways. First, the progressive normative content of the rights-expanding component of the judicialization project has often been out of sync with social norms in a region where socially conservative values are still predominant. As a result, progressive judicial interventions in policy debates put the judiciary in a difficult position. Safeguarding the rights of minorities often has these institutions making unpopular decisions that fail to galvanize widespread popular support and are seen as top-down or even foreign impositions.

For example, judicialization has played an important role in efforts to advance same-sex marriage as well as sexual and reproductive rights, including access to abortion. Yet legal mobilization to advance these issues has taken place amidst publics that do not view these changes favorably. A 2016 ILGA/RIWI survey in the Americas by the International Lesbian, Gay, Bisexual, Trans, and Intersex Association in cooperation with the RIWI corporation (the ILGA/RIWI survey) found that on average, 40 percent of respondents opposed the legalization of same-sex marriage, with 35 percent supporting it. Public support never breaks into a majority (it was highest in Chile, at 48 percent); while the rate of rejection ran as high as 49 percent (in Ecuador). Public opinion in the region has historically been even more negative toward abortion. Data from the 2015 Latin American Public Opinion Project's (LAPOP) national surveys show that 75 percent of those interviewed in Ecuador, 70 percent in Colombia, and 66 percent in Brazil stated that abortion was justifiable under no circumstances. Things appear to be shifting, but in an incremental and selective manner. By 2018, for example, the approval level for abortion when the woman's health is at risk was over 60 percent for most countries in Latin America, except Jamaica and Paraguay, according to LAPOP. Approval rates for abortion decriminalization in cases of rape or incest, and other causes, which are at the center of contemporary debates, remain low.

Going against the grain to protect rights can raise serious problems for institutional legitimacy and for the acceptance of specific decisions among the public. How can Latin American courts build much-needed legitimacy in such contexts? The chapter by Forero-Alba and Rodríguez-Raga (Chapter 7) explores the effect that different types of arguments (scientific, religious, majoritarian, legal) have on support for Colombia's Constitutional Court. This tribunal has distinguished itself in the region for its groundbreaking jurisprudence expanding and enforcing socioeconomic rights amid a conservative public. Their findings call attention to the power of ideas to legitimize judicial interventions, and echo the overall shift in culture toward legality and technocracy. They show that by relying on legalistic and scientific arguments the court can accrue more support when deciding on a highly contested issue like abortion.

Second, the growing NGOization of progressive social movements has meant, in some cases, the detachment of rights advocacy organizations at the forefront of progressive socio-legal mobilization from grassroots movements. Where progressive grassroots activism is absent, and where conservative values continue to have wide resonance among mass publics, it can be easier for counter-movements to organize in response to the judicialization promoted by elite NGOs. Moreover, taking a page from the progressive playbook, groups defending more conservative approaches to rights and their enforcement also turn to the language of rights, strategic litigation, and legal advocacy as counter-mobilization strategies, making use of the very same superstructure to advance their cause (Lehoucq 2021). The counter-movements that emerged after initial advances in sexual and reproductive rights in Colombia (Ruibal 2014) and Argentina (Peñas Defago and Morán Faúndes 2014) are excellent examples of religious and conservative groups deploying the strategies traditionally used by progressive civil society organizations in response to court and legislative victories.

Several chapters in this volume detail how the absence of solid roots in society limits the impact and effectiveness of judicialization. As Gianella's chapter on Peru (Chapter 3) shows, sophisticated legal advocacy efforts around sexual and reproductive rights have achieved key supranational judicial victories. But on the ground, rights realization is blocked by two separate fractures: on the one hand, by the chasm that separates litigation groups oriented toward the superstructure from grassroots activism; and on the other, by conservative Catholic counter-movements with much stronger political allies, new mobilization strategies and stronger social roots. Similarly, Ruibal's chapter (Chapter 4) compares the counter-movements against abortion in Latin America. She identifies countries in which judicial intervention fueled a conservative reaction that has relied on legal mobilization and rights talk, as in Colombia. At the same time, she cautions us against a one-dimensional understanding of backlash. Instead, she delves deep into the realities of the abortion counter-movements in Brazil, Colombia, Mexico, and Argentina. Ruibal identifies and explores key elements that help us better understand the different national trajectories: the counter-movement's connections to legislatures, whether the Supreme Court provided a favorable forum for conservatism, and the strength of their support structures. Finally, Gallagher and Contesse (Chapter 2) show that the absence of professionalized and resourceful grassroots activism in Mexico is one of the reasons why local courts and prosecutors struggle to find the means and the willingness to go after human rights criminals.

Third, some of the disconnect between the superstructure and society is not a bug but a – possibly misguided – feature of the system. Many reform efforts sought to insulate the institutions charged with rights enforcement from politics altogether. The CICIG, for instance, was composed of internationally appointed figures precisely to ensure that it would have no ties to Guatemala's politics; the Brazilian Ministério Público was similarly imagined as insulated from politicians and the judiciary, and afforded the same guarantees of independence granted to the judiciary. Rather than seek to design institutions that could secure broad-based support and ensure impartiality through the inclusion of a diverse set of voices in their governance (see Brinks and Blass 2018: 24–27), these organizations sought to cut all ties to a politics and society that was perceived as exactly the problem. In the case of the CICIG, Bowen's chapter (Chapter 5) shows that this original design eventually proved the downfall of the institution. She explores shifts in the balance of power between reformist and obstructionist coalitions, and how the political influence of entrenched criminal networks in Guatemala was only kept at bay when the CICIG received strong support from the international community. In the absence of strong roots in Guatemalan society, a fatal backlash followed close on the heels of a loss of international support after 2016.

Fourth, efforts to enforce human rights and the rule of law continue to run up against resistance from powerful societal actors that can effectively block the most ambitious and well-thought-out institutional reforms. Institutional strength is a relational concept – strength relative to the capacity of its opponents to resist (Brinks, Levitsky, and Murillo 2019). Bernal-Bermúdez's chapter on attempts in Colombia to hold private businesses accountable for their role in human rights violations during the armed conflict (Chapter 6) demonstrates this clearly. She shows that after relative success with convictions and truth-telling a decade ago, businesses have successfully pushed back on institutional efforts for greater accountability in the context of recent peace negotiations with the FARC. Read alongside the chapters by Bowen on Guatemala

(Chapter 5) and Gallagher and Contesse on Mexico (Chapter 2), Bernal's work suggests that the fight against structural corruption and state capture by criminal groups depends crucially on establishing a strong social base of support. In the absence of that social base, efforts that seek to challenge deeply entrenched power structures often rely on a highly unusual and unstable constellation of conditions that can vanish shortly after institutional reforms are put in place.

In sum, the failure to build stronger and more transparent states often leads to the deficient implementation of court-mandated reforms and constrains the ability of law enforcement actors to behave in accordance with the values and ideals that inspired judicial reformism in the first place. Problems of state capacity thus limit the impact of judicialization, in terms of both rights expansion and greater accountability of public officials. Likewise, the failure to build social support, coupled with the distance between the progressive movements that spearhead socio-legal mobilization and the wider public, opens up space for reactions against judicialization that capitalize on the existing conservative orientation of the mass public or politically influential religious movements. These counter-movements can be more narrowly legal, resting on conservative laws and courts, or based in a broader politics, all the way up to a regressive populist backlash.

While in many instances the superstructure had a tenuous impact on social reality due to these deficits, it sometimes worked as expected – and on a few occasions it did so perhaps too well. This points to another form of disconnect, one in which the goals and aspirations of superstructural change were not aligned with the kind of changes that "really existing" Latin American democracies could tolerate or support. As a result, some forms of judicialization violently crashed against reality, wreaking havoc on the political order, and threatening to undermine the very same institutions that made them possible. Nowhere is this crash seen more clearly than in the recent battles between judicial and political elites over the criminalization of systemic corruption, which came to define the contemporary politics of countries such as Brazil, Peru, and Ecuador (Gonzalez-Ocantos and Baraybar 2019). As we saw, judicial reformism in Latin America created new accountability institutions and empowered new actors, especially prosecutors, to police the exercise of power. But this new emphasis took place in the context of rampant corruption and compromised judiciaries and prosecution services. When a handful of judges and prosecutors put these tools to work in the various national chapters of the ongoing Lava Jato investigation, four possibilities began to loom large.

First, the efforts of going after complex networks of white-collar criminals embedded in the state apparatus often led prosecutors and judges to bend due process in order to circumvent innumerable evidentiary, political, and bureaucratic obstacles. Some prosecutors justified extreme forms of legal unorthodoxy arguing that traditional uses of the law were ineffective in these cases and thwarted accountability efforts. Second, judges and prosecutors at the forefront of these probes sometimes became tools at the service of political agendas and partisan advantage-taking. When judges abused their prerogatives, embraced controversial innovations to make laws actually "bite," or overtly served political interests, the legitimacy of both the courts and their anti-corruption agenda suffered. Third, the absence of a uniform institutional commitment to fight corruption among members of the judicial branch meant that the victories orchestrated by a zealous minority were precarious, with limited success in the protracted appeals structure. Coupled with the aforementioned legitimacy costs, the paucity of robust results often fueled disillusionment and deepened political cynicism. Finally, perhaps more worrying is that committed judges and prosecutors entered into a collision course with political and judicial actors implicated in systemic corruption. This invariably had problematic implications for political stability and governability, on the one hand, and the integrity of judicial institutions, on the other.

The lesson may be that these reforms sought to do too much too fast. When these superstructural changes work well in contexts where corruption is not systemic, they do not pose an existential threat to the establishment. But when they work half as well in places like Latin America, they can unleash a dangerous dialectic in which judicialization (in this case, the criminalization of politicians and their accepted way of doing politics), encourages elites to decisively turn against judicial and prosecutorial power.

As mentioned, the Lava Jato case in Brazil, and its regional ramifications, embody an extreme example of this disjuncture between the superstructure and its context. Four separate chapters explore different dimensions of the resulting clashes. They complement the analysis presented in the other chapters by highlighting judicial agency as yet another contributor to backlash and broken promises. What started as an investigation into a money-laundering and illegal campaign-financing scheme quickly morphed into an existential threat for politicians throughout Latin America (Taylor 2018). The chapter by Da Ros and Taylor (Chapter 10) shows how Brazilian judges and prosecutors profited from the new tools and institutional structures created by superstructural reforms and used them to take on the political class. But as Mota Prado and Rodríguez Machado explain in their chapter (Chapter 11), prosecutorial zeal, coupled with the difficulties they encountered when trying to investigate deeply entrenched corruption, induced judges and prosecutors to overstep their prerogatives and undermine due process. Aware of the importance of anchoring criminalization in social support structures, especially to justify breaking the rules, the Lava Jato task force reached out to the public. This gave the embattled investigators some breathing space, but also catalyzed a process of political polarization that turned citizens against part of the political class, and eventually also against the inquiry. More worrying, Bastos dos Santos and Solano Gallego's analysis of the discursive dimension of Lava Jato (Chapter 12), demonstrates how the moralizing discourse espoused by Brazilian judges and prosecutors to galvanize support for their cause found an elective affinity with conservative, anti-rights, and anti-leftist forces, a synergy that ultimately opened up space for the rise of Bolsonaro, a populist president.

Lava Jato soon acquired a transnational dimension, pushing prosecutors in other countries to launch their own investigations. Baraybar and Gonzalez-Ocantos (Chapter 13) explore the Peruvian chapter of Lava Jato, which, like the Brazilian one, has had far-reaching political implications. Echoing the analysis presented in Mota Prado and Rodríguez Machado's chapter (Chapter 11), they show how a handful of prosecutors embraced innovative and controversial prosecutorial strategies to take on the political class. And – picking up and expanding on a theme already present in Da Ros and Taylor's chapter (Chapter 10) – the Peruvian case study documents the dynamics of backlash engendered by the criminalization of corruption. In both cases, politicians and high-level judicial actors turned against the task forces created to investigate corruption, jeopardizing the promise of greater accountability.

When read together, these four chapters suggest that a wholesale clash between members of the legal and political establishments, in a weak institutional context, risks undermining the integrity and legitimacy of courts and prosecution services. In a similar vein, Bowen's chapter on the CICIG (Chapter 5) also chronicles the backlash that inevitably ensues when empowered accountability actors try to dismantle deeply entrenched corruption networks. In the Guatemalan case, at least part of the institutional superstructure suffered a definitive defeat when the CICIG was expelled from the country. Da Ros and Taylor (Chapter 10) conclude that Lava Jato in Brazil is also likely to lose steam and ultimately fail, with negative consequences for the judiciary, the Ministério Público, and future efforts to contain corruption. The lesson seems clear: judicial actors that decide to take on politicians without a broad base of social support, in contexts where institutions are weak and corrupt interests dominate the scene, are ill-prepared to resist a political class that sees judicialization as an existential threat. Their own maverick and controversial investigative tactics are often part of the reason why they fail to legitimize accountability efforts in the face of backlash.

CONCLUSION

Despite the focus on weaknesses and shortcomings, at the end of the day our overall evaluation of the net balance left by judicialization in Latin America is more optimistic than our observations thus far might suggest. In assembling case studies that could shed light on the shortcomings of judicialization, we purposefully selected areas or cases in which judicialization has been problematic or fallen short of reformers' originally high expectations, including struggles over organized crime, abortion rights, transitional justice, and political malfeasance. The book therefore leaves out – although it is informed by all the collaborators' expertise in – other areas such as indigenous rights, individual freedoms, and access to health, for which there is an already vast literature that documents significant, if not unmixed, successes. In each of these areas, the emergence of a more judicialized politics has enabled many formerly excluded populations to press their claims. This is particularly true for people with HIV and AIDS, gender nonconforming people, and indigenous peoples. In many, though not all, countries women have found their voices amplified by constitutional values and the language of rights. Environmental and consumer groups have found new purchase on public policy through constitutionalized debates. In short, in many places and for many people, judicialization has meant an improvement in their ability to shape outcomes, and much of the literature has focused on the successes, and sometimes the excesses, of this new way of doing politics.

But our goal was to identify instances that would enable us to shine a light on less frequently examined areas like backlash; zoom in on elusive phenomena such as judicial corruption; explore tensions between the aspirations of judicialization and other cherished goals such as democratic stability; and provide a counterbalance to analyses that too often select on positive values of the dependent variable. In this sense, rather than removing all hope in courts and the law as instruments of social change and more transparent politics, or suggesting that the entire project ought to be abandoned, we aim to paint a more comprehensive picture of the heterogeneity of outcomes that ensue when judicial institutions undergo historic processes of empowerment.

Latin America, as we noted at the outset, may well be the region with the most experience in this regard. At the same time, the factors identified in this volume as barriers for realizing the potential of judicialization as a path to social progress apply well beyond the region. Indeed, deficient states, weak societal roots, corruption, and backlash-inducing forms of judicial or prosecutorial zeal have also led to disappointment with the judicialization project in Africa, Asia, and Eastern Europe.

South Africa is often cited as a paradigmatic case of transformative constitutionalism. After the transition to democracy, a progressive constitution and active civil society organizations mobilized through the legal system to enforce new rights and seek structural change. By and large, the South African Constitutional Court's cautious response to these overtures has prevented serious backlash, while earning some criticism from activists and scholars who would like to see a more assertive court (see, e.g., Bilchitz 2013; Langford et al. 2014). Yet scholars have noted that limited state capacity often conditions the impact of its more ambitious rulings. According to Langford's (2014) assessment of several housing rights litigation cases, including the famous *Grootboom* case, which declared that housing rights were justiciable, economic limitations as well as bureaucratic dysfunction hindered the full potential of these legal victories. On the one hand, the decision eventually led to an increase in emergency housing programs across the country, and even a public housing program for the Wallacedene community, which had triggered the case. On the other hand, housing remains an unmet need in South Africa, and housing rights litigation continues to struggle to bridge the gap between the constitutional promise and the reality of unsafe and inadequate housing for many South Africans, as evidenced by the *Olivia Street* case.

The history of housing rights in South Africa is, in a way, a microcosm of what we have described in Latin America. On the one hand, for reasons of sheer state incapacity, state capture, and mismanagement, the constitution's and the courts' mandates for adequate housing (and health care, and social provision) for all South Africans are still far from being met. On the other hand, by hearing the cases, requiring the government to engage in meaningful conversations with the plaintiffs (as it did in *Olivia Road*), and insisting that the government must both address acute situations and take reasonable steps toward the progressive realization of the right more broadly, the system of constitutional justice has transformed the politics of housing rights – as well as the politics of health care, social provision, and many other acute problems in South Africa – giving greater voice to urban squatters, shantytown dwellers, prison inmates seeking health care, and more.

India's Supreme Court has been similarly hailed for its progressive intervention in key policy debates, including on the right to food, the right to health, the right to work, and other seemingly intractable problems afflicting the subcontinent. Gauri (2014) examines the country's experience with public interest litigation (PIL), an institutional innovation that has supplied the court with the cases it needs to raise its public profile. In doing so, he reminds us of the huge variation that still exists in judicial effectiveness. He explains that success hinges in no small part on the capacity and authority commanded by the agencies responsible for implementing court-mandated policies. Thus, for example, bowing to the lack of state capacity, the court's most assertive interventions on the right to health tend to be limited to, say, civil servants, who are already within the reach of the state and its public health system, rather than to the millions who have little or no access to health care at all; and in addressing the right to food, the court worked with and through the government's existing grain reserves and the public school system, already in place, to provide a cooked noonday meal for students (Drèze 2004). Gauri and Brinks (2008) find that the Indian court suffers from a chronic lack of compliance, due primarily to state weakness, diminishing the expected impact of its decisions by at least 50 percent. In short, it is, unsurprisingly, also true in other regions of the world that the most far-reaching judicialized attempts at social transformation often founder on the shoals of weak states.

Judiciaries outside Latin America have also sought to advance minority rights in the absence of broad support from coalitions in civil society. In some Asian countries we see evidence that this disconnect has stalled implementation and generated tensions, if not outright backlash. The persistence of violence against women in India, despite multiple judicial attempts to improve gender equality, testifies to the court's difficulty in overcoming strong social norms. In Taiwan, Kuo and Chen (2018) describe how the Council of Grand Justices' (the constitutional tribunal) granted a two-year remedial grace period for the government to implement a decision recognizing same-sex marriage because of social resistance to the ruling. The court's goal was to afford time to legitimize the ruling. In its aftermath, however, opponents called for a national referendum and counter-mobilization thrived (Lau 2020). Beyond Taiwan, compliance with the decisions of the Indian and Nepalese Supreme Courts with regard to reforms to gender-identity laws have also had limited reach due to a gap in public support (Lau 2020). Similarly, Dotan's (2015) research into legal mobilization efforts by women's and LGBT rights advocates in Israel dovetails with our own claim that in the absence of coalitions of broader support results usually fall short of expectations. In the Israeli case, LGBT activists worked from the grass-roots up, combining litigation with other strategies to expand and support reforms, while women's movements (akin to what Gianella documents for Peru in Chapter 3) focused on an elitist strategic litigation strategy that has been less successful. The comparative evidence – from Latin America and elsewhere – thus points to the importance of paying attention to societal support and how it interacts with the judiciary and other actors involved in crafting social change.

Examples of institutional pathologies that undermine the integrity of judicial institutions and condition the promise of judicialization abound in other world regions too. For example, Dzmitryieva (2021) discusses the absence of meritocracy in Russia, where senior judges informally sponsor candidates for vacant positions in the judiciary, in echoes of the dynamic Ríos-Figueroa documents in this volume (Chapter 8). Trochev (2018) reports similar hierarchical judicial networks in post-Soviet Ukraine. A system that strongly favors insiders via patronage networks does not necessarily undermine competence to deal with bread-and-butter cases. It does, however, bias the judiciary when it comes to sensitive cases because it limits the types of voices that circulate within the organization and conditions levels of internal independence. Put differently, as in many Latin American countries, the mundane is dealt with technocratically, whereas the non-mundane is dealt with politically. As Stroh (2018) notes with regard to Benin, the emergence of judicial networks linked to specific sectoral interests may also compromise the legitimacy of the courts and reduce their ability to serve as credible arbiters of sociopolitical conflict.

Finally, democratization led to a more robust institutional infrastructure for investigating and punishing high-level political wrongdoing in many countries throughout the developing world. Latin America is therefore not alone in experiencing ambitious anti-corruption crusades by zealous judges and prosecutors. While there is a lot to commend in these steps toward greater horizontal accountability, the comparative record confirms our claim that the criminalization of corruption in contexts where corruption is systemic can sometimes prove highly disruptive of democratic politics.

One latent risk is the weaponization of law enforcement for political gain. For example, Shen-Bayh's (2018) work on Sub-Saharan Africa shows the use of judicial rituals to legitimize repression against insider-challengers. Chapman and Chaudoin (2013) show that most countries joined the International Criminal Court in order to prosecute their political opponents. Corruption prosecutions have also become quite common in Eastern Europe, but as Popova and Post (2018) show convincingly, these are often targeted against weak actors, for instance, junior coalition partners. The results are politically compromised investigations rather than bona fide attempts to curb wrongdoing. In this regard, the authors note that while the creation of specialized anti-corruption agencies has endowed states with more committed and capable watchdogs, these agencies "can become overzealous and trample civil rights" and when their "political independence gets compromised" they gravely endanger the rule of law and the competitiveness of elections (Popova and Post 2018: 236).

Also in line with the Latin American experience, corruption investigations in other regions of the world too often turn into institutional bombshells that trigger fierce backlash. For instance, created in the early 2000s, Nigeria's Economic and Financial Crimes Commission quickly became a nightmare for the establishment (Adebanwi and Obadare 2011). Critics eventually mounted a campaign to reduce the institution to a paper tiger, depicting its aggressive approach to law enforcement as Gestapo-like. Some former commission members reportedly regretted "strategic choices" that were necessary to succeed in an "ocean of corruption," but which legitimized these objections, creating a "moral platform for rogues" (Adebanwi and Obadare 2011: 201). Worryingly, backlash against resolute anti-corruption efforts is not limited to weak democracies. Reflecting on the end of the Mani Pulite operation in Italy, Della Porta and Vannucci (2007: 844) note that the "revolution of the judges" led to a "counter-revolution of the political class." This severely weakened the impetus for change.

All in all, the limits to the promise of a judicialized politics we identify in this book are present in a variety of contexts. They stem from deficient states, distant or hostile publics and entrenched vested interests, but also from the choices judges and prosecutors make. When backlash and ineffectiveness are part and parcel of the politics of judicialization, a lot is at stake, including the legitimacy of the judicial complex, the staying power of well-meaning reforms, the livelihoods of millions, and in more extreme circumstances, such as widespread corruption prosecutions, the very same structures of political representation upon which democracy relies. In this sense, our volume offers lessons for institutional engineers. To avoid superstructural change becoming a house of cards or a disappointment, fine print and connections to grassroots matter. It is paramount to pay attention to bread-and-butter issues of infrastructural capacity, and make sure formal institutions result from and are sustained by widespread participatory processes. It is also critical to remember that judicialization, and the legal creativity that often fuels it, ought to be exercised with caution, and within the bounds of the law, in order to preserve and promote values central to democracy.

References

Adebanwi, W., and Obadare, E. (2011) When Corruption Fights Back: Democracy and Elite Interest in Nigeria's Anti-Corruption War. *Journal of Modern African Studies* 49(2), 185–213.

Albarracín, M. (2011) Corte Constitucional y movimientos sociales: el reconocimiento judicial de los derechos de las parejas del mismo sexo en Colombia. *Sur: International Journal on Human Rights* 8(14), 7–33.

Antía, F., and Vairo, D. (2019) Política y Justicia en Uruguay: el poder de la Suprema Corte de Justicia (1990–2018). *Revista Uruguaya de Ciencia Política* 28(2), 61–86.

Baxi, U. (1985) Taking Suffering Seriously: Social Action Litigation in the Supreme Court of India. In S. Ramaswamy and S. K. Dhavan, eds., *The Judicial Power*. Delhi: Tripathi, Sweet-Maxwell.

Bilchitz, D. (2013) Constitutionalism, the Global South, and Economic Justice. In D. Bonilla-Maldonado, ed., *Constitutionalism of the Global South: The Activist Tribunals of India, South Africa, and Colombia*. New York: Cambridge University Press.

Bonilla-Maldonado, D., ed. (2013) *Constitutionalism of the Global South: The Activist Tribunals of India, South Africa and Colombia*. Cambridge: Cambridge University Press.

Botero, S. (2017) Agents of Neoliberalism? High Courts, Legal Preferences and Rights in Latin America. In T. Falletti and E. Parrado, eds., *Latin America since the Left Turn*. Philadelphia: University of Pennsylvania Press.

(2018) Judicial Impact and Court Promoted Monitoring in Argentina. *Comparative Politics* 50(2), 169–87.

Braconnier De León, A. I. (2021) Disputing Extractivism at the Court: Elite Countermobilization and Backlash in a (Still) Colonial Guatemala. PhD Dissertation, University of Texas at Austin.

Brinks, D. M. (2012) The Transformation of the Latin American State-as-Law: State Capacity and the Rule of Law. *Revista de Ciencia Política* 32, 561–83.

Brinks, D. M., and Blass, A. (2017) Rethinking Judicial Empowerment: The New Foundations of Constitutional Justice. *International Journal of Constitutional Law* 15(2), 296–331.

(2018) *The DNA of Constitutional Justice in Latin America: Politics, Governance and Judicial Design*. Cambridge: Cambridge University Press.

Brinks, D. M., and Botero, S. (2014) Inequality and the Rule of Law: Ineffective Rights in Latin American Democracies. In D. M. Brinks, M. Leiras, and S. Mainwaring, eds., *Reflections on Uneven Democracies: The Legacy of Guillermo O'Donnell*. Baltimore, MD: Johns Hopkins University Press.

Brinks, D. M., and Forbath, W. (2014) The Role of Courts and Constitutions in the New Politics of Welfare in Latin America. In R. Peerenboom and T. Ginsburg, eds., *Law and Development of Middle-Income Countries: Avoiding the Middle-Income Trap*. Cambridge: Cambridge University Press.

Brinks, D. M., Gauri, V., and Shen, K. (2015) Social Rights Constitutionalism: Negotiating the Tension between the Universal and the Particular. *Annual Review of Law and Social Science* 11, 289–308.

Brinks, D. M, Levitsky, S., and Murillo, M. V. (2019) *Understanding Institutional Weakness: Power and Design in Latin American Institutions*. Cambridge: Cambridge University Press.

eds. (2020) *The Politics of Institutional Weakness in Latin America*. Cambridge: Cambridge University Press.

Brinks, D. M., and Sandoval Rojas, N. (2019) Entrenching Social Constitutionalism? Contributions and Challenges of the Left in Latin American Constitutionalism. In M. Balan and F. Montambeault, eds., *Legacies of the Left Turn in Latin America: The Promise of Inclusive Citizenship*. Notre Dame, IN: Notre Dame University Press.

Chapman, T. L., and Chaudoin, S. (2013). Ratification Patterns and the International Criminal Court. *International Studies Quarterly* 57(2), 400–09.

Cano Blandón, L. F. (2017) Constitucionalismo Experimental y Protección Judicial del Derecho al Agua en Colombia. PhD Dissertation, Universidad de Los Andes.

Contesse, J. (2018) The International Authority of the Inter-American Court of Human Rights: A Critique of the Conventionality Control Doctrine. *International Journal of Human Rights* 22(9), 1168–91.

Couso, J., Huneeus, A., and Sieder, R., eds. (2010) *Cultures of Legality: Judicialization and Political Activism in Latin America*. Cambridge: Cambridge University Press.

Della Porta, D., and Vannucci, A. (2007). Corruption and Anti-Corruption: The Political Defeat of "Clean Hands" in Italy. *West European Politics* 30(4), 830–53.

Dembowski, H. (2001) *Taking the State to Court: Public Interest Litigation and the Public Sphere in Metropolitan India*. New Delhi: Oxford University Press.

Díez, J. (2015) *The Politics of Gay Marriage in Latin America*. Cambridge: Cambridge University Press.

Domingo, D. (1999) Judicial Independence and Judicial Reform in Latin America. In A. Schedler, L. Diamond, and M. Plattner, eds., *The Self Restraining State: Power and Accountability in New Democracies*. London: Lynne Reinner.

Domingo, P. (2000) Judicial Independence: The Politics of the Supreme Court in Mexico. *Journal of Latin American Studies* 32(3), 705–35.

Domingo, P., and Sieder, R., eds. (2001) *Rule of Law in Latin America: The International Promotion of Judicial Reform*. London: Institute of Latin American Studies.

Dotan, Y. (2015) The Boundaries of Social Transformation through Litigation: Women's and LGBT Rights in Israel, 1970–2010. *Israel Law Review* 48, 3–38.

Drèze, J. (2004) Democracy and the Right to Food. *Economic and Political Weekly*, April 24, 2004, 1723–31.

Dulitzky, A. (2015) An Inter-American Constitutional Court? The Invention of the Conventionality Control by the Inter-American Court of Human Rights. *Texas International Law Journal* 50, 45–93.

Dzmitryieva, A. (2021) 2021. Becoming a Judge in Russia: An Analysis of Judicial Biographies. *Europe–Asia Studies* 73(1), 131–56.

Engstrom, P., ed. (2019) *The Inter-American Human Rights System: Impact Beyond Compliance*. London: Palgrave Macmillan.

Epp, C. (2009) *Making Rights Real: Activists, Bureaucrats, and the Creation of the Legalistic State*. Chicago, IL: University of Chicago Press.

Finkel, J. (2008) *Judicial Reform as Political Insurance*. Notre Dame, IN: University of Notre Dame Press.

Gauri, V. (2014) Fundamental Rights and Public Interest Litigation in India. In M. Suresh and S. Narrain, eds., *The Shifting Scales of Justice: The Supreme Court in Neo-Liberal India*. New Delhi: Orient BlackSwan.

Gauri, V., and Brinks, D. M. (2008) *Courting Social Justice: Judicial Enforcement of Social and Economic Rights in the Developing World*. Cambridge: Cambridge University Press.

Gathii, J. (2019) Recharacterizing Corruption to Encompass Illicit Financial Flows. *AJIL Unbound* 113, 336–40.

Gonzalez-Ocantos, E. (2016) *Shifting Legal Visions: Judicial Change and Human Rights Trials in Latin America*. Cambridge: Cambridge University Press.

(2018) Communicative Entrepreneurs: The Inter-American Court of Human Rights' Dialogue with National Judges. *International Studies Quarterly* 62 (4), 737–50.

(2019) Courts in Latin America. In G. Prevost and H. Vanden, eds., *The Oxford Encyclopedia of Latin American Politics*. Oxford: Oxford University Press.

Gonzalez-Ocantos, E., and Baraybar, V. (2019) Lava Jato beyond Borders: The Uneven Performance of Anti-Corruption Judicial Efforts in Latin America. *Taiwan Journal of Democracy* 15(1), 63–89.

Gonzalez-Ocantos, E., and Sandholtz, W. (2021) Constructing a Regional Human Rights Legal Order: The Inter-American Court, National Courts, and Judicial Dialogue, 1988–2014. *International Journal of Constitutional Law* 9(5), 1559–96.

Hammergren, L. (1998) *The Politics of Justice and Justice Reform in Latin America: The Peruvian Case in Comparative Perspective.* Boulder, CO: Westview Press.

(2002) Fifteen Years of Justice and Justice Reform in Latin America: Where We Are and Why We Haven't Made More Progress. Unpublished manuscript.

Helmke, G., and Ríos Figueroa, J., eds. (2011) *Courts in Latin America.* Cambridge: Cambridge University Press.

Herrero, A. (2011) La incidencia de La Corte Suprema de Justicia en la formulación de políticas públicas: Una exploración empírica del caso argentino. *Revista Política* 49(1), 71–106.

Huneeus, A. (2016) Constitutional Lawyers and the Inter-American Court's Varied Authority. *Law and Contemporary Problems* 79, 179–207.

Huneeus, A., and Madsen, M. (2019) Between Universalism and Regional Law and Politics: A Comparative History of the American, European, and African Human Rights Systems. *International Journal of Constitutional Law* 16(1), 136–60.

Ingram, I. (2015) *Crafting Courts in New Democracies: The Politics of Subnational Judicial Reform in Brazil and Mexico.* Cambridge: Cambridge University Press.

Ingram, M., and Kapiszewski, D., eds. (2019) *Beyond High Courts: The Justice Complex in Latin America.* Notre Dame, IN: University of Notre Dame Press.

Kapiszewski, D. (2012) *High Courts and Economic Governance in Argentina and Brazil.* Cambridge: Cambridge University Press.

Kapiszewski, D., Silverstein, G., and Kagan, R., eds. (2013) *Consequential Courts: Judicial Roles in Global Perspective.* Cambridge: Cambridge University Press.

Kapiszewski, D., and Taylor, M. (2008) Doing Courts Justice? Studying Judicial Politics in Latin America. *Perspectives on Politics* 6(4), 741–67.

Keck, T. (2009) Beyond Backlash: Assessing the Impact of Judicial Decisions on LGBT Rights. *Law & Society Review* 43(1), 151–86.

Klarman, M. (1994) Brown, Racial Change, and the Civil Rights Movement. *Virginia Law Review* 80(1), 7–150.

(2006) *From Jim Crow to Civil Rights: The Supreme Court and the Struggle for Racial Equality.* Oxford: Oxford University Press.

Kuo, M. S., and Chen, H. W. (2018) The Brown Moment in Taiwan: Making Sense of the Law and Politics of the Taiwanese Same-Sex Marriage Case in a Comparative Light. *Columbia Journal of Asian Law* 31, 1–81.

Langer, M. (2004) From Legal Transplants to Legal Translations: The Globalization of Plea Bargaining and the Americanization Thesis in Criminal Procedure. *Harvard International Law Journal* 45(1), 1–64.

(2007) Revolution in Latin American Criminal Procedure: Diffusion of Legal Ideas from the Periphery. *American Journal of Comparative Law* 55(4), 617–76.

Langford, M. (2014) Housing Rights Litigation: Grootboom and Beyond. In M. Langford, B. Cousins, J. Dugard, and T. Madlingozi, eds., *Socio-Economic*

Rights in South Africa: Symbols or Substance? New York: Cambridge University Press.

Langford, M., Cousins, B., Dugard, J., and Madlingozi, T. (2011) *Symbols or Substance? The Role and Impact of Socio-Economic Rights Strategies in South Africa*. Cambridge: Cambridge University Press.

Langford, M., Cousins, B., Dugard, J., and Madlingozi, T., eds. (2014) *Socio-Economic Rights in South Africa: Symbols or Substance?* New York: Cambridge University Press.

Langford, M., Rodríguez Garavito, C., and Rossi, J., eds. (2017) *Social Rights Judgments and the Politics of Compliance: Making It Stick*. Cambridge: Cambridge University Press.

Lau, H. Courts, the Law, and LGBT Rights in Asia. Oxford Research Encyclopedia of Politics. May 29, 2020; accessed Oct. 29, 2021. https://doi.org/10.1093/acrefore/9780190228637.013.1230

Lehoucq, E. (2021) Legal Threats and the Emergence of Legal Mobilization: Conservative Mobilization in Colombia. *Law & Social Inquiry* 46(2), 299–330.

Magaloni, B. (2003) Authoritarianism, Democracy and the Supreme Court: Horizontal Exchange and the Rule of Law in Mexico. In S. Mainwaring and C. Welna, eds., *Democratic Accountability in Latin America*. Oxford: Oxford University Press.

Mainwaring, S., and Welna, C., eds. (2003) *Democratic Accountability in Latin America*. Oxford: Oxford University Press.

Merlinsky, M. G. (2009) Atravesando el rio: la construcción social y política de la cuestión ambiental en Argentina. PhD Dissertation, Universidad de Buenos Aires/Paris 8.

Michel, V. (2018) *Prosecutorial Accountability and Victims' Rights in Latin America*. Cambridge: Cambridge University Press.

Nunes, R. (2010) Ideational Origins of Progressive Judicial Activism: The Colombian Constitutional Court and the Right to Health. *Latin American Politics and Society* 52(3), 67–97.

O'Donnell, G. (1999) Horizontal Accountability and New Polyarchies. In A. Schedler, L. Diamond, and M. Plattner, eds., *The Self-Restraining State: Power and Accountability in New Democracies*. London: Lynne Rienner.

Pasqualucci, J. (2013) *The Practice and Procedure of the Inter-American Court of Human Rights*. Cambridge: Cambridge University Press.

Peñas Defago, M. A., and Morán Faúndes, J. (2014) Conservative Litigation against Sexual and Reproductive Health Policies in Argentina. *Reproductive Health Matters* 22(44), 82–90.

Popova, M., and Post, V. (2018) Prosecuting High-Level Corruption in Eastern Europe. *Communist and Post-Communist Studies* 5(3), 231–44.

Ríos-Figueroa, J. (2007) Fragmentation of Power and the Emergence of an Effective Judiciary in Mexico, 1994–2002. *Latin American Politics and Society* 49(1), 31–57.

(2011) Institutions of Constitutional Justice in Latin America. In G. Helmke and J. Ríos-Figueroa, eds., *Courts in Latin America*. Cambridge: Cambridge University Press.

(2016) *Constitutional Courts as Mediators: Armed Conflict, Civil–Military Relations, and the Rule of Law in Latin America*. Cambridge: Cambridge University Press.

Roa Roa, J. (2019) Justicia constitucional, deliberación y democracia en Colombia: Jeremy Waldron reflexivo en Bogotá. *Revista Derecho del Estado* 44, 57–98.

Rodriguez Raga, J. C. (2011) Strategic Deference in the Colombian Constitutional Court, 1992–2006. In G. Helmke and J. Ríos-Figueroa, eds., *Courts in Latin America*. Cambridge: Cambridge University Press.

Rodríguez-Garavito, C. (2010) Toward a Sociology of the Global Rule of Law Field: Neoliberalism, Neoconstitutionalism, and the Contest over Judicial Reform in Latin America. In B. Garth and Y. Dezalay, eds., *Lawyers and the Rule of Law in an Era of Globalization*. London: Routledge.

(2011) Latin American Constitutionalism: Social and Economic Rights: Beyond the Courtroom: The Impact of Judicial Activism on Socioeconomic Rights in Latin America. *Texas Law Review* 89: 1669–98.

Rodríguez-Garavito, C., and Rodríguez-Franco, D. (2015) *Radical Deprivation on Trial: The Impact of Judicial Activism on Socioeconomic Rights in the Global South*. Cambridge: Cambridge University Press.

Rosenberg, G. (1991) *The Hollow Hope: Can Courts Bring about Social Change?* Chicago, IL: University of Chicago Press.

Ruibal, A. (2014) Movement and Counter-Movement: A History of Abortion Law Reform and the Backlash in Colombia 2006–2014. *Reproductive Health Matters* 22(44), 42–51.

Sandoval Rojas, N. (2013) La movilización social en tiempos de la constitución: feministas, indígenas y víctimas de crímenes de estado ante la Corte Constitucional colombiana. *Colombia Internacional* 79, 191–217.

Schedler, A. (1999) Conceptualizing Accountability. In A. Schedler, L. Diamond, and M. Plattner, eds., *The Self Restraining State: Power and Accountability in New Democracies*. London: Lynne Reinner.

Shen-Bayh, F. (2018) Strategies of Repression. *World Politics* 70(3), 321–57.

Sieder, R., Schjolden, L., and Angell, A., eds. (2005) *The Judicialization of Politics in Latin America*. London: Palgrave Macmillan.

Sigal, M., Rossi, J., and Morales, D. (2017) Argentina: Implementation of Collective Cases. In M. Langford, C. Rodríguez Garavito, and J. Rossi, eds., *Social Rights Judgments and the Politics of Compliance: Making It Stick*, 140–75. Cambridge: Cambridge University Press.

Stroh, A. (2018) Sustaining and Jeopardising a Credible Arbiter: Judicial Networks in Benin's Consolidating Democracy. *International Political Science Review* 39(5), 600–15.

Taylor, M. (2018) Getting to Accountability: A Framework for Planning and Implementing Anti-Corruption Strategies. *Daedalus* 147(3), 63–82.

Trochev, A. (2018) Patronal Politics, Judicial Networks and Collective Judicial Autonomy in Post-Soviet Ukraine. *International Political Science Review* 39 (5), 662–78.

Uprimny, D., and Durán, J. (2014) *Equidad y Protección Judicial del Derecho a La Salud en Colombia*. Santiago de Chile: CEPAL/Naciones Unidas.

Voeten, E. (2020) Populism and Backlashes against International Courts. *Perspectives on Politics* 18(2), 407–22.

Von Bogdandy, A. (2015) Ius Constitutionale Commune in Latin America: Observations on Transformative Constitutionalism. *AJIL Unbound* 109, 109–14.

Waldron, J. (2006) The Core Case against Judicial Review. *Yale Law Journal* 115 (6), 1346–406.

White, L., and Perelman, J. (2011) *Stones of Hope: How African Activists Reclaim Human Rights to Challenge Global Poverty*. Stanford, CA: Stanford University Press.

Wilson, B. (2009) Rights Revolutions in Unlikely Places: Colombia and Costa Rica. *Journal of Politics in Latin America* 1(2), 59–85.

(2011) Litigating Health Rights in Costa Rica. In A. E. Yamin and S. Gloppen, eds., *Health Rights in Comparative Perspective*. Cambridge, MA: Harvard University Press.

Yashar, D. (2018) *Homicidal Ecologies: Illicit Economies and Complicit States in Latin America*. Cambridge: Cambridge University Press.

2

Critical Disconnects

Progressive Jurisprudence and Tenacious Impunity in Mexico

Janice K. Gallagher and Jorge Contesse

> Technical [investigation] capacities are next to non-existent. The bigger issue is that basically they [Mexican authorities] aren't able to investigate crime in general. And then there are those individual cases where ... there's a political order: You have to give me results. And these are the four methods they know to get results: beating, asphyxiation, electric shocks and rape.
>
> Author Interview with Jan Jarab, High Commission for Human Rights in Mexico, 2019

INTRODUCTION

The year 2011 should have been a watershed year for Mexican human rights. In June, Mexico amended its constitution to fully incorporate international human rights standards in their national legal landscape. A month later, Mexico's Supreme Court decided to comply with a far-reaching Inter-American Court ruling on the 1974 enforced disappearance of activist Rosendo Radilla. Under this ruling, military jurisdiction would be limited and Mexican judges would be required to ensure domestic legislation was compatible with the American Convention on Human Rights. Mexico was also in the midst of a transition from a written to an oral system of justice, which it was hoped would revolutionize the slow, corrupt Mexican judicial system, known for reliably generating reams of case files and impunity, but little else. All of these institutional changes were occurring amid mass mobilization of civil society precisely around the issue of disappearances and human rights: in early May 2011, poet and journalist Javier Sicilia led a march which grew to over 100,000 people: the collective cry was "*estamos hasta la madre*" (we have had it) with violence, and they demanded peace with justice and dignity.

Much extant literature on judicial politics in Latin America would view these developments as auspicious for strengthening Mexico's historically weak judicial performance (see Taylor 1997).[1] These jurisprudential and constitutional developments all indicated a strengthening of vertical accountability (O'Donnell 1998; Helmke and Ríos-Figueroa 2011). Scholars, advocates and policymakers hoped that these reforms would further strengthen a supreme court empowered after the democratic transition of 2000 (Magaloni 2003; Ríos-Figueroa 2007; Staton 2010). However, many judicial politics scholars focused on Mexico have long cautioned that implementation does not necessarily follow institutional change, and that political incentives must be taken seriously when we consider judicial performance (Finkel 2008; Davis 2009; Knight 2012).

What has been the result of these institutional changes and popular mobilization? By nearly any measure, reality has fallen tragically short of the plans and hopes of legal reformers and civil society activists. The unprecedented wave of violence that triggered the 2011 mobilizations has not relented: by the state's own measure, between 2011 and 2017 there were more than 140,000 intentional homicides, 94,000 rapes and 40,000 disappearances.[2] This violence has been met by a legal system incapable of and/or unwilling to meaningfully address widespread impunity – and this has proved especially true in cases involving federal security forces. The involvement of the army in the 2014 disappearance of 43 students from the radical Ayotzinapa teachers' college; the execution of 22 civilians by the army in Tlatlaya also in 2014; and the alleged involvement of 257 marines in 36 cases of enforced disappearances in Nuevo Laredo in 2018 are the most well-known cases – and despite their notoriety, no federal state agents have been prosecuted for these crimes.[3]

[1] We use Carolyn Beer's (2006: 33–34) conception of judicial performance: "a broad concept encompassing the behavior of the supreme court, criminal and civil courts, prosecutors and police, as well as crime, corruption and human rights violations."

[2] Data from *Sistema Nacional de Seguridad Pública*, which aggregates state and national-level data.

[3] While there is no public information which indicates that federal officials have been convicted for their involvement in the Ayotzinapa disappearances, there have been several arrests. In September 2020 it was announced that arrest warrants had been issued for members of the military and federal police. In March 2020, four government officials and a marine were charged with torture and obstruction of justice in the investigation. See Maureen Meyer and Moses Ngong, "6 Years after Ayotzinapa Disappearances, Mexico's

How do we understand the spectacular and tragically costly failure of Mexico's judicial system to strengthen human rights protections and break patterns of impunity over the course of the past decade? In this chapter, we argue that the disconnect between progressive human rights jurisprudence in Mexico and the investigation and prosecution of cases of lethal violence stems from two intersecting dynamics. First, we argue that the Mexican state's historically weak, fragmented, federal nature has resulted in the institutionalization of mechanisms that enable impunity. Neither the state nor mobilized civil society have focused on addressing the training, incentives and resources of investigators, prosecutors and judges – and this lack of attention has helped to make impunity exceptionally tenacious in Mexico. Second, we argue that socio-legal mobilization has not coalesced around demands for effective implementation of progressive jurisprudence or basic tenets of the rule of law. We have instead seen human rights litigation proceed simultaneously on two distinct tracks: on the one hand, the strategic litigation of a small number of paradigmatic cases connected to, or in relation with, the inter-American human rights system; and the advocacy and collaborative investigation of cases by small, state-based organizations, on the other.

CONTRADICTIONS AND INSTITUTIONAL DYSFUNCTION

Mexico under the rule of the *Partido Revolucionario Institucional* (PRI, 1929–2000) was full of contradictions. The PRI claimed to represent the interests of Mexico's workers, peasants, military and common people, while presiding over sham elections. It violated human rights at home, especially during the Dirty War of the 1960s–1980s, while championing human rights abroad and accepting political exiles from the rest of Latin America. It relied on clientelistic social goods distribution and grew a bloated, inefficient state bureaucracy, while at the same time adopting neoliberal economic policies. The progressive 1917 constitution, in place throughout PRI rule, set the standard for guaranteeing social rights at the time, but shortcomings in its implementation left Mexicans without redress for violations of their civil, political and social rights. Perhaps most relevant for this chapter: it was at once a political system with highly centralized power concentrated in a single political party, but at the same

Government Must Build on Its Efforts to Provide Truth and Justice," *WOLA*, September 24, 2020.

time highly fragmented, with states and localities run by cabals of local *caudillos* (strongmen) and politicians.

The centralized-yet-fragmented nature of Mexican politics was ingrained under PRI rule, and continued to shape politics after the PRI lost the presidency in 2000. The rough agreement between local leaders and national politicians under PRI rule was to keep the peace, or at least enough peace to allow the federal government to keep up the veneer that in Mexico "*no pasa nada*" – that nothing happens and nothing is wrong. This local-level stability, managed by the governing coalition of local politicians/*caudillos*, created a dynamic in which power, politics and the rule of law were "personal, informal, to a degree reciprocal, and resistant to formal laws and regulations" (Knight and Pansters 2005: 3). As a result of these local power dynamics, Mexican judicial and security institutions were rendered largely irrelevant: instead of police, courts, or legislatures mediating conflict, local power-sharing coalitions meted out justice according to their own political calculations. When crimes were investigated, torture was commonly used to extract confessions. As Magaloni and Rodriguez (2020: 1031) argue, "institutions that began relying on coerced confessions never invested in investigative capacity, which meant that the Mexican criminal justice system became utterly incapable of sorting criminals from innocent people." Added to this dynamic, the Mexican constitution provides for significant state autonomy, including different criminal codes and barriers to implementing national laws without state legislative authorization. Together, these dynamics rendered local judicial institutions largely inert and/or wholly ineffective through the early 2000s.

While Mexico's institutions had a veneer of power and centralization, but were in fact fragmented and weak at the time of the democratic transition, the control of Mexico's illicit markets was increasingly consolidated by powerful drug trafficking organizations (DTOs). Beginning in the late 1980s, Mexican DTOs began to gain power and wealth, disrupting the stable relationships they had negotiated with local politicians. As US demand for drugs increased and Colombian cartels weakened, DTOs' economic prospects exploded. Even as the PRI showed cracks in its stranglehold on Mexican electoral politics, the PRI's party structure facilitated DTO operations. As Shirk (2011: 9) summarizes: "Mexico's centralized, single-party political system enabled DTOs to create a system-wide network of corruption that ensured distribution rights, market access, and even official government protection for drug traffickers in exchange for lucrative bribes." These dynamics gave rise to unprecedented wealth and power for Mexican cartels in the early 2000s.

While the PRI's 2000 election defeat marked a new era in Mexican politics, newly democratic Mexico quickly disappointed most of its citizens. Under center-right president Vicente Fox (2000–2006), efforts at reform and economic growth stalled, while inequality, unemployment, crime and corruption rose. When fellow PAN (*Partido Acción Nacional*) President Felipe Calderón took power in 2006, he perceived that organized crime, especially drug traffickers, had never been more powerful, and that they were further weakening the power and legitimacy of the Mexican state, particularly the federal forces. "The Calderón team argued that past administrations had not effectively confronted criminal organizations and that the threat had reached a tipping point in perhaps six or so of Mexico's 32 states" (Bailey 2014: 5). Calderón responded to this threat by sending the military into cartel hotspots, with an explicit strategy to take out the leaders of DTOs. While the government succeeded in taking down cartel leaders, highly visible violence erupted in many of Mexico's cities. Destabilized cartels, together with their respective allies within the Mexican state (including local and state police, politicians and/or federal forces), engaged in grisly and open combat, frequently killing civilians.

FEDERAL ADVANCES IN HUMAN RIGHTS JURISPRUDENCE

Running parallel to, and separate from, the institutional weakness and fragmented Mexican state, the Mexican Supreme Court and Mexican Constitution have been developing a backbone of internationally recognized human rights jurisprudence. Compelled by rulings from the Inter-American Court of Human Rights (IACtHR), developments of conventionality control[4] and the influence of Mexican legal scholars through the expansion of the *ius constitutionale commune* school, which originated in the Max Planck Institute in Heidelberg, have been lauded internationally (Pelayo Moller 2012: 1033). Scholars affiliated with the *ius constitutionale commune* work closely with Mexican jurists based at the

[4] The conventionality control doctrine breaks ground insofar as it creates *domestic* judicial power by an *international* court: the court seeks to transfer authority to domestic judges, bypassing domestic legislatures. For example, if in a given jurisdiction, district judges are not allowed under their domestic constitution to give preference to international treaties over domestic law then conventionality control overrides this.

Universidad Nacional Autónoma de México (UNAM), Latin America's largest public university. Publications on the influence of the *Ius Constitutionale Commune in Latin America* (ICCAL) on inter-American human rights law abound; academic exchanges are recurrent, and the dissemination of a normative language on democracy and human rights seems hegemonic in Mexico. If one looked only at the literature, one could have the impression that Mexico is a place where human rights litigation is deeply "transformative" (von Bogdandy 2015). The reality is, however, very different. In this section, we discuss these progressive federal decisions and constitutional provisions. In the rest of the chapter, we discuss the reasons for the gap between these elegant, progressive decisions and the widespread impunity in Mexico.

Campo Algodonero: Political and Social Movement Context

In the decade before Mexico's "democratic transition," the first alarm bells were sounded about the killing of women. With the first cases taking place in the northern border state of Chihuahua among young women working in the border factories known as *maquiladoras*, a coalition of families began to organize.[5] They called the phenomenon of the killing of women *feminicidio*, femicide, and by 2003 Amnesty International had adopted the new analytical category, documenting 370 femicides (Amnesty International 2003; Anaya 2011; Staudt 2009: 107). As the occurrence of femicides coincided with the 1994 implementation of the North American Free Trade Agreement (NAFTA), the US press became particularly interested in the story. By 1998, news of femicides in Chihuahua reached the *New York Times* and CNN. By 2004, there were large international protests[6] on the US–Mexico border with celebrity endorsers.

While international attention flourished, family members of victims were slowly becoming disillusioned by the state's lack of action.

[5] The members of the Coordinadora en Pro de los Derechos de la Mujer (CPDM) included Comité Independiente de los Derechos Humanos de Chihuahua (CICH), Centro de Orientación de la Mujer Obrera (COMO), Salud y Desarrollo Comunitario (SADEC), Organización Popular Independiente (OPI), Centro de Investigación y Solidaridad Obrera (CISO), Compañeros, Mujeres por Juárez, 8 de Marzo, Asociación de Trabajadores Sociales de la UACJ, Centro para el Desarrollo Integral de la Mujer (CEDIMAC), Comité de Lucha contra la Violencia, Centro de Estudios y Taller Laboral AC (CETLAC), Tonanzin, Voces sin Eco y Red de Mujeres.

[6] On Valentines' Day 2004, for example, between 5,000 and 8,000 people mobilized on both sides of the border. Promoters included Jane Fonda, Sally Field and other celebrities (Staudt, 2009, 121).

In 1994, the governor of Chihuahua appointed a special prosecutor to look into the femicides in Juárez, and in 1998, the Special Prosecutor's Office for the Investigation of Murders of Women was created (Amnesty International 2003). None of these prosecutors lasted long – by 2003 there had been seven prosecutors. In 2004, a special prosecutor accused 120 current and former Chihuahua state officials of failing to provide justice in the case of femicides (Mueller, Hansen, and Qualtire 2009: 147). Unsurprisingly, she was subsequently removed from her position.

Meanwhile, one of the best-known cases of femicide in Juárez, the case of the *Campo Algodonero* (Cotton Field), was making its way, slowly, through the Inter-American system. In 2001, the remains of three young females were found murdered near a factory on a former cotton field. The case was reported to the Inter-American Commission on Human Rights (IACoHR) in March 2002, and the IACtHR took until 2009 to issue a decision.[7] Both commentators and activists praised the decision as "groundbreaking": the Inter-American Court had not just ordered structural remedies but it had done so through the lens of gender justice. Three years after the court's decision, the Mexican Federal Criminal Code was finally amended to incorporate the crime, defined as the killing of a woman for "gender reasons" under multiple specified circumstances (Art. 325, Federal Criminal Code). Thus, Mexico implemented some of the most important orders of the Inter-American Court.

The decision's impact went beyond the federal level: between 2009 and 2017, many states in Mexico also codified the crime of femicide. However, many states did so just to "cultivate an image of responsibility" (García-Del Moral 2019). The enactment of new laws seemed to satisfy legal elites but the process of actual implementation of those new laws took too long – if it occurred at all. Some state penal codes failed to include penalties for the offense. Others added amendments to favor law enforcement officers accused of killing women. Still others defined the crime in vague terms, which created enforcement problems since criminal law principles require a clear definition of the punishable conduct. Even in

[7] Part of the IACoHR's ruling called for the national implementation of a rapid, coordinated response to reports of the disappearance of women, called the Alba Protocol. The Alba Protocol was pioneered in Juárez in 1993, and requires that DNA of the missing person be taken; that authorities at all levels of government, along with NGOs and the media, be alerted immediately of the disappearance; and that the local Public Prosecutor coordinate the investigation. Civil society advocates have critiqued the implementation of the protocol, claiming it is activated rarely and incompletely. See Ruben Villalpando, "Entra en vigor Protocolo Alba en todo Mexico," *La Jornada*, July 26, 2012.

those cases where laws were effectively amended, prosecutors and judges failed to follow the gender perspective introduced by the Inter-American Court, many times addressing these cases as simple homicides, not *femicides*. Only in 2015 did the Mexican Supreme Court confront the situation, ruling that prosecutors must adopt a gender perspective in cases of gender violence.[8] The judgment, however, has also faced pushback, even from the Office of the Attorney General (García-Del Moral 2019), and the case's petitioner has declared that the Supreme Court has failed to incorporate the gender perspective into its adjudicative protocols.[9]

Constitutional Reform and the Case of Rosendo Radilla Pacheco

A week after the Inter-American Court issued its judgment in the *Cotton Field* case, the court handed down another landmark decision – the *Radilla Pacheco* judgment. In August 1974, members of the army in the Mexican state of Guerrero arrested and disappeared activist Rosendo Radilla Pacheco. His family initiated several judicial proceedings to determine who was responsible for the enforced disappearance, but they failed to obtain any results. This prompted Radilla's daughter to take the case to the IACoHR in 2001. The Commission ruled that Mexico had violated a series of rights detailed in the Convention and brought the case before the Inter-American Court.[10] In November 2009, the court ruled against Mexico for failing to exercise due diligence in the investigation of Radilla's disappearance, and for giving a military tribunal jurisdiction in a criminal case in which the victim was a civilian.[11] The IACtHR ordered a new criminal investigation that would identify those responsible for the crime and decide the appropriate punishment, and ruled that in all cases of a criminal violation by state security forces against a civilian, the proceedings must be carried out under the rules and regulations of ordinary criminal jurisdiction, not military jurisdiction.[12]

8 Case of Mariana Lima Buendía, Amparo en revisión 554/2013, decided on March 25, 2015. Petitioner: Irinea Buendía Cortez (mother of Mariana Lima Buendía).

9 Irinea Buendía, Mariana Lima Buendía's mother, has actively advocated in favor of the need for courts to adopt a gender perspective when they adjudicate feminicide cases. See "Continúa SCJN sin incorporar sentencia de Mariana Lima en su protocolo para juzgar con perspectiva de género," *Cimanoticias*, March 25, 2021.

10 The Inter-American Commission found that Mexico had violated the right to recognition of the juridical personality of the individual, the right to life, the right to personal integrity, the right to personal liberty, certain other juridical guarantees and the right to the legal protection of certain relative of Rosendo Radilla.

11 *Radilla Pacheco*, Inter-Am. Ct. H.R. (ser. C) No. 209.

12 *Id.*, para. 331.

The petitioners had solicited the IACtHR to call for the reform of Article 13 of the Mexican Constitution, which despite its unambiguous language, had lent itself to interpretations that conflict with the American Convention on Human Rights.[13] The Court, however, dismissed the request, observing that the crucial issue was the judiciary's *interpretation* of the reach of military justice. What was unacceptable, the Court determined, was the implementation of Article 13: The Court found that it was clear under the existing law that those charged with a crime against humanity (such as enforced disappearance) should not be judged in military courts, but rather in civilian courts. In its decision, the IACtHR reiterated the doctrine of conventionality control, whereby the Court understands that all domestic judges are directly bound by the American Convention and the interpretation of the Convention carried out by the Court.[14] The Court concluded that "constitutional and legislative determinations regarding the criteria of substantive and personal jurisdiction of military tribunals in Mexico must adhere to the principles established in the jurisprudence of this Court,"[15] a message directed to the judiciary.

Mexico's reaction to this decision is remarkable. In June 2011, the Legislative Assembly passed a constitutional amendment which gave prominence to international human rights treaties in domestic law. According to the Mexican government, this amendment was "the most important reform since 1917,"[16] which "changed the relationship between state and society."[17] As part of a process that began more than two decades earlier in other parts of Latin America, Mexico too decided to give human rights treaties an enhanced place within the domestic legal

[13] The relevant provision of the Mexican Constitution, art. 13 provides: Military jurisdiction shall be recognized for the trial of crimes against and violation of military discipline, but the military tribunals shall in no case have jurisdiction over persons who do not belong to the army. Whenever a civilian is implicated in a military crime or violation, the respective civil authority shall deal with the case.

[14] *Radilla Pacheco*, Inter-Am. Ct. H.R. (ser. C) No. 209, para. 339.

[15] *Id.* para. 340.

[16] Gobierno de México, Secretaría de la Gobernación, *¿Qué sabes sobre #DDHH y la Reforma Constitucional de 2011? 11 puntos clave para entender y ejercer tus derechos*, www.gob.mx/segob/articulos/que-sabes-sobre-ddhh-y-la-reforma-constitucional-de-2011-11-puntos-clave-para-entender-y-ejercer-tus-derechos (January 12, 2016).

[17] Gobierno de México, Secretaría de la Gobernación, *¿Por qué la Reforma Constitucional de Derechos Humanos de 2011 modificó la relación entre el gobierno y la sociedad?*, www.gob.mx/segob/articulos/por-que-la-reforma-constitucional-de-derechos-humanos-de-2011-cambio-la-forma-de-ver-la-relacion-entre-el-gobierno-y-la-sociedad?idiom=es (June 9, 2017).

system.[18] The constitutional reform effectively placed human rights treaties at the same level as the national constitution, codifying what is known in other jurisdictions as the "block of constitutionality" doctrine – that is, an understanding that individuals are protected not only by domestic guarantees (such as a bill of rights), but also – and directly – by international norms. With the constitutional amendment, Mexico signaled its unequivocal commitment to a *legalized* protection of human rights: those whose rights were violated could seek redress, resorting to claims based on both domestic and international law.

Following the June 2011 constitutional reform, the Mexican Supreme Court of Justice convened itself for a deliberation over the ways in which the judiciary should address the definitive points of the Inter-American Court's decision in *Radilla Pacheco*. Specifically, the issue was the importance that domestic judges would give to the Inter-American Court's rulings, and the ways in which they should apply the American Convention on Human Rights through the use of the conventionality control doctrine.[19] The Supreme Court devoted several days of this plenary session to reaching an agreement which held three key elements: (a) judges should conduct conventionality control *ex officio* in a model of decentralized constitutional interpretation; (b) the application of military justice must be restricted to certain concrete cases; and (c) the federal judiciary shall implement administrative measures proceeding from the holding reached by the Inter-American Court in the *Radilla Pacheco* case.[20]

The Supreme Court's reasoning on how courts should carry out their duty to exercise conventionality control was remarkable, observing that the Inter-American Court's decision together with the June 2011 constitutional reform *had altered* the conventional control regime in place until then, yielding one that did not arise from any particular constitutional rule but rather was the product of "diverse jurisprudential

[18] Cases include the Brazilian Constitution of 1988, the Chilean constitutional amendment of 1989, the Colombian Constitution of 1991, the Peruvian Constitution of 1993, and the Argentinean constitutional reform of 1994.

[19] Miscellaneous Case 912/2010, Conventionality control *ex officio* in human rights matters. Mechanism must observe the general constitutional model of control, which stems from the systematic analysis of Articles 1 and 133 of the Constitution of Mexico, Supreme Court Grand Chamber, *Judicial Weekly Gazette*, Tenth Period, Book I, Vol. I, October 2011, 313. See English translation, https://law.utexas.edu/colloquia/archive/papers-public/2011-2012/03-19-12_The%20Rosendo%20Radilla%20Case%20(2010).pdf

[20] *Id.*, para. 22.

constructions."[21] Latin American constitutional courts had already explored jurisprudential mechanisms to expand the scope of rights protection; Mexico, as González-Ocantos (2016: 253) observes, lagged behind these jurisprudential developments.

Specifically, the Mexican court believed judges to be unable to make general declarations about the validity of norms or, further, to eliminate them from the legal system. Judges would, however, be obligated to refuse to apply them in order to give preference to the constitutional text – which would now also include international treaties. In doing so, the Mexican court observed, judges should follow a three-pronged test aimed at allowing for judicial interpretation "consistent" with treaties. Only where these alternatives are impossible to carry out should the law then be nullified.[22] Lastly, the Supreme Court examined the legal foundations for the types of constitutionality control existing in Mexico and how district judges should employ them to achieve the obligation of exercising conventionality control and the mandate established in the (new) Article 1 of the Mexican Constitution.[23]

GROUNDING JURISPRUDENTIAL ELEGANCE: INSIDE STATE-LEVEL JUDICIAL BUREAUCRACIES

How did these new mandates to strengthen human rights protection and to rule in line with international law filter down to Mexico's state-based investigators and prosecutors? First, it must be noted that concurrent with the implementation of the 2011 Supreme Court decisions, Mexico was also in the midst of transitioning to the adversarial or accusatory system. In 2008, Mexico passed another set of constitutional reforms which

[21] *Id.*, para. 25.

[22] *Id.*, para. 33 (invalidating a legal rule "shall neither affect nor disrupt the logic of the principle of separation of powers and federalism, but instead strengthens the role of the judiciary as the last resort to guarantee the primacy and effective application of human rights established in the Constitution and in the international treaties to which the Mexican state is a party").

[23] The Supreme Court also held that lower courts must adhere to the interpretation arising out of the IACtHR's judgment with respect to the incompatibility of Mexico's Military Justice Code (Código de Justicia Militar [CJM; Military Justice Code], art. 57, § II (Mex.)), which permitted, before an amendment that the Mexican's Legislative Assembly passed in June 2014, for crimes or violations committed by military personnel against civilians, even those constituting crimes against humanity, to be tried in special military courts. For that reason, the Supreme Court held that from now on, "military jurisdiction shall under no circumstances be applied in situations where the human rights of civilians are violated" (Supreme Court of Mexico, Autos 912/2010, para. 44).

guaranteed a transition from the outdated written inquisitorial judicial system to a more modern oral system by 2016. This reform was intended to increase the transparency, efficiency and efficacy of the justice system. Its implementation, however, was costly and arduous, requiring everything from the retrofitting of all of Mexico's courtrooms to the extensive retraining of all judicial officials.

A significant effect of the 2008 reforms has been to significantly empower the prosecutorial arm of the Mexican judicial system and to weaken the power of judges. Under the old inquisitorial system, judges carried out both prosecutorial and judicial functions. Under the new system, judges assume only judicial functions – that is, they are not expected to investigate but to adjudicate only. The investigative function is now vested in prosecutors, who must adapt to a new environment of direct examination and cross-examination (as opposed to written and, for that matter, highly formalistic legal proceedings). While all justice systems are divided into what Ríos-Figueroa (2015) calls the "prosecutorial set" and the "administration of justice" set, it remains true that most judicial politics literature is focused on judges, relatively neglecting the investigators and prosecutors,[24] "as if scholars working on these topics had never watched an episode of *Law & Order*" (Ríos-Figueroa 2015: 196). This focus on judges is particularly problematic in Mexico in the wake of their transition to the accusatory system.

In this section, and in response to the lacunae of research on the "prosecutorial set," we focus on the structure and incentives of the *ministerio público* (MP), or lead investigator/prosecutor, under Mexico's new accusatory system. We argue that MP's institutional incentives have led directly to the non-implementation of human rights standards. We also discuss the politicized nature of state-level Mexican judges, which exacerbate the weaknesses of the MPs.

The Responsibilities and Incentives of the Ministerio Público[25]

The MP in Mexico is both the lead investigator and prosecutor in all criminal investigations. From the moment that a case enters Mexico's criminal courts, the MP makes consequential decisions: they decide how to file the cases which come to them; whether to ask that the case be

[24] Notable exceptions include Brinks (2008), Gonzalez-Ocantos (2016), Michel (2018), and Shirk (2011).

[25] This section draws from Gallagher (2022).

transferred to the *fuero federal* (the federal system); and whether to seriously investigate the case. When a person reports a disappearance, for example, the MP has the option to register the case as a missing person, a kidnapping, an illegal deprivation of liberty, or as an enforced disappearance. If it is classified as an enforced disappearance, or if the MP indicates that organized crime is involved, the MP can ask that the case be transferred to the federal system. The MP then decides if and how they will proceed with the investigation.

The importance of this aspect of judicial institutional design is hard to overstate: as Ríos-Figueroa (2015: 197) explains, this reality means not only that prosecutors are active and judges are passive – "in other words, judges can only decide the cases that are brought to the court by someone else"; it also means that the MP in effect controls the *jurisdiction* of the case, whether the case is classified as violations of *human rights*, and how rigorously, or not, a case is investigated.

In one interview, for example, one of us talked to a mother who had been present as the municipal police removed her son from their house and forced him into their truck, never to be heard from again. When she went to report the enforced disappearance of her son, the case was registered as an illegal deprivation of liberty, despite it being a textbook case of enforced disappearance. If it had been registered as an enforced disappearance, the jurisprudence stemming from the *Radilla Pacheco* case would have been applied and it could have been referred to the federal system. In the case of homicides, the decision of how to register the case is similar: while "extrajudicial execution" is not on the books in Mexico, homicides can be registered as being committed by state forces. In the *Ayotzinapa* case, this is highly relevant: many of the indicted local police officers and members of organized crime have been released because they were being investigated for kidnapping, not illegal deprivation of liberty or enforced disappearance. Since cases of kidnapping need to include a demand for ransom – something never asked for in the Ayotzinapa case – the charges filed against these officials and individuals are being dismissed.

What are the institutional incentives for MPs given this configuration of power and responsibilities? There have been some efforts to insulate the MPs from being politically driven positions. MPs gain employment through a series of exams, including a subject area exam, and psychological, medical, toxicology and socioeconomic evaluations. There is no evaluation mechanism for MPs, a provision intended to preserve their impartiality. While this is part of what has made it difficult to fire an MP, they can be informally sanctioned by giving them a heavy caseload, transferring them to a different office, or take cases away from them so they only have administrative, rather than investigative, tasks. While many MPs have indefinite contracts, new positions often have limited renewable contracts of one to three years – and not renewing a contract can be another way of sanctioning an MP. In short, while certain institutional provisions insulate MPs from the everyday politics of the local contexts, there are still mechanisms through which MPs may be pressured to operate according to the political preferences of their superiors, namely the state attorney general and governor.

MPs' vulnerability to political dynamics plays a role in their decisions about how to classify cases, as well as whether to refer them to the federal system. If we think of MPs as at least partially motivated by rational incentives (see Beer 2006), we would expect there to be strong personal and systemic incentives against filing cases in ways that implicate fellow state agents, and an aversion to creating more work. While systematic evidence of this is difficult, a former judicial official told one of us in an anonymous interview that a federal attorney general who served under Peña Nieto had laid out two institutional directives in disappearance cases: (1) do everything possible so that the number of cases of enforced disappearance are limited; (2) send as many cases as possible back to state jurisdiction. They were encouraged to question evidence that pointed to the involvement of state officials. For example, it was suggested that an investigator introduce the possibility that criminals could have dressed as security forces in order to justify the classification of a case as something other than enforced disappearance. These strategies were explicitly political: the attorney general saw it as in the interest of the administration to decrease indicators which imply federal government responsibility. Fewer cases in the federal system, and fewer enforced disappearances, help make the case that disappearances were not the state's fault.

For MPs based outside Mexico City, however, the incentives to transfer cases to the federal government are more complicated. On the one hand, cases which involve state responsibility and human rights violations (for example, torture, enforced disappearances, or homicides by a member of the state forces) are notoriously time-consuming. In a meeting with the head of the *Unidad de Búsqueda*, the unit within the attorney general's office tasked with investigating disappearances, for example, he expressed that an MP really cannot investigate more than 12–15 cases at a time, and urged victims to re-channel their advocacy efforts to pressure

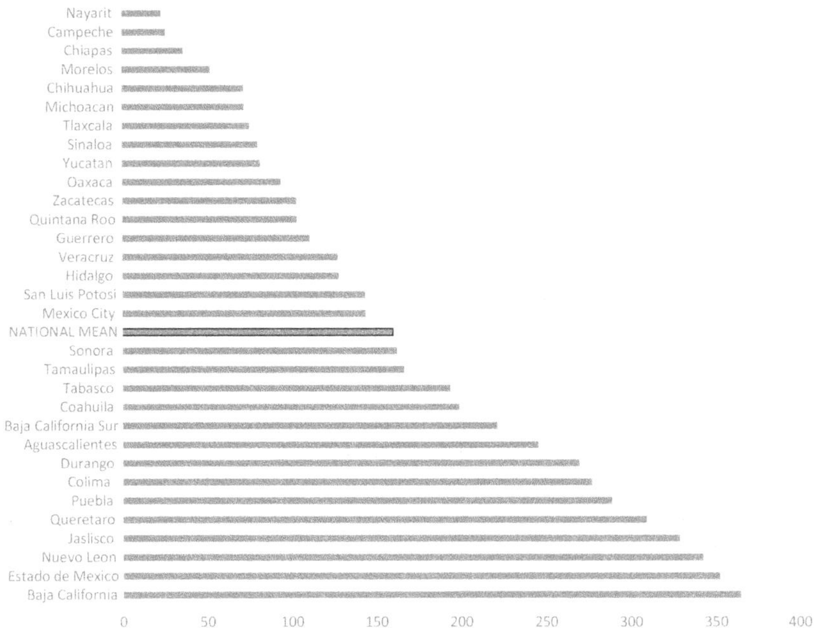

FIGURE 2.1. Median caseloads per state-based MP
Source: Reproduced from Zepeda Lecuona and Jiménez Rodríguez (2019).

the ministry charged with managing departmental budget allocations to increase the number of MPs available to investigate their cases.

As shown in Figure 2.1, the national median caseload is 160. Given this, we might think local MPs would want to transfer these cases out of their jurisdiction – and therefore incentivize the classification of cases as enforced disappearance or as involving organized crime, since those cases can be taken up under federal jurisdiction. Additionally, the influx of homicide cases shown in Figure 2.2 (from 2011 to 2017) was more than 140,000, while in the seven years prior, there had been slightly over 94,000 – a rise of nearly 40 percent that exacerbated an already high caseload. MPs, however, report that there is often pressure from their superiors to report judicial advances in politically important cases of disappearance. Successfully investigating and prosecuting cases of disappearances can be important to a governor's reelection or attorney general's appointment and career trajectory. Which of these countervailing forces has shaped how MPs classify and route cases? Since disappearances can readily be classified as so many different crimes and can be sent to the state or federal justice system, analyzing how they are classified provides us with insight into the decision-making of MPs.

TABLE 2.1. *Disappearances/enforced disappearances (2006–2018)*

Disappearances in the federal system	1,121
Disappearances in state legal systems	36,076
Enforced disappearances	1,144 registered cases investigations initiated 62 sentences * 34 sentences in federal system * 28 sentences in state judicial system 380 complaints to the National Human Rights Commission (CNDH); 20 recommendations

Sources: Mexican Government, National Public Security System www.gob.mx/sesnsp/acciones-y-programas/registro-nacional-de-datos-de-personas-extraviadas-o-desaparecidas-rnped (Consulted January 13, 2020; Data has since been removed).

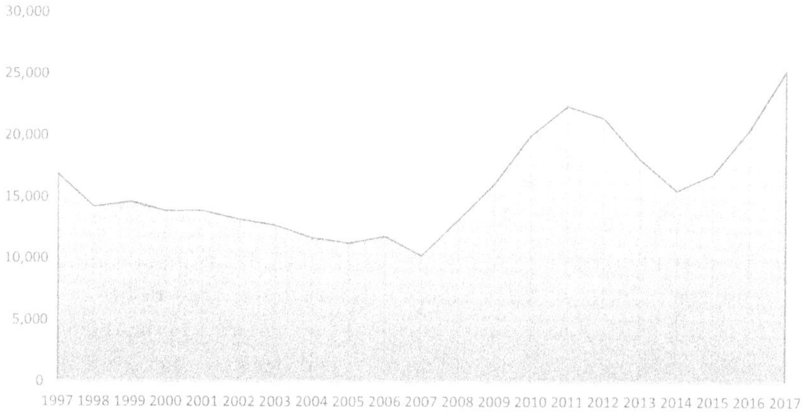

FIGURE 2.2. Reported intentional homicides in Mexico (1997–2017)
Source: INEGI (Instituto Nacional de Estadística y Geografía / National Institute of Statistics and Geography).

As shown in Table 2.1, of the more than 137,000 cases of disappearances reported in Mexico between 2006 and 2018, only 1,121 are in the federal system and only 1,144 are registered as enforced disappearances. That is, 3 percent of cases are in the federal system, leaving 97 percent to be adjudicated in the state-level courts. Likewise, only 3 percent of cases have been registered as enforced disappearances. While this 3 percent could, in theory, accurately represent state involvement in cases of disappearances, the nature of Mexican violence makes this highly unlikely.

In the next section we provide evidence to illustrate this point through a case study analysis of disappearances in the state of Nuevo León. While some of the underreporting of enforced disappearances can be attributed to the fact that enforced disappearance did not exist in the criminal codes of many states during this time, we see that even in states which had "enforced disappearance" on the books for years before the general law on enforced disappearance was passed in 2017, there is a paucity of reported cases.

Apart from playing a primary role in determining the jurisdiction of a case and whether it is a human rights violation, MPs also make the decision of when to bring a case to a judge – that is, when they have enough evidence to indict, or *consignar*, a case. In the vast majority of cases, indictments are never made. For all crimes, only 21 percent of investigations which are opened have any resolution, and of those only 5 percent have indictments issued, with an additional 3 percent being resolved through "alternative justice" or being settled. While there is sometimes simply not enough evidence to issue an indictment, which by its nature indicates a responsible party, Gallagher (2017) argues that more than 65 percent of homicides and 75 percent of disappearances show no evidence that the case has been opened after it was filed, confirming anecdotal evidence in which family members of victims gain access to their case files after months or even years have passed since they recorded the crime – only to find that the case file is empty, indicating no action has been taken by the MP.

Finally, it has long been accepted practice for MPs to ignore certain human rights violations, most notably torture (Magaloni, Magaloni, and Razu 2018). While more progressive jurisprudence and recognition of international legal jurisprudence should, in theory, override older legal precedent in the area of human rights, it is important to note that prior to the cases discussed in the previous section, the Mexican Supreme Court had ruled, essentially, that confessions extracted through torture were admissible under any circumstance,[26] and established that state agents would not be held accountable for torture. These Supreme Court decisions gave police free rein to torture: cases in which there was evidence that a confession had been attained from a suspect who had been a victim

[26] "The verification by the accused of traces of physical abuse caused during the detention did not invalidate the confession if it was corroborated by other evidence in the file" (Tesis 139–44, Séptima época, Primera Sala, *Seminario Judicial de la Federación*, noviembre 1980: 36).

of chokings, beatings, subject to electric shocks or deprived of a lawyer were given full evidentiary value. This judicial approval of torture "contributed to making torture in a practice used to extract confessions in trials" (Magaloni, Magaloni, and Razu 2018: 233), and to establishing a firm base of non-prosecution of state officials for rampant and widespread human rights abuses.

In sum, MPs play a decisive role in determining the legal filing of all cases. They are key players in understanding why the lethal violence that has plagued Mexico in the past twelve years has not translated into the justice system as human rights violations – and triggered the relevant progressive human rights jurisprudence – despite the well-documented involvement of state forces. The politics which motivate MPs' decisions are, in the end, tied to the electoral logics. This inscribes a lack of judicial independence into the classification and prosecution of lethal violence, including the investigation of human rights abuses which should be subject to the highly developed jurisprudence discussed in the previous section.

The Responsibilities and Incentives of State-Level Judges in Mexico

While significant effort is expended to make MPs' positions appear free from political influence, state judges' careers are more explicitly tied to politics. Judges are all trained as lawyers, and must work within the judicial arm of the Mexican government as *secretarios* or *actuarios* prior to becoming judges, most commonly managing the various processes and paperwork required to make the system work: notifying all parties to a case about required paperwork and appearances; reviewing all decisions and case files; and registering decisions, appeals and sentences. To become a judge, a lawyer working for the state must first pass a number of exams. Apart from this, it helps to know a magistrate, judge or politician, whose recommendation can ensure that a successful exam translates into a position as a judge.

All lawyers who become judges follow a strict hierarchy: they enter as a *juez/jueza de primera instancia* (judge of first instance). These judges do the work of everyday justice provision: deciding cases, imposing sentences, resolving *amparos* and receiving initial appeals. Next, judges may ask to be promoted to be the judge of the *tribunal unitario*, essentially an appellate court which resolves complaints made against the first instance court. Finally, judges may seek a promotion to be a magistrate in the *Sala de Segunda Estancia*, the highest court in each state.[27] The promotion to this court is based on both their record and ongoing education – as well as a nomination by the governor, and congressional approval. Governors usually present a list of nominees to the state legislature, which then confirms a subset of those nominees.

Since the highest state court judges need gubernatorial and congressional support, and these judges control the promotion of lower-level judges, this structurally politicizes all judicial positions. Added to this dynamic, the tribunal president – the most powerful judge in the state – is selected by the other magistrates, though the governor may weigh in and influence the election.[28] Finally, there is a term limit for all judicial positions. While the term varies between states (from four to six years), all states have a limit of two terms for each judicial appointment. This means that they either must ascend through the judicial appointment ladder, being sure to serve gubernatorial and congressional interests, or they will cease to be judges.

While considerations of state legislatures' and governors' preferences are built into a judge's career, as the most visible members of the judicial bureaucracy, we argue that considerations of DTO preferences should also be expected to influence their decisions. Recent literature has argued both for the importance of judges' social and professional networks in shaping their opinions (Ingram 2016), as well as for the importance of human rights NGOs and progressive members of civil society in the diffusion of new ideas about the judiciary (González-Ocantos 2016). Ingram (2016: 766–67), in a study of the diffusion of ideas in Michoacán, persuasively argues that we should think about judges

> as interconnected or interrelated with each other in ways that affect how they think about the law and legal institutions ... For [reform] projects to be most successful, the findings suggest reform advocates need to have a better sense of the social or relational architecture in which these advocates operate.

In this regard, a recent survey of judges revealed that increased state–DTO contact not only changes the political context of judges and prosecutors, but also the security context (Cortés, Ferreira, and Shirk 2016). As Mexico's security situation has worsened, judicial officials have increasingly had to take into account their own safety as they decide

[27] Each state has one *Sala de Segunda Instancia* in five different legal areas: administrative, criminal, civil, labor and family law.

[28] This infamously happened in Coahuila, when magistrates defied notoriously corrupt governor Ruben Moreira, refusing to vote for his selection for tribunal president. Moreira then refused to reappoint the magistrates for a second term.

cases. These considerations undoubtedly skew the system toward even greater levels of impunity.

Relatively little has been written about how the increasing power of criminal networks and the deepening of ties between the state and DTOs has affected the calculations of judicial officials.[29] While comprehensive data does not exist to document the extent of direct ties between organized crime and judicial system officials, collaboration between DTOs and judges became a sufficiently prominent issue that President López Obrador declared it a prosecutorial priority in May 2019,[30] emphasizing that he would pursue cases of corruption against not only federal, but also state-level judges. Collaboration between governors, their attorney generals and cartels (e.g., Fidel Herrera and Javier Duarte and fiscal Jorge Winckler in Veracruz; the Moreira brothers in Coahuila), however, have been extensively documented and prosecuted.

The deepening patterns of DTO–state collaboration have implications for the social and professional networks of both judges and prosecutors. In this environment, impunity is a lynchpin in the protective racket that is bargained over by criminal networks and corrupt state agents (Snyder and Durán Martinez 2009; Durán-Martinez 2018; Moncada 2019; Gallagher 2021). In practice, this most often means not investigating possible links between violent crime and members of organized crime; perhaps taking direct bribes; publicly challenging DTOs only when it is politically expedient; and actively working to prevent any real change in the status quo protection racket (Snyder and Durán Martinez 2009) between state officials and members of DTOs.

STATE-BASED COLLABORATIVE INVESTIGATIONS: THE NEW FACE OF HUMAN RIGHTS LITIGATION

Against this backdrop of political and institutional fragmentation, a lack of state capacity to perform a minimum level of administering justice, and the growing power of DTOs and accompanying violence, how has civil society responded? What strategies has it adopted, and what institutional barriers has it confronted as it has sought to address impunity?

[29] Magaloni and Rodríguez (2020) is an exception: their study focuses on the incentives of police and investigators around using torture to extract confessions in the context of increased militarization of security forces

[30] Following the president's commitment to prosecuting judicial corruption, charges have been brought against several judges for corruption and collusion with organized crime. "Destituyen a 15 jueces por acoso y corrupción," *El Univeral*, April 6, 2019.

Civil Society Mismatch: The Failure of Socio-Legal Mobilization

Ideas of and movements in support of human rights came about in Mexico, as in many places in the world and especially its southern cone neighbors, as a response to the violent repression of political dissent by a dictatorship. Mexico's human rights movement has its roots in the response to the 1968 Tlatelolco massacre, in which unarmed student protestors were killed by government troops, and the subsequent Dirty War, which was focused against student movements and resistance groups mainly in Guerrero and Mexico City: The paradigmatic case was that discussed earlier of Rosendo Radilla, the teacher and musician who was part of the Guerrero-based resistance and was forcibly disappeared because of his involvement in that group. Human rights activists responded to this centrally organized violence by adopting international human rights frameworks that regard the state as a coherent actor with a presumed monopoly of violence that can and should be held responsible for all violence within its borders. Groups that emerged during this time have worked to criminalize human rights abuses in domestic law through the strategic litigation of representative legal cases – including *Cotton Field* and *Radilla Pacheco*.

Given this history of human rights movements in Mexico, when violence exploded between government and DTOs following Calderón's declaration of war on organized crime, civil society was caught largely unprepared. Not only were human rights violations not meaningfully distinguishable from criminal violence in terms of how the cases were filed in the legal system, but in many cases the perpetrators were not clearly distinguishable between the state or the DTOs, and the victims were very different from the politicized students and activists of the Dirty War. The Mexico City-based human rights community did not, initially, see the violence as human rights violations, and therefore did not accompany the cases or provide their legal expertise. This left victims of state and DTO violence with very limited access to civil society allies, and without the capacity to address the structural problems of the new justice system, namely the incentives of MPs and the politicization of judges. While civil society dynamics shifted somewhat after the 2014 disappearance of the forty-three Ayotzinapa students, the human rights community has remained largely focused on the strategic litigation of a small number of cases while advocating for legislative changes.

Given these advances in human rights jurisprudence and challenges to implementation, what has civil society advocacy and human rights litigation looked like on the ground, and what impact has it had? The combination of the pushing of cases to the state-level courts and the absence of large human rights organizations in Mexico's thirty-two state capitals have meant that small, regional human rights organizations, which often have a religious affiliation, together with small victims' collectives have been left to accompany and advocate cases of lethal violence (homicides and disappearances) in state-based courts. These small state-based victims' collectives emerged mostly in the wake of the Movement for Peace with Justice and Dignity's (MPJD) mass protests of 2011. While the MPJD itself would fade, the victims who came out to protest in 2011 seeded the founding of more than sixty victims' collectives in nearly every state touched by violence. These collectives diffused and institutionalized participatory investigations[31] in at least eighteen of Mexico's thirty-two states, successfully pushed through national legislation, met with presidents and made themselves known internationally. They have led efforts to get the Mexican state to search for victims of disappearances, resulting in hundreds of remains being identified and returned to their families – something which undoubtedly would not have happened without their pressure. And while judicial results remain abysmal in these cases, they have succeeded in persuading the state to take some investigatory steps in nearly all cases, and in a limited number of cases, in this inauspicious legal environment, these cases have resulted in prosecutions and convictions.

Achievements of Local Organization: Cracks in the Wall of Impunity

In order to more fully understand the role, challenges and achievements of these small state-based victims' collectives and human rights organizations, in this section we focus on one human rights NGO in Nuevo León, *Ciudadanos en Apoyo de los Derechos Humanos AC* (CADHAC). CADHAC is arguably a crucial, rather than representative case: it is one of the oldest human rights organizations in the country, it is a faith-based NGO, and it also works closely with a long-standing, victim-led collective. After Nuevo León experienced a historic wave of violence and disappearances between 2009 and 2012, CADHAC was among the first organizations in Mexico to establish participatory investigations with the state, which have been held sporadically since then. The MPJD

[31] Participatory investigations: Regular meetings between state investigators and family members of victims in which investigatory goals are collectively set and both states and victims provide information and take actions to move the investigation forward.

TABLE 2.2. *Judicial and investigatory results for disappearances committed in Nuevo León (2009–2012)*

Summary judicial results (as of 2019)	
Total disappearances documented by CADHAC	269
Disappearances with no indictments	232
Disappearances with at least one indicted perpetrator	37
Total number of perpetrators indicted	53
Likely perpetrator:[a] by state affiliation	
Federal agents	32
...federal agents indicted for enforced disappearance	0
Local officials	22
...local officials indicted for enforced disappearance	6
Indictments: crime perpetrator was charged with (in cases of disappearances)[b]	
Illegal deprivation of liberty	26
Kidnapping	21
Organized crime	17
Other/unknown	12
Aggravated kidnapping	7
Enforced disappearance	**6**
Robbery	2
Sentences	
Found not guilty	9
Found guilty	12
Found guilty of enforced disappearance	0
Pending	33

[a] One author reviewed CADHAC's case files and attended participatory investigations held with members of the state attorney general's office. If there was an indication (witness testimony, video footage, last known location) that federal or local forces had been involved in the disappearance, we classified these cases as "likely" to have federal/local involvement.
[b] A perpetrator can be charged with multiple crimes associated with committing a single disappearance.
Source: Analysis of original data. Disaggregated data to be published in Gallagher (forthcoming)

brokered them into an advocacy role with the state attorney general (Gallagher 2019), and they formed a close and functional working relationship with the state prosecutors' office.

As summarized in Table 2.2, CADHAC documented the disappearance of 269 people between 2009 and 2012. Each of these cases was brought to the NGO by a friend or family member, and CADHAC agreed to accompany cases in which the victims' family member was able to come to regular meetings with other victims of violence and the NGO's staff. Of these 269 disappearances, only twelve cases that include the disappearance of thirty-seven people had at least one indicted perpetrator, and in four cases there have been at least one guilty sentence. If we think of the disappearance of one person as a case, 14 percent of the cases that CADHAC documented had an indicted perpetrator.

From these results it is evident that while CADHAC's advocacy on behalf of these cases has led to indictments, achieving guilty sentences has been much more difficult. We see that many cases that involve state forces, and all cases involving federal agents, that could be classified as enforced disappearance are instead being processed as illegal deprivation of liberty, kidnapping, or under organized crime. There have been only six indictments of local security officials for enforced disappearance, and none of these has resulted in a conviction.

In addition to these very limited judicial advances, CADHAC has facilitated the location of 56 of the 269 (21 percent) people that were reported to them as missing. In 27 of the cases in which the disappeared person was located, they assisted family members in identifying the remains of their loved ones through DNA analysis. In 21 of these cases, the disappeared person was found alive in the same year they disappeared – and in most of these cases the disappeared person was found within the first month. In only two cases was a person found alive after more than a year, and in 79 percent of cases – that is, 213 of 269 people – the person remains missing.

CONCLUSION

Mexico remains the site of intense contradictions. In this chapter, we have seen how the historical roots of fragmentation, corruption and institutional weakness have frustrated the intentions of state reformers. The overhaul of the justice system, innovations in the constitutional positioning of international law, and trailblazing jurisprudence around femicide and disappearances have been met with a powerful *ministerio público* who is not incentivized or held accountable for acting in accordance with these high-minded human rights standards. As a result, human rights violations are rendered legally invisible, and investigations and prosecutions are stalled. Increasing strength of DTOs, and their links with the same politicians who appoint and confirm judges, exacerbate these dynamics. While understandable given their historical roots, mainstream human rights advocacy's focus on high-level institutional reform, rather than on the implementation of justice and close attention to the vital work of investigators, prosecutors and judges, has failed to undo persistent patterns and practices of impunity. Small organizations propelled by victim advocacy and activism continue to fight valiantly in state-level courts, but their possibilities for success are limited given the deep-seated structural problems within the Mexican justice system.

We understand stubborn impunity and judicial dysfunction not as a backlash, but as a continuation of the duplicity of the Mexican state. The Mexican judiciary has never provided effective vertical accountability, and these reforms can be understood as altering the form but not the substance of the operation of the Mexican justice system. If we characterize the Mexican justice system as being designed as a sponge to absorb the ire of the citizens when their rights are violated, without any intention to deliver substantive or systemic redress, we can see that despite these apparent disruptions, this function has been preserved. While talented lawyers and lawmakers have focused their attention on altering the law on paper, and on-the-ground activists and advocates have likewise expended tireless efforts, justice remains out of reach for Mexican citizens.

References

Amnesty International (2003) *Mexico: Intolerable Killings. Ten Years of Abductions and Murders in Ciudad Juárez and Chihuahua*. London: Amnesty International.

Anaya, A. (2011) Explaining High Levels of Transnational Pressure Over Mexico: The Case of the Disappearances and Killings of Women in Ciudad Juárez. The International Journal of Human Rights 15(3), 339–58.

Bailey, J. (2014) *The Politics of Crime in Mexico: Democratic Governance in a Security Trap*. Boulder, CO: First Forum Press.

Beer, C. (2006) Judicial Performance and the Rule of Law in the Mexican States. *Latin American Politics and Society* 48(3), 33–61.

Brinks, D. M. (2008) *The Judicial Response to Police Killings in Latin America*. New York: Cambridge University Press.

Chapman, T. L., and Chaudoin, S. (2013) Ratification Patterns and the International Criminal Court. *International Studies Quarterly* 57(2), 400–09.

Cortés, N. G., Ferreira, O. R., and Shirk, D. A. (2016) *Justiciabarómetro – Perspectives on Mexico's Criminal Justice System: What Do Its Operators Think?* San Diego, CA: Justice in Mexico.

Davis, D. E. (2009) Non-State Armed Actors, New Imagined Communities, and Shifting Patterns of Sovereignty and Insecurity in the Modern World. *Contemporary Security Policy* 30(2), 221–45.

Finkel, J. S. (2008) *Judicial Reform as Insurance Policy: Argentina, Peru, and Mexico in the 1990s*. Notre Dame, IN: University of Notre Dame Press.

Gallagher, J. (2017) The Last Mile Problem: Activists, Advocates, and the Struggle for Justice in Domestic Courts. *Comparative Political Studies* 50(12), 1666–98.

(2019). The Judicial Breakthrough Model: Transnational Advocacy Networks and Lethal Violence. In A. Alejandro and B. Frey, eds., *The Human Rights Crisis in Mexico*. Philadelphia, PA: University of Pennsylvania Press.

(2022) *Bootstrap Justice: The Search for Mexico's Disappeared*. Oxford: Oxford University Press.

García-Del Moral, P. (2019) The "Formally Feminist State": A Potential New Player in the Inter-American Human Rights System? *American Journal of International Law Unbound* 113, 365–69.

González-Ocantos, E. A. (2016) *Shifting Legal Visions: Judicial Change and Human Rights Trials in Latin America*. Cambridge: Cambridge University Press.

Helmke, G., and Ríos-Figueroa, J., eds. (2011) *Courts in Latin America*. Cambridge: Cambridge University Press.

Ingram, M. (2016) *Crafting Courts in New Democracies: The Politics of Subnational Judicial Reform in Brazil and Mexico*. New York: Cambridge University Press.

Knight, A. (2012) Narco-Violence and the State in Modern Mexico. In W. Pansters, ed., *Violence, Coercion, and State-Making in Twentieth-Century Mexico: The Other Half of the Centaur*. Palo Alto, CA: Stanford University Press.

Knight, A., and Pansters, W. G., eds. (2005) *Caciquismo in Twentieth-Century Mexico*. London: Institute for the Study of the Americas.

Magaloni, B. (2003) Authoritarianism, Democracy and the Supreme Court: Horizontal Exchange. In S. Mainwaring and C. Welna, eds., *Democratic Accountability in Latin America*. Oxford: Oxford University Press.

Magaloni, B., and Rodriguez, L. (2020). Institutionalized Police Brutality: Torture, the Militarization of Security, and the Reform of Inquisitorial Criminal Justice in Mexico. *American Political Science Review* 114(4), 1013–34.

Magaloni, B., Magaloni, A. L., and Razu, Z. (2018) La tortura como método de investigación criminal: El impacto de la guerra contra las drogas en México. *Política y gobierno* 25(2), 223–61.

Michel, V. (2018) *Prosecutorial Accountability and Victims' Rights in Latin America*. New York: Cambridge University Press.

Mueller, C., Hansen, M., and Qualtire, K. (2009). Femicide on the Border and New Forms of Protest. In K. Staudt, T. Payan, and Z. A. Kruszewski, eds., *Human Rights along the US–Mexico Border: Gendered Violence and Insecurity*. Tucson: University of Arizona Press.

O'Donnell, G. A. (1998). Horizontal Accountability in New Democracies. *Journal of Democracy* 9(3), 112–26.

Pelayo Moller, C. M. (2012) Book review of Ferrer Mac-Gregor, E. & Silva García, F. (2012). Jurisdicción militar y derechos humanos. *El caso Radilla ante la Corte Interamericana de Derechos Humanos, published in Anuario Mexicano de Derecho Internacional* 12, 1029–35.

Ríos-Figueroa, J. (2007) Fragmentation of Power and the Emergence of an Effective Judiciary in Mexico, 1994–2002. *Latin American Politics and Society* 49(1), 31–57.

(2015) Judicial Institutions. In J. RioGandhi and R. Ruiz-Rufino, eds., *Routledge Handbook of Comparative Political Institutions*. New York: Routledge.

Shirk, D. A. (2011) The Drug War in Mexico: Confronting a Shared Threat. Working Paper No. 60 Council on Foreign Relations.

Snyder, R., and Duran-Martinez, A. (2009) Does Illegality Breed Violence? Drug Trafficking and State-Sponsored Protection Rackets. *Crime, Law and Social Change* 52(3), 253–73.

Staton, J. (2010) *Judicial Power and Strategic Communication in Mexico*. New York: Cambridge University Press.

Staudt, K. (2009) *Violence and Activism at the Border: Gender, Fear, and Everyday Life in Ciudad Juárez*. Austin: University of Texas Press.

Taylor, M. C. (1997) Why No Rule of Law in Mexico – Explaining the Weaknesses of Mexico's Judicial Branch. *New Mexico Law Review* 27, 141–66.

Von Bogdandy, A. (2015) Ius Constitutionale Commune en América Latina: una mirada a un constitucionalismo transformador. *Revista Derecho del Estado* 34, 3–50.

Zepeda-Lecuona, G., and Jiménez Rodríguez, P. G. (2019) Índice estatal de desempeño de las procuradurías y fiscalías 2019. *Impunidad Cero*. www.impunidadcero.org/uploads/app/articulo/123/contenido/1567527134U67.pdf

3

When Winning in the Courts Is Not Enough

Abortion and the Limits of Legal Mobilization without Grassroots Involvement in Peru

Camila Gianella

INTRODUCTION

Peru is often cited as an example of the internationalization of sexual and reproductive health and rights (SRHR) norms through supranational litigation. Yet the impact on petitioners and other similarly situated women in Peruvian society has fallen far short of expectations (Gianella & Yamin, 2018). Moreover, success before international tribunals, as well as in national courts, has not prevented the rise of contestation around sexual and reproductive health and rights in the country. This chapter argues that the professionalization and specialization of Peruvian feminist NGOs, which allowed these organizations to become key actors in the institutionalization of a gendered approach at different levels of the state, also detached these organizations from grassroots movements. This detachment ultimately limited the capacity of the NGOs involved in litigation to access a network of political support and to leverage the opportunities presented by litigation. In contrast, anti-abortion organizations are closely connected to grassroots organizations and have developed links to political organizations that allow them to deploy different strategies to stall efforts at expanding the right to abortion.

Since the early 2000s, highly professionalized and well-connected Peruvian feminist NGOs secured important normative victories at the international level, and more recently in national higher courts. These victories have, however, failed to trigger broader social change. As Epp (1998) notes, the limited impact of successful legal mobilization is closely linked to the core characteristics of the actors involved in litigation and their limited capacity to create a strong network of support. This condition has been described by others as key to advancing abortion rights in Latin America (Roa & Klugman, 2014; Ruibal, Chapter 4 in this volume). My study of Peru confirms its centrality.

In striking contrast to progressive litigants, conservative actors, in alliance with religious groups who have deep grassroots movements and are well connected in Congress, have successfully responded to court outcomes by blocking bills to expand the grounds for legal abortion, and making abortion an important issue during political campaigns. Since 2011, presidential and congressional candidates are asked to stand against abortion in public campaigns.[1] Additionally (as documented in other Latin American countries) abortion, sexual and reproductive rights issues, as well as gender equality, have become part of opposition politics (Vaggione et al., 2018). This chapter aims at shedding some light on the risk of an overspecialization of strategic litigation detached from social movements.

The socio-legal studies literature on abortion rights disputes across the globe and particularly in Latin America has analysed the key role played by the courts (Ansolabehere, 2009; Ruibal, 2014) and the strategies deployed by activists contesting access to legal abortion (Morán Faúndes & Peñas Defago, 2016). This includes the emergence of conservative legal mobilization (Lemaitre, 2014; Lemaitre & Sieder, 2017; Bergallo et al., 2018) and the legal frames developed during these disputes (Lemaitre, 2014; Bergallo & Ramón Michel, 2016; Ramón Michel & Bergallo, 2018). Other scholars have analysed the relationship between political parties and churches (Morán Faúndes & Peñas Defago, 2016), including a focus on the role of religious groups in local politics (Machado Campos, 2012; Montero, 2012; Vaggione & Machado Campos, 2020). This chapter aims to provide a different, but complementary angle. While recognizing the key role played by conservative actors in the litigation of sexual and reproductive rights, I assess whether progressive legal strategies, as well as the type of actors behind those strategies, shape the precarity of court victories that expand and enforce

[1] For example, during the campaign, the presidential candidate Pedro Pablo Kuczynski signed a commitment in which he promised to reject abortion (except in life-threatening situations) and to recognize the value of the "natural family" (i.e., only those unions comprising a woman and a man). In March 2011, in a meeting with the archbishop of Lima and a leader of the Peruvian Catholic Church, presidential candidate Ollanta Humala confirmed his conservative Catholic upbringing, his commitment to respecting family values as defined by the Catholic Church, and his position against abortion and same-sex marriage.

abortion rights in Peru. To be sure, the chapter does not dismiss the positive developments towards the decriminalization of abortion in Latin America. But as stated in the Introduction to this collection (Chapter 1), there is a need to better understand why, despite these victories, judicialization has often fallen short of the high expectations it created.

ACCESS TO ABORTION IN PERU: A BRIEF HISTORY

Historically, access to legal and safe abortion has been a contested issue in Peru. Since the beginning of the 2000s, some feminist organizations started to mobilize to undermine the informal rules and procedures that established a de facto prohibition of legal abortion services. These rules and procedures are usually created and enforced outside officially sanctioned channels, but they shape how democratic institutions work, often overturning formal rules. The recognition of the formal and informal dimensions of institutions such as health-care systems, is well established in the literature. Institutions consist of formal and informal rules, monitoring and compliance mechanisms, and meaning systems that define the context in which actors interact. Institutions arise from struggles and compromises, reflect the resources of those who create the rules, and ultimately affect the distribution of power in society (Campbell & Pedersen, 1996, p. 4). As described by Ruibal (2018), in the field of sexual and reproductive rights in Latin America, views regarding the separation of State and Church are a key part of the informal norms that effectively condition access to abortion. Furthermore, Bergallo (2014, p. 146) shows that gaps and incomplete legal regulations – for example, the lack of a clear definition of the scope of the rape exception, or of a clear specification of the type of danger that justifies a legal abortion – produces uncertainty. This could partially account for the failure of the health-care community to offer legal abortion services.

In Peru, therapeutic abortion – abortion to save the life and protect the health of pregnant women – has been legal since 1924. However, for many years, Peruvian authorities failed to develop and implement regulations and national-level guidelines for the implementation of therapeutic abortions, or offer training for health workers. The lack of an enforcement mechanism allowed for the emergence of informal rules and procedures to deny access to safe abortion. For example, not all medical procedures have national administrative procedural guidelines. Interestingly, the lack of such instruments has not implied denial of treatment for many other medical conditions, but it has been used as grounds to refuse therapeutic abortions (PROMSEX, 2012).

In Latin America, one of the tools used to undermine these informal rules has been legal mobilization, including litigation seeking the recognition of administrative procedural guidelines (Bergallo, 2014; González Vélez & Bergallo, 2017). In the case of Peru, the strategy included the development of examples of procedural guidelines, such as the therapeutic abortion guidelines developed in some public hospitals for internal use. It also included national and international litigation which resulted in two decisions from UN bodies: the Human Rights Committee (*KL v. Peru*) and the Committee on the Elimination of Discrimination against Women (CEDAW, *LC v. Peru*). The decisions from these UN bodies are technically "recommendation reports". In any case, these legal battles had tangible results in Peru: the issuing of the Therapeutic Abortion Guidelines in 2014.

KL and *LC* are landmark cases (Table 3.1). Both tested the capacity of some international mechanisms to deal with issues related to abortion rights, and clarified the responsibility of the state with respect to the regulation of safe abortion. Moreover, both have been referred to in other UN decisions and have also informed national cases regarding similar issues in other countries (Gianella & Yamin, 2018). Unfortunately, while

TABLE 3.1. *KL and LC cases*

Case	Court/body	Submitted	Decision	Observations
KL v. Peru. Access to Therapeutic Abortion	United Nations Human Rights Committee	2002	2005	Recommends issuing therapeutic abortion guidelines
LC v. Peru. Access to Therapeutic Abortion	Committee on the Elimination of Discrimination Against Women	2009	2011	Recommends taking measures to allow safe abortion services for girls and adolescent victims of sexual abuse

KL and *LC* could be labelled as "innovative" decisions due to their contributions to international jurisprudence on abortion, effectively recognizing abortion as a human right (Ngwena, 2013), domestic courts have been less innovative. In 2009, when there was no therapeutic abortion protocol, the Superior Court of Lima did not order one, as the Committee on the Elimination of Discrimination Against Women (CEDAW) did. A decade later, the court upheld the new Therapeutic Abortion Guidelines when these were challenged by conservative groups, but did so on relatively narrow grounds. In its 2019 and 2020 decisions, the court quoted and described the policy-making process as its core (formalistic) argument to dismiss plaintiffs' opposition to the protocol. This suggests that in the field of public policies, Peru has judges who are more comfortable deciding within the parameters created by the executive and legislative branches than innovating. This puts into question the suitability of national courts as the best arena to develop new, transformative and more progressive understandings of abortion rights in Peru (Gianella & Álvarez, 2021).

The implementation of new therapeutic guidelines has also been deficient (Bergallo, 2014). For example, for five years the procedure did not have a code in the Ministry of Health's information system. Consequently, health authorities did not have a tool to monitor the number of therapeutic abortions performed in the country, systematize the type of conditions behind the requests, or detect delays in access to the procedure. Against this backdrop, studies have shown poor implementation of therapeutic abortion. Most of the procedures are still performed at the Maternal Perinatal Institute in Lima, a specialized public hospital that has been applying its own therapeutic abortion guidelines since 2010. Some hospitals stated that they did not perform the procedure due to a lack of demand (ForoSalud, 2018). This is problematic because the guidelines establish a procedure that must be started by a physician or health worker, not by user demand. For instance, women need to be informed by their physicians that the possibility exists. Every year, Peru reports maternal deaths related to the conditions included in the guidelines, such as respiratory diseases (7.6 per cent of all maternal deaths and 12.5 per cent among women under nineteen years old) and oncological conditions (6.6 per cent of all maternal deaths and 8.3 per cent among women under nineteen years old) (Gil, 2018). While it would be inaccurate to assume that all these pregnancies would have ended in a therapeutic abortion, the data collected across the country by organizations such as ForoSalud (2018) cast doubt regarding female patients' autonomy in deciding whether to continue with their pregnancies, and also regarding access to information about their right to access a therapeutic abortion. Further compounding the problems, women face delays in diagnosis (therapeutic abortion is only allowed until week 22), which results in few women having access to legal abortion (Guerrero et al., 2019).

The evidence collected by civil society organizations and media outlets indicates that the recognition of administrative procedural guidelines for therapeutic abortion has not overturned the informal rules that effectively block access to abortion rights in Peru. In May 2019, the media reported the cases of two adolescents who were raped, became pregnant as a result of sexual abuse, and suffered complications that put their health and lives at risk. One of the girls died after a caesarean section. A second thirteen-year-old girl suffered severe pain during the pregnancy, for which medical doctors at public health facilities recommended that she rested. Only on week 21 of her pregnancy, when it was too late to initiate the abortion procedure, did the doctors inform her about this possibility. The girl delivered her new-born, which only survived a few hours. Journalists cited the *LC* case, arguing that despite international legal victories, informal rules in the country were still a problem.

In response to these cases, and as a strategy to overturn the informal rule creating barriers to accessing therapeutic abortions, the Peruvian Ombudsman issued a statement asking the Ministry of Health to issue special guidelines for therapeutic abortion in the case of adolescents. This was not welcomed by the Ministry of Health. According to the director of the National Programme on Sexual and Reproductive Health, the requirement was nonsense because a pregnant adolescent requires the same medical care as an adult.[2] Some politicians condemned the ombudsman's request. Refusing to recognize legal access to therapeutic abortion, the then president of the Peruvian women legislators' caucus, the neo-Pentecostal priest Tamar Arimborgo, and legislator Julio Rosas, another neo-Pentecostal priest, stated that the ombudsman was an apologist of manslaughter, excusing taking the life of the unborn child (*"apología de tentativa de homicidio" en agravio del feto*). Both reactions illustrate well the degree of opposition to abortion in Peru.

Furthermore, despite legal victories at the domestic level backing the Therapeutic Abortion Guidelines, in the context of the COVID-19 pandemic the Ministry of Health has been asked to explain the inclusion of

[2] Jaqueline Fowks, "El aborto terapéutico en adolescentes desata la controversia en Perú", *El País* (28 May 2019).

therapeutic abortion within the guidelines for treatment, care and support for pregnant women infected with COVID-19. The guidelines state that health-care personnel must evaluate the termination of the pregnancy when the life of a woman infected with COVID-19 is at risk. The request, filed by congresswoman Luz Cayguaray,[3] disregards recent jurisprudence, and states that in Peru abortion is unconstitutional.[4]

In sum, neither the early victories in international fora nor the proceduralization of therapeutic abortion have prompted the development of other governmental indications expanding the grounds for legal abortion. In other words, such gains did not expand the legal grounds for abortion, nor have they reinforced the normative claims for decriminalization, as has been the case in other Latin American countries such as Argentina and Colombia (Bergallo, 2014; Cabrera & Reingold, 2018; La Mesa por la Vida y la Salud de las Mujeres, 2009).

THE DEVELOPMENT OF PERUVIAN FEMINIST NGOS

The development of know-how around strategic litigation is part of the evolution of the Peruvian feminist movement, know-how that was crucial in securing the legal victories mentioned in the previous section. In this section I describe the trajectory of feminist NGOs in Peru, highlighting the absence of connection to political parties and other grassroots organizations. A highly professionalized and institutionalized NGO-based feminist movement has successfully used legal mobilization to advance access to abortion and made important contributions to women's rights, but has failed to connect with a broad-based and popular women's movement. This renders court victories highly precarious.

The feminist movement in Peru was always neglected by progressive parties. This detachment, coupled with a limited interest in the feminist agenda, including sexual and reproductive rights, fuelled the emergence of a feminist movement independent from party structures in the early 1980s (Barrientos Silva & Muñoz Cabrejo, 2014). The professionalization and institutionalization of the movement was not an isolated phenomenon, but was part of Latin America's second-wave feminism (Alvarez, 1999), which has been the target of a variety of critiques. One highlights the risk

[3] Cayguaray is a right-wing congresswoman representing the *Frente Popular Agrícola del Perú* – FREPAP.

[4] "Colectivos conservadores aprovechan cuarentena para campaña contra aborto terapéutico", *Wayka* (7 May 2020).

of NGOs becoming a surrogate for civil society. Even if feminist NGOs are aware of the fact that they do not represent a broader social or political movement, professionalized NGOs have become convenient substitutes for civil society. The process of accreditation to attend certain spaces framed as open to civil society, such as UN meetings or the hearings of the Inter-American Commission on Human Rights, are examples of the implicit, sometimes acritical role adopted by some feminist NGOs. A second critique relates to their autonomy. Some question the extent to which organizations dependent on national and international funding sources are movement-oriented, and the extent to which their struggles reflect grassroots concerns rather than foreign interests (Riquer Fernández, 2005).

In the case of Peru, NGOs' organizational structure, i.e. hierarchical with non-participatory decision-making spaces, tasks and goals determined by funders, and a technocratic approach, contributed to the weakening of the feminist movement. In 1991, the Feminist Movement Coordination Committee, which had been in place since 1986, was dissolved, and the organizations decided to continue with their track towards professionalization (Barrientos Silva & Muñoz Cabrejo, 2014). After this schism, in 1996 and 1997 other initiatives such as the *Movimiento Amplio de Mujeres* (MAM) and the *Movimiento de Mujeres por la Democracia* (MUDE) emerged. These organizations, with members employed by feminist NGOs, aimed to channel feminist political positions against Alberto Fujimori's regime. As described by Rousseau (2012), the creation of platforms where feminists could participate as individuals without an organizational label was the result of a combination of factors: attacks against institutions deemed political opponents by the government, the distrust of international donors who hesitated to support organizations labelled as opposition, and the lack of consensus within the organizations. Though important at the time, these platforms weakened after the collapse of Fujimori's regime in 2000.

The Peruvian feminist movement is therefore politically weak. While highly professionalized, it is characterized by a lack of grassroots anchoring (Barrig, 2002; Rousseau, 2012). In this sense, salient features of the movement are (1) its strong connections with transnational networks; and (2) its commitment to the process of institutionalization of gender policies at the level of the state.

The strong connections to transnational networks and the legal expertise of some feminist organizations have been central to the development of jurisprudence on sexual and reproductive rights in Peru, as well as to the mounting of legal responses to the aforementioned suits against the implementation of the Therapeutic Abortion Guidelines. High levels of professionalization are an asset that allows NGOs with support from external funders to intervene (as litigants, or through *amicus curiae*) in judicial cases. Moreover, the work of these feminists has also been key in framing women's struggles as human rights issues during the process of institutionalizing liberal gender policies (e.g., gender quotas or legislation on violence against women). This happened with the support of international organizations and donors, and the process was aligned with global development policies that started to portray women's issues as central to development. For example, as in other countries, Peruvian feminist NGOs became a key source of technical assistance for the state. This technical assistance led to the emergence of participatory mechanisms at the level of local and regional governments (such as gender concertation boards in local governments) and within other civil society organizations, including indigenous groups. As described by Rousseau and Morales (2018), the programme National Network of Rural Women, developed in the early 2000s by the NGO Flora Tristan, was key in the emergence of indigenous female leaders at local and regional levels.

The institutional activism that emerged from the professionalization of the feminist NGOs framed women's issues as technical ones, independent of specific political positions. This allowed feminist NGOs to lobby mainly the executive branch, and to some extent the legislature, and, through this, to achieve significant results, such as the first law addressing violence against women in 1993. The law was amended several times, until a new law was issued in 2015 (Law No. 30394). This bill adopts a more comprehensive approach, as it is a law against "gender-based" violence. In addition, starting in 1999 governments have created women's emergency centres for female victims of gender violence across the country. Moreover, in 1996 the Ministry of Women's Affairs was created, which, after several reforms, became the Ministry of Women's Affairs and Vulnerable Populations (MIMP). This ministry is the governing body of national and sectorial policies on women, providing a focal point for institutional activism. Finally, Peruvian feminists have been involved with supporting national policies for equal opportunities. Since 2000, five-year plans for Equal Opportunities for Women and Men have been approved. In 2012, the plans explicitly adopted a gendered approach.[5]

[5] In 2012, the title changed from Equal Opportunities for Women and Men to National Plan for Gender Equality.

Despite these positive legal and policy developments, major gender gaps prevail in Peru: there are more women in the informal sector (i.e., without access to social security or pensions) than men; illiteracy rates among women are higher than among men; adolescent pregnancy is rising; and early parenthood is a challenge mainly faced by female adolescents (Instituto Nacional de Estadística e Informática, 2017, 2020; Mesa de Concertación Para La Lucha Contra la Pobreza, 2018). The evidence also reveals major pitfalls in the implementation of these policies, highlighting the limits of institutional activism.

It can be argued that in Peru, as a country with weak social movements (World Bank, 2020), the shortcomings of institutional activism are a foregone conclusion. However, recent events show that even in this context, when social protests converge with feminist institutional activism they can produce major transformations. The 2016 *#NiUnaMenos* protest in Lima against violence against women is a case in point. As stressed by Ramírez Huaroto (2020), despite the presence of a legislative majority that espoused a strong anti-gender discourse, the size of the protest (approximately 300,000 people, the biggest street demonstration recorded in Lima in recent years), gave media visibility to the topic and fuelled public debate. The protest prompted not only the approval of new laws on gender violence, but also the implementation of existing laws and regulations, leading, for example, to the allocation of resources to improve the attention to and protection of victims of gender-based violence (Rousseau et al., 2019). To be sure, feminist NGOs were not the main force behind the protest or the main players. However, because violence against women and impunity for this type of violence had been one of the central concerns of the institutional feminist agenda (Muñoz Cabrejo, 2019), many organizations embraced the *#NiUnaMenos* initiative and welcomed alliances with other actors, showing the transformative capacity of such action.

There are, however, limits to coalition building. For instance, abortion was perceived as a contested issue, and therefore intentionally excluded from *#NiUnaMenos* (Caballero Rojas, 2018). For some of the actors involved, this was a strategic decision aimed at gaining a wider appeal. For others, there are no natural convergence points between the agenda of institutional feminists regarding sexual and reproductive rights and that of grassroots movements. For the latter, institutional feminists' focus on individual reproductive rights has neglected the concerns of working women and women from poor neighbourhoods (Caballero Rojas, 2018), showing major cracks within the Peruvian feminist movement.

GROUND-LEVEL SHORTCOMINGS OF STRATEGIC LITIGATION AS A TOOL TO EXPAND ABORTION IN PERU

As in other countries and fields, the professionalization of Peruvian feminist NGOs has included the development of links to transnational networks. Members of Peruvian feminist organizations participated in key international events that defined new paradigms of development focused on women's rights: The International Conference on Population and Development (ICPD) in 1994 and the Fourth World Conference on Women (Beijing) in 1995. Engagement in these initiatives motivated feminist advocates across the globe to use domestic law to "vernacularize" – appropriate, adopt and adapt – global conceptions of women's rights to their local contexts (Gianella & Yamin, 2018; Merry, 2017). Peruvian NGOs such as *Centro de Promocion y Defensa de los Derechos Sexuales y Reproductivos* (PROMSEX), have also been key actors on regional platforms (such as the Latin American and Caribbean Consortium against Unsafe Abortion, CLACAI, created in 2005), where legal strategies were developed and discussed. The development of health as legal grounds for abortion (*causal salud*) in Latin America has been described as a regional, collaborative effort of feminist groups (González Vélez & Bergallo, 2017).

For transnational networks of sexual and reproductive rights, alliances with local organizations enabled them to put into practice their plans to use the supranational bodies to advance their agenda. For example, *KL v. Peru* showed that access to abortion was a core concern for the Peruvian feminist movement, but it is also true that *KL* was part of a broader strategy designed by international women's rights organizations. The objective was twofold: (1) ensure that national-level legislation, policies and jurisprudence were aligned with the international recognition of sexual and reproductive rights; and (2) push for new standards in international law for the protection of reproductive rights (Cabal et al., 2003). When defining the strategy, international "litigants" did not prioritize a comprehensive assessment of local civil society capacity to frame abortion as a rights violation, or the existence of networks to support and leverage the opportunities created by international litigation, including the capacity of the local NGOs to monitor the enforcement of the decision (interview, feminist NGO lawyer, Lima, July 2014).

Moreover, the actors and organizations involved in the public debate on abortion in Peru have usually framed abortion as a technical issue. Jurisprudence, state obligations and public health data (maternal morbidity and mortality) have been quoted as scientific evidence in attempts to portray positions as neutral and objective, distant from ideological grandstanding. As a result, in contrast with what has been documented in countries such as Argentina (Benford & Snow, 2000), the social justice framing has not emerged in Peru. Abortion rights are not linked by Peruvian activists to matters of economic and social justice (Beavin et al., 2019). The economic argument reflects a concern for poor women who shoulder a greater burden from unwanted pregnancies or economic costs of abortion, but in general, in Peru, the frames used by institutional feminist NGOs do not appeal to other civil society movements addressing issues such as poverty, unemployment or social violence, as has been described in other Latin American countries. This furthers the gap between the two arms of the movement.

Another central characteristic of strategic litigation by feminist NGOs in Peru is that it has been most successful with international bodies. At the national level, the know-how of Peruvian NGO feminist lawyers, such as PROMSEX, has allowed them to defend, in alliance with state actors, the national guidelines for therapeutic abortions as well as some of the victims of the criminalization of abortion. Undoubtedly, these efforts have led to important judicial victories. However, in contrast with what has been documented in countries such as Colombia (Roa & Klugman, 2014; Stifani et al., 2018), which is also characterized as a country with weak "social mobilization", Peruvian courts have not become epicentres of more ambitious legal struggles. For instance, feminist NGOs have not sued the Ministry of Health for the failures in implementation of the national guidelines, nor have they used national courts to expand the grounds for legal abortion. In other words, interventions in national courts have become a resistance strategy (Ramírez Huaroto, 2020).

This brief overview points to significant differences between the actors involved in struggles for access to abortion in Peru, including differences regarding the strategies they should deploy and the issues they should prioritize. Importantly, the most relevant players in the progressive camp are still those who favour institutional advocacy via NGOs. They have the capacity and know-how to litigate in court and influence policies at the national level in a technocratic fashion. What they lack is a strong connection to a broad-based feminist movement that can activate additional pressure points in order to promote rights expansion. The result is deficient implementation of ambitious legal frameworks inspired by global liberal scripts, and a focus on protecting narrow victories. By contrast, as I will show in the next section, the actors that oppose expanding abortion rights are a more heterogenous group, with elite and grassroots members. They share religious values and are therefore able to present a more united front, complementing each other's strategies. This heterogeneity has been key in helping them block the expansion of abortion rights.

A SUCCESSFUL RESISTANCE AGAINST INTERNATIONAL LEGAL VICTORIES: WORKING WITH GRASSROOTS RELIGIOUS MOVEMENTS

Despite victories in strategic litigation and advances at the international level seeking to safeguard the right to abortion in Peru, the feminist movement has lost a connection to grassroots organizations that could help make those victories a reality. In contrast, actors against expanding abortion rights have successfully built ties with religious groups that have the grassroots power as well as presence and connections in Congress. Religious groups can thus successfully stall pro-abortion initiatives in the legislature, and spread a message against abortion rights.

The movement opposing the expansion of grounds for legal abortion brings together a number of actors and religious groups. Such movements have at various points functioned as interfaith alliances where different groups play different roles. To better understand the mosaic of organizations, recall that religious affiliation is a central issue in Latin America. It is the region with the largest Catholic population in the world but has in recent decades seen a rapid increase in Evangelical church membership: from 4 per cent in 1974 to 20 per cent in 2014 (Christensen Bjune, 2016). Evangelicals in Latin America are significantly more conservative than Catholics and are more likely to be opposed to abortion rights, same-sex marriage and gender policies (Corporación Latinobarómetro, 2018).[6] However, as Fonseca (2018) notes, there are differences among Evangelical churches. The more "conservative", politically active and right-wing are the so-called charismatic churches. Like other Evangelical churches, charismatic churches have strong social roots: one of their sources of outreach power, or "evangelizing action", is grassroots work, based on door-to-door contact at the community level, as well as through Evangelical radio stations (Albañil, 2016). Finally, Evangelical churches in Peru also have a tradition of providing local public services, including food and education.

[6] Neha Sahgal, "500 Years after the Reformation, 5 Facts about Protestants around the World", *Pew Research Center* (25 October 2017).

In sharp contrast, since the 1990s, feminist groups have gradually lost that type of community connection. Their dedication to work with and in the state and to policy reform (providing technical support and advice) have detached these organizations from broader social movements. This process has denied them the possibility to build a more critical approach to the structural conditions that limit the implementation of the institutions and policies that they helped design.

The capacity to reach local communities is a major political asset in Peru, a country where the collapse of political parties (Levitsky & Zavaleta, 2019, p. 23) has reshaped the relationship between politicians and voters. In this regard, one of the core characteristics of Peru's "democracy without parties" is the proliferation of coalitions of independents at the local, regional and national levels, which generates disincentives for rebuilding national parties (Muñoz & Dargent, 2016). Candidates for office are free agents, recruited by parties on an ad hoc basis, mainly because of their financial resources and capacity to attract votes. In other words, parties select independent candidates who are able to win on their own merit but who cannot compete without a formally recognized party label. Ideology or party identification are therefore not central concerns when it comes to candidate recruitment (Levitsky & Zavaleta, 2019). Candidates, in turn, have no incentives to invest in party strength, furthering the weakness of party organizations at the national level.

The need for financial resources as well as the capacity to attract votes have contributed to the emergence of parties rooted in economic corporations. These political parties not only stress values linked to entrepreneurship and the image of the candidates; they also allow the use of corporations to build new types of clientelism, providing access to graduate education, health care or day care for infants, among others (Levitsky & Zavaleta, 2019). The ownership of mass media outlets, such as local radio stations, also allows these amateur politicians to reach a wider population. In this context, the resources offered by Evangelical leaders at the local level have become particularly coveted. For example, in the 2001 elections, there were twenty-eight priests running as candidates in nine lists for a seat at the national parliament, and only one was elected. By 2006, the number of candidates who were priests had risen to 120 in thirteen lists, and from those, five were elected to office.[7] It is worth noting that in in 2006, *Restauración Nacional*, an Evangelical party, also

[7] Martin Hidalgo, "La influencia evangélica en el Congreso", *El Comercio*, (12 November 2017).

ran a presidential candidate and won enough votes to have two representatives in Congress. Five years later, in 2011, there were no Evangelical or neo-Pentecostal parties competing for seats in parliament, but in 2016, seven priests participated in elections in five lists, and two won seats.

As a result of the growing participation of religious personalities in elections, moral and religious values have gained relevance in Peruvian electoral and non-electoral politics. For instance, during the 2011 presidential campaign, the leaders of the Catholic Church addressed presidential candidates, asking that they all commit to banning abortion upon taking office. In 2016, abortion again came up as a central issue during the presidential campaign. In her attempt to win the run-off election against Pedro Pablo Kuczynski, the leader of *Fuerza Popular*, Keiko Fujimori, signed an agreement with neo-Pentecostal charismatic leaders, stating her opposition to abortion and same-sex civil unions. After she lost, moral issues emerged as a core component of Fujimori's strategy to attack the government. This approach spread to other groups too. For instance, in 2019, one year after the resignation of President Kuczynski, his former co-partisans Gilbert Violeta, Juan Sheput, Pedro Olaechea and Salvador Heresi, created two new groups in Congress, *Contigo* and *Acción Republicana*, with both adopting ultra-conservative positions. While in the 2020 legislative election some of these actors did not do well,[8] other parties with a strong religious conservative bent gained a large number of seats. Not surprisingly, these parties, including the *Frente Popular Agrícola del Perú* (FREPAP) and *Unión por el Perú*,[9] have roots at the community level. FREPAP is an organization with a tradition of providing local services. Once in Congress, and in the context of the COVID-19 pandemic, its representatives championed bills to expand social protection and access to generic drugs (@FrepapBancada, 2020a, 2020b).

The tactics used by the actors against expanding abortion rights in Peru are multiple. Here I have grouped them into six, non-mutually exclusive categories. The first is institutional activism. As Alba Ruibal shows in her chapter in this volume (Chapter 4), institutional activism has

[8] Contigo Peru only got 0.9 per cent of the votes. Similarly, Rosa Bartra, a former Fujimorista congresswoman who adopted a radical religious position, claiming, for example, that female empowerment is akin to promoting masturbation, did not got elected.

[9] FREPAP obtained 8.36 per cent of the votes and fifteen representatives, Unión por el Perú get 6.77 per cent of the votes and thirteen representatives. Maria Eugenia Ulfe, "El Frepap y las preguntas que dejamos de hacernos", *La Mula* (27 January 2021).

not been a strategy used exclusively by feminists. Peru has also experienced counter-activism from within the state. Notable examples are two of the ministers of health during Alejandro Toledo's government (2001–2006): Luis Solari, member of *Sodalicio de Vida Cristiana*, and Fernando Carbone, former representative in Peru of Human Life International, an international association known for its work against modern contraceptive methods (Rousseau, 2007). During their terms in office (mid-2001 to mid-2003) both implemented key reforms, with an emphasis on distorting sexual and reproductive rights policies. While they focused on preventing maternal deaths, they did not pay attention to abortion as one of the main contributing factors and made modern contraception less widely available (Aramburu, 2014). Both ministers framed their arguments as technocratic, referring to indicators and the need for prioritization within the public sector. As medical doctors, these two actors also used "scientific arguments". With regard to the debate on the use of emergency contraception, for example, Carbone warned about its potentially negative side effects.[10]

A second tactic is the use of legislative oversight mechanisms. For example, during the debate on the implementation of the free distribution of the emergency contraception at public health facilities in 2004, two Catholic conservative congressmen, Hector Chávez Chuchon MD and Rafael Rey, filed a constitutionality challenge against the then minister of health, Pilar Mazzeti, accusing her of promoting the distribution of emergency contraception. Similarly, during the legislative period 2016–2019, Fujimori's party made use of its absolute majority in Congress to censor two ministers of education (Jaime Saavedra and his successor, Marilú Martens) with the support of the protest movement #*ConMisHijosNoTeMeta*s (#DoNotMessWithMyChildren). A more recent example of these conservative legislative tactics is the information request filed by FREPAP congresswomen Luz Cayguaray regarding the inclusion of therapeutic abortion as one of the services to be offered to pregnant women affected by COVID-19. Her goal, as mentioned previously, was to make access more difficult.

The third tactic is blocking legislative debates. Political representation in Congress has provided conservative actors with the power to block debates. By controlling leadership positions within parliament, they have had the power to block broader debates on abortion bills. Peru has seen

[10] See, for example, "Cuidado con Píldoras Anticonceptivas. Algunas podrían ser abortivas, teme ministro Carbone", *La República* (19 December 2002).

legislative attempts to expand the legal grounds for abortion, including debates that took place between 2014 and 2015. During the legislative period 2011–2016, Martha Chavez (*Fuerza Popular*) and Juan Carlos Eguren (*Partido Popular Cristiano*), both linked to the more conservative sectors of the Catholic Church, were full members of the Justice and Human Rights Commission. Eguren was the president of the commission when the abortion bill was introduced, and therefore had the power to postpone the debate. Ultimately, the project was rejected by the commission. In 2016 another bill to decriminalize abortion on three grounds was introduced. *Fuerza Popular*, which still controlled parliament, kept the bill at the commission level and refused to debate it.

A fourth strategy is promoting bills and adopting new legislation. Political representation in parliament provides the power to promote new legislation. For example, in 2004, following a trend in Latin America, Congress passed Law 27654 establishing 25 March as the "Day of the Unborn". The bill was submitted by former minister of health, Luis Solari. Similarly, during the 2011–2016 legislative period, in parallel to the bills to decriminalize abortion mentioned earlier, legislators introduced a bill to make the regulations on abortion stricter and more wide-ranging. All the bills were dismissed. However, the victory was for the conservatives, who managed to keep the status quo and prevent liberalization.

A fifth tactic is the use of social protest. As mentioned, social protest has emerged as an effective mechanism to galvanize people around specific demands. Recent protests in Peru, especially in urban areas, have used social media as one of the main means to communicate and to convene street demonstrations (Chavez, 2020). Recognizing the power of this type of protest, in November 2016 the hashtag *#ConMisHijosNoTeMetas* (#DoNotMessWithMyChildren) was created. At the time, the Fujimorismo-controlled Congress had trained its sights on Jaime Saavedra, a progressive minister of education. While it is possible to argue that *#ConMisHijosNoTeMetas* lost appeal over time (such protests are often short-lived), the protesters achieved their goals: two ministers of education were censored by Congress.

The last, and least successful, strategy has been litigation. As in the case of feminist NGOs, litigation is led by a more institutionalized sector of the movement, such as *Acción de Lucha anticorrupción Alas Sin Componenda*, created in 2002, and the Association Centre for Legal Studies Santo Tomás Moro, established in 2016. Since its inception, *Alas Sin Componenda* has participated in three judicial cases to limit access to oral emergency contraception and to limit therapeutic abortion. The Centre for Legal Studies Santo Tomás Moro has been involved in two judicial cases against the state: one against the implementation of the national school curriculum,[11] and the case against the Therapeutic Abortion Protocol. These actors are, like their feminist counterparts, linked to transnational networks with which they share legal strategies and legal arguments. Despite their lack of success in the courts, it is important to note that the strategic use of litigation goes beyond winning. As McCann (1994) stated, the judicialization of politics through litigation can be employed as part of a broader strategy to increase an issue's visibility, gain more popular support, or as a recruitment tool. Litigation can be also used to increase pressure on policy makers (Langford, 2013).

The cases filed by anti-abortion actors in national courts aim to overturn the few victories secured by Peruvian feminist organizations. This counter-litigation triggered an alliance between feminist NGOs and progressive state officers, with a narrow focus on protecting the Therapeutic Abortion Guidelines. As a result, the judicial tactics orchestrated by conservative actors have the potential to delay or block attempts to develop more ambitious progressive litigation efforts. They put feminists and their few allies on the defensive. The know-how to take sexual and reproductive rights to court is mainly concentrated in two NGOs based in Lima: the *Centro de Promocion y Defensa de los Derechos Sexuales y Reproductivos* (PROMSEX) and the Office for the Defence of Women's Rights (DEMUS). Resources are scarce, and it is difficult for these feminist NGOs to spread their efforts beyond merely defensive litigation.

CONCLUSION

The analysis presented in this chapter shows that the NGOization of the Peruvian feminist movement and its professionalization, which involved developing close links with transnational actors, allowed feminist NGOs to develop the skills to implement sophisticated legal strategies. These gave them national and international recognition, and allowed them to work with state officials to institutionalize global liberal gender policy

[11] The case was built around the component of sex education (if the parents can prevent the state from teaching sex education in schools) and was linked to the broader debate regarding the inclusion of gender approach (talking about gender violence and power relations) in the school curricula.

scripts. Unfortunately, activists were less successful at building a political support structure in the form of links to political parties or grassroots organizations. This sophisticated, progressive and highly technical approach therefore had limited effects when it came to overturning informal barriers to therapeutic abortion or expanding the grounds for legal abortion. It also contributed to the precarity of judicial victories. This technocratic orientation has deep historical roots. In this sense, the so-called *ONGización* (Alvarez, 1999) of the feminist movement in Peru is an extreme example of the lack of social rootedness of the NGO-based feminist movement in Latin America.

This detachment can be seen in the design of pro-abortion legal mobilization strategies. The overly technical approach has not contributed to promoting grassroots organizations' ownership of the abortion issue. For example, the exclusion of abortion from the *#NiUnaMenos* social protest, at a time when NGOs and congresswomen were working on a bill to expand legal abortion, is one of the examples that show the chasm that separates institutional feminists from feminist social organizations. In a context where conservative values continue to have wider resonance, this kind of detachment is a major blind spot of judicialization.

By contrast, the counter-movement against abortion rights has been able to expand its repertoires of action and build broader, more impactful alliances. As Ruibal states in her chapter (Chapter 4), opposition to reproductive rights by religious fundamentalists in Latin America, and the organizational infrastructure for political and legal activism, sometimes pre-dates court rulings. Peru is one of those cases. However, as described in this chapter, opposition to reproductive rights by religious actors has the capacity to innovate as the counterpoint between conservatives and feminists intensifies and becomes more salient. Crucially, in the wake of and in response to progressive legal victories, conservatives were able to amplify their repertoires of action, developing technical expertise and secular discourses, as well as the capacity to reach formal positions within the government. In other words, they also became institutional activists. Additionally, they have built interfaith alliances with strong grassroots components, which has allowed them to disseminate the message and maintain political power and influence in the national Congress. Interfaith alliances also had the capacity to successfully organize massive social protests around moral agendas.

The case of the Peruvian abortion counter-movement, financed by deep-pocketed national and international groups, deserves more attention from scholars of judicialization. In Latin America, religious conservative groups are gaining political power, due in no small part to their networking capacity at community level, as well as to their capacity to convene social protests. The Peruvian experience of a highly professionalized feminist NGO movement that achieved crucial international victories but lacks the grassroots and political connections that the conservative counter-movement so successfully cultivated, can teach us much about where other countries that also witnessed progressive court victories might be headed in the coming years.

References

@FrepapBancada. 2020a. En el Perú existen grandes compañías que generan millones de soles anuales y que no contribuyen de manera justa con nuestro país. Por ello, nuestra congresista @LuzCayguaray presentó el PL 4887, el cual crea un impuesto solidario a las grandes fortunas (1/3). 10 June, https://twitter.com/FrepapBancada/status/1270898195439255552

2020b. ¡Lo logramos!. Hoy se aprobó por insistencia en el #PlenoVirtual del @congresoperu, nuestro PL 5251 de nuestra vocera titular @MariaCespedesc, el cual busca una adecuada accesibilidad a medicamentos genéricos para el tratamiento de #covid19. Nuestra iniciativa garantiza el (1/2). 25 June, https://twitter.com/FrepapBancada/status/1276339228025204737

Albañil, I. (2016) Evangélicos y política en el Perú: la gesta de un outsider. In F. d. C. Universidad de Lima, ed., *Concurso de Investigación en Comunicación*. 9th ed. Lima: Universidad de Lima.

Alvarez, S. E. (1999) Advocating Feminism: The Latin American Feminist NGO "Boom". *International Feminist Journal of Politics* 1(2), 181–209.

Ansolabehere, K. (2009). *Oportunidades y Decisiones: la judicialización del aborto en perspectiva comparada* SELA 2009, Asunción, Paraguay, 11–14 June.

Aramburu, C. E. (2014) Idas y vueltasLos programas de planificación familiar en el Perú. *Revista Latinoamericana de Población* 8(14), 81–103.

Barrientos Silva, V., & Muñoz Cabrejo, F. (2014) Un bosquejo del feminismo/s peruano/s: los múltiples desafíos. *Revista Estudos Feministas* 22, 637–45.

Barrig, M. (2002) La Persistencia de la Memoria: Feminismo y Estado en el Perú de los 90. In A. Panfichi, ed., *Sociedad Civil, Esfera Pública y Democratización en América Latina: Andes y Cono Sur*. Lima: Pontificia Universidad Católica del Perú – Fondo de Cultura Económica.

Beavin, C., Billings, D. L., & Chávez, S. (2019) Activist Framing of Abortion and Use for Policy Change in Peru. *Sexual and Reproductive Health Matters* 27(1), 160–67.

Benford, R. D., & Snow, D. A. (2000) Framing Processes and Social Movements: An Overview and Assessment. *Annual Review of Sociology* 26, 611–39.

Bergallo, P. (2014) The Struggle against Informal Rules on Abortion in Argentina. In R. Cook, J. Erdman, & B. Dickens, eds., *Abortion Law in Transnational Perspective*. University Park, PA: University of Pennsylvania Press.

Bergallo, P., & Ramón Michel, A. (2016) Abortion. In R. Gargarella & J. González, eds., *The Latin America Casebook: Courts, Constitutions and Rights*. London: Routledge.

Bergallo, P., Jaramillo Sierra, I. C., & Vaggione, J. M., eds. (2018) *El aborto en América Latina: Estrategias jurídicas para luchar por su legalización y enfrentar las resistencias conservadoras*. Buenos Aires: Siglo 21.

Cabal, L., Roa, M., & Sepúlveda-Oliva, L. (2003) What Role Can International Litigation Play in the Promotion and Advancement of Reproductive Rights in Latin America? *Health and Human Rights* 7(1), 50–88.

Caballero Rojas, G. (2018) *Redes sociales y feminismos en la acción colectiva: el caso de "Ni Una Menos" en el Perú*. Lima: Pontificia Universidad Católica del Perú.

Cabrera, O., & Reingold, R. B. (2018) De la teoría a la práctica: La aplicabilidad del principio de no regresividad para proteger avances en la liberalización del aborto. In P. Bergallo, I. C. Jaramillo, & J. M. Vaggione, eds., *El aborto en América Latina: Estrategias jurídicas para luchar por su legalización y enfrentar las resistencias conservadoras*. Buenos Aires: Siglo 21.

Campbell, J. L., & Pedersen, O. K. (1996) *Legacies of Change: Transformations of Postcommunist European Economies*. Berlin: Aldine de Gruyter.

Chavez, N. (2020) Movilizaciones sociales en Lima: Redes, identidades y oportunidades en Los Pulpines y Toma el Bypass. Cuaderno de Trabajo No. 54, Departamento Academico de Ciencias Sociales, Pontificia Universidad Catolica del Peru.

Christensen Bjune, M. (2016). *Religious Change and Political Continuity: The Evangelical Church in Guatemalan Politics*. Bergen: University of Bergen.

Corporación Latinobarómetro (2018) *El Papa Francisco y la religión en Chile y América Latina. Latinobarómetro 1995–2017*. Santiago: Corporación Latinobarómetro.

Epps, C. (1998) *The Rights Revolution: Lawyers, Activists, and Supreme Courts in Comparative Perspective*. Chicago, IL: University of Chicago Press.

Fonseca, J. (2018) Conceptos básicos para comprender el mundo evangélico en el Perú. *Argumentos* 12(1), 34–41.

ForoSalud (2018) *Vigilancia Ciudadana en Salud: Aplicación del Protocolo de Aborto Terapéutico en establecimientos públicos de salud a nivel nacional*. Lima: ForoSalud.

Gianella, C., & Álvarez, B. (2021) Judicial Lawfare: Analysis of Legal Arguments against Abortion Rights in Peruvian Courts. *Revista Direito GV* [online] 17 (3). https://doi.org/10.1590/2317-6172202146

Gianella, C., & Yamin, A. (2018) Struggle and Resistance: Using International Bodies to Advance Sexual and Reproductive Rights in Peru. *Berkeley Journal of Gender, Law, and Justice* 33(1), 41–73.

Gil, F. (2018) Situación Epidemiológica de la muerte materna en el Peru. *Boletin Epidiemologico (MINSA)* 25, 66–74.

González Vélez, A. C., & Bergallo, P. (2017) The Health Exception in Latin America: An Autochtonous Experience of Transnational Advocacy. Paper presented at the Annual Meeting of the Latin America Studies Association, Lima, 29 April.

Guerrero, R., Ramírez, S., & Gonzalez, M. (2019) *Relatos de Mujeres*. Lima: PROMSEX.

Instituto Nacional de Estadística e Informática (2017) *Perú: Brechas de Género, 2017: Avances hacia la igualdad de mujeres y hombres*. Lima: Instituto Nacional de Estadística e Informática.

(2020) *Informe Técnico: Comportamiento de los indicadores del mercado laboral a nivel nacional*. Lima: Instituto Nacional de Estadística e Informática.

La Mesa por la Vida y la Salud de las Mujeres (2009) *Un derecho para las mujeres: La Despenalización parcial del Aborto en Colombia*. Bogota: La mesa por la vida y la salud de las Mujeres.

Langford, M. (2013) Housing Rights Litigation: Grootboom and Beyond. In M. Langford, B. Cousins, & J. Dugard, eds., *Symbols or Substance? The Role and Impact of Socio-Economic Rights Strategies in South Africa*. Cambridge: Cambridge University Press.

Lemaitre, J. (2014) Catholic Constitutionalism on Sex, Women and the Beginning of Life. In R. Cook, J. Erdman, & B. Dickens, eds., *Abortion Law in Transnational Perspective*. University Park: University of Pennsylvania Press.

Lemaitre, J., & Sieder, R. (2017) The Moderating Influence of International Courts on Social Movements: Evidence from the IVF Case against Costa Rica. *Health and Human Rights Journal* 19(1), 150–60.

Levitsky, S., & Zavaleta, M. (2019) *¿Por qué no hay partidos políticos en el Perú?* Lima: Planeta.

Machado Campos, M. d. D. (2012) Aborto e ativismo religioso nas eleições de 2010. *Revista Brasileira de Ciência Política* 7, 25–54.

McCann, M. (1994) *Rights at Work: Pay Equity Reform and the Politics of Legal Mobilization*. Chicago, IL: University of Chicago Press.

Merry, S. (2017, 11 May) The Global Travel of Women's Human Rights. *The Silver Dialogues*, New York University.

Mesa de Concertación Para La Lucha Contra la Pobreza (2018) *Equipo de Seguimiento Concertado a las Políticas de Salud Sub Grupo "Prevención del Embarazo en Adolescentes". ALERTA No. 1-2018-SC/MCLCP*.

Montero, P. (2012) Controvérsias Religiosas e Esfera Pública: Repensando as Religiões como discurso. *Religião e Sociedade* 32(1), 167–83.

Morán Faúndes, J. M., & Peñas Defago, M. A. (2016) Strategies of Self-Proclaimed Pro-Life Groups in Argentina: Effect of New Religious Actors on Sexual Policies. *Latin America Perspectives* 43(2), 144–62.

Muñoz, P., & Dargent, E. (2016) Patronage, Subnational Linkages, and Party-Building. In B. Van Dyck, J. Loxton, J. I. Domínguez, & S. Levitsky, eds., *Challenges of Party-Building in Latin America*. Cambridge: Cambridge University Press.

Muñoz Cabrejo, F. (2019) Ni Una Menos, más allá de la marcha, el campo en disputa. *Discursos del Sur* 4, 9–24.

Ngwena, C. (2013) A Commentary on *LC v Peru*: The CEDAW Committee's First Decision on Abortion. *Journal of African Law Review* 57, 1–15.

PROMSEX (2012) *Aborto terapéutico: El camino recorrido por el acceso a un derecho 2007–2011*. Buenos Aires: CALCAI.

Ramírez Huaroto, B. (2020) Intervention at roundtable ¿Sin Movilización Social Los Derechos de las Mujeres se Diluyen? Paper presented at the Meeting Jornadas sobre Perspectivas de Género en Tiempos de Distanciamiento Social.

Ramón Michel, A., & Bergallo, P. (2018) *La reproducción en cuestión: Investigaciones y argumentos jurídicos sobre el aborto*. Buenos Aires: EUDEBA.

Riquer Fernández, F. (2005) *Del Movimiento Feminista a la Institución: ¿Una historia que aún no puede contarse?* Mexico: Universidad Veracruzana.

Roa, M., & Klugman, B. (2014) Considering Strategic Litigation as an Advocacy Tool: A Case Study of the Defence of Reproductive Rights in Colombia. *Reproductive Health Matters* 22(44), 31–41.

Rousseau, S. (2007) Las políticas de salud reproductiva en el Perú: reformas sociales y derechos ciudadanos. *Revista Estudos Feministas* 15, 309–31.

(2012) *Mujeres y Ciudadanía: Las paradojas del neopopulismo en el Perú de los noventa*. Lima: IEP.

Rousseau, S., & Morales, A. (2018) *Movimientos de mujeres indígenas en Latinoamérica*. Lima: Fondo Editorial de la Pontificia Universidad Católica del Perú.

Rousseau, S., Dargent, E., & Escudero, A. (2019) *Rutas de atención estatal a las víctimas de violencia de género: Entre legados e innovaciones Proyecto de investigación. Informe Final*. Lima: CIES-PUCP.

Ruibal, A. (2014) Movilización y contra-movilización legal: Propuesta para su análisis en América Latina. *Política y Gobierno* 22(1), 137–44.

(2018). Federalism, Two-Level Games and the Politics of Abortion Rights Implementation in Subnational Argentina. *Reproductive Health Matters* 26 (54), 137–44.

Stifani, B. M., Gil Urbano, L., Gonzalez Velez, A. C., & Villarreal Velásquez, C. (2018) Abortion as a Human Right: The Struggle to Implement the Abortion Law in Colombia. *International Journal of Gynecology & Obstetrics* 143 (S4), 12–18.

Vaggione, J. M., & Machado Campos, M. D. D. (2020) Religious Patterns of Neoconservatism in Latin America. *Politics & Gender* 16(1), 6–10.

Vaggione, J. M., Peñas Defago, M. A., Rodrigues de Assis Machado, M., & Gianella, C. (2018) *UPON LA: Understanding the Politics of Neo-Conservative Mobilization in Latin America*. Unpublished manuscript.

World Bank (2020) *TCdata360: Civil Society Participation*. Washington, DC: World Bank.

4

Forms of Countermovement and Counter-Reform in Latin America

Judicial Backlash or Resources and Political and Legal Opportunities?

Alba Ruibal

INTRODUCTION

In Latin America, the fear of judicial backlash has not been at the center of the discussion on courts and social change. Perhaps because of the historically weak and dependent role of the judiciary in the region's political systems, the literature has focused more on judicial independence, and the empowerment and effectiveness of courts to process social demands. However, the judicial backlash thesis has recently emerged in current discussions on judicial politics in the region, particularly in the field of abortion rights. This has been more evident in the Brazilian case, where opponents of sexual and reproductive rights frequently argue against the legitimacy of courts to decide on these issues. More recently, however, progressive voices have expressed concern over the potentially counterproductive effects of the judicialization of abortion, not only for women's rights, but also for its possible backlash effects on other rights and the political system as a whole (see Diniz and Carino 2019).

The backlash question is at the core of the discussion of the role of judicial review in the democratic process. However, the conventional judicial backlash thesis, with its causal claim regarding the role of courts in producing strong reactions against progressive politics (Sunstein 1999; Tushnet 1999; Klarman 2013), does not seem apt to account for the wave of anti-gender campaigns that has been at the center of Latin American politics in recent years. Courts have been key actors in the expansion of abortion rights in the region since the mid-2000s and, certainly, even limited feminist gains in this area of rights have met with strong countermovements and attempts at counter-reform. Furthermore, the abortion rights issue has been pivotal to a larger conservative reaction against progressive politics that has recently swept across the region. The question, though, is how to understand counter-mobilization and backlash vis-à-vis the role of courts. In this study, I define backlash as the reaction against the advancement of equality claims, in the form of countermovement and counter-reform. In this context, I discuss the soundness of the court-centered approach that is crucial to the theory of judicial backlash in accounting for antiabortion rights movements in contemporary Latin America.

Instead of characterizing these processes as a reaction to judicial intervention, provoked by intrinsic features of courts, I seek to understand the particular characteristics and timing of antiabortion countermovements in the region. I argue that the analysis of social movement dynamics, and in particular the countermovement's resources and opportunities in each context, offers a better lens to understand these backlash processes. The study draws on frameworks from social movement studies, such as political opportunities and resource mobilization (McAdam, McCarthy, and Zald 1996), and the further development of these analytical frameworks by legal mobilization scholars through the conceptualization of *legal opportunities* (Hilson 2002) – which includes accessible institutional rules and courts' receptivity to social movement claims – and *support structures for legal mobilization* (Epp 1998) – which takes into special account the presence of organizations with legal capacities and resources to sustain litigation.

Through the study of countermovement and counter-reform processes in the field of abortion law in Mexico, Colombia, Brazil, and Argentina over the past two decades, this chapter argues that this conservative reaction cannot be explained as a direct or specific response to court decisions. The a priori stance against the role of courts that characterizes the judicial backlash thesis (Greenhouse and Siegel 2011) is replaced by an empirical examination of the different pathways and mechanisms of this reaction, and the different forms that the interventions of conservative actors have taken in the field of abortion rights in four countries in the region. My analysis intends to contribute to understanding under what conditions countermovements can develop, and what leads them to adopt a particular form of influence on the political and legal fields in the Latin American context, by tracing them back to their interaction with political and legal opportunities. In this way, following Greenhouse and Siegel's (2011) approach, it addresses the key role played by legal strategies and courts in the abortion rights controversy in the region, as part of larger social and political processes in which courts' decisions are one element. In line with a central claim of social movement researchers, according to whom organized opposition in the form of a countermovement is a normal consequence of a movement that achieves substantial success in its call for equal rights (Meyer and Staggenborg 1996), Greenhouse and Siegel (2011: 2077) claim that conflict or backlash is a normal feature of constitutional politics when equality claims achieve increased support, and that judicial review may or may not play a role in these processes.

The study identifies four types of counter-mobilization and counter-reform, according to the predominant and most successful strategy of conservative actors against the advancement of abortion rights in each of those countries, and explains their variation on grounds of their resources and their relationship to the political and legal opportunities in each context. The four countries under study are those in which constitutional courts have had the most relevant role in the liberalization of abortion laws in the region; in each of them, we can identify a particular kind of backlash, or a central form of counter-mobilization and counter-reform. In this account, Brazil is analyzed as an emblematic case of the influence of conservative forces on the legislature and the formation of an interreligious caucus at the national Congress; Mexico as a case of pressure on the subnational legislative processes; Colombia as a case of counter-legal mobilization by institutional activists within the national state structure; and Argentina as the most notable case of counter-legal mobilization in civil society and the use of courts by the countermovement. The empirical research for this study draws on fieldwork carried out between 2010 and 2019 in Mexico, Colombia, Brazil, and Argentina, including in-person interviews conducted with social movement activists, lawyers, health professionals, and academics.

The abortion rights controversy in Latin America is especially suited to analyze backlash dynamics and the role of courts in these processes. The legalization of abortion has been a core claim of one of the most important contemporary movements in the region, and the dispute around this issue is a paradigmatic case of interaction between movement and countermovement. Moreover, recent reform processes in this area of rights have prominently involved constitutional courts, which, since the mid-2000s, have, for the first time, upheld feminists' claims to liberalize the normative framework in this field.[1] Furthermore, as shown in the cases under study,

[1] In 2006, the Colombian Constitutional Court established that abortion should be legal in cases of rape, risk to the woman's life or health, and serious fetal malformation. As this book went to print in 2022, the Constitutional Court handed down a new ruling which

and as Gianella's chapter in this book (Chapter 3) discusses in more detail, the abortion rights dispute in Latin America prominently features the crucial problem of the implementation of regulatory frameworks in the cases allowed by the law. As pointed out in the Introduction to this volume (Chapter 1), the strong resonance of conservative values and their organizational capacity in Latin American societies presents huge challenges for the use of courts for progressive social change.

The abortion question highlights, perhaps more clearly than any other issue, the tension between the aspirations of liberal democratic regimes and the still-powerful influence of religious institutions on Latin American states. In fact, since the democratization process in the region, feminism has been the movement that placed at the center of the political agenda, and more strongly than any other actor, the claim for state laicity and secularity. This claim has been a crucial political demand of the region's liberal elites since the nineteenth century. This explains the centrality of the abortion issue for contemporary religious politics in the region, as well as the dimension of the conservative reaction against sexual and reproductive rights. This issue has also become a focal point of reference for diverse types of conservatism, galvanizing various conservative and right-wing aims and projects. In sum, abortion politics and the legal struggle for abortion offer a particularly appropriate field in which to analyze legal processes as part of wide-ranging social and political conflicts, which neither begin nor end with court decisions.

A synthetic panorama of the recent history of the conservative reaction against abortion rights in Latin America will allow us to contextualize its role in the four case studies that follow. Conservative religious actors in the region – mostly the Catholic Church and increasingly also neo-Pentecostal churches – continue to exert influence as a de facto power on state institutions. These actors use traditional and often informal types of pressure over the political system. However, especially since the 1990s, conservative actors in the field of sexual and reproductive rights in the region have developed new repertoires of collective action that make them

decriminalized abortion in the first twenty-four weeks of pregnancy. In 2008, the Mexican court upheld Mexico City's legalization of first-trimester abortion. In 2012, the Brazilian *Supremo Tribunal Federal* legalized abortion in cases of anencephaly. Also in 2012, Argentina's Supreme Court established that abortion was legal in all cases of rape, and the Uruguayan Congress decriminalized first-trimester abortion. In 2017, the Chilean Congress liberalized the abortion law in cases of risk to the woman's life, rape, and fetal malformations. The legislative assembly of the state of Oaxaca, Mexico, legalized first-trimester abortion in 2019, and Argentina did so in 2020.

similar to a social movement, or a countermovement. They have created new types of organizations and support structures in civil society, have developed a framing more in keeping with the discourse of democracy and human rights, and have used the institutional channels provided by the democratic system (see González Ruiz 2005; Vaggione 2005; Amuchástegui et al. 2010; Lemaitre 2012) – i.e., they have seized political and legal opportunities to advance their cause. They have done so as a reaction to the advancement of feminism and the movement for sexual and reproductive rights since the democratization processes. In the context of democratic transitions, the first relevant intervention by antiabortion actors in the legal field was their attempt to influence constituent processes. In that setting, they lobbied for the introduction of a clause to protect the right to life "from the moment of conception until natural death", following the Vatican's campaign in this regard, particularly since the papacy of John Paul II (Pitanguy 2011: 39; Tamés and Andión 2012: 9–10). These attempts were successfully resisted by feminist mobilization in the constituent processes of Brazil (1988), Colombia (1991), and Argentina (1994), while in countries such as Chile, Guatemala, Honduras, Dominican Republic, and El Salvador they succeeded in doing so (Tamés and Andión 2012: 9–10).

Later on, conservative religious actors in the region developed diverse repertoires of actions against feminist advances in the field of reproductive rights, including legal strategies from civil society and state institutions. They also turned their attention to local-level politics by attempting to, for example, stop the local implementation of regulations on lawful abortions, or by influencing legal and constitutional change at the subnational level in federal countries. More recently, the reaction against abortion rights movements has been a pillar and precedent for the development of the contemporary wave of conservative reactions in Latin America. In this regard, Corrêa and Kalil (2020: 33) observe that the campaigns against so-called gender ideology that have recently swept through the region have built up from the preexistent interconfessional coalitions and organizational infrastructure of antiabortion campaigns. As the analysis of the four cases that follow shows, to attribute these backlash processes to the use of rights strategies and judicial decisions is a disproportionate causal claim.

ABORTION COUNTERMOVEMENTS IN LATIN AMERICA: AN OVERVIEW

The typology presented in Table 4.1 is built on three questions that identify the key elements that help us explain the main form of backlash

TABLE 4.1. *A typology of abortion countermovements in Latin America*

	Legal strategy, in civil society Argentina	Political strategy, national level Brazil	Legal strategy, within the state Colombia	Political strategy, subnational level Mexico
Do religious conservatives have a political party or allies in legislatures?	Does not have a consolidated conservative party or a religious coalition in Congress.	Strong interconfessional and interparty conservative caucus at the House of Representatives.	Conservative party, with religious links, and recently a pro-life coalition in Congress.	Strong conservative party, with religious links.
Did the countermovement find a favorable opportunity at the Supreme Court?	Conservative majority and conservative doctrine at Supreme Court during part of the 2000s.	Supremo Tribunal Federal generally favorable to abortion rights.	Constitutional Court systematically favorable to abortion rights.	Majority of justices favorable to abortion rights, but institutional rules favor deference of Supreme Court toward any subnational legislative reforms.
Did the countermovement have a support structure for legal mobilization?	Strong support structure for legal mobilization by NGOs.	Weak support structure for legal mobilization	Strong support structure, and strong conservative legal institutional activism.	Weak support structure for legal mobilization

in each country: (1) the strength of the political opportunity in terms of presence in parties and legislatures; (2) the existence of a legal opportunity at the Supreme Court; (3) the countermovement's legal resources, or support structure.

The categories are not necessarily mutually exclusive, but the typology corresponds to the major and most effective strategies of conservative actors to deter the advancement of abortion rights in each case so far. However, it should be noted that in recent years, as sexual and reproductive rights were brought to the center of the contemporary political dispute in Latin America, conservative political strategies have been strengthened in the four countries. As highlighted in the case studies, a distinctive element of this process has been the emergence in Colombia, Mexico, and Argentina, and their consolidation in Brazil, of religious conservative political parties, mostly neo-Pentecostal. These parties have the opposition to sexual and reproductive rights at the center of their political platforms, and they turn to a strategic alliance with traditional Catholic groups when dealing with political or legal reforms on this area of rights. Another component of relevance to this process is the presence, for the first time, of presidential candidates running on an anti-gender platform, as happened in recent elections in Brazil and Argentina. Furthermore, conservative religious actors with an anti-gender discourse have led the downfall of democratic elected governments, as in the cases of Brazil and Bolivia. Finally, the use of the anti-gender discourse, with antiabortion claims at the center, by the right-wing opposition to the peace processes in Colombia, has been an acute instance of the role of sexual and reproductive rights, and abortion in particular, in the development of conservative projects in Latin America.

COUNTER-LEGAL MOBILIZATION IN CIVIL SOCIETY: ARGENTINA

Argentina is a case that clearly shows the inadequacy of the judicial backlash thesis to account for conservative reactions, as the most important instances of conservative mobilization against reproductive rights did not take place after feminists' gains in courts, but in the aftermath of advances in the National Congress. In fact, in Argentina, conservative groups set out to use courts and legal opportunities before the feminist movement started developing legal strategies; indeed, they have led the field of litigation strategies on reproductive rights at the Supreme Court. They have pursued strategic litigation that motivated the development of the court's conservative doctrine on the absolute right to life from conception, which stood between the early 2000s until 2012. Even the court's progressive decision on abortion rights in the 2012 *F, AL* case was motivated by a legal claim submitted by a conservative actor.

One of the first organized actions by conservative forces in the field of abortion rights in Argentina was their mobilization against the first bill to reform the country's abortion law, presented in 1989 by a female deputy from the *Unión Cívica Radical* party. But during the 1980s and at the beginning of the 1990s, a proper conservative movement against reproductive rights in Argentina did not yet exist, and the church's reaction against the bill consisted mainly of mobilizing Catholic school students to attend public demonstrations (Blofield 2006: 132).

However, at the beginning of the 2000s conservative Catholic groups implemented new repertoires of action, mostly based on counter-legal mobilization against reproductive rights by organizations in civil society. Regarding the support structure for counter-legal mobilization, two of the main conservative organizations working against reproductive rights in Argentina are *Portal de Belén* and *Mujeres por la Vida*, based in the city of Córdoba, which have been central actors in the judicialization of reproductive rights in the country. These organizations seized the new legal opportunity created by the constitutional reform of 1994, which extended legal standing to social actors through the introduction of collective *amparo* briefs, and incorporated human rights treaties in the constitution. The main argument of antiabortion activists in the country is that Article 4 of the American Convention on Human Rights, which includes the right to life from conception, entails the prohibition of abortion under all circumstances. Their litigation strategies led to the two most important Supreme Court decisions on reproductive rights in the country (*Portal de Belén* and *Mujeres por la Vida*), until the court issued its progressive decision in the *F, AL* case in 2012 and clarified the scope of legal abortions under the rape exception.[2]

Prior to *F, AL*, the Supreme Court's abortion-related jurisprudence had been motivated by a collective *amparo* claim against emergency contraception pills filed by *Portal de Belén*, on grounds of their alleged abortive effects. This claim was upheld by the court in 2002,[3] and it had significant effects on subsequent reproductive rights cases in lower courts,

[2] CSJN, "F.,A.L. s/medida autosatisfactiva," March 13, 2012.

[3] CSJN, "Portal de Belén c. Ministerio de Salud y Acción Social de la Nación s/amparo," March 5, 2002.

as well as on a decision the court made in 2006. That year, the court upheld a claim submitted by *Mujeres por la Vida*, in which it analyzed whether this NGO had legal standing to challenge the constitutionality of the law that created, in 2002, the National Program for Sexual Health and Responsible Procreation.[4] Based on the precedent set in *Portal de Belén*, the plaintiff had argued in 2003, before a local court, that the program allowed for the distribution of emergency contraception pills that had abortive effects and were, therefore, against the right to life of the unborn. The case reached the court through extraordinary appeal. In a brief decision, a majority of justices said that the NGO had legal standing to challenge that law through an *amparo* brief, because it had among its organizational aims "to promote and defend the establishment of social conditions that allow the effective enforcement of the right to life from conception." The case was about legal standing, but to justify the organization's interest in the case, the court had to accept the plaintiff's claim that emergency contraception drugs were abortive.

More recently, soon after the Supreme Court's *F, AL* decision urged subnational authorities to issue protocols for the implementation of lawful abortions, *Portal de Belén* challenged the constitutionality of the protocol enacted in the province of Córdoba, through a collective *amparo* claim. This led to a 2012 decision from a provincial court that suspended, for seven years, the implementation of that directive in the province. The blockage of the local protocol ended when in December 2018 the highest provincial court (*Tribunal Superior de Justicia de Córdoba*) rejected *Portal de Belén*'s claim. One year later, the same court denied that organization's extraordinary appeal to the national Supreme Court.

Some of the features of this countermovement contribute to explaining their use of litigation strategies, as well as their success in court. In the first place, in contrast with the feminist movement, conservative religious actors in Argentina did not have a wide constituency, but were "elite-oriented" and had strong contacts and familiarity with the judicial power (Bascary, author interview 2010). Second, they have counted on material resources for litigation, provided mainly by Human Life International (Juliá, author interview, 2010).[5] Third, at the beginning of their litigation

[4] CSJN, "Mujeres por la Vida c/ E.N.-P.E.N.-Ministerio de Salud y Acción Social de la Nación s/amparo," October 31, 2006.

[5] Human Life International is a coalition of antiabortion groups, founded in the United States in 1981, which has an office for Latin America in Miami, as well as affiliates in most countries across the region (Htun 2003: 152).

campaign in 2000, conservative organizations took advantage of the favorable legal opportunity created by the presence of a conservative majority at the Supreme Court, appointed under the presidency of Carlos Menem (1989–1999). Some of those justices belonged to Opus Dei, the branch of Catholicism most against abortion rights in Argentina. Finally, regarding the political opportunities, in particular those related to their capability to pursue legislative bills, it can be highlighted that conservative religious actors in Argentina can count neither on a strong congressional coalition, as in the case of Brazil, nor on a consolidated political party, such as *Partido Acción Nacional* in Mexico or the *Conservador* party in Colombia. When in the mid-2000s fundamentalist actors within the National Congress – in particular, Congresswomen Cynthia Hotton, of Evangelical affiliation, and Liliana Negre, from the Opus Dei – tried to form an antiabortion caucus, they did not gain attention for their proposal (Díaz, author interview, 2013).

However, conservative political actors gained new strength and renewed their attempts to organize in the political sphere as part of the backlash that ensued in the aftermath of the defeat of the bill to legalize abortion in the Senate, in August 2018. The legislative process of that bill, approved by the Chamber of Deputies in June that year, showcased the strength of the feminist movement, with massive public manifestations of support. This represented a real threat to conservative sectors. Immediately after the rejection of the bill, conservative actors redoubled their activism, with a focus on opposing sexual education, joining the "Don't mess with my children" movement, set up in Lima at the end of 2016. This movement, which is part of the larger campaign against so-called gender ideology, had a strong presence in other countries throughout the region (see Gutiérrez 2018) but did not have a footing in Argentina until the backlash started in 2018. In this context, fundamentalist religious actors, with strong Evangelical presence, launched anti-choice parties and electoral coalitions, with an eye to the 2019 elections. For example, on March 28, 2019, Hotton relaunched the party *Valores para mi País*, gathering antichoice political actors from different religious and party affiliations. She also allied with an ultranationalist conservative actor to run for the country's presidency in 2019 under an electoral front (*Frente Nos*) that obtained enough votes in the primary to compete in the first round of the presidential election. This was the first time that a presidential candidate in the country had focused their electoral platform on opposition to sexual and reproductive rights, and abortion in particular. Furthermore, in June of that same year, a provincial coalition of anti-gender Catholic and Evangelical actors founded by an Evangelical pastor (*Frente Unite por la Vida y la Familia*) obtained 20 percent of the vote in elections for national legislators in one of the country's most progressive jurisdictions, Santa Fe province, running on an antiabortion campaign financed by Evangelical groups. In this way, the movement/countermovement dynamics created a new opportunity for conservative actors and helps explain the backlash and their renewed momentum to act in the political sphere.

CONTROLLING THE LEGISLATIVE PROCESS AT THE NATIONAL LEVEL: BRAZIL

In Brazil, the epicenter of conservative mobilization and the stronghold of abortion opponents is the Federal Chamber of Deputies. In contrast to the Argentine case, conservative mobilization in Brazil is not predominantly based on the development of NGOs as an expression of religious groups in civil society, and it does not use litigation as a central strategy. The two distinctive aspects of conservative mobilization in Brazil are its direct participation in the legislative process and the coalition between Catholic and Evangelical actors in Congress, forming a religious caucus. This has created an increasingly favorable political atmosphere for conservatives' opposition to abortion rights, and for their intervention in the country's political process more generally.

The Catholic Church has been a traditional opponent of abortion rights in the country, and as early as 1949 it promoted a legislative project aimed at eliminating the two exceptions to criminalization of abortion in the penal code (Casanova 2000: 71). Besides this early relevance of Catholicism, Brazil has become the most striking example of the increasing influence of Evangelical, mostly neo-Pentecostal churches, in the region's politics. The Brazilian Universal Church of the Kingdom of God (*Igreja Universal do Reino de Deus*), the main neo-Pentecostal church in the country, got its first federal deputy elected as early as 1986. Since then, its influence on the National Congress, together with *Assambleia de Deus* and other Evangelical groups, has continued (Almeida 2017). The presence of these groups in the Chamber of Deputies has been crucial for the recent ascent of extreme-right forces to national power with the presidency of Jair Bolsonaro.

Conservative groups in Brazil argue that their reluctance to use legal strategies is due to the lack of legitimacy of courts to decide on abortion, and on so-called moral issues in general. As such, their strategy has been to delegitimize the role of the country's highest court, the *Supremo Tribunal Federal* (STF) in the advancement of abortion rights (Rondon, interview 2019). The only change to the abortion law over the past decades has been motivated by litigation strategies before the STF, carried out by the feminist NGO ANIS, *Instituto de Bioética*. In responding to these legal challenges, in 2012 the STF expanded the framework of abortion law by incorporating a new exception to its criminalization, in cases of fetal anencephaly.[6] Furthermore, in 2017 the STF received a challenge to legalize first-trimester abortion, becoming the first constitutional court in the region to face this request, on which it has yet to decide.[7] In this context, conservative legislators have argued that the intervention of the STF in this field violates the division of powers, by surpassing legislative competences, and that it is contrary to popular sovereignty (Coutinho 2019: 139). As observed by Batista (interview, 2019), it remains to be seen what their position in this regard would be in case the legal opportunity changes at the STF, if new justices with a conservative position on abortion rights are appointed.

The strength of this religious legislative coalition is due in part to the cross-party and cross-religious alliance among different conservative actors in the Brazilian Congress. The so-called *bancada evangélica* (Evangelical caucus) is the main articulator of antiabortion parliamentary fronts. The conservative influence in the legislature started gaining prominence from the beginning of the 1990s (Corrêa and McIntyre 2003: 36). During the period that elapsed from that time through the beginning of the 2000s, the correlation of forces between defenders and opponents of abortion rights in Congress was more balanced, and legislators from different confessions worked separately (Rodrigues, interview 2012). But since the mid-2000s, religious groups have developed more coordinated actions, mostly through the creation, in 2005, of the Evangelical Parliamentary Front (*Frente Parlamentar Evangélico*) and the Parliamentary Front for the Defense of Life against Abortion (*Frente Parlamentar Mista em Defesa da Vida Contra o Aborto*). At crucial junctures, the religious caucus presided over the most important legislative commissions dealing with the abortion issue: the Commission on Social Security and Family and the Commission on Human Rights and Citizenship, both at the Chamber of Deputies (Almeida 2017). Moreover, since 2007 there has been a constant increase in the number of religious

[6] STF, ADPF 54, July 1, 2004. [7] STF, ADPF 44, March 8, 2017.

legislators from different parties who vote together to block the advance of abortion rights, as well as the rights of sexual minorities (Viana 2011: 168). In 2014, the interparty religious caucus represented almost one-third of the members of the chamber (Miguel, Biroli, and Mariano 2017: 231).

Over the past fifteen years, these congressional groups have presented more than thirty projects against reproductive rights (Batista, interview 2019). One of the most important legislative initiatives presented by conservative legislators at the Chamber of Deputies has been the bill on the so-called Statute of the Unborn. This bill aimed to eliminate the right to abortion in all circumstances, even those currently allowed by the law (PL 478/2007). More recently, the focus of these legislative groups has been on a constitutional reform proposal aimed at introducing a constitutional clause on the right to life from conception and an explicit prohibition of abortion under all circumstances (PEC 181/2015, so-called *PEC da vida*). Thus far they have not achieved any legislative victories. However, they have successfully stopped progressive initiatives to change the country's abortion law, which is among the most restrictive in the world, as it does not include an exception in cases of risk to women's health.

Beyond their incidence in the field of sexual and reproductive rights as a single-issue caucus, this conservative religious bloc in Congress has been a crucial actor in the process that led to the removal of President Dilma Rousseff and, eventually, to the ascent of the extreme right to the national government. The abortion issue was a central element in the offensive against the Workers' Party (PT), and in the conservative turn in Brazilian politics. During the 2010 presidential race, and due to pressures from Catholic and Evangelical sectors, abortion became the single most relevant issue (Pitanguy 2011: 42). During the second round, and at the insistence of religious leaders, then-candidate Rousseff signed a public commitment pledging not to promote changes in the abortion law or any other issue related to the family. Eventually, Rousseff was elected as Brazil's first female president, and during her government she adhered to that commitment, while affirming a compromise to grant access to lawful abortion (Negrão, interview 2012). It was precisely around the regulation of legal abortions that conflict escalated, in 2014, between the government and religious deputies, over the enactment of an executive order (*Portaria* 415) aimed at regulating access to legal abortions in the public health system (Coutinho 2019). The successful opposition to this measure, which forced the government to cancel that measure seven days after its enactment, was led by Eduardo Cunha, then leader of PMDB (Party of the Brazilian Democratic Movement) at the Chamber of Deputies. This victory gave Cunha a prominent role in leading the Evangelical caucus and allowed him to become the chamber's president in 2015, defeating the PT's candidate in the first round (Coutinho 2019). From that position, Cunha headed the parliamentary coup against President Rousseff in 2015–2016, which led to the provisional presidency of Michel Temer (see Limongi 2015) and eventually to the election of Jair Bolsonaro in 2018.

This political process, led from the lower chamber of Congress, and aimed at banishing the PT from the country's political scene, was articulated through a broader process of polarization in Brazilian politics, which allowed right-wing political forces to capitalize on the social unrest manifested in the cycle of street protests started in June 2013. Progressive sectors of the legal profession pointed to the judicialization of abortion as the cause of backlash when the action of unconstitutionality (APDF 442) asking for the legalization of first-trimester abortion was filed in 2017. However, given the dynamics of the political conflict in the country at that time, this appears as a disproportionate attribution.

CONSERVATIVE INSTITUTIONAL ACTIVISTS AND COUNTER-LEGAL MOBILIZATION WITHIN THE STATE: COLOMBIA

In Colombia, conservative institutional activists working at a key national-level institution, the Office of the Inspector General (*Procuraduría General de la República*), headed the main form of backlash against abortion rights so far in the country. In 2006, the Constitutional Court issued its landmark decision C-355/2006, which decriminalized abortion under three circumstances.[8] When the unconstitutionality challenge was filed in 2005, and when it was discussed in the court, conservative President Alvaro Uribe did not intervene in the public discussion, and he did not exert pressure on the court, allegedly due to his intention to win reelection, for which he needed the court's approval to reform the constitution (Cuéllar, interview 2013). However, the political opportunity changed after his reelection, and he appointed an ultraconservative institutional activist, Alejandro Ordoñez, at the *Procuraduría*

[8] Corte Constitucional, C-355/06, May 10, 2006. The court established that abortion would not be a crime in cases of risk to the woman's life or health, serious fetal malformations, and rape.

(Office of the Inspector General). Ordoñez systematically worked to block implementation of the court's decision.

The traditional opposition to sexual and reproductive rights in Colombia came mainly from the Catholic Church and, more recently, also from neo-Pentecostal churches, which have started gaining influence in the political sphere. The Catholic Church's influence on the state was exercised through the National Conference of Bishops and other Catholic leaders (Lemaitre 2012: 497). However, since the mid-2000s, and in line with similar trends in other Latin American countries, a new type of religious mobilization emerged in the country. Based on civil society organizations and led by lay Catholics – most prominently from Opus Dei – these organizations started using the same methods as other social movements, such as legislative lobbying and strategic litigation (Lemaitre 2012: 498). This process entailed the formation of a support structure for counter-legal mobilization, helped by the presence of *Universidad de la Sabana* – an Opus Dei university that has been a seedbed for conservative legal activists. Among the main Catholic organizations working in the sphere of civil society are *Red Futuro Colombia*, *Unidos a Dios Salvaremos a Colombia*, *Legión de María*, and the *Consejo Nacional de Laicos* (Mazo 2006: 80).

When the Colombian office of the feminist organization Women's Link Worldwide presented the action of unconstitutionality that motivated the Constitutional Court's decision C-355/2006, the Catholic network set out to campaign against it. With support from Human Life International and its Colombian affiliate (Löfgren 2008: 40), lay Catholic actors presented forty lawsuits against the decision (Lemaitre 2012: 498) and lobbied state institutions to obstruct its implementation. However, until 2009 that reaction was not coordinated and had no leadership.

In 2009, Uribe appointed a conservative lawyer linked to Opus Dei, Alejandro Ordoñez, as the head of the crucial *Procuraduría*. This office had, until then, been favorable to the implementation of the court's decision. This powerful institution is charged with enforcing human rights and has the competence to investigate public officials, even those publicly elected, and to remove them from office for noncompliance with their duties, without criminal trial. Before taking office, Ordoñez had openly expressed fundamentalist positions against abortion and gay marriage, and as a former judge at the *Consejo de Estado* he had issued decisions based on Catholic doctrine (Lemaitre 2012: 497). One of his first actions as inspector general was the appointment of lawyer Myriam Hoyos, professor at *Universidad de la Sabana* and former president of *Red*

Futuro Colombia, to the office in charge of the protection of sexual and reproductive rights and of overseeing the implementation of Decision 355/06 (see Parra 2010: 41). Hoyos had presented forty-seven amicus curiae briefs during the decision-making process of ruling C-355/2006 and had stated that she would take action against a court decision that liberalized abortion (Parra 2010: 41).

From their institutional positions, these actors developed a backlash legal strategy aimed at blocking the implementation of Decision 355/06, and ultimately at reversing this jurisprudence. Their actions had a chilling effect on other state officials, given, for example, the indication of the inspector general to public officials in charge of the implementation of abortion services that misoprostol was an unsafe method, and more expensive than others, and that, therefore, they could go to jail for damaging public finances (Tovar, interview 2013). The role of these conservative institutional activists also encouraged other public officials to be vocal in the public sphere about their convictions against sexual and reproductive rights (Tovar, interview 2013).

In this process, the Constitutional Court was the most important actor within the state structure with the capacity and willingness to oppose the conservative reaction. The court's position in this regard configured a steadily favorable legal opportunity for feminist struggles to achieve the implementation of the new legal framework, and to resist backlash. Feminist organizations used strategic litigation and other legal actions to counter the backlash, and the Constitutional Court responded to their petitions, ensuring the implementation of its decision, and also preserving its institutional standing vis-à-vis other state powers. In the first place, the court rejected several actions of nullity presented by the inspector general against ruling C-355/2006. In T-388/2009, for example, the Office of the Inspector General demanded the annulment of the court's decision on grounds of procedural failures. This was the first time that an inspector general presented a demand for annulment against a decision by the Constitutional Court protecting rights (Parra 2010: 41). The court rejected the petition and its arguments in 2010.

The most significant court decision to counter the backlash was motivated by a *tutela* writ filed on September 21, 2011 by Women's Link and signed by 1,201 Colombian women. In the writ, they denounced the inspector general as well as two other officials from his office, including Myriam Hoyos, for having systematically transmitted false and misleading information regarding women's reproductive rights, violating in this way their right to receive accurate and high-quality information.

The *tutela* was filed before Bogota's section of the Judicial Council, and it was rejected in the first and second instances. The Constitutional Court decided to consider it on appeal. In ruling T-627/2012, it upheld the claim, reaffirmed the duty of state officials to provide accurate and truthful information as a basic requirement for the exercise of fundamental rights. The court ordered the inspector general and the other two officials to rectify the information they had disseminated. The inspector general complied with the court's decision – had he not done so, he could have been charged with contempt (Tovar, interview 2013). This is considered a highly relevant and unprecedented decision, and the first case worldwide in which a court recognized the right to information as a receptor's right to receive quality information (Tovar, interview 2013).

More recently, on October 11, 2018, the court issued ruling SU-096/2018, in which it unified and consolidated its progressive jurisprudence regarding the implementation of C-355/2006. This decision is considered the most significant since 2006, in that it was the only abortion rights decision by the court sitting in full (*Sala Plena*). In it, the court exhorted Congress to advance the liberalization of the abortion law, and ordered the Ministry of Health to unify all the criteria previously established by the court and to translate them into public policy (Ardila, interview 2019; Martinez, interview 2019; Mazo, interview 2019).

The court ruled in 2018 in the context of the ascent of right-wing actors to the national government. Ivan Duque, from the *Uribista Centro Democrático* party, won the presidential elections in May that year, after a fierce struggle over the ratification of the Peace Agreement for the termination of the conflict between the Colombian government and the FARC (Revolutionary Armed Forces of Colombia) at the plebiscite of October 2016. The mobilization against the peace process is considered as a watershed (Martínez, interview 2019). It showed the increasing political presence of neo-Pentecostal churches (Mazo, interview 2019) as well as the centrality of anti-gender and antiabortion positions in the more general political contest. Conservative forces led by ex-President Uribe mobilized neo-Pentecostal constituencies to vote "No" on the plebiscite, on grounds that the text of the Peace Agreement promoted gender ideology and abortion (see Botero 2017; Gil 2020). On that occasion, there was a strategic use of the gender issue by these sectors to mobilize religious constituencies, and there was a disinformation campaign, claiming that the agreement said things that were not in the text (Ardila, interview 2019). The political victory of rightist sectors at the plebiscite paved the way for their victory in the 2018 elections, and for the consolidation of a conservative anti-gender coalition in Congress. This coalition includes parties with a clear religious affiliation, as well as conservative politicians from different parties opposed to so-called gender ideology. Together, this group constitutes a majority in both legislative chambers (Gil 2020: 56, 64). The political opposition to sexual and reproductive rights is led by the party *Centro Democrático* (Ardila, interview 2019; Martínez, interview 2019), but they form a coalition with the traditional *Conservador* party, as well as with neo-Pentecostal parties, most prominently MIRA (*Movimiento Independiente de Revolución Absoluta*) founded in 2000, and *Colombia Justa Libres*, created in 2017 (Mazo, interview 2019). In this context, the Constitutional Court continues to be trusted by feminist activists as an institutional venue that can guarantee the implementation of abortion rights and deter conservative reactions in this field (Ardila, interview 2019).

INFLUENCING THE LEGISLATIVE PROCESS AT THE SUBNATIONAL LEVEL: MEXICO

In Mexico, the main backlash against abortion rights has taken place in state legislatures. In 2007, Mexico City's Legislative Assembly legalized first-trimester abortion, which placed the city at the vanguard of abortion rights in Latin America. The reform was challenged before the Supreme Court by the Federal Prosecutor's Office (PGR) and the president of the National Human Rights Commission (CNDH). In 2008, the court approved the new law. This triggered a counter-reform process in Mexican states: since 2008, seventeen have modified their constitutions to include the right to life from conception. In 2011, the Supreme Court also validated these changes. As a result of the backlash, these local constitutions – as well as the constitution of the state of Chihuahua since 1994 – now contain a similar provision that declares the protection of life from the moment of fertilization.

Notably, the constitutional reforms have not produced changes in the states' criminal codes, all of which contain exceptions to the criminalization of abortion – including a rape exception that is common to all states. Moreover, although the counter-reforms were meant to deter the occurrence elsewhere of reforms similar to Mexico City's (Mejía, interview 2017), on September 25, 2019, the Legislative Assembly of the state of Oaxaca legalized first-trimester abortion. Oaxaca, whose constitution is among those that enshrine the right to life from conception, thus became the second jurisdiction in the country to legalize abortion. Still, the legislative counter-reforms have had a negative impact on women's rights and liberties at the state level. Among their chief consequences are the creation of uncertainty regarding the legal status of abortion (Mejía, interview 2017; Díaz de León, interview 2020), as well as further obstacles to women's access to reproductive health, and the prosecution of women who decide to terminate their pregnancies or suffer spontaneous abortions (Tamés and Andión 2012: 6).

Conservative groups reacted strongly to the process of abortion law reform in Mexico City in 2007. For example, the Catholic hierarchy threatened any person promoting the bill, and in particular the deputies who voted for it, with summary excommunication (Lamas and Bissell 2000: 20). However, after the Supreme Court decision in 2008, a truly coordinated strategy developed against the reform. The constitutional challenge against Mexico City's law nationalized the abortion discussion. According to an active participant in this process, the fact that the abortion question reached the Supreme Court gave this issue a national platform that it would not have enjoyed had it remained only as a legislative decision in Mexico City (Ortiz-Millán, interview 2011). In the same sense, it was observed that many sectors of the country had been unaware of the debate in Mexico City, mostly because there was a favorable majority at the city's Legislative Assembly and there was no need for a massive feminist mobilization, but when the issue reached the Supreme Court, it became a national debate (Cruz Parcero, interview 2011).

However, this does not mean that the Supreme Court as such triggered a backlash. The conservative movement was established in Mexico long before Mexico City's reform. The largest antiabortion organization working in Mexico at that time was the National Pro-Life Committee, *Provida*, which was composed of more than 140 organizations (González Ruiz 2005: 71). The countermovement had significant resources, mainly from Human Life International (González Ruiz 2005), and increasingly from prominent Mexican business actors. The daughters of Lorenzo Servitje (Bimbo Group) and the daughter of Carlos Slim reportedly financed several conservative campaigns. More recently, and in line with similar developments throughout Latin America, the influence of Evangelical churches in Mexico's political sphere has been growing, and the countermovement against sexual and reproductive rights in the country has joined the crusade against so-called gender ideology, mostly through the formation of the National Front for the Family (*Frente Nacional por la Familia*). This umbrella organization was created in

2016 by more than 1,000 Catholic and neo-Pentecostal churches, organizations, and political actors. At present, this is the main anti-gender and antiabortion coalition in the country (Romero, interview 2019; Moneta, interview 2019).

A core purpose of conservative mobilization in Mexico since the 1990s had been the introduction of the Vatican-sponsored phrasing regarding the right to life into state and federal constitutions and laws. Since 1995, *Provida* has been advised by Human Life International in its attempt to introduce constitutional reforms that incorporated this provision in Chihuahua, Nuevo León, Guanajuato, and Jalisco, states that were governed by the Catholic National Action Party, PAN (Lamas 2003: 97). For many years, these attempts failed, except in Chihuahua in 1994 (González Ruiz 2005). However, the PAN continued to pursue bills on this issue in legislative debates at the state level (Lamas 2003: 98).

The political and legal opportunities in the aftermath of Mexico City's reform contribute to explaining the success of this conservative project in effecting counter-reforms in state constitutions since 2008. Mexico is the only Latin American country where civil and criminal codes are determined by each of the thirty-one states and Mexico City, and thus it is the only country in the region where abortion laws can be enacted at the local level (Htun 2003: 10). The location of abortion policy in Mexico was favorable both to the feminist movement in Mexico City, where there was a progressive government from 1997, and to the countermovement at the state level, as it allowed Catholic conservative forces to influence regional local elites. Most surely, it would have been much harder, for both reformers and counter-reformers, to achieve desired changes at the national level, where inter- and intraparty disputes are much heightened, and political majorities for and against abortion rights would have probably been much more difficult to reach.

The political opportunity in the states was favorable to conservative claims. Three main factors contribute to explaining the backlash. In the first place, although formal church–state relations are a national-level variable, regulated by the constitution and national laws, which express the long Mexican tradition of secularity and state–church separation, there exist subnational differences in terms of informal rules and de facto influence of the Catholic Church over local politics. The influence of the church is much stronger at the state level than in Mexico City or at the national level (Moneta, interview 2019). Conservative religious actors were able to influence legal change in the states through their influence as a de facto power over governors and local legislators (Mejía, interview

2017; Moneta, interview 2019; Romero, interview 2019). Second, at the state level there are fewer visibility and accountability mechanisms. By contrast to the process in Mexico City, where there was an intense legislative and public discussion, the counter-reforms were passed without public or legislative debate (Lamas, interview 2011).

Third, national electoral incentives and politicians' search for support from the Catholic Church at the local level help explain the political incentives for the backlash. The counter-reforms were promoted by conservative subnational governments headed by PAN, but they would not have been passed by local legislatures without support from the PRI (Institutional Revolutionary Party). The PRI is a historically anticlerical party, which had developed progressive policies in the field of reproductive health. At the time of the reforms, the party was led by self-declared feminist Beatriz Paredes. So the party's position in this process was surprising to activists and observers (Lamas, interview 2011). After the first counter-reforms took place, feminist organizations demanded that national authorities of political parties, in particular Paredes, stop the backlash. However, Paredes only addressed her party on this issue through a letter presented at the PRI annual meeting in 2010, when the bulk of counter-reforms had already been passed (Beltrán and Díaz de León, interview 2011). The explanation given by relevant actors in this process is that PRI made pacts with the Catholic hierarchy, seeking their support for the presidential election in 2012 (Beltrán and Díaz de León, interview 2011; Ortiz-Millán, interview 2011). At the time of the counter-reforms, PRI's main concern was to regain its hegemony at the national level, which it had lost in 2000 for the first time after governing the country for seven decades. In that pre-electoral context, the support of the church at the local level was fundamental.

A seemingly puzzling aspect of the process of reform and counter-reform in Mexico is that the Supreme Court upheld both types of legal change, in a short time period and without significant changes in the court's composition. The institutional rules that shape judicial review in Mexico contributed to the configuration of a favorable legal opportunity for counter-reforms, despite the presence of a favorable majority in the court for the expansion of abortion rights. The rules governing actions of unconstitutionality require a qualified majority of eight out of eleven justices to declare unconstitutional a law sanctioned by federal or state legislatures (Article 105 of the National Constitution). In the case of subnational laws, this requirement favors a strong form of federalism. This institutional feature helps explain why, while a majority of justices at the court voted consistently in favor of the legalization of abortion in Mexico City in 2008 (eight out of eleven justices voted in favor of the new law),[9] and against the counter-reforms in 2011 (seven out of eleven justices voted against their constitutionality),[10] the resulting court decisions were favorable to both types of subnational reforms. In fact, given the supermajority rule, a significant majority fell short by one vote of rejecting the counter-reforms, and the decision of four justices to leave them standing ultimately prevailed.

After the cycle of abortion law reform and counter-reform, in which abstract actions of unconstitutionality had a prominent role, feminist organizations started pursuing strategic litigation on concrete cases, through *amparo* claims (Díaz de León, interview 2019; Méndez, interview 2019; Romero, interview 2019). These actions resulted in significant decisions by the court, in 2018 and 2019, regarding the interpretation of subnational abortion laws in cases of rape and risk to the woman's health.[11] As explained by a key litigant lawyer in this process, these claims aimed at obtaining the same type of protection throughout the country, on grounds of constitutional rights (Méndez, interview 2019).

CONCLUSION

Through the analysis of the main forms of counter-mobilization and counter-reform in the field of abortion law in four Latin American countries, this study intended to question in empirical terms the applicability of the judicial backlash thesis as a lens through which to read the constitutional controversies over abortion rights in Latin America. In contrast to the judicial backlash thesis, which attributes a causal role to courts in provoking conservative reactions when adjudicating on so-called hard cases, this study showed that distinct conditions in different countries have shaped the ways the antiabortion countermovements have developed. To understand these, we need to look at the countermovement's resources and the prevailing legal and political opportunity structures that are linked to these forms of mobilization.

[9] AI 146/2007 and *Acumulada* 147/2007. [10] AI 11/2009 and AI 62/2009.

[11] In 2018, the court established that access to abortion services in cases of rape should be granted without a police attestation or an authorization by the Public Ministry (*Amparo en Revisión* 601/2017 and *Amparo en Revisión* 1170/2017). In 2019, the court established that abortion should be considered legal when the woman's health is at risk, on grounds of the constitutional right to health (*Amparo en Revisión* 1388/2015).

The study showed that, in some instances, the opposition to reproductive rights by religious fundamentalism in the region, and its organization for political and legal activism, is prior to courts' intervention in the field of abortion rights. In Argentina, conservatives were indeed the first to use the courts, and the only ones to have appealed to the National Supreme Court through strategic litigation. Second, the Colombian case showed that constitutional courts can play an active role in countering backlash, which is usually overlooked in the examination of the use of courts for policy change. Finally, the four cases show an increasing centrality of sexual and reproductive rights, and abortion in particular, in the region's contemporary political dispute, with a growing presence from neo-Pentecostal actors in the opposition to sexual and reproductive rights, as well as an alliance between Evangelical and Catholic sectors in their anti-gender struggle. In this regard, the study shows that the abortion issue has been strategically used in the process of polarization linked to the ascendancy of right-wing forces to power in cases such as Brazil and Colombia. In this context, given, among other aspects, the dimension of the conservative offensive against progressive politics, it appears disproportionate to blame the use of litigation and courts for provoking backlash.

References

Almeida, R. (2017) A onda-quebrada – evangélicos e conservadorismo. *Cadernos Pagu* 50, 1–27.

Amuchástegui, A., Cruz, G., Aldaz, E., & Mejía, M. C. (2010) Politics, Religion and Gender Equality in Contemporary Mexico: Women's Sexuality and Reproductive Rights in a Contested Secular State. *Third World Quarterly* 31(6), 989–1005.

Blofield, M. (2006) *The Politics of Moral Sin: Abortion and Divorce in Spain, Chile and Argentina*. New York: Routledge.

Casanova, A. (2000) Abortion in Brazil: Legislation, Reality and Options. *Reproductive Health Matters* 8(16), 66–76.

Botero, S. (2017) El plebiscito y los desafíos políticos de consolidar la paz negociada en Colombia. *Revista de ciencia política* 37(2), 369–88.

Corrêa, S., & Kalil, I. (2020) *Políticas antigénero en América Latina: Brasil – ¿la catástrofe perfecta?* Rio de Janeiro: Observatorio de Sexualidad y Política, ABIA, eBook.

Corrêa, S., & McIntyre, P. (2003) *The John and Catherine MacArthur Foundation, 1990–2002. The Population and Reproductive Health Program in Brazil: Lessons Learned*. Chicago, IL: The John and Catherine MacArthur Foundation.

Coutinho, A. (2019) A Câmara dos Deputados e a questão do aborto: tensionamento no século XXI *Faces de Clio* 5(9), 123–44.

Diniz, D., & Carino, G. (2019) É injusto acusar movimentos sociais de judicializar a política, *El Pais – Brasil*, June 19.

Epp, C. (1998) *The Rights Revolution: Lawyers, Activists, and Supreme Courts in Comparative Perspective*. Chicago, IL: University of Chicago Press.

Gil, F. (2020) *Políticas antigénero en América Latina: Colombia*. Rio de Janeiro: Observatorio de Sexualidad y Política, ABIA, eBook.

González Ruiz, E. (2005) *Cruces y sombras: Perfiles del conservadurismo en América Latina*. Ciudad de México: Promsex.

Greenhouse, L., & Siegel, R. (2011) Before (and after) Roe v. Wade: New Questions about Backlash. *Yale Law Journal* 128, 2028–87.

Gutiérrez, M. A. (2018) Entrevista con Sonia Corrêa. Significante vacío: ideología de género, conceptualizaciones y estrategias. *Observatorio Latinoamericano y Caribeño* 2(1), 106–13.

Hilson, C. (2002) New Social Movements: The Role of Legal Opportunity. *Journal of European Public Policy* 9(2), 238–55.

Htun, M. (2003) *Sex and the State: Abortion, Divorce, and the Family under Latin American Dictatorships and Democracies*. Cambridge: Cambridge University Press.

Klarman, M. (2013) *From the Closet to the Altar: Courts, Backlash, and the Struggle for Same-Sex Marriage*. New York: Oxford University Press.

Lamas, M. (2003) La lucha por modificar las leyes de aborto en México. In M. Castañeda, ed., *Interrupción voluntaria del embarazo: Reflexiones teóricas, filosóficas y políticas*. Ciudad de México: CEICH, UNAM – Plaza y Valdés, pp. 83–105.

Lamas, M., & Bissell, S. (2000) Abortion and Politics in Mexico: Context Is All. *Reproductive Health Matters* 8(16), 10–23.

Lemaitre, J. (2012). By Reason Alone: Catholicism, Constitutions, and Sex in the Americas. *International Journal of Constitutional Law* 10(2), 493–511.

Limongi, F. (2015) O passaporte de cunha e o impeachment a crônica de uma tragédia anunciada. *Novos estudos CEBRAP* 103: 99–112.

Löfgren, S. (2008) Framing and Shaming. Transnational Networks and the Decriminalization of Abortion in Colombia. Master's dissertation, Goteborgs University. https://gupea.ub.gu.se/bitstream/2077/17861/1/gupea_2077_17861_1.pdf

Mazo, S. (2006) A propósito de los fundamentalismos en Colombia. In *Defensa de los Derechos Sexuales en Contextos Fundamentalistas*. Córdoba: Católicas por el Derecho a Decidir, pp. 78–84.

McAdam, D., McCarthy, J., & Zald, M. (1996) Introduction: Opportunities, Mobilizing Structures, and Framing Processes. In D. McAdam, J. McCarthy, & M. Zald, eds., *Comparative Perspectives on Social Movements*. New York: Cambridge University Press, pp. 1–22.

Meyer, D. & Staggenborg, S. (1996) Movements, Countermovements, and the Structure of Political Opportunity. *American Journal of Sociology* 101(6), 1628–60.

Miguel, L. F., Biroli, F., & Mariano, R. (2017) O direito ao aborto no debate legislativo brasileiro: a ofensiva conservadora na Câmara dos Deputados. *Opinião Pública* 23(1), 230–60.

Parra, A. (2010) Sentencia T-388 de 2009: Consolidación del derecho al aborto oportuno y seguro y los esfuerzos para menoscabarlo. In Articulación Regional Feminista, ed., *Derechos de las mujeres y discurso jurídico*, Bogotá: Humanas Colombia, pp. 29–46.

Pitanguy, J. (2011) Advocacy: um processo histórico. In L. Linhares & J. Pitanguy, *O Progresso das Mulheres no Brasil 2003–2010*. Rio de Janeiro: CEPIA, ONU Mulheres, pp. 22–56.

Sunstein, C. (1999) *One Case at a Time: Judicial Minimalism on the Supreme Court*. Cambridge, MA: Harvard University Press.

Tamés, R., & Andión, X. (2012) *Derechos humanos de las mujeres y protección de la vida prenatal en México*. Ciudad de México: GIRE.

Tushnet, M. (1999) *Taking the Constitution Away from the Courts*. Princeton, NJ: Princeton University Press.

Vaggione, J. M. (2005) Reactive Politicization and Religious Dissidence: The Political Mutations of the Religious. *Social Theory and Practice* 31(2), 233–55.

Viana, P. (2011) Presentación de Brasil. In R. Soares, ed., *Quem controla as mulheres? Direitos reprodutivos e fundamentalismos religiosos na América Latina*. São Paulo: Católicas pelo Direito a Decidir, pp. 167–69.

Interviews

Ardila, Mariana (2019) Director of the Legal Area, Women's Link Colombia. Bogota, November 29.

Bascary, Lourdes (2010) Member of the Area of Economic, Social and Cultural Rights, Center for Legal and Social Studies (CELS). Buenos Aires, December 20.

Batista, Jolúzia (2019) Senior Technical Advisor at Centro Feminista de Estudos e Assessoria (CFEMEA). Brasilia, August 23.

Beltrán, Alma, and Fernanda Díaz de León (2011) Members of the Legal Area of GIRE. Ciudad de México, September 29.

Cruz Parcero, Juan Antonio (2011) Professor Institute of Philosophical Research-UNAM. Ciudad de México, September 14.

Cuéllar, Guillermo (2013) Director of Brújula Comunicaciones. Bogotá, February 21.

Díaz, Estela (2013) Gender Secretary, Confederation of Argentine Workers (CTA) and member of the National Campaign for the Right to Legal, Safe and Free Abortion. Buenos Aires, September 12.

Díaz de león, Fernanda (2019) Coordinator of Policy and Advocacy for Ipas Mexico. Ciudad de México, September 25.

Juliá, Silvia (2010) Executive Director at Catholics for Choice Argentina. Córdoba, December 18.

Lamas, Marta (2011) Director of Debate Feminista; ex Director of GIRE. Ciudad de México, September 29.

Martínez, Juliana (2019) Coordinator Mesa por la Vida y la Salud de las Mujeres. Bogotá, November 6.

Mazo, Sandra (2019) Director Catholics for Choice Colombia. Bogotá, November 7.

Mejía, María Consuelo (2017) Director of Catholics for Choice Mexico. Ciudad de México, August 5.

Méndez, Alex Ali (2019) Coordinator of the Case Documentation and Litigation Department at GIRE. Ciudad de México, September 24.

Moneta, Fátima (2019) Member of Catholics for Choice Mexico, Ciudad de México, September 26.

Negrão, Telia (2012) Executive Secretary of the National Feminist Network for Sexual and Reproductive Health and Rights (2006–2012). Porto Alegre, August 8.

Ortiz-Millán, Gustavo (2011) Professor Institute of Philosophical Research-UNAM, member of the College of Bioethics. Ciudad de México, September 26.

Rodrigues, Kauara (2012) Member of CFEMEA (Feminist Centre for Studies and Advisory Services). Brasilia, August 13.

Romero, María Eugenia (2019) Director of Equidad de Género, Familia y Trabajo. Ciudad de México, September 26.

Rondon, Gabriela (2019) Senior Legal Researcher at ANIS. Institute of Bioethics, Human Rights, and Gender. Brasilia, August 30.

Tovar, Ariadna (2013) Senior Lawyer at Women's Link Worldwide. Bogotá, February 22.

5

Backlash against State Strengthening Reforms

The Rise and Fall of the CICIG in Guatemala

Rachel E. Bowen

INTRODUCTION

For many observers of Central America, the 2015 removal of Guatemalan President Otto Perez Molina to stand trial for corruption appeared to be a clear step toward cementing the rule of law in that country. The International Commission against Impunity in Guatemala, or CICIG, was lauded for its role in the investigation into the customs scandal that ultimately brought down first the vice-president and then the president. Activists in neighboring countries who had been demanding similar international anti-corruption commissions found their political environments suddenly more receptive to those demands as a result of renewed international pressure. Indeed, Honduras adopted its own variation of the CICIG and El Salvador entered into a partnership with the United Nations Office on Drugs and Crime in the subsequent months. The CICIG, which was ultimately shuttered in 2019 by President Jimmy Morales, offers lessons about the opportunities for leveraging international alliances to fight grand corruption as well as the challenges inherent in pursuing such strategies against powerful domestic anti-reform coalitions.

Activists often pursue international allies when facing an inhospitable domestic environment. Especially in internationally weak and economically dependent countries, international actors can wield significant influence over domestic governments. Indeed, Guatemala has been no stranger to foreign intervention. Despite violent histories of intervention, Guatemalan proponents of peace processes, democratization, and rule of law construction have routinely sought international support to counteract the influence of powerful domestic actors such as the military, economic elites, and criminal networks. In the quarter-century since the signing of the Peace Accords, the CICIG has been the single most prominent and active form of international participation in Guatemala's domestic governance. The CICIG was a unique form of international cooperation, through which international jurists, prosecutors, and investigators helped to strengthen the Guatemalan justice system, most notably the prosecutorial service (Zimmerman 2019). However, the persistence of that international cooperation depended on the willingness of powerful international actors and donors to support it and to maintain pressure on the domestic government to tolerate it – or even comply with it. Despite – and because of – its notable accomplishments and its continuing popularity in Guatemala, President Morales felt free to close the CICIG following shifts in the priorities and engagement of international actors, most notably the United States.

Guatemalan opponents of the CICIG decried it as an international imposition from the beginning, particularly objecting to the power imbalance between Guatemala and a United States government that would not consider Guatemalan concerns regarding US immigration law (Zimmerman 2017, 174). It is unclear whether any Guatemalan president had the genuine will to fight impunity with the support of the CICIG, but the combination of pro-reform advocacy from influential sectors of Guatemalan society and international pressure substituted for that will for a period. During that time, the CICIG was able to grow the law enforcement capacity of the Guatemalan state, resulting in reductions in impunity and the overall violent crime rate. The CICIG helped to bring to Guatemala investigative and prosecutorial tools similar to those that Brazilian prosecutors used to prosecute the *Lava Jato* scandal, as described by Da Ros and Taylor (Chapter 10 in this volume). Although the CICIG departed Guatemala in 2019, those tools remain. Indeed, the popular will in favor of ending impunity is still there. The question, however, is how to end impunity when the minority in power have long benefited from rampant organized criminality.

The trajectory of the CICIG in Guatemala also complicates the ways in which we think about corruption control and transitional justice. Transitional justice is often understood as focusing on the sidelining and prosecution of former dictators, on the one hand, and the vindication of human rights more broadly through truth commissions, trials, and other measures (Olsen, Payne, and Reiter 2010; Sikkink 2011; Skaar, García-Godos, and Collins 2016). There are clear overlaps between transitional justice and judicial reform processes that promote judicial independence, although that relationship is somewhat murky as we get further from the original "transition" (Bowen 2019; Collins 2010; McAuliffe 2013; Skaar 2011). Especially complicated is the relationship between the prosecution of past human rights violations and the prosecution of gross corruption, particularly when, as in Guatemala, many of the perpetrators are the same or connected to each other across both kinds of cases. Nonetheless, "[a]lthough still incomplete, Guatemala's progress in accountability is striking precisely because it has happened against all odds, in a politically hostile and impunity-prone context" (García-Godos and Salvadó 2016, 218).

This chapter provides an overview of the rise and fall of the CICIG. Following the substantial international negotiations involved in creating the CICIG, especially following the rejection of a previous attempt by the Guatemalan Constitutional Court, the CICIG spent the first several years of its existence building and strengthening Guatemala's institutions. Partnerships were forged, new laws relating to criminal procedure were proposed and ultimately passed, new "high-risk tribunals" were created, justice sector officials were offered training, and a slow crescendo of investigations into criminal networks was initiated. By the end of its twelve years of operation, the CICIG had participated in the investigation of more than sixty criminal networks and the charging of more than 300 officials. Its lasting impact, however, will come from the institutions and officials it developed and not any single prosecution. Only strong and independent courts and prosecutorial agencies can establish and institutionalize accountability. The experience of the CICIG in Guatemala suggests that the justice system alone does not have the capacity to reorder a corrupt state, especially given institutional and political relationships between high-ranking members of the justice system and those within networks of corruption.

REVISITING THE RULE OF LAW

Constructing the rule of law, specifically the development of processes, institutions, and even cultures of accountability and law-abidingness, is routinely considered an essential component of democratic deepening (Diamond 1999; Gloppen 2004; Hammergren 2007; Helmke and Ríos

Figueroa 2011; Ulfelder 2010). Scholars and international donors suggest that various aspects of the rule of law, such as independent courts, have benefits for democratic governance, human rights protection, economic development, and the control of corruption (Helmke and McLean 2014; Ríos-Figueroa and Staton 2014). As such, international support for a variety of efforts to build the rule of law was plentiful as the Cold War ended and the "third wave of democratization" reached a crescendo (e.g., Carothers 2006; Domingo and Sieder 2001; Girod, Krasner, and Stoner-Weiss 2009; Popkin 2000; Prillaman 2000). These international efforts included projects to modernize judicial administration, reform criminal codes, engage justice sector officials in local and international training programs, and disseminate public education campaigns, among others, in the service of enhancing access to justice, independence of courts and judges, control of corruption, and a variety of associated goals (Hammergren 2008). Notably, these efforts depended heavily on funds, organization, and leadership from outside the democratizing countries, often working under the assumption that domestic actors would eventually take over leadership of these efforts (Díaz Rivillas and Linares Lejarraga 2005; Salas 2001; Santiso 2004; Sieder 2004). As a deeply impoverished country democratizing in the wake of a lengthy civil war, Guatemala ultimately hosted a substantial number of international programs.

What predicts the success and persistence of the institutional changes intended to enhance the rule of law in weak states? Brinks and Blass have argued that the relative power of the coalition seeking to reform the justice system over the "original coalition" that benefits from the unreformed system will drive the development of constitutional justice (Brinks and Blass 2018). In Guatemala, the reform coalition never eclipsed the power of the original coalition during the design of the 1985 constitution, the 1996 peace accords, or since. Given the persistent ties between the judiciary and powerful groups within the anti-reform coalition, the CICIG was created as an alternative to the weak and compromised national investigative and prosecutorial services. The CICIG can be understood as creating a sort of "institutional bypass" to allow interested parties to pursue their justice goals without being blocked in the preexisting justice sector institutions (Mota Prado and Trebilcock 2019). For a time, the CICIG flourished in this capacity, but its design as a "layered" reform that did not fundamentally or permanently alter the preexisting institutions (Thelen 2004) ultimately allowed the anti-reform coalition to reassert control.

While international support can bolster reform for a time, I argue that a strong, broad domestic coalition in support of the institutional reforms is necessary to resist backlash and outlast the eventual withdrawal of international backing. In weak states, especially those that are experiencing regime transitions, domestic political actors do not presumptively support those changes; some actors and coalitions can expect to lose a variety of benefits they enjoyed in the current or immediately prior regime. Where those benefits are acquired through undemocratic, corrupt, and/or criminal activities, as in Guatemala, those actors and coalitions are likely to be especially resistant. In Guatemala, the organized business sector has long been influential in determining the outcome of major political crises (McCleary 1999). The defection of the major business federation from President Perez Molina was an important step in his resignation and subsequent arrest. However, when the CICIG subsequently turned its attention to the business sector's involvement in corrupt campaign finance schemes, that same business federation turned against the CICIG.

REFORM COALITIONS AND BACKLASH IN GUATEMALA

The case of the CICIG demonstrates the necessity of the backing of a powerful coalition for substantial institutional reforms. Where domestic actors that support the rule of law lack power or financial resources, those coalitions will often involve international actors. In Guatemala and a handful of other weak states that have attempted regime change, international involvement was far more extensive than models around international pressure such as Keck and Sikkink's (1998) "boomerang" model would suggest. In Guatemala, the United Nations, along with the "Group of Friends" that included Colombia, Mexico, Norway, Spain, the United States, and Venezuela, sponsored peace processes, actively monitored the implementation of the peace accords through an in-country UN mission that lasted ten years, and funded and directed numerous institutional reform programs (Misión de Verificación de las Naciones Unidas en Guatemala 2000). The subsequent establishment of the CICIG involved yet more extensive international involvement to try to build the rule of law.

When previously powerful coalitions continue to operate through a transitional period, backlash against institutional reforms is all but inevitable. That backlash will be better able to impede institutional reform efforts when pro-reform domestic coalitions are weak or fragmented.

International reform sponsors may be able to bolster the pro-reform coalition and limit the impact of backlash if they exercise sufficiently powerful pressure on the state – and the pro-reform coalition has the will, backed by sufficient state capacity, to resist the backlash. Given that international actors are likely to withdraw their support over time as priorities shift, the long-term persistence of institutional reforms and accompanying gains in the rule of law depend on shifts in domestic coalitions, the availability of continued funding for institutional reform, and the strength and independence of specific actors such as chief prosecutors or courts.

In Guatemala, I emphasize two primary concerns. First, domestic political actors in Guatemala were at best divided on the desirability of constructing the rule of law as envisioned by international donors – and even some of those who supported the goals of the endeavor were skeptical of processes that seemed like international imposition of programs, legal reforms, and related projects. These divisions overlapped with underlying political divisions in Guatemala around issues of human rights, transitional justice, and priorities for economic development, along with more explicit differences over political parties and political ideologies. Although democratic Guatemala has supported a party system that has been largely feckless, there have nonetheless been dominant strains of political ideologies and political alliances. Indeed, the right-wing and pro-military Guatemalan Republican Front (*Frente Republicano Guatemalteco*, FRG), which was led by former military president Efrain Rios Montt until his death in 2018, had been the only party to truly persist throughout the democratic era, even if it lost relevance in the 2019 election. Other parties and coalitions have come and gone, largely existing primarily to back particular politicians.

The second concern that needs to be emphasized is that the international donor community was also divided on many of these programs and projects. Donors had different preferences about reform strategies, institutional structures, and legal models. They did not always coordinate their separate projects well, sometimes leaving room for reform projects to be used to aggrandize the power of individuals within the domestic justice sector or the political system more generally. So long as the major, wealthy powers of the world were in an ideologically liberal period, however, these problems remained in the realm of implementation. As major international players, including the United States and European Union, shifted their attention further and further from democracy promotion, the landscape of aid changed as well. Until 2017, the United States retained an interest in promoting a version of the rule of law in Guatemala to try to combat drug trafficking and related organized criminality in the service of its own national security. However, aid from the United States increasingly focused on professionalizing and, at times, militarizing law enforcement, in contrast to the broader and less militarized priorities of European donors.

Donald Trump's assumption of the presidency of the United States in January 2017 altered the reform landscape in Guatemala dramatically. Trump built much of his 2016 campaign around opposition to Latin American immigration, vilifying undocumented migrants from Mexico and Central America specifically. Building democracy, the rule of law, and economic development in Guatemala was not among his political priorities. His nativism was paired with foreign policy isolationism, a combination that made continued aid to Guatemala of no value to him. Indeed, the Trump administration cut off aid to Guatemala, along with El Salvador and Honduras, in retaliation for increased immigration pressure along the US–Mexico border. The damage to efforts to construct the rule of law in Guatemala went beyond the financial realm, however. When Guatemalan President Jimmy Morales announced that he would not renew the mandate of the CICIG in 2018 and subsequently barred its head from entering Guatemala in January 2019, the US government showed no evidence of concern. Guatemala was no longer a priority. Meanwhile, the European Union also shifted its attention to its own continental crises, including the protracted process of British departure from the union and the refugee crisis sparked by the Syrian civil war.

The Guatemalan case, in particular the rise and fall of the CICIG, can help us understand construction of rule of law at the intersection of domestic democratization processes and international influences. While international support can indeed bolster democratic institutions in a country with a weak or transitional democracy, domestic actors remain powerful and may take opportunities to shift trajectories when the international donor community is divided or distracted. An account of the shifting efforts of both domestic and international actors is essential for explaining the persistence of corruption in Guatemala and the backlash against efforts to combat impunity there. While presidents and their administrations are no doubt important players, the Guatemala system staggers appointments of attorneys general, Constitutional Court magistrates, and magistrates of the appellate courts and the Supreme Court. These staggered appointments generally prevent incoming presidents from being able to transform the justice system in their own images upon entering office. These actors then become potential opponents of presidents; their independence from political and societal influences are necessary as well.

Development of rule of law, then, is not simply an outgrowth of democratization processes. It is its own process that is no less affected by alliances and political conflict than is democratization writ large. International funds and programs have been an especially significant component of those alliances. Seen from this perspective, the creation of the CICIG was, in large part, the product of an alliance between only some domestic political and legal actors and powerful international actors to try to limit the power of other domestic political actors. The anti-reform coalition persisted through a decade of reform efforts and took the opportunity to dismantle the CICIG when the reform coalition fractured. The shuttering of the CICIG was made possible not just because Guatemala's president wanted it, but because important international and domestic actors were not able – or willing – to stop him. President Morales was hardly the first Guatemalan president to threaten not to renew the CICIG's two-year mandates, but he was the first to be met with ineffective opposition.

The remainder of this chapter will seek to explain the conception, creation, progress, and ultimate downfall of the CICIG through the lens of these shifting alliances between and within international actors and domestic actors. Within Guatemala, we will see that important actors go beyond politicians and political parties to include the military and criminal and other informal networks. Additional actors, such as attorneys general, became increasingly significant in the years after the CICIG had begun its work. Major international actors in Guatemala since the peace process have included the United States, the European Union and several of its member states, and the United Nations. As the inter-American system became more active in this period, various of its institutions exerted some influence as well. In particular, this chapter looks to explain the success of the domestic backlash against the CICIG as a product of the shifting power and influence of domestic actors in a period of diminishing engagement from international actors.

PEACE, CRIME, AND CORRUPTION: GUATEMALA BACKGROUND

Guatemala experienced a civil war for thirty-six years beginning in 1960, following a coup against an elected socialist president. Although the rhetoric of the war was consistently framed in Cold War terms of communist guerrillas fighting to subvert democracy, in fact democratic governance was the exception during the war years. The war reached its peak in the first half of the 1980s, when genocidal warfare under military governments produced an estimated 100,000 deaths and disappearances, fully half of the total over the entire war (Comisión para el Esclarecimiento Histórico (Guatemala) 2000; Proyecto Interdiocesano Recuperación de la Memoria Histórica (Guatemala) 1998). The 1985 adoption of the democratic constitution that came into force in 1986 was, in actuality, a superficial transition. While it instituted elections and formally democratic governance, it did nothing to end the war or to curtail military abuses. Indeed, many Guatemalans will cite "democratization" as occurring a decade later with the signing of the peace accords, which included a robust vision of a transformed Guatemala.

When, after the war ended in 1996, the military began to retract some of its repressive capabilities, organized criminal violence expanded its reach. This violence included organized crime rings engaged in smuggling all manner of goods, narco-trafficking networks with ties to international cartels, and ordinary street crime, all of which exploded in the years after the peace accords. In the context of this extreme criminal violence, threats against judges and other inducements to judicial corruption became common. In significant ways, this organized crime was an extension of wartime authoritarianism. Many criminal networks had past and current ties to the military (Peacock and Beltrán 2003). Moreover, family and marital ties connected many powerful families in politics, the military, and criminal networks. Roberto López Villatoro, "the tennis shoe king," is an excellent example: he made a fortune in smuggling; was married to Zury Rios, four-time member of Congress and daughter of former military dictator Efrain Rios Montt (1982–1983); and exerted massive influence over the judiciary through corruption in the judicial selection processes prior to his 2018 arrest.

The CICIG, ultimately created in 2007, was the most far-reaching effort to control corruption in Guatemala. Many hoped that controlling corruption would also aid in reducing violent crime since there were so many ties between security forces and criminal networks; police officers made excellent enforcers and assassins. The rates of violent crime, especially homicide, did go down during the CICIG's twelve-year tenure. There may have been many reasons for that, but the work of the CICIG likely contributed. Indeed, the International Crisis Group estimated in a 2018 report that the CICIG was responsible for preventing approximately 4,500 homicides between 2007 and 2017 (International Crisis

Group 2018). Among the networks investigated by the CICIG and dismantled by Guatemalan authorities in that period were many members of the security forces. The most prominent corruption investigation carried out by the CICIG was the customs scandal known as *La Linea* (the line), which ultimately resulted in the 2015 resignations and ultimate prosecution of both the sitting vice president and president. However, the CICIG was shut down before it could dismantle what its last commissioner referred to as the "Captured State."

THE FAILURE OF THE PEACE PROCESS TO ROOT OUT CORRUPTION

While the peace process that ultimately culminated in the 1996 "Firm and Lasting Peace" officially ended Guatemala's thirty-six-year civil war, it didn't go far enough in dismantling the structures of power and corruption that had developed during the war years. The civil war had provided a fertile environment for the growth of increasingly sophisticated and far-reaching clandestine operations involved in smuggling and other illegal businesses. These operations were built on the foundation of networks of politicians and businessmen, as well as military members. The broad scope of the peace accords as written suggested that significant efforts would be made to improve politics in a variety of ways, including expanding the role of civil society, incorporating rebel groups into political life, and codifying human rights and indigenous rights into national policies. These grand promises were never realized, in no small part because those powerful networks were able to persist.

In the Peace Accords, these networks were known as *cuerpos ilegales y aparatos clandestinos de seguridad* (illegal clandestine security apparatuses), or CIACS. The CIACS have their roots in relationships formed within the Guatemalan army's intelligence services, especially in the *Estado Mayor Presidencial* (EMP), a unit originally created to protect the president and his family that ultimately was implicated in numerous disappearances and the murders of anthropologist Myrna Mack in 1990 and Bishop Juan Gerardi in 1998 before being abolished in 2003. Other intelligence units have also formed the nuclei of CIACS. The resumption of formal democracy in January 1986 did little to limit the growth of the CIACS; the military was largely allowed to continue to operate unfettered behind the scenes of elected government (Jonas 2000).

The peace process emerged in the context of a military stalemate in which armed revolutionaries had been rendered ineffective yet could not be successfully routed by the Guatemalan military. It gained much more international cooperation, coming under the direction of the United Nations, following the failed autogolpe by President Jorge Serrano Elías in 1993. The *Serranazo*, as Serrano's autogolpe is known, provided the impetus for a short-lived unity of purpose, during which most sectors of Guatemalan society, including the military and the Constitutional Court, supported Serrano's ouster. With the guidance of the United Nations, the peace process expanded to cover many areas that went well beyond the mere cessation of armed hostilities. Many of the far-reaching goals of the ten-part peace accords have never been fully implemented, however. While the war ended, many underlying issues continued. The CIACS continued to operate even as civilians governed on the surface (Brands 2010; Comisión para el Esclarecimiento Histórico (Guatemala) 2000; Peacock and Beltrán 2003; Stanley 2007).

These "hidden powers," as some termed the CIACS, were "partially revealed" during the 2003 showdown over the presidential candidacy of Rios Montt (Hernandez Pico 2003). At issue was the prohibition in the 1985 constitution on former coup-makers being able to become president again. When the Supreme Electoral Tribunal rejected Rios Montt's candidacy, citing that constitutional provision, Rios Montt appealed to the Supreme Court, ultimately setting off a back-and-forth conflict between the Supreme Court and the Constitutional Court. Because of Guatemala's unusual constitutional structure in which the Constitutional Court is not a part of the judiciary, there are areas of jurisdictional overlap that can be exploited by entrepreneurial attorneys and their clients. As this conflict escalated, Rios Montt and his party staged a riot in Guatemala City, backed up by *campesinos* and former members of the war-era self-defense patrols, or "ex-PACs," who had been bused in for this purpose. In the aftermath of these events, Rios Montt was put forward as a presidential candidate, although he went on to lose the election in the first round.

The "Black Thursday" riots, as they were known, gave added support for those in Guatemalan society and government who sought the creation of a body that would reign in the CIACS. The first attempt to create an international commission – the CICIACS – was found by the Constitutional Court in 2004 to violate several measures in the Guatemalan Constitution. The Constitutional Court notably insisted that an international body could not be given prosecutorial powers in Guatemalan courts. In 2006, a new agreement between the Guatemalan government and the United Nations authorized the establishment of the CICIG, which began its first two-year mandate in 2007. Crucially, the CICIG was designed as a partner to Guatemalan institutions, intended to strengthen them, thus avoiding the problems that derailed the CICIACS.

THE GRADUAL PROGRESS OF THE CICIG AGAINST SUSTAINED RESISTANCE

Because of its institutional structure and its location within Guatemala but institutionally adjacent to Guatemalan institutions, the CICIG's progress was heavily dependent on the ability of its commissioners and other personnel to build strong relationships with their Guatemalan counterparts. These efforts proved challenging in the first years of the CICIG's operation. Its first few annual reports chronicled frustrations with lack of cooperation within the national justice sector. Indeed, when I was interviewing judges in 2010, I heard a chorus of complaints from a subset of judges against new laws and initiatives, promoted by the CICIG, that sought to combat corruption within the judiciary. These initiatives were perceived as interfering inappropriately in the independence and authority of Guatemalan judges. The 2009 annual report complains in particular of the difficulties associated with high turnover in the high ranks of the National Civilian Police (CICIG 2009, 8). Nonetheless, successes grew, notably with the early creation of the *Fiscalia Especial Contra la Impunidad* (Special Prosecutor's Office against Impunity, or FECI) and the creation of the High-Risk Tribunals in 2009. In 2010, however, President Alvaro Colom appointed Conrado Reyes to the post of attorney general. A week later, CICIG Commissioner Carlos Castresana resigned in protest over Reyes' alleged drug ties, which the CICIG had investigated and made known to the president. The ensuing scandal led to Reyes' resignation from the post before the end of the year, necessitating a new appointment.

The appointment of Claudia Paz y Paz as attorney general in 2010 provided the CICIG with an outspoken and active ally at a high level in the Guatemalan justice sector. The presence of an activist attorney general meant support for the FECI's efforts as well as an advocate for the CICIG's projects within the Guatemalan government. Her tenure included prosecutions and conviction in the High-Risk Tribunals of military officers in multiple cases. Most prominent among these cases was the

2013 conviction of General Rios Montt for genocide, although the decision was quickly overturned by the Constitutional Court on an evidentiary matter. An ordered retrial was delayed multiple times, ultimately being rendered moot by Rios Montt's death in 2018. These high-profile cases against prominent figures in Guatemala who continued to have ties to powerful and wealthy figures in the political and criminal worlds, were routinely cheered by the international community. Within Guatemala, however, they were highly dangerous for the judges involved.

Paz y Paz received considerable praise and support from international actors, bolstering her status in Guatemala. At the same time, her activities earned her many enemies in Guatemala. The timing of her 2014 departure from her position was controversial. Because she had assumed the position in December, rather than May, 2010, some believed that her four-year term should extend until December 2014. Some within Guatemala's old guard of elites considered her a threat. Ultimately, the Constitutional Court ruled that her term was to end in May 2014. To her supporters, this was a harsh rebuke of her and her accomplishments. She had, during her tenure, put numerous organized crime figures in jail. In the process, she had helped to reduce the crime rate by 9 percent in just three years. Her tenure represented a sea change in Guatemala, one that traditional right-wing elites wanted to halt. Paz y Paz would ultimately go into exile.

When Thelma Aldana was appointed in May 2014 by President Otto Perez Molina, she was criticized for being too close to the president, too partisan, and connected to Rios Montt's Guatemalan Republican Front. By its September 2014 annual report, however, the CICIG praised its relations with Aldana as being one of good will and the Public Ministry as being an "ideal partner" (CICIG 2014, 40). Its November 2015 annual report praised Aldana even more extravagantly, indicating that her excellent relationship with the CICIG had allowed for ever-improving inter-institutional cooperation (CICIG 2015, 61). Whether or not Aldana as a Supreme Court magistrate had been too cozy with Perez Molina, she certainly was not as attorney general. Before the end of her first year in the post, she would announce a joint investigation with the CICIG that would ultimately bring down the president himself.

In April 2015, the National Civilian Police arrested a number of customs officers as part of an investigation known as *La Linea*. This kind of arrest had become common in Guatemala. That same month, President Perez Molina and his vice president, Roxana Baldetti, argued to the United Nations that the CICIG was no longer needed in Guatemala, suggesting that he did not plan to renew the commission for another two-year mandate. As evidence mounted that both Perez Molina and Baldetti were connected to the customs scandal, perhaps even directing it, international pressure grew to renew the mandate. Domestic pressure grew as well, leading to the renewal of the CICIG until 2017.

Domestic opposition to the president and vice president grew over that summer, organized through social media with the hashtags #JusticiaYa and #RenunciaYa (Justice Now and Resign Now). Major public demonstrations began on April 25 and culminated in a national strike on August 27. These protests were large, peaceful, and did not appear to be centrally coordinated. They were also successful. Vice President Baldetti resigned on May 9. Perez Molina resisted longer, only resigning after the National Strike, when he was already subject to an arrest warrant and the Congress had stripped him of his presidential immunity from prosecution. He resigned on September 2 and was arrested on September 3. The world was stunned. The November 2015 CICIG report suggests that the majority of analysts, journalist, political actors, and the society in general viewed the result positively (CICIG 2015, 10).

GROWING BACKLASH AND THE DISMANTLING OF THE CICIG

In retrospect, the latter half of 2015, when a mass popular movement was galvanized by one of the CICIG's investigations, would be the peak of the power and influence of the commission. The resignation and subsequent arrest of President Perez Molina in 2015 happened mere days before the presidential election runoff. One candidate was Sandra Torres, the former wife of President Alvaro Colom, who had divorced her husband in order to be able to run for president herself, employing a literal interpretation of a constitutional provision preventing direct family relations of a former president from becoming president. The other candidate was a former television comedian and political outsider, Jimmy Morales. Morales was running under the campaign slogan "Not corrupt, not a thief" and enjoyed the support of powerful members of the armed forces. Despite calls to delay the election in light of the tremendous political upheaval, the election went ahead as planned. Morales won the election and assumed the presidency in January 2016.

It was not long after Morales' election that his showdown with the CICIG began. Early in Morales' presidency, while he still voiced substantial support for anticorruption reforms, an investigation was initiated into the president's son and brother for falsifying receipts to the government;

they were ultimately acquitted in 2019. Once they stood accused, Morales stopped cooperating with anti-corruption efforts. Within the first year of Morales' presidency, the CICIG began an extensive investigation of campaign finance irregularities. By 2017, Morales stood accused of accepting $1 million in illegal campaign donations. In retaliation, Morales attempted to expel the head of the CICIG, Ivan Velasquez, from the country. The Constitutional Court quickly struck down the president's actions. Facing substantial international and domestic pressure to comply with the Constitutional Court's order, Morales abandoned his efforts, but not before firing his foreign minister for not having carried out the order.

However, one year later, in August 2018, Guatemalan prosecutors from the FECI, with the support of the CICIG, successfully petitioned the Supreme Court to authorize a vote in Congress to strip the president of his legal immunity so that he could be made to face prosecution. In response, Morales announced the immediate revocation of the commission's mandate and the transfer of its responsibilities to Guatemalan institutions. At the same time, Morales sent army vehicles to surround the CICIG's headquarters. During a tense standoff, US Secretary of State Mike Pompeo spoke with Morales, expressing his support for Guatemala's sovereignty and reforms to the CICIG. Guatemala's Constitutional Court repeatedly overruled the president's orders, leading to a dramatic showdown at Guatemala City's La Aurora airport when a CICIG investigator was detained upon arrival, sparking popular protests outside the airport and another rebuke from the Constitutional Court, but Morales' decision remained in force. The CICIG's presence in Guatemala always depended on the national government's willingness to renew its mandates, such that its power ultimately depended on the amount of influence that the reform coalition could wield.

The CICIG spent 2019 largely finalizing its mandate, which expired on September 3, 2019. The United Nations maintained its support for Velasquez as the chief of the commission, but he was not able to reenter Guatemala and completed his duties from overseas. There had always been resistance to the reforms and investigations that the CICIG promoted. Prior to 2018, however, the CICIG appeared to be gradually winning over an increasing share of Guatemalan actors in civil society as well as in the state sector. Many of their strongest opponents had been arrested and seemingly sidelined. As the CICIG departed, it still enjoyed the support of more than 70 percent of Guatemalans. What changed during 2018 to make it impossible to restrain Morales from acting against the CICIG?

Even prior to 2018, alliances had been shifting in Guatemala. Morales had long been allied with the military, finding common cause around, among other things, harsh crime control tactics. In 2017, members of Congress introduced bill 5377, an amnesty law. Members of Congress who supported the military and the amnesty law attacked the Constitutional Court and successfully petitioned the Supreme Court to allow the Congress to open impeachment proceedings in 2019 against three Constitutional Court magistrates who had most consistently opposed President Morales. In his frequent disregard of the Constitutional Court, Morales was finding strong support within the Guatemalan Congress. In May 2018, Morales was also able to appoint a new attorney general, María Consuelo Porras, when Thelma Aldana's term expired. While Porras did take steps to enforce the Constitutional Court's rulings regarding the CICIG investigator held at La Aurora airport, she did not challenge Morales in the ways that Aldana had. Moreover, the long-powerful business sector found itself under scrutiny and was threatened by the CICIG's investigation into Morales' campaign finances. With domestic backlash growing and a diminishing coalition supporting the CICIG, the work of the commission was likely to survive only with pressure from international actors.

Internationally, the United States made clear that it was no longer going to push Guatemala to accept the presence of an international body that might question the power and legitimacy of Guatemala's president. Now in an anti-internationalist presidency, the United States signaled its support for unfettered sovereignty. Moreover, the United States was politically focused on the flow of Central American migrants at its southern border and sought more stringent crime and border control from Guatemala – notably without pairing those demands with even so much as rhetoric about human rights or the rule of law. At the same time, Sweden's pro-CICIG ambassador to Guatemala was expelled. The European Union and its member states were increasingly distracted from aid activities by the fallout from their own migrant crisis and the potential unraveling of the union associated with the United Kingdom's gradual exit from the EU. While the United Nations remained supportive of the CICIG to the end, it had little enforcement power without the intervention of the United States and European Union. International actors that had put pressure on previous presidents to extend the CICIG's mandate and cooperate with its investigations did not apply similar pressure in late 2018.

Guatemala held its presidential election in 2019. Thelma Aldana was initially a candidate for the Semilla party before she was charged with corruption by Morales' government. In May, the Constitutional Court rejected her candidacy. She has remained abroad since and was granted political asylum in the United States in April 2020. General Rios Montt's daughter Zury Rios was also disqualified because she is a direct relative of a coup-maker. Another candidate was arrested for allegedly accepting millions of dollars in campaign contributions from the Sinaloa cartel. In the second round, conservative former prison director Alejandro Giammattei defeated Sandra Torres. Giammattei has promised *mano dura* policies against crime as well as corruption, but is a critic of the CICIG dating back to the 2010 CICIG investigation of extrajudicial killings at El Pavón prison while he was prisons director. As of this writing, just over a year into his presidency, Giammattei's commitment to combatting corruption is questionable. Among his early actions were the creation of a new anti-graft commission housed in the president's office and the reappointment of police chiefs that Morales had dismissed in retaliation for their work with the CICIG. However, he has surrounded himself with advisors from Morales' circle and from the military. The 2020–2021 process of selecting judges for the Constitutional Court has evidenced substantial influence of corruption.

LOOKING AHEAD: AFTER THE CICIG

How, then, should we assess the CICIG's tenure in light of how it ended? One narrative of Velasquez's expulsion from Guatemala and the subsequent shuttering of the commission is that a corrupt president eliminated an international anti-corruption commission that had attempted to investigate his own corruption. That narrative, while accurate, would be incomplete. The CICIG did more than conduct investigations and its work had ripples throughout Guatemalan legal institutions as well as in popular opinion and mobilization around issues of corruption and justice. While it is possible but highly unlikely that a new international commission could be created in Guatemala, the real question looking forward is whether Guatemalan institutions themselves can maintain their independence from politicians as well as the myriad of societal actors that would seek to influence them. If they can, progress against corruption in Guatemala may continue. There are reasons to believe that such progress is possible, but also reasons for concern.

One reason for optimism is the new institutions and laws that were created during the CICIG's mandate. Many efforts were far-reaching, such as legal reforms that allowed Guatemalan investigators for the first time to use tools such as wiretapping and witness protection measures. Those measures were instrumental in investigations of organized crime rings and other conspiracies. Larger projects included the creation of whole new offices and institutions. The FECI was created to be the CICIG's partner in prosecution and continues to operate. Because Guatemalan law would not allow the CICIG to prosecute cases directly, this special corps of prosecutors handled all of the prosecutions that flowed from the CICIG's investigations. One result of that endeavor is a cohort of highly experienced and knowledgeable prosecutors specialized in anti-corruption efforts. The high-risk tribunals were also created during this period. These trial-level courts, which offer special security measures along with public recognition and the ability to develop specialized knowledge for their judges, focus on cases involving crimes such as drug trafficking or human trafficking, as well as trials of military officers for human rights offenses, including the Rios Montt trial. Those courts also continue to operate.

The period in which the CICIG operated also saw significant growth in civil society activity against corruption. These activities included monitoring the appointment processes that selected magistrates of the appeals courts and the Supreme Court as well as the attorneys general and others. These efforts enjoyed the support of international actors such as Transparency International; there is no reason why the CICIG's absence would change such support. The Justicia Ya/Renuncia Ya protests reflected broad changes in Guatemala's political culture that may bolster further civil society activism. While finding common cause among such a broad and multisectoral group of actors is unlikely to be a routine occurrence, those demonstrations reflected a reduction in fear-based public reticence around politics and the rise of a youthful activism that uses new tools such as social media for organizing.

It will be more difficult, albeit not impossible, for future Guatemalan presidents to reverse these institutional developments than it was to not renew the CICIG's mandate. Guatemalan authorities are likely to be more reluctant to openly intimidate large urban protests in the contemporary era than they were during the war years, for example. With the 2015 protests, what had long been unimaginable in Guatemala became imaginable. Civil society organizations continue to enjoy international support, but they may be vulnerable nonetheless; some of Guatemala's neighbors have taken subtle but effective measures to hinder the work of civil society organizations and limit their access to international funding. Moreover, politicians are now expected to at least publicly oppose corruption. These developments are hardly a firewall against corruption, but they nonetheless suggest that local anti-corruption efforts may be able to continue.

Combatting corruption in Guatemala is likely to remain a struggle, however. Even with the illegal networks and corrupt individuals investigated by the CICIG, many of whom were ultimately tried and imprisoned, there remain ties between politicians, businessmen, the military, and criminal and drug trafficking gangs. Because the material incentives to engage in corruption are substantial, there is every reason to believe that corrupt individuals will continue to try to place allies in Guatemalan institutions. Selection processes for powerful officials in the justice sector, including the attorney general, are designed to limit the exclusive power of the president to influence those appointments. However, the design of these nominating committees incorporates diffuse participation in ways that make it easy to introduce corrupt individuals to the slates and also difficult to hold anyone in particular accountable for those actions. Monitoring of these processes by civil society organizations helps somewhat, but those unofficial monitors rarely have the authority to go beyond public denunciations.

An additional cause for concern is that the progress we have seen in Guatemala has taken place predominately in Guatemala City and several secondary cities. In much of the rest of the country, corruption continues to proliferate. Indeed, rural activists face threats and even lethal violence at the hands of not only criminal gangs, but also paramilitaries and members of state security forces who are protecting the interests of major international corporations. Activists who seek to defend their communities from environmental devastation threatened by extractive industries face substantial danger. Moreover, there is often not the political will to enforce the law against corrupt officers or corrupt international businesses. Although it has become possible to pierce the impunity of military figures for human rights violations carried out during the war years, it remains difficult to do so for ongoing abuses.

CONCLUSION

This examination of the Guatemalan experience with the CICIG has elucidated the important overlaps between domestic democratization and international influence. Domestic democratization efforts stumbled in the face of the persistence of the CIACS. In Guatemala's feckless party system, partisan relationships are infrequently stable and only rarely predict actual networks and loyalties. Collusion happens rather between politicians, military, and criminals in often shifting coalitions. Thus, it can be difficult to prove and prosecute the CIACS. The international community, through the United Nations, supported the CICIG just as earlier it had supported the peace negotiations. However, the international community has its own shifting coalitions, which are often influenced by the domestic politics of states. When the United States elected an isolationist and nativist president, while the European Union was also focused on the Brexit crisis, it provided an opening to attack the CICIG and allied institutions such as the Constitutional Court without consequence.

One cannot discuss Guatemalan society without recognizing the extensive interactions between legal economic activity and officially illegal activity such as smuggling and money laundering. The line between the black market and the legal market is often quite porous and the beneficiaries of that lax enforcement and associated corruption include powerful politicians. Guatemala City has enjoyed a real estate boom that has frequently been financed by money laundering, for example. Both national and international firms have made use of the easy corruption of security forces to eliminate opponents, especially in the more rural areas of the country. Relationships between politicians and organized criminals, be they "love matches" or marriages of convenience, pose a substantial danger to Guatemalan democracy. When one turns against the other, which has more firepower? In Guatemala, the answer to that has often been organized crime.

The tenure and demise of the CICIG also provides important lessons for other anti-corruption efforts. Honduras adopted its own variation of the CICIG and El Salvador entered into a partnership with the United Nations Office of Drugs and Crime in the months following President Perez Molina's resignation and arrest. These more recent institutions had significant differences from the original CICIG that have made them far easier for their host governments to contain. The CICIG experience teaches us the importance of strong relationships with domestic actors and institutions, preferably ones with power. With the short terms of most judges and attorneys general in Central America, not including Costa Rica, those relationships may be, at best, unstable. To the extent that these important justice sector actors can be made independent of the political and societal actors they are intended to monitor, there may be greater success against corruption – but selection and renewal processes may be more fraught. Given that it is not clear that the current governments of Honduras and El Salvador prefer strong accountability measures for government officials, it would behoove anti-corruption institutions to be highly strategic in fostering relationships with more stable institutions or even in creating partner institutions such as Guatemala's FECI.

Guatemala's experience with the CICIG tells us that it is possible to interrupt impunity. However, the backlash sparked by that interruption will seek to neutralize newly empowered judges and prosecutors. Guatemala is not a case where the public turned away from reform, but rather one of an elite that was willing to tolerate and even support reforms until investigators came too close to them. Unlike Brazil or even Peru, the institution that became such an irritant was not a national institution and could be far more easily removed as a result. Indeed, had President Morales shuttered the judiciary or the prosecutorial service, he would have invited international condemnation and possibly a repeat of the popular uprisings that brought down his predecessor. The state remains captured.

References

Bowen, R. E. (2019). The Weight of the Continuous Past: Transitional (In)Justice and Impunity States in Central America. *Latin American Politics and Society* 61(1), 126–47.

Brands, H. (2010). *Crime, Violence, and the Crisis in Guatemala: A Case Study in the Erosion of the State*. Carlisle, PA: US Army War College.

Brinks, D. M. & Blass, A. (2018). *The DNA of Constitutional Justice in Latin America: Politics, Governance, and Judicial Design*. Cambridge: Cambridge University Press.

Carothers, T. (2006). *Promoting the Rule of Law Abroad: In Search of Knowledge*. Washington, DC: Carnegie Endowment for International Peace.

CICIG (2009). *Two Years of Work: A Commitment to Justice, Guatemala, Guatemala: International Commission against Impunity in Guatemala*. Annual Report, Guatemala: CICIG.

(2014). *Informe de La Comisión Internacional Contra La Impunidad En Guatemala con Ocasión de Su Séptimo Año de Labores, Guatemala, Guatemala: International Commission against Impunity in Guatemala*. Annual Report, Guatemala: CICIG.

(2015). *Informe de La Comisión Internacional Contra La Impunidad En Guatemala con Ocasión de Su Octavo Año de Labores, Guatemala, Guatemala: International Commission against Impunity in Guatemala*. Annual Report, Guatemala: CICIG.

Collins, C. (2010). *Post-Transitional Justice: Human Rights Trials in Chile and El Salvador*. University Park, PA: Pennsylvania State University Press.

Comisión para el Esclarecimiento Histórico (Guatemala) (2000). *Guatemala, Memory of Silence = Tz'inil Na'tab'al: Report of the Commission for Historical Clarification, Conclusions and Recommendations*. 2nd ed. Guatemala: CEH.

Diamond, L. (1999). *Developing Democracy: Toward Consolidation*. Baltimore, MD: Johns Hopkins University Press.

Díaz Rivillas, B. & Linares Lejarraga, S. (2005). Fortalecimiento de la Independencia Judicial en Centroamérica: Un Balance Tras Veinte Años de Reformas. *América Latina Hoy* 39, 47–96.

Domingo, P. & Sieder, R. (2001). *Rule of Law in Latin America: The International Promotion of Judicial Reform*. London: Institute of Latin American Studies.

García-Godos, J. & Salvadó, L. R. (2016). Guatemala: Truth and Memory on Trial. In E. Skaar, J. García-Godos & C. Collins, eds., *Transitional Justice in Latin America: The Uneven Road from Impunity towards Accountability*. New York: Routledge, pp. 203–26.

Girod, D. M., Krasner, S. D. & Stoner-Weiss, K. (2009). Governance and Foreign Assistance: The Imperfect Translation of Ideas into Outcomes. In A. Magen, T. Risse & M. A. McFaul, eds., *Promoting Democracy and the Rule of Law: American and European Strategies*. New York: Palgrave MacMillan, pp. 61–92.

Gloppen, S. (2004).The Accountability Function of the Courts in Tanzania and Zambia. In S. Gloppen, R. Gargarella & E. Skaar, eds., *Democratization and the Judiciary: The Accountability Function of Courts in New Democracies*. London: Frank Cass, pp. 112–36.

Hammergren, L. A. (2007). *Envisioning Reform: Improving Judicial Performance in Latin America*. University Park, PA: Pennsylvania State University Press.

(2008). Twenty-Five Years of Latin American Judicial Reforms: Achievements, Disappointments, and Emerging Issues. *Whitehead Journal of Diplomacy and International Relations* 9(1), 89–104.

Helmke, G. & McLean, E. V. (2014). Inducing Independence: A Strategic Model of World Bank Assistance and Legal Reform. *Conflict Management and Peace Science* 31(4), 383–405.

Helmke, G. & Ríos Figueroa, J. (2011). *Courts in Latin America*. Cambridge: Cambridge University Press.

Hernandez Pico, J. (2003). La Revelación Parcial de Los Poderes Ocultos. *Política y Sociedad* 41, 9–24.

International Crisis Group (2018). *Saving Guatemala's Fight against Crime and Impunity*. Latin America Report No. 70. Brussels: International Crisis Group.

Jonas, S. (2000). Democratization through Peace: The Difficult Case of Guatemala. *Journal of Interamerican Studies and World Affairs* 42(4), 9–38.

Keck, M. & Sikkink, K. (1998). *Activists beyond Borders: Transnational Advocacy Networks in International Politics*. Ithaca, NY: Cornell University Press.

McAuliffe, P. (2013). *Transitional Justice and Rule of Law Reconstruction: A Contentious Relationship*. London: Routledge.

McCleary, R. M. (1999). *Dictating Democracy: Guatemala and the End of Violent Revolution*. Gainesville: University Press of Florida.

Misión de Verificación de las Naciones Unidas en Guatemala (2000). *Compendio General Sobre El Proceso de Paz de Guatemala*. Guatemala: Misión de Verificación de las Naciones Unidas en Guatemala (MINUGUA).

Mota Prado, M. & Trebilcock, M. J. (2019). *Institutional Bypasses: A Strategy to Promote Reforms for Development*. Cambridge: Cambridge University Press.

Olsen, T. D., Payne, L. A. & Reiter, A. G. (2010). *Transitional Justice in the Balance: Comparing Processes, Weighing Efficacy*. Washington, DC: United States Institute of Peace.

Peacock, S. C. & Beltrán, A. (2003). *Hidden Powers in Post-Conflict Guatemala: Illegal Armed Groups and the Forces behind Them*. Washington, DC: Washington Office on Latin America.

Popkin, M. (2000). *Peace without Justice: Obstacles to Building the Rule of Law in El Salvador*. University Park, PA: Pennsylvania State University Press.

Prillaman, W. (2000). *The Judiciary and Democratic Decay in Latin America: Declining Confidence in the Rule of Law*. Westport, CT: Praeger.

Proyecto Interdiocesano Recuperación de la Memoria Histórica (Guatemala) (1998). *Guatemala, Nunca Más: Informe Del Proyecto Interdiocesano Recuperación de la Memoria Histórica Versión resumida*. San Sebastián: Tercera Prensa.

Ríos-Figueroa, J. & Staton, J. K. (2014). An Evaluation of Cross-National Measures of Judicial Independence. *Journal of Law, Economics, and Organization* 30(1), 104–37.

Salas, L. (2001). From Law and Development to the Rule of Law: New and Old Issues in Justice Reform in Latin America. In P. Domingo & R. Seider, eds., *Rule of Law in Latin America: The International Promotion of Judicial Reform*. London: Institute of Latin American Studies, pp. 17–46.

Santiso, C. (2004). Economic Reform and Judicial Governance in Brazil: Balancing Independence with Accountability. In S. Gloppen, R. Gargarella & E. Skaar, eds., *Democratization and the Judiciary: The Accountability Function of Courts in New Democracies*. London: Frank Cass, pp. 161–80.

Sieder, R. (2004). Renegotiating "Law and Order": Judicial Reform and Citizen Responses in Post-War Guatemala. In S. Gloppen, R. Gargarella & E. Skaar, eds., *Democratization and the Judiciary: The Accountability Function of Courts in New Democracies*. London: Frank Cass, pp. 137–69.

Sikkink, K. (2011).*The Justice Cascade: How Human Rights Prosecutions Are Changing World Politics*. New York: W. W. Norton.

Skaar, E. (2011). *Judicial Independence and Human Rights in Latin America: Violations, Politics, and Prosecution*. New York: Palgrave MacMillan.

Skaar, E., García-Godos, J. & Collins, C. (2016). Introduction: The Accountability Challenge. In E. Skaar, J. García-Godos & C. Collins, eds., *Transitional Justice in Latin America: The Uneven Road from Impunity towards Accountability*. New York: Routledge, pp. 1–24.

Stanley, W. (2007). Business as Usual? Justice and Policing Reform in Postwar Guatemala. In C. T. Call, ed., *Constructing Justice and Security after War*. Washington, DC: United States Institute of Peace, pp. 113–55.

Thelen, K. (2004). *How Institutions Evolve: The Political Economy of Skills in Germany, Britain, the United States, and Japan*. Cambridge: Cambridge University Press.

Ulfelder, J. (2010). *Dilemmas of Democratic Consolidation: A Game-Theory Approach*. Boulder, CO: First Forum Press.

Zimmerman, L. (2017). *Global Norms with a Local Face: Rule-of-Law Promotion and Norm Translation*. Cambridge: Cambridge University Press.

(2019). Beyond Diffusion: Cyclical Translation of International Rule-of-Law Commission Models in Guatemala. *Journal of International Relations and Development* 22(1), 28–49.

6

Backlash against Corporate Accountability for Grave Human Rights Violations in Colombia

Laura Bernal-Bermúdez

INTRODUCTION

Between 1958 and 2019, the Registry of Victims counted nearly 9 million victims of the armed conflict in Colombia, i.e. nearly one-fourth of the total population of the country today. With over sixty peace negotiations between the government and armed actors (including guerrilla and paramilitary groups) (Chaparro González and Martínez Osorio 2017: 11), Colombians have struggled to come to terms with past atrocities and hold those responsible to account. Nearly all signed peace agreements[1] focused solely on those bearing arms (mostly through amnesties and commissions to investigate past violence), and memory exercises have been largely limited to those actors (Jaramillo Marín 2014). However, when the *Autodefensas Unidas de Colombia* (AUC – United Self-Defense Forces of Colombia), the largest paramilitary group, demobilized in 2003,[2] the context changed. The reference to the role of economic elites and economic actors that was present in isolated academic studies and reports from NGOs became more tangible. As part of the demobilization process, a transitional justice framework known as *Justicia y Paz* (Justice and Peace) was created. The paramilitary leaders, tried by the Justice

[1] According to Pizarro Leongómez (2017), Colombia concluded fifteen peace negotiations from 1981 until 2016.

[2] The AUC emerged in 1996, when Carlos Castaño managed to bring together all the paramilitary groups operating in the country under one umbrella organization. See Verdad Abierta, Expansión de las Autodefensas Unidas de Colombia, https://verdadabierta.com/expansion-de-las-autodefensas-unidas-de-colombia/ (accessed May 7, 2021); Centro Nacional de Memoria Histórica (2013); Romero (2003).

and Peace magistrates, recounted how certain economic actors were complicit in forced displacement, murder, torture, as well as in creating and financing paramilitary groups (Bernal-Bermudez and Marín López 2018).[3]

These rulings started to suggest the complexity of the phenomenon, of the actors involved and their heterogeneity. Allegedly, some actors voluntarily collaborated with paramilitary groups, while others were forced to collaborate to protect their lives and/or their business operations. For the purposes of this chapter, by economic actors I mean those individuals or entities that develop an economic activity that is part of the licit economy. This broad definition accommodates the variety of actors that were named in the Justice and Peace rulings, including businesspeople, small, medium-size and large domestic companies, companies with national and local reach, business associations and multinational companies. However, individuals with more complex identities were also named: politicians who were economic actors, drug traffickers who participated in licit businesses, or paramilitaries with economic ventures (some were businessmen before they joined the paramilitaries and others were paramilitaries and drug traffickers who later ventured into licit economic projects).

The political opportunities created by the Justice and Peace process brought about two avenues of accountability. One was accountability through truth. By including economic actors in the narrative of paramilitary violence, the courts limited the number of permissible lies allowed in the public discourse (Ignatieff 1997) about the economic dimension of the conflict. The other was accountability through judicial actions. Though the Justice and Peace magistrates did not have a mandate to hold economic actors to account, they did urge prosecutors to pursue investigations of some of the economic actors involved, and they provided victims with additional evidence to pursue their cases in the courts.[4]

With fifteen rulings issued by the ordinary criminal jurisdiction since the early 2000s, convicting dozens of businesspeople, the prosecutors and courts have made significant progress untangling some of the processes of complicity. They traced how these businesspeople colluded with

[3] While this chapter refers to the role of certain economic actors in the atrocities of the conflict, I do not mean to set aside those businesspeople who were also victims of the armed conflict. The National Center of Historical Memory has produced several reports bringing their memories to the public and dignifying their experiences.

[4] By March 1, 2021, the Prosecutor's Office was conducting 625 investigations against businesspeople, of which 576 had started at the request of the Justice and Peace magistrates.

paramilitary forces and used violence to do business in some of the regions most affected by the conflict, which were also resource-rich.

As a result of these advances in truth and accountability regarding corporate complicity with the armed conflict, when the FARC guerrilla group – the oldest guerrilla group in the world and largest in Colombia – engaged in a peace process with the government in 2012, discussions about accountability for past atrocities included economic actors. They were no longer left out of the narrative of accountability. This seemed the next natural step in what may have been regarded as a progressive path towards accountability. However, as I show in this chapter, that path found resistance in the organized opposition (Meyer and Staggenborg 1996) of the largest business associations of the country, which set out to limit the reach of the transitional justice mechanisms that came out of the peace process. I argue that the organized opposition from a part of the business community was a reaction, or backlash, to the relative success of the movement toward accountability with the Justice and Peace process, increased threats to their interests and the result of effective work by these associations with political allies in the government. There is a sharp divergence between the comprehensive accountability that was discussed at the negotiation table between the government and FARC in Havana, and what we have today in the implementation of the Peace Agreement signed in 2016.

In this chapter I show how an absence of societal support to legitimize court-promoted changes can trump accountability efforts. In this case, low-level judges and prosecutors, supported by the superstructure created to protect the rights of victims through the courts,[5] managed to secure advances in accountability for business actors. However, these steps not only lacked mainstream societal support, but also produced a backlash from a very powerful sector of society. Similar to what Camila Gianella and Alba Ruibal find in their chapters in this volume (Chapters 3 and 4), judicialization can unleash opposition that affects the extent to which these efforts can build solid social roots. This chapter provides a unique contribution by tracing a process that has been understudied in two sets of literature: transitional justice and business and human rights, i.e. the ways in which the economic elite works as an organized opposition to thwart accountability efforts.

[5] Colombia has a very active Constitutional Court (Landau and López Murcia 2009), which has helped to advance the rights of victims of the conflict.

The strategies and mechanisms of opposition that I record in this chapter are the result of my own personal experience working with Dejusticia – an NGO that has actively advocated for the pursuit of corporate accountability through transitional justice mechanisms – and with a group of actors supporting the Truth Commission to devise a methodology to investigate this phenomenon. In that sense, this chapter is written as a chronicle of my own experience and perceptions throughout the negotiations and the implementation of the agreement with the FARC, coupled with archival work and documentary evidence.

A MOVEMENT TOWARDS CORPORATE ACCOUNTABILITY: BACKGROUND (1980–2005)

The story of accountability for corporate complicity with violence in Colombia is part of a broader story of struggle by victims of the armed conflict for the recognition and guarantee of their rights to truth, justice, remedy and guarantees of non-repetition. Ever since the first efforts from the state in the 1950s to come to terms with the violence, victims were left at the margins of state efforts, and there was particular emphasis on broader structural causal explanations of violence (Jaramillo Marín 2014: 74). Peace negotiations with the different armed groups in the past fifty years have ended largely with amnesties and impunity. However, as I will describe, a change in the domestic and international context led to a change in that pattern that started with the Justice and Peace process in the early 2000s.

In the mid-1980s, the government estimated that only 20 percent of crimes were investigated by the state, and only in 4 percent of those cases were any rulings issued (Centro Nacional de Memoria Histórica 2015). However, in the midst of increased state, paramilitary and guerrilla violence, a consolidated movement of victims started to emerge in the 1970s and 1980s, demanding justice and truth. They used human rights language to make violence legible to society, and to catch the attention of international actors (Sánchez-Mejía 2017: 3–5; Tate 2007). It was a heterogeneous group, supported by grassroots organizations, and the increased emergence of professional human rights NGOs and INGOs[6]

[6] The human rights movement is different from the victims' movement. The former takes collective action to defend the rights of others, while the victims' movement is made up of victims. There are debates about how much the human rights movement in Colombia represents the victims' movement (Tate 2007). However, this controversy is not the object

(Centro Nacional de Memoria Histórica 2015). In the 1990s, civil society organizations in Colombia had mastered the human rights language and countered the increased violence of the 1997–2004 period with claims made before domestic courts, but more effectively before the inter-American system of human rights (Centro Nacional de Memoria Histórica 2015).[7] The increased sophistication in the claims-making machinery of the human rights bureaucracy in NGOs and INGOs put enough pressure on the state to open up political opportunities to seek institutional change and avenues of redress before domestic courts (Keck and Sikkink 1998). There was increased legal mobilization through claims filed before domestic courts and increased success before the Inter-American Court, which issued ten convictions between 2004 and 2012 (Centro Nacional de Memoria Histórica 2015).

Demand from the human rights movement produced important institutional changes that, for some, opened avenues for remedy. In 1991, a new constitution was drafted, but more than a constitution, it was yet one more peace agreement between the state and several left-wing guerrilla groups. The *tutela*, or constitutional action for the protection of fundamental rights included in the constitution, emerged as one of the most significant avenues of redress for human rights violations. It allowed victims to access the courts directly and receive a fast-track response to their demands. The National Prosecutor's Office was also created with the new constitution, and in 1994 a human rights unit was formed, evidencing how the human rights language was influencing the institutional growth of the state. The Constitutional Court – also a creation of the constitution – has championed the rights of victims of the armed conflict and put their claims at the forefront of state policy.[8] The law was also changed, aiming to create institutional paths to seek redress, for example with the inclusion of enforced disappearance as a crime in 2000, or the law on forced displacement issued in 1997.[9]

of this chapter. Here, I simply recognize the role that NGOs and international NGOs (INGOs) have had in the accountability path, even if at times there are differences and ruptures between the human rights movement and the victims' movement (Tate 2007).

7 In 1995, the Inter-American Court issued the first conviction of the Colombian state for the Massacre of Trujillo. There are over 250 decisions by the Inter-American Court involving the Colombian state.

8 See, e.g., rulings T-268 of 2003, T-611 of 2007, T-821 of 2007, T-402 of 2011 and T-083 of 2017.

9 Some contend that the translation of victims' rights into these laws, as well as transitional justice mechanisms created from 2003 onwards, were the result of the struggle between victims' and other groups, where the victims lost, and as a result their rights have been

CORPORATE ACCOUNTABILITY IN THE CONTEXT OF JUSTICE AND PEACE (2005–2016)

In this context of increased mobilization for accountability, in 2003 the government started negotiations with the AUC.[10] The context of heightened demand for accountability by a more consolidated human rights movement, plus increased international surveillance,[11] led to the design of a transitional justice mechanism where accountability was the rule, and not the exception (Payne 2008). Law 975 of 2005 (Justice and Peace Law),[12] created a transitional justice mechanism where paramilitaries would face trial, and receive reduced sentences, in exchange for truth and reparation. I do not mean to suggest that the Justice and Peace process brought encompassing accountability and no impunity, as that was not the case. The process has been accused of being too slow and costly (Contraloría General de la República 2017), and the effective participation of victims has faced serious obstacles (Comisión Colombiana de Juristas 2007). Others have argued that the law significantly limited the definition of violence, the actors involved in the violence, and the identity of victims (Castillejo-Cuéllar 2014). Nonetheless, the limitations that several actors (academics and activists) see in the law do not efface the fact that the Justice and Peace Law represented a change in the way Colombians dealt with the past by attending to the rights of individual victims and trials.

Created in 1996, the AUC was the largest paramilitary group in the country, and with its demobilization over 20,000 men and women gave up their weapons and started a process of being reincorporated into

ended (Castillejo-Cuéllar 2014; Vidal López 1997). However, in my view, the laws did provide an institutional framework to pursue justice and a space to debate the interpretation of the law. These laws represent another front of controversy, but they do bring the debate to the public space.

10 On July 15, 2003, the government and leaders of the AUC signed the *Acuerdo de Ralito* (Agreement of Ralito), where they committed to starting negotiations for the demobilization of the AUC.

11 The Statute of the International Criminal Court entered into force on June 1, 2002, and the court was attentive to the negotiations in Colombia, since it was clear that certain crimes could not be subject to amnesties. The Inter-American System of Human Rights had also produced several decisions regarding the rights of victims to truth, justice, reparations and guarantees of nonrepetition, which limited the options available to the state. There was also increased surveillance by INGOs that could affect the claims of victims at the international level.

12 See www.secretariasenado.gov.co/senado/basedoc/ley_0975_2005.html (accessed May 7, 2021).

civilian life. The Justice and Peace process, broadly, consisted of granting lighter sentences in exchange for truth and reparations.[13] Accountability was, therefore, at its core. Justice and Peace chambers were created inside certain tribunals to hold paramilitary leaders to account.[14] Several memory institutions[15] were also created. In its dozens of reports, the Center for Historical Memory[16] has recorded the suffering of millions of Colombians, and has attempted to explain some of the violence and stories of resistance and resiliency.

As the accountability path continued to evolve, in 2011 the Victims and Land Restitution Law was enacted.[17] This law attempted to include an integral approach to the reparation of victims. There are, broadly, two avenues for redress. On the one hand, there is an administrative reparations program for victims handled by the Victim's Unit; and, on the other hand, a lands restitution system led by the Lands Restitution Unit and lands restitution courts. By January 2022, the lands system had received 135,997 requests, and the courts had issued nearly 6,791 rulings regarding the restitution of 177,539 hectares of land.[18] Again, while there are increasing reservations about the actual impact of these systems on the guarantee of the rights of victims (Amnesty International 2014; Sánchez and Acosta 2021), in my view they did open opportunities for redress.

As Winifred Tate (2007) suggests, this struggle for accountability included ruptures and controversies amongst the human rights movement to establish which actors should be held to account. Some focused on state actors and others on guerrillas and paramilitary groups. Yet others, following the versions of victims and their own experiences on the ground, started to demand a more comprehensive look into the dynamics behind the violence, which included several state and nonstate actors. The

[13] See Law 975 of 2005, www.secretariasenado.gov.co/senado/basedoc/ley_0975_2005.html (accessed May 7, 2021).

[14] These Justice and Peace chambers were created inside the tribunals of Medellín, Bogotá, Barranquilla and Bucaramanga. See www.ramajudicial.gov.co/web/10228/1136 (accessed May 7, 2021).

[15] The Group of Historical Memory first, and then the National Center of Historical Memory (CNMH in Spanish).

[16] See http://centrodememoriahistorica.gov.co/ (accessed May 7, 2021).

[17] Law 1448 of 2011, www.secretariasenado.gov.co/senado/basedoc/ley_1448_2011.html (accessed May 7, 2021).

[18] See www.restituciondetierras.gov.co/estadisticas-de-restitucion-de-tierras (accessed May 7, 2021).

role of businesses in the atrocities of the past started to emerge in the public discourse, as victims' grievances started to translate from the private sphere into claims in public fora (Felstiner, Abel, and Sarat 1980).

In the early 1990s, local NGOs, such as the *Comisión Intereclesial de Justicia y Paz* (CIJP), started demanding a broader spectrum of accountability – one that included economic actors and other nonarmed actors that had promoted or benefited from the violence in the territories. Around 1994, the paramilitary groups led by Carlos Castaño (later called AUC) entered the Urabá region in the Department of Chocó. They justified the massacres, tortures, rapes, selective killings and forced displacement as part of a strategy to rid the area of the influence of the FARC, but they also had economic interests in mind.[19] They colluded with palm oil businesspeople from the region of Madgalena Medio to appropriate the lands of the communities of Curvaradó and Jiguamiandó and start large-scale monocultures (Bernal-Bermúdez 2017). In what became known as the Urapalma case, the CIJP supported the communities on the ground and, together with the Dioceses of Quibdó, they brought a case against the businesses in regional fora (the Inter-American Commission and Court) and in domestic courts (constitutional and criminal jurisdictions). In 2014, nearly a decade after the communities had filed their claims with local prosecutors, a court in Medellin convicted fifteen businesspeople for their role in the forced displacement of these communities.

This has not been the only conviction of economic actors for their role in the violence of the conflict. While there is no dataset that records all convictions of businesses in Colombia, up until March 2021, the Prosecutor's Office was able to trace fifteen rulings – issued between 2005 and 2021 – where dozens of economic actors have been convicted for colluding with paramilitaries to perpetrate violence in the territories. The Urapalma case, described earlier, is only one of such cases. The rulings convicted businesspeople from the agriculture sector, cattle ranchers and local merchants. The Human Rights Unit of the Prosecutor's Office has also prioritized the investigation of those involved in funding paramilitary groups,[20] and consequently, for example, there are two open preliminary investigations against executives of two

[19] Interview with Danilo Rueda from the Comisión Intereclesial de Justicia y Paz, 2014. Interview with former prosecutor Héctor Cruz, 2019.

[20] Interview with a former public servant working with the Context Unit of the Prosecutor's Office, 2018. The public servant asked to remain anonymous.

multinationals registered in the United States: Chiquita Brands and Drummond.

As previously mentioned, transitional justice mechanisms have also contributed to further the path to accountability. The Justice and Peace and lands restitution processes also opened up avenues of enquiry into corporate complicity with past violence. Regarding corporate accountability, they made visible a phenomenon that had been reported by scholarly work and local communities, but that had broadly been left out of the public discourse. The Justice and Peace process was not designed to put economic actors on trial, as the courts could only decide on the legal accountability of paramilitaries. However, the Justice and Peace magistrates and prosecutors were innovators, and they found a way to bring businesses to account. They created a section in the rulings called "Context," where they explored the context in which paramilitary cells emerged and operated. As part of this context, the rulings include economic actors named as allegedly complicit with paramilitary violence. They also devised a system where, if the court found enough evidence to suggest complicity, they would send a formal notice (*compulsa* in Spanish) to the Prosecutor's Office so that they could conduct a preliminary investigation and pursue a trial if they considered it viable.[21] In this way, the Justice and Peace process was a stage in corporate accountability through truth (Payne, Pereira, and Bernal-Bermúdez 2020).

The lands restitution process also, unintendedly, became a stage for corporate accountability when economic actors are found to be aligned with armed actors to cause dispossession, or that after dispossession occurred, took advantage of the situation of violence to acquire lands (Bernal-Bermúdez and Sanchez 2022). Just like the Justice and Peace process, the restitution courts were not asked to investigate extensively the relationship between the company and the violence that led to dispossession or displacement. While a decision to restore lands does not necessarily mean that the company involved is responsible for a human rights violation, the work of the courts and the evidence provided by victims have allowed for some public reflection around the accountability of those who occupied lands that were only available because of violent displacement or dispossession. The processes do prompt reflection around the different levels of accountability within Colombian society (Bernal-Bermúdez and Sanchez 2022).

[21] Interview with Justice and Peace Magistrate Uldi Teresa Jiménez, 2014.

Considering the success that some NGOs had uncovering patterns of complicity – through the decisions of judges in the ordinary jurisdiction, the Justice and Peace chambers and the lands restitution courts – there was a move to seek a more systematic and less case-by-case approach to the accountability of businesses in the violence of the conflict. In this way, a group of NGOs that closely followed the negotiations with the FARC at Havana pushed for the inclusion of a broad spectrum of accountability in the competence of two of the transitional justice mechanisms that would come out of the negotiations: the Special Jurisdiction for Peace (JEP) and the Truth Commission (CEV). The accountability of third parties to the conflict – including businesspeople – was an important point of negotiation but, as I will suggest, it triggered an organized opposition from the business community that in the end limited the channels of accountability.

In the next section, I describe how the opposition organized by the business community manifested itself from 2012 to the date of writing this chapter, and the effects it has had in the path of accountability.

AVOIDING A "WITCH-HUNT" (2012–PRESENT): TRACING ORGANIZED OPPOSITION

According to Meyer and Staggenborg (1996: 1635), there are "three conditions [that] promote the rise of countermovements: first, the movement shows signs of success; second, the interests of some population are threatened by movement goals; and third, political allies are available to aid oppositional mobilization." As NGOs were increasingly successful in presenting corporate complicity as a more systematic phenomenon, and as the accountability movement shifted tactics to achieve more sustainable policy reforms, certain business associations were put on the defensive, and opposition emerged (Meyer and Staggenborg 1996). While I do not suggest that we have gone from some accountability to no accountability, the result of this engagement between movement and counter-movement has made it more difficult for victims to seek accountability under the current transitional justice (TJ) system in Colombia. In this section, I will first show evidence to suggest the emergence of an organized business opposition to accountability efforts, and then use Meyer and Staggenborg's conditions to explain the emergence and impact of this opposition.

Meyer and Staggenborg (1996: 1632) define counter-movements as "networks of individuals and organizations that share many of the same objects of concern as the social movements that they oppose. They make competing claims on the state on matters of policy and politics (see Gale 1986) and vie for attention from mass media and the broader public." They represent an organized attempt to resist or reverse social change and, in that way, they are reactionary. In my view, social movements are easier to trace, as they mostly use strategies that are visible to the public; counter-movements, particularly those that involve elites, are harder to trace. However, although their tactics tend to stay in the background, in this section I describe some actions that taken together suggest organized action by some of the most representative business associations in the country to impact the design of accountability mechanisms.

There is a marked change in the attitude of certain business associations regarding accountability efforts that can be traced to the start of the peace negotiations in Havana between the government of Colombia and the FARC. They went from hardly engaging with the discussion around accountability in the Justice and Peace process, to engaging with the media and the government in efforts to shape the design of the accountability mechanisms that were included in the peace agreement. As part of a group pushing for broader accountability and a multi-actor understanding of the conflict, we witnessed an organized attempt to resist social change. This was a backlash from corporate actors in response to a social change that was being imagined because of the empowerment of certain groups through truth and trials that stemmed from the Justice and Peace process: a social change in the understanding of past and future accountability.

We saw business associations use social movement tactics to oppose further advances of the accountability path, seeking and having a presence in all stages where civil society had a voice. This includes: actively engaging in the peace negotiations, creating organizations to push for a particular agenda regarding peace, using media to influence public debate, participating in law-making debates in Congress; producing reports with their narrative of the conflict; engaging with the TJ mechanisms that came out of the peace agreement; and actively lobbying for a candidate in the presidential elections where the implementation of the peace agreement was at stake. The power of businesses to trump accountability efforts was exercised effectively, making it more difficult for victims to pursue the guarantee of their rights to truth, justice, remedy, and guarantees of nonrepetition.

While business associations largely agreed that the competence of TJ mechanisms to put third parties on trial needed to be limited, they did not agree on the extent of that limitation. In this way, this organized opposition was not without fragmentations and ruptures (De la Calle 2019).[22] Particularly regarding the justice component of the peace agreement, certain business associations (for example those close to the agriculture and cattle ranchers sector) had strong views about the JEP not having competence regarding any conduct of third parties to the conflict. Others, mainly industrialists and business associations that bring together some of the largest companies in the country, advocated for a more restricted definition of the cases where the JEP could judge the conduct of third parties to the conflict.[23] However, even given these ruptures, there was a coordinated move towards limiting (partly or totally) the use of TJ mechanisms to put economic actors on trial, and there was a coordinated effort at different stages to achieve that goal. I now turn to an explanation of the different scenarios in which the backlash played out.

Strategies of Opposition: Vetoing Corporate Accountability through TJ Mechanisms

In the following pages I describe the different stages and strategies that certain business actors used to undermine the discourse and tools geared at making possible corporate accountability: the public sphere (specifically during the last stage of the peace negotiations), Congress and the Constitutional Court (both involved in the discussion of the transitional justice framework) and the work of the Truth Commission.

During the Peace Negotiations

During the Justice and Peace process, and throughout the series of convictions issued by ordinary courts, the business associations that bring together some of the largest companies in Colombia[24] remained untouched. The rotten apple theory appeared perfectly suited to explain the phenomenon: It was "them" (a few rotten apples) and not "us." Furthermore, there was great effort to differentiate the different types of businesses in Colombia, suggesting that not all apples belonged in the

[22] Interview with Sebastián González, former Asociación Nacional de Empresarios (ANDI) consultant, February 2020. Interview with Julián Correa, former official from Proantioquia, March 2020.

[23] Interview with Sebastián González, former ANDI consultant, February 2020. Interview with Julián Correa, former official from Proantioquia, March 2020.

[24] These include ANDI, Proantioquia and Grupo Empresarial Antioqueño.

same bag.[25] In the view of the leaders of some of the largest business associations, those with proven ties to armed groups and drug-trafficking renounced the privilege of being called businesspeople. However, when human rights defenders moved to broaden the spectrum of accountability through TJ mechanisms during the peace negotiations in Havana, the groups that were more heavily questioned could not stay out of the discussion. In the view of these associations, there was a risk of it all becoming a "witch-hunt," i.e. very public investigations of businesses, based solely on the word of *guerrilleros*, which could produce a high reputational risk that could not be erased even if businesses were absolved in the end (Amat 2017; León 2016).

For example, a business leader was recorded saying about the JEP:

> Yes. We have to make sure that [the JEP] has all the safeguards to avoid anyone abusing it. Apart from the economic danger that it represents. Surely many of the people who will be brought [to the JEP] or who are involved in processes will prove their innocence in the end, but they will do so after a proceeding that has already left them with a mark, and the effect of the bad reputation can translate into negative effects for their businesses and revenues.
>
> (Amat 2017)

This illustrates those concerns perfectly as they perceived that most claims would have no legal grounding, but would produce great economic harm to businesses.

Throughout the peace negotiations, the media covered the concerns of the business community over the negotiation (León 2016), and their trips to Havana to participate in the discussion on rural reform and justice (Caracol Radio 2015). In the memoirs of Humberto de la Calle, lead negotiator of the government in Havana, he recalled his meetings with different business associations (De la Calle 2019). The government needed businesses to invest in peace-building, and, at the same time, they were being pressured by the FARC and civil society to include economic actors in the accountability efforts of the JEP and the CEV. Some business associations remained in favor of the negotiations but against certain points of the agreement, and others, like the Colombian Farmers Association (SAC in Spanish), opposed the whole negotiation (De la Calle 2019: 86).

[25] This was a perspective that was made clear by business leaders on several occasions. For example, the leader of the largest industrialists' association in the country said in the course of a meeting with representatives from Dejusticia and academia that those willingly engaging with paramilitary groups could not be called businesspeople.

The idea of including businesspeople in the JEP and CEV was initially pitched as a guarantee for all those economic actors that feared convictions for their proximity to guerrilla or paramilitary groups (De la Calle 2019: 111). This, however, was far from the understanding of the business community, which saw it as a risk and not a guarantee (León 2016). There were three business leaders in the team of negotiators of the government – Luis Carlos Villegas, Gabriel Echavarría and Gonzalo Restrepo – and they all expressed their concern about the use of TJ mechanisms by guerrilla and other groups to set up what they later called in the media a "witch-hunt" against the economic elite (De la Calle 2019: 111). In their view, this would allow the FARC to change the narrative of the conflict by suggesting that they were the victims and the "establishment" the perpetrators (De la Calle 2019: 111). As De la Calle (2019: 238) recalls, business associations were constantly calling them to meetings, presenting recommendations and critiques. As he describes them, these were stages of negotiations, away from Havana, but with serious implications for the content of the agreement.

The FARC argued that "to reach a reconciliation of the Colombian family, there is an underlying moral and political obligation of all sectors of society with truth, justice, reparation and guarantees of non-repetition"[26] (León 2015). On the other hand, businesses were concerned about the agreement giving the JEP competence to prosecute indirect participation in the violence of the armed conflict (Amat 2017; León 2015). It was public knowledge that the ordinary jurisdiction had received thousands of calls from Justice and Peace magistrates to pursue further investigations into the role that some businesspeople had had in paramilitary violence. Some of these cases could be viewed as indirect participation in the conflict, as they referred to funding (voluntary or coerced) of paramilitary groups (Bernal-Bermudez and Marín López 2018; El Tiempo 2015).

President Santos and the FARC signed a first version of the agreement on September 26, 2016, and it was put to a vote of the people through a plebiscite on October 2, 2016. The result was a marginal victory for those who advocated for "No ratification of the agreement" (BBC Mundo 2016). While certain business associations had voiced their concerns about the scope of the transitional justice mechanisms (found in Point

[26] Translation by the author. Original text in Spanish: "Alcanzar la reconciliación de la familia colombiana presupone una obligación moral y política para todos los sectores de la sociedad, con la verdad, la justicia, la reparación y la garantía de no repetición."

5 of the agreement about victims), the *Consejo Nacional Gremial* (National Guild Council), which brings together some of the strongest businesses in Colombia,[27] supported the "Yes" campaign, arguing that peace would also enhance business performance (Lewin and Vélez 2016).

There was, however, some variation among the members of the business associations (Lewin and Vélez 2016), and more broadly among economic actors. Other economic actors funded the "No" campaign, arguing against a broader scope of accountability. This included, among others, businesspeople and associations involved in the production and commercialization of bananas (Revista Dinero 2016) and cattle ranchers (CONtexto Ganadero 2016), two of the groups of economic actors most mentioned by paramilitaries as complicit with their acts of violence (Bernal-Bermudez and Marín López 2018). As an investigative journalist found, for example, three firms and a businessman that financed the "No" campaign had been named by a paramilitary leader as having funded the Banana Bloc of the AUC in the first decade of the 2000s (Rodriguez 2017). In addition, the *Centro Democrático* political party, traditionally linked to certain economic actors in the agricultural sector, supported the "No" campaign.[28]

When the "No" campaign won, the government was forced to sit down with the opposition and make certain adjustments to the Peace Agreement. A revised agreement was signed on November 24, 2016, and ratified by Congress (Casey 2016). The recently created Business Council for Peace was one of the actors that actively engaged in this conversation and sent the government a document called "Basic Proposals to adjust the text of the final peace agreement and its implementation." Although several adjustments were introduced to the definition of the competence of the JEP (Semana.com 2016),[29] it did not exclude economic actors. The agreement even said that the Prosecutor's Office had to send all ongoing investigations against third parties to the conflict, including businesspeople, to the JEP (Cote 2019).

27 The Guild Council is a permanent forum of deliberation made up of the most representative associations of the following sectors: industry, services, agriculture, financial and commerce. It is meant to consolidate the position of the business sector and act on their behalf in areas that include economic policy and peace. See www.cgn.org.co/. This Council brings together some of the largest business associations in the country, including the financial, industry, agricultural and public utilities sectors.

28 The leader of the party, former president Alvaro Uribe Vélez, owns land in rural Colombia, and is also a well-known businessman.

29 For example, a more precise definition of indirect and direct crimes related to the conflict, or the fact that the JEP needed to triangulate the confession of former FARC combatants with other sources.

The business associations that supported the "Yes" campaign later engaged in the next stage of negotiation: the translation of the agreement into domestic law and policy. Congress was mandated to issue a series of laws to implement the agreement, among them a Legislative Act that regulated the JEP and the CEV. In the next section, I will present some evidence to show the role that certain business associations had in the design of the JEP during congressional debates.

In the Congress: Legislative Act 01 of 2017

The National Guild Council and the Business Association for Peace made sure to have their say in Congress. They used their political alliances through the representatives of the *Centro Democrático* and *Cambio Radical* political parties. Two of the political leaders who were more outspoken against the JEP putting economic actors on trial were former president Álvaro Uribe Velez and then presidential candidate, Germán Vargas Lleras (Revista Dinero 2017).

The large business associations were constantly asking for technical advice from lawyers in preparation to participate in the debate in Congress.[30] A business leader said at the time that they had "successfully" spoken to the minister of interior. In his view, they had made observations to ensure that the draft of the Legislative Act did not allow for a "witch-hunt," and their observations had been taken on board by the government. He also stated that they had reached out to the Prosecutor General with their concerns about the JEP (Amat 2017). Their strategy to avoid a "witch-hunt" was to limit the extent of the universe of cases that could be taken to the JEP. They fell back on the rotten apples discourse that has been consistent throughout: it was certain types of businesspeople who engaged in complicity, not all types. They wanted to make sure that the distinction was made and that they had a say in the way that distinction was incorporated into the law. They insisted that the law should only allow the JEP to put third parties on trial when they had had an active and determinant role in the violence. And this terminology was left in the Legislative Act that was approved.

On April 4, 2017, Congress issued Legislative Act No. 01 of 2017[31] to include in the Constitution a set of transitory norms to end the armed conflict and build a stable and lasting peace. Chapter III of the Legislative

30 Interview with Julián Correa, former Proantioquia official, March 2020.

31 See www.unidadvictimas.gov.co/es/acto-legislativo-01-4-de-abril-de-2017/38922 (accessed May 7, 2021).

Act referred to the JEP, particularly in Article 16, establishing that the transitional justice tribunal could call on third parties to the conflict (including businesspeople) to account for their role in past atrocities if they had an *active* and *determinant* role in the crimes. The participation was qualified, and therefore a higher threshold was set for cases to reach the JEP. This was considered a victory by the larger business associations that had not opposed all accountability efforts, but just indiscriminate accountability efforts.[32]

In the Constitutional Court

The Legislative Act, as part of its natural course through the legal system, was sent to the Constitutional Court so that it could determine whether the procedural rules to issue Legislative Acts were met and whether the Legislative Act was trying to substitute the constitution, i.e. change some of the founding principles of the 1991 Constitution. The second paragraph of Article 16 established that third parties could be forced to present themselves before the JEP if they had an *active* or *determinant* role in the perpetration of genocide, crimes against humanity, war crimes, torture, forced displacement, forced disappearances and other crimes listed (Cote 2020: 120–21).

Civil society organizations that are part of the human rights movement for accountability presented *amicus curiae* to the court asking it to declare the JEP's competence to put economic actors on trial constitutional. Some even went as far as to ask the court to give a broader interpretation to the terms "active" and "determinant."[33] Nonetheless, in November 2017, the Constitutional Court declared the second paragraph of Article 16 unconstitutional, because it violated the natural judge principle. The natural judge principle states that a person can only be tried by a court that predates the crime. This means that an ad hoc tribunal can only try a person if they expressly renounce their natural judge. In the view of the court, third parties to the conflict (including businesspeople) did not participate in the peace negotiations, and therefore did not renounce their right to be tried by the ordinary jurisdiction. In view of the court, the state renounced this right only on behalf of the members of the Colombian armed forces, and the FARC only on behalf of the members of that guerrilla group. In that sense, everyone else who wants their case to be

[32] Interview with Sebastián González, former consultant to ANDI, March 2019.

[33] See, e.g., the interventions of Dejusticia, the University of Oxford and the University of Essex.

brought before the JEP (to receive the benefits), needs to voluntarily come before this jurisdiction. With this decision, as the system stands today, businesspeople cannot be forced to come before the JEP, they can only volunteer to be included.

The strategies of certain business associations in Havana and in Congress were covered by the media and are included in the memoirs of peace negotiators, but when it comes to the Constitutional Court, it seemed as though the opposition had come to a complete stop. The decision of the court was apparently reached without the participation of economic actors. A magistrate of the court said that they relied on the law, the public hearing that they held[34] and the amicus curiae that they received. He said that they were never approached by businesses formally or informally.[35] In that sense, he said, the court made a technical decision, not trying to favor the interests of a particular group.[36]

Despite what the magistrate said, and what the list of organizations participating in the debate showed, a group of business associations (*ANDI*, *Proantioquia* and the *Grupo Empresarial Antioqueño*) did participate in the public hearings, but they did so through a think tank called *Instituto de Ciencia Política Hernán Echavarría Olózaga*.[37] While their presentation to the court did not refer specifically to economic actors, it did emphasize an issue that had concerned economic actors in the past: the need for a more detailed and restrictive delimitation of the conduct that would be considered related to the conflict (Correa 2017).

Speaking to people who advised these large business associations throughout the peace negotiations and the implementation of the agreement, I was able to understand why the opposition slowed down when the issue reached the Constitutional Court.[38] In their view, the large business associations that had remained unengaged in the debate with the Justice and Peace law were content with the results that came out of the Congress. They were not advocating for the complete removal of economic actors from the competence of the JEP, as they recognized that

[34] See recording of hearings in: www.youtube.com/watch?v=g1JTrNTmAiE; www.youtube.com/watch?v=O-OKm4xrg4s (accessed May 7, 2021).

[35] See Appendix 1 of Ruling C-674/17 of the Constitutional Court, www.corteconstitucional.gov.co/relatoria/2017/C-674-17.htm (accessed May 7, 2021).

[36] Interview with Miguel Polo, Assistant Magistrate of the Constitutional Court, February 2020.

[37] Interview with Julián Correa, former official of Proantioquia, March 2020.

[38] Interview with Sebastián González, former consultant to ANDI, February 2020; Interview with Julián Correa, former official of Proantioquia, March 2020.

there were cases of complicity that merited being investigated, but rather a stricter delimitation of the types of conduct that the JEP could prosecute. That purpose was served when Congress introduced the words "active and determinant role." In that sense, they did not find it necessary to have a visible role in the debate in the Constitutional Court.

When the court decided to leave third parties outside of the compulsory jurisdiction of the JEP, some of these business associations were surprised and concerned with the result. Politically, they thought that they would be accused of interfering with the court to secure impunity. And legally, the decision of the court made two moves that they thought were unfavorable to third parties. First, it removed a set of detailed constraints on the type of acts that the JEP could judge, and second, it ordered the National Prosecutors' Office to prioritize all the cases against third parties who did not voluntarily ask to be prosecuted by the JEP.

While I was unable to trace how the organized opposition had any bearing on the results in the Constitutional Court, its decision had a significant impact on accountability for corporate complicity in Colombia. On June 6, 2017, the JEP opened a three-month period for all those third parties to the conflict who were involved in an ongoing criminal investigation to voluntarily bring their cases to the JEP (Special Jurisdiction for Peace 2019). By the end of this three-month period, the JEP recorded around 657 petitions from third parties to the conflict, out of which 540 involve civilians that are not state officials (different from the armed forces) and include businesspeople (Semana.com 2019). All of them had ongoing investigations in the ordinary jurisdiction and one of the possible reasons for coming to the JEP is that in a cost–benefit analysis they feared higher sentences in the ordinary jurisdiction. This means that the JEP is not receiving those who have historically and systematically escaped prosecution because of their veto power, but rather mostly those who were already facing prosecution.

The Truth Commission: Contesting Memory

Regarding the Truth Commission, during the negotiations of the Peace Agreement, members of the business community devoted most of their efforts to the competence of the JEP. All they said about the Truth Commission, at the time, was that they were not concerned with it because historians would write the history of Colombia. However, afterwards, having realized the importance of the struggle over memory, they made efforts to counter the CEV's role once it started to operate. They largely abstained from participating in the national dialogue that the CEV attempted to build in order to secure reconciliation and peaceful coexistence in the territories. On the one hand, they decided to conduct their own memory exercises where they emphasize their role as victims, neglecting to explore other aspects of their involvement in the conflict, or to engage with victims of the conflict in the regions where they operate. On the other hand, their limited engagement with the CEV focused on procedural discussions that for over a year diverted its mandate to clarify the past (*esclarecimiento*). To date, only one businessperson recognized their responsibility in paramilitary violence.

Chief among these memory efforts – that exist at company and industry level – was a report of the largest business association in the country written with the support of academics of a university in Medellín. In a meeting with the president of this business association in 2017, I heard about the initial intention of publishing this report to counter – in a way – the work of the CEV in reconstructing the memory of the conflict. Here, again, the witch-hunt framework emerged: The members of this business association believed that the Truth Commission did not provide any guarantees to economic actors and it could end up heading a "witch-hunt" that would not provide all the nuances and detail needed to understand the phenomenon.

In light of the efforts from civil society organizations and from business associations to investigate the role of economic actors in the conflict (as victims and perpetrators), in 2018 the CEV decided to create an advisory group (*Mesa Técnica*) that could provide reports and publications on the role of businesses in past atrocities, but could also help the commission devise a methodology to engage with businesses. This group included representatives from civil society organizations, a group of academics from various universities around the country (including myself) and, more importantly, representatives from business associations. In the context of this advisory group, the Truth Commission asked representatives of business associations and academics what conditions were needed for them to participate in the truth-telling and memory-building exercises that the CEV is leading.

So far, in my view, there are at least two ways in which the veto power of businesses to trump accountability efforts has been made visible in the work of the CEV. First, after all the participants in the advisory group presented the methodology and findings of their own work on businesses' involvement in the conflict, the business associations failed to share their own work. They informed us that while the report they had produced (based on hundreds of interviews to members of the business communities) was completed, the members of the board of directors had decided not to make the report public. In this way, after months of waiting to gain access to the report, the Truth Commission – as well as all other actors – was denied access to very rich qualitative work by rigorous academics and involving some of the largest companies in the country.

Secondly, the CEV spent one year (out of its three-year mandate) devising a protocol of engagement with the business actors. This instrument was negotiated every step of the way with representatives of the business community. The *Fundación Ideas para la Paz*, an NGO created by businesses, held several workshops and interviews with businesspeople in the country, asking them what they would need in terms of procedural guarantees. The protocol, which was yet to be made public at the time of writing, included (particularly) stringent rules on anonymity and control of the information at all stages of the process. So far, three years after the Truth Commission began knocking on the doors of different businesses and business associations, very few businesses agreed to participate in the truth-telling exercises. In this way it appears that accountability efforts through truth are at a standstill because the CEV, just like the JEP, requires businesses to share voluntarily their side of the story. At the time of writing, the CEV is working on the final report with the limited participation that they managed to obtain.

CONCLUSION: EXPLAINING ORGANIZED OPPOSITION IN COLOMBIA

In Colombia, starting in the early 2000s, NGOs achieved advances on the path of corporate accountability. The superstructure created through domestic and regional courts to protect the rights of victims of the armed conflict was a stepping-stone to push for these outcomes. However, these efforts lacked mainstream societal support and set off organized opposition from a powerful group in society: large business associations. As a result, the changes that were achieved in terms of a broader understanding of accountability have seen some significant setbacks.

In the 1970s and 1980s, a human rights movement for accountability emerged. It emerged at a time when peace agreements had used amnesties in an attempt to end conflict, and victims' rights to truth, justice, reparations and guarantees of nonrepetition had been put aside. The movement managed to change the paradigm of peacebuilding, producing changes in the design of the state (e.g. the Constitutional Court and the Human Rights Unit in the Prosecutors' Office) and the content of the law (e.g. the forced displacement law). And with time, the TJ mechanisms that came out of peace negotiations started to include trials and truth telling. In 2003, when the AUC paramilitary group demobilized with the Justice and Peace process, the rule was accountability and not amnesty. Both the domestic and the international context made sure amnesties were not the only means of ending a conflict. The ordinary criminal courts started to convict businesspeople in the early 2000s for their role in the violence, and the Justice and Peace process and the lands restitution processes also opened up spaces of business accountability through truth.

Nonetheless, in 2012, when the government started negotiating with the FARC guerrilla group, the path of accountability for corporate complicity took a turn. While some may have expected a continued and intensified path to wider access for victims to the courts and truth and memory institutions, the path moved to more restricted access to justice through transitional justice mechanisms. In this chapter I showed that what explains the change in the path is the emergence of an organized opposition from the business community, which, using tactics and strategies similar to the accountability movement, sought to reduce access. This organized opposition started to emerge in 2012, when the accountability movement changed venues and started lobbying for TJ mechanisms that came out of the peace agreement with the FARC to include a broad understanding of accountability. A combination of factors explains the intervention of the countermovement in the design and work of the JEP and the CEV: increased success in the courts (even if relative in numbers) and at the policy level for the human rights movement, tied to the interests of a wider community being affected, and access to political allies.

Victims now face great difficulties in bringing economic actors to account, with only one path to accountability: the ordinary jurisdiction, which has been constantly criticized for its inefficacy in the investigation of human rights violations. The difficulties for those acting to push for accountability is even more grim if we consider that there is increased violence in the territories (Johnson 2019) and violence against social leaders and human rights defenders, with over 257 social leaders and human rights defenders killed between November 2016 and July 2018 (Comisión Colombiana de Juristas et al. 2018). As violence surges, forced displacement of communities continues to occur, with over 8,000 people displaced during the first semester of 2019 (El Espectador 2019). This context of violence, combined with the exercise of veto power by economic actors at the national and local level, make mobilization by civil society increasingly more costly.

References

Amat, Y. (2017). Dos Caras de la Posición Empresarial Frente a la Reglamentación de JEP. *El Tiempo*, October 28,.

Amnesty International (2014). *Un Título de Propiedad No Basta: Por una Restitución Sostenible de Tierras en Colombia.* London: Amnesty International.

BBC Mundo (2016). Colombia: Ganó el "No" en el Plebiscito por los Acuerdos de Paz con las FARC. *BBC Mundo*, October 2.

Bernal-Bermúdez, L. (2017). The Power of Business and the Power of People: Understanding Remedy and Corporate Accountability for Human Rights Violations. Colombia 1970–2014. DPhil thesis. University of Oxford.

Bernal-Bermudez, L. & Marín López, D. (2018). Los Empresarios en la Guerra: Verdad Judicial Sobre la Complicidad Empresarial en Colombia. In C. Sánchez et al., eds., *Cuentas Claras: El papel de la Comisión de la Verdad en la develación de la responsabilidad de empresas en el conflicto armado colombiano.* Bogotá: Dejusticia, pp. 39–68.

Bernal-Bermúdez, L. & Sanchez, N. C. (2022). Innovation from the Bench: Judges, Prosecutors and Analysts Advancing Truth and Accountability for Conflict-Related Corporate Complicity in Colombia. In L. Payne, L. Bernal-Bermúdez, & G. Pereira, eds., *Economic Actors and the Limits of Transitional Justice: Truth and Justice for Business Complicity in Human Rights Violations.* Oxford: Oxford University Press.

Caracol Radio (2015). Los Empresarios van a La Habana ¿Por Qué Es Importante? *Caracol Radio*, November 11.

Casey, N. (2016). El Gobierno de Colombia y las FARC Firman Un Nuevo Acuerdo Que No Será Sometido a Votación. *New York Times*, November 24.

Castillejo-Cuéllar, A. (2014). Historical Injuries, Temporality and the Law: Articulations of a Violent Past in Two Transitional Scenarios. *Law Critique* 25, 47–66.

Centro Nacional de Memoria Histórica.(2013). *Basta Ya: Colombia Memorias de Guerra y Dignidad.* Bogotá: Centro Nacional de Memoria Histórica.

(2015). *El Derecho a la Justicia Como Garantía de No Repetición* Vol. I. Bogotá: Centro Nacional de Memoria Histórica.

Chaparro González, N. & Martínez Osorio, M. (2017). *Negotiating from the Margins: The Political Participation of Women in the Peace Processes of Colombia (1982–2016).* Bogotá: Dejusticia.

Comisión Colombiana de Juristas (2007). *Anotaciones Sobre la Ley de "Justicia y Paz" una Mirada Desde los Derechos de las Víctimas.* Bogotá: Opciones Gráficas Editores Ltda.

Comisión Colombiana de Juristas, IEPRI, Verdadabierta.com, Cinep, & Movimiento Ríos Vivos (2018). *¿Cuáles Son los Patrones? Asesinatos de Líderes Sociales en el Post Acuerdo.* Bogotá: Comisión Colombiana de Juristas, IEPRI, Verdadabierta.com, Cinep, & Movimiento Ríos Vivos.

CONtexto Ganadero (2016). Ganaderos Explican Porqué Sus Regiones Dijeron No en el Plebiscito. *CONtexto Ganadero*, October 5.

Contraloría General de la República (2017). *Análisis Sobre los Resultados y Costos de la Ley de Justicia y Paz*. Bogotá: Contraloría General de la República.

Correa, J. (2017). *Contribución Para la Intervención del ICP Hernán Echavarría Olózaga en la Audiencia Pública Convocada por la Corte Constitucional*. Bogotá: ICP Hernán Echavarría Olózaga.

Cote, G. (2019). Complicidad, Responsabilidad Penal de Directivos Empresariales y Violaciones de Derechos Humanos Cometidas por Grupos Armados Ilegales: Lecciones del Derecho Penal Internacional Para Colombia. *Vniversitas* 68(138), pp. 1–39.

ed. (2020). *Régimen Jurídico de la Jurisdicción Especial Para la Paz – Concordancias Normativas y Extractos Jurisprudenciales*. Bogotá: Procuraduría General de la Nación.

El Espectador (2019). Durante el Primer Semestre de 2019 Se Desplazaron 8223 Personas en el País. *El Espectador*, June 12.

El Tiempo (2015). Justicia Investiga a 12 Mil Empresarios Que Financiaron a Paramilitares. *El Tiempo*, May 9.

Felstiner, W., Abel, R. L. & Sarat, A. (1980). The Emergence and Transformation of Disputes: Naming, Blaming. Claiming. *Law & Society Review* 15(3/4), pp. 631–54.

Gale, R. P. (1986). Social Movements and the State: The Environmental Movement, Countermovement, and Government Agencies. *Sociological Perspectives* 29(2), pp. 202–40.

Ignatieff, M. (1997). *The Warrior's Honor: Ethnic War and the Modern Conscience*. New York: Henry Holt and Company.

Jaramillo Marín, J. (2014). *Pasados y Presentes de la Violencia en Colombia Estudio Sobre las Comisiones de Investigación (1958–2011)*. Bogotá: Editorial Pontificia Universidad Javeriana.

Johnson, K. (2019). Where the Peace Has No Name: (Post)Conflict along Colombia's Pacific Coast. Paper presented at the 2019 Annual Congress of the Latin American Studies Association in Boston, May 25.

Keck, M. E. & Sikkink, K. (1998). *Activists beyond Borders: Advocacy Networks in International Politics*. New York: Cornell University Press.

De la Calle, H. (2019). *Revelaciones al Final de la Guerra*. Bogotá: Debate.

Landau, D. & López Murcia, J. D. (2009). Political Institutions and Judicial Role: An Approach in Context, the Case of the Colombian Constitutional Court. *Vniversitas* 119(1), pp. 55–90.

León, J. (2015). El Abismo y el Puente Entre las Farc y los Empresarios. *La Silla Vacía*, November 15.

(2016). Las Diez Preguntas de los Empresarios Sobre la Habana. *La Silla Vacía*, May 16.

Lewin, J. E. & Vélez, J. (2016). Estos Son los Activos del No y del Sí en la Recta Final del Plebiscito. *La Silla Vacía*, September 28.

Meyer, D. & Staggenborg, S. (1996). Movements, Countermovements, and the Structure of Political Opportunity. *American Journal of Sociology* 101(6). pp. 1628–60.

Payne, L. A. (2008). Performances of Power: Paramilitary Confessions in Colombia. Paper presented at Coming to Terms with the Past, Yale University (Conference), October 13.

Payne, L. A., Pereira, G. & Bernal-Bermúdez, L. (2020). *Transitional Justice and Corporate Accountability from Below: Deploying Archimedes' Lever*. Cambridge: Cambridge University Press.

Pizarro Leongómez, E. (2017). *Cambiar El Futuro: Historia de Los Procesos de Paz en Colombia 1981–2016*. Bogotá: Debate.

Revista Dinero (2016). Aquí El Listado de Donantes a Campaña del No... y No Está Ardila Lulle. *Revista Dinero*, October 6.

(2017). Con Su Fallo, la Corte Blindó a los Empresarios de la JEP. *Revista Dinero*, November 15.

Rodriguez, I. (2017). Los Cuestionamientos a Bananeros Detrás del "No." *Verdadabierta.com*, https://verdadabierta.com/los-cuestionamientos-a-los-bananeros-detras-del-no/

Romero, Ma. (2003). *Paramilitares y Autodefensas 1982–2003*. Bogotá: IEPRI & Editorial Planeta Colombiana, S. A.

Sánchez, N. C. & Acosta, A. A. (2021) *¿Barreras Insuperables? Un Análisis de la Etapa Administrative del Proceso de Restitución de Tierras*. Bogotá: Editorial Dejusticia.

Sánchez-Mejía, A. L. (2017). *Victims' Rights in Flux: Criminal Justice Reform in Colombia*. Cham, Switzerland: Springer.

Semana.com (2016). Los 68 Cambios del Acuerdo en Materia de Justicia. *Semana.com*, November 14.

(2019). Cierre de Plazo: 657 Civiles Piden Ser Acogidos por la JEP. *Semana.com*, September 9.

Special Jurisdiction for Peace (2019). Comunicado 087 – Empiezan a Correr Plazos Para Sometimiento Voluntario a la JEP de Terceros Civiles y Agentes del Estado No Miembros de la Fuerza Pública, Bogota, June 1, www.jep.gov.co/Sala-de-Prensa/Paginas/Empiezan-a-correr-plazos-para-sometimiento-voluntario-a-la-JEP-de-terceros-civiles-y-agentes-del-Estado.aspx

Tate, W. (2007). *Counting the Dead: The Culture and Politics of Human Rights Activism in Colombia*. Berkeley: University of California Press.

Vidal López, R. (1997). El Régimen Jurídico de Protección a los Desplazados por la Violencia. *Universitas Jurídica* 47, pp. 98–120.

7

Courting Judicial Legitimacy

An Experimental Study of the Colombian Constitutional Court

Sofía Forero-Alba and Juan Carlos Rodríguez-Raga

INTRODUCTION

Since World War II, the world has seen an unprecedented expansion of the judiciary's power (Hirschl, 2004).[1] Many of those countries adopted new constitutions that include a bill of rights and different forms of judicial review. The emergence of new mechanisms for protecting rights has enabled the judiciary to make decisions on substantial issues regarding the social, political, economic, and cultural realms. High courts with constitutional review powers not only have taken charge of the protection of fundamental rights, they have also become involved in the design of public policy, as well as in making the other branches of government accountable for those policies. This transformation of the political-legal systems in many countries, known as judicialization of politics, has also taken place in Latin America (Sieder, Schjolden and Angel, 2005) and Colombia (Cepeda, 2005).

As the introduction to this volume pointed out, judicial legitimacy is acutely in question when support for a more central role of courts in the political arena lacks a dependable social base. This is particularly true in policy areas where courts attempt legal developments that run against deeply ingrained conservative values in society. In fact, even in those rare cases where their institutional foundations lie on solid ground, courts often face a dilemma that emerges as a result of their assigned task of

[1] We want to thank the editors for their valuable and helpful comments. We also appreciate the insights of those who participated in the seminar *Política y derecho en América Latina: Nuevas preguntas, viejos desafíos*, held in Bogotá (October 2019), where we presented a preliminary version of this chapter.

protecting minority rights, especially when the exercise of those rights goes against the opinion of the majority of the population. When such rights enjoy majoritarian support in a country, it is usually the legislature that plays the central role in their protection. Constitutional review by courts comes into play precisely when the majority (of the population, of the lawmaking body) is unwilling to grant those rights. Courts are asked to step in and make unpopular decisions in order to provide them with constitutional protection. To be able to make those decisions palatable while preserving its status in the political arena, a court requires a reservoir of citizen support while, at the same time, those rulings may eventually undermine such legitimacy.

In this chapter we attempt an exploration of the extent to which a court can cultivate its public legitimacy through the manner in which it frames the arguments that sustain controversial and potentially unpopular decisions. In order to achieve that goal, we conducted a vignette survey experiment on college students in Colombia aimed at determining what types of arguments are more likely to provide the Constitutional Court with *diffuse support* – a set of favorable attitudes that help citizens stomach judicial decisions they dislike – or to what extent the court's legitimacy depends on the public's evaluation of its overall performance (*specific support*). The vignettes presented to the respondents include a fictional news piece reporting on a decision by the court that completely decriminalizes abortion. The experiment randomly divides the sample into four treatment groups. Each one is assigned a vignette depicting the court arguing its ruling based one of four types of arguments: legalistic, scientific, public opinion-based, and religious. We hypothesize that decisions supported on legalistic and scientific reasonings better convey the kind of principled argumentation that may summon the sense of procedural fairness that furthers public legitimacy (Ruibal, 2010).

Analyzing the Colombian Constitutional Court (CCC) offers a suitable case for understanding the way in which people award legitimacy to courts. Our findings suggest that the way in which a court frames its decisions mediates the relationship between its specific and diffuse support. Approval of a court's past performance (specific support) translates better into loyalty (diffuse support) when the court issues rulings grounded on arguments that convey an aura of neutrality. This is particularly true when judicial decisions make use of scientific reasonings, a proposition which, to our knowledge, had not been tested using an experimental design of the sort we describe later.

It is also substantively relevant to assess the key role that the CCC has played in the Colombian polity three decades into its lifetime, asking how it can contribute to maintaining the public's goodwill. The results of our inquiry indicate that, aside from summoning the advice of experts both in public hearings and as *amicus curiae* submissions, adopting the language of those experts in its decisions might help boost the CCC's legitimacy. In controversial and divisive issues such as women's right to abortion, courting citizens' loyalty might prove crucial to preserving its institutional status as guardian of the constitution and champion of fundamental rights.

THEORETICAL PERSPECTIVES ON COURTS' LEGITIMACY

Constitutional judges play a role that goes beyond that of mere interpreters of the law and the constitution. By reviewing acts issued by the executive and the legislature, judges become key players in the political arena (Hirschl, 2008; Tate and Vallinder, 1995; Ginsburg, 2008).

It is in the very ability to review acts issued by popularly elected officials that the legitimacy of the judiciary becomes problematic. It entails a tension between the democratic majoritarian principle and the rights of minorities: a counter-majoritarian dilemma that exposes the legitimacy of the judiciary (Linares, 2008; Gargarella, 1996), and which shows the relevance of studying the public's perception of courts deciding on controversial issues. "A Court whose public support rests on popular approval of its decisions, rather than a long-standing deep pool of public esteem, should be less likely to issue decisions that protect the rights of minorities, to exercise the power of judicial review ..., and to issue decisions that counter the wishes of a majority" (Gibson and Nelson, 2014: 207).

To better understand legitimacy, scholars have identified two types of public support, based on the distinctions made by Easton (1965). *Diffuse support* can be defined as a "reservoir of favorable attitudes or good will that helps members to accept or tolerate outputs to which they are opposed or the effects of which they see as damaging their wants" (Easton, 1965: 273). *Specific support* refers to the "satisfaction with the performance of a political institution" (Gibson and Caldeira, 1992: 1126). The conceptual distinction between diffuse and specific support in analyzing and understanding judicial legitimacy has been central in studies of the US Supreme Court.

Recent research on that court's legitimacy has found evidence that connects specific and diffuse support. Bartels and Johnston (2013) suggest that individual dissatisfaction with the court's performance translates directly and immediately into a decrease in diffuse support. This finding implies that if the latter cannot shield the court when it makes unpopular decisions, then the court's independence could be questionable. However, most theoretical and empirical works suggest that diffuse support is somewhat immune to short-term changes in specific support; the individual-level change in the court's specific support is momentary (Caldeira and Gibson, 1992; Gibson and Caldeira, 1992; Gibson and Nelson, 2014). These authors find that the US Supreme Court at least "has a sufficiently deep reservoir of goodwill that allows it to rise above the contemporary divisions in the American polity" (Gibson and Nelson, 2015: 173).[2]

Almost all research that seeks to understand a high court's legitimacy, however, focuses on the US Supreme Court or, to a lesser extent, on lower level American courts. An exception to this pattern is the work by Gibson, Caldeira, and Baird (1998). In their study of high courts in eighteen countries, mainly in Europe, they find that "a tendency of people to credit [a court] for pleasing decisions but not to penalize it for displeasing ones" is not unique to the US case (Gibson, Caldeira, and Baird, 1998: 343).

Studies on the legitimacy of high courts in Latin America are even scarcer, and only recently have scholars begun to examine the issue of legitimacy in Colombian high courts. In focusing on the CCC's diffuse support, Botero (2020) finds that citizens' support for democracy is associated with higher levels of trust in the court, while perceptions of corruption promote public distrust. We contend, however, that the two dimensions of legitimacy – diffuse and specific support – are not well understood in isolation; they are constantly interacting. However, this interaction "is a key unresolved area in the literature, with enormous substantive importance for our understanding of both the Court's role in the political system and its decision making" (Gibson and Nelson, 2014: 208).

Crucially, Farganis (2012) suggests that in order to understand the legitimacy of a court it is important to pay attention to the type of arguments that judges use to justify their rulings. Depending on the framing of a decision's reasoning, the decision can gather more or less

[2] However, some authors suggest that the increasing partisan polarization in American society, Congress, and the court itself may be eroding the latter's legitimacy (Hasen, 2013).

public support and, eventually, such framing may increase or lessen citizens' diffuse support. Some authors have also found that reasoning that makes apparent the complexity and uncertainty of a decision may increase legitimacy (Simon and Scurich, 2011), although this may only be true when citizens disagree with the court's outcome (Scurich, 2018).

Our aim is to build on these ideas and evaluate to what extent the types of arguments used by the Colombian Constitutional Court to frame its rulings impact its legitimacy. In the next section, we introduce the tribunal itself, describe the role it has played in Colombian politics since its creation, discuss some of the mechanisms through which this relatively young court has built its legitimacy, and introduce an analytical framework on how different types of case law may distinctively affect the public's response.

THE COLOMBIAN CONSTITUTIONAL COURT

The CCC, created in 1991, is the highest tribunal in the nation's constitutional jurisdiction. On the one hand, it acts as the court of last resort for *tutela* cases that citizens file when they see their fundamental rights violated. These concrete review cases usually start at a lower court and may eventually advance all the way up to the Constitutional Court for a final decision. On the other hand, the CCC also performs abstract review of legislative acts either automatically or upon a legal action submitted directly to the court by any citizen arguing that such an act is contrary to specific constitutional provisions.

In three decades, the court has played a central role not only in adjudicating constitutional issues but also in shaping public policy in different areas. The court has issued highly controversial decisions that have put it at odds not only with the executive and significant portions of Congress, but also with majoritarian attitudes and opinions of Colombians. In most instances, though, the court has prevailed and has been relatively successful in establishing a new policy status quo.

Figure 7.1 shows that for most of the past two decades the CCC has enjoyed the support of a majority of the population (Invamer, 2021: 96). Moreover, contrasting the timing of some arguably unpopular decisions – marked as milestones in the figure's timeline and described later – and the trends of the court's approval rates over time in Figure 7.1 shows no evidence that the former have had a significant negative impact on the latter.

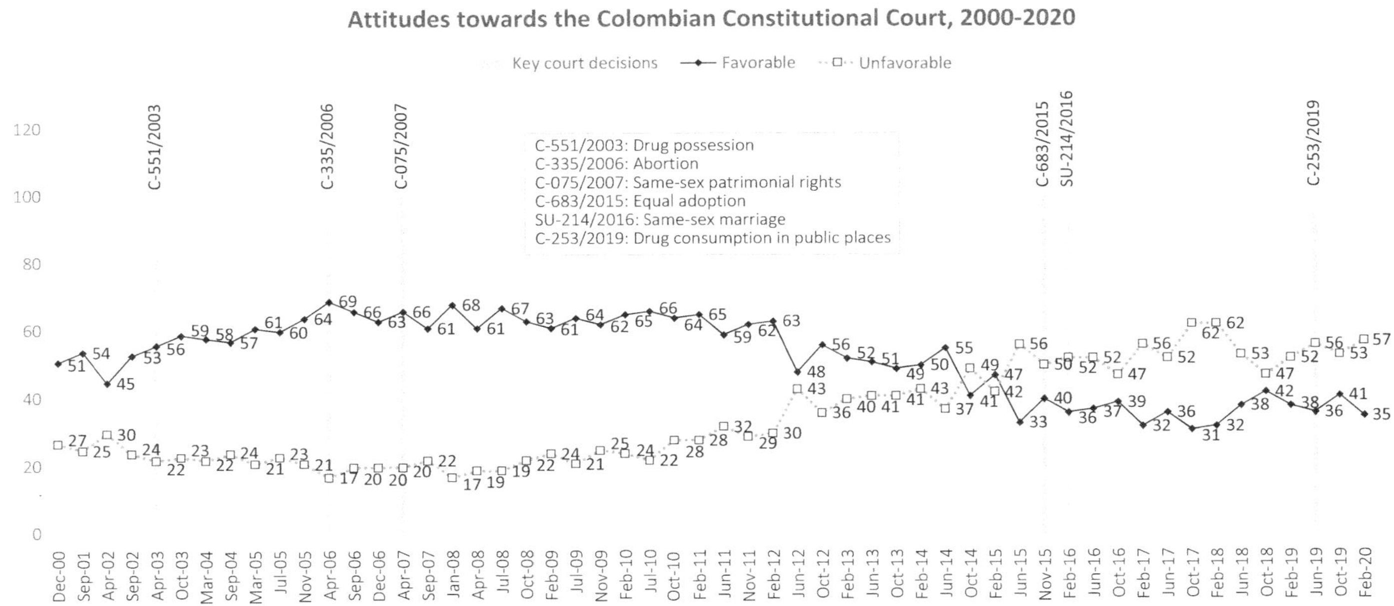

FIGURE 7.1. Attitudes towards the Colombian Constitutional Court (2000–2020)
Source: The authors, based on Invamer (2021: 96).

However, since around 2014, the court seems to have lost the favor of the majority. Botero (2020) finds that, at the individual level, perceptions of corruption negatively impact the public's trust in the Constitutional Court. Indeed, studies of public opinion have found that corruption has become one of the most salient issues for citizens. While in 2010 only 4 percent of the population mentioned corruption as the most serious problem in the nation, this increased four-fold to reach 16.2 percent eight years later (Rivera, Plata, and Rodríguez-Raga, 2019: 16).

Although corruption has in fact tainted the Constitutional Court,[3] the problem appears to be systemic: there is a rather generalized perception that the whole polity has been pervaded by this problem. In fact, in 2018 three out of four Colombians responded that "more than half" or "all" politicians are corrupt (Rivera, Plata, and Rodríguez-Raga, 2019: 25).

This perception of generalized corruption has been added to (and certainly has fueled) a general decline in the public's support for political institutions in Colombia in the midst of the peace talks between the Santos administration and the FARC guerrillas. Data from the AmericasBarometer in Colombia show that the decline started between 2012 and 2013, just when those negotiations were made public and a sharp divide between President Santos and former president Uribe emerged, creating a highly polarized atmosphere around the peace agreement (Rivera, Plata, and Rodríguez-Raga, 2019). This in turn has impacted Colombians' support for democratic values and has hit the CCC's legitimacy (Botero, 2020).

Decline in trust notwithstanding, some features in the CCC's institutional framework and its behavior may have contributed to preserving the public's support for the court over the past decades. On the one hand, its creation occurred within the drafting and enactment of the 1991 Constitution, which enjoyed in its origins significant levels of hopefulness and legitimacy. The newly created court inherited that initial aura. Moreover, the constitutional review instruments granted to the court were designed, in the words of Manuel J. Cepeda, former CCC justice, to build "a bridge between reality and the Constitution" (Bustamante, 2011; Merhof, 2015), that is, to bring the institutions of constitutional rights protection much closer to the common citizen's needs. To the *actio popularis* by which any citizen could prompt an abstract review case

[3] Justice José I. Pretelt was charged with requesting bribes to influence the court's decisions and was removed from office in 2015 (Botero, 2020).

against any piece of legislation, which existed in Colombia since 1910, the constitution added the *tutela* action which can be filed, with few requirements, by any citizens seeking enforcement of their rights when they feel that those rights are being violated by the action or omission of a public official or a private actor. This triggers a concrete review case that starts at a lower court and can eventually be heard by the CCC. These instruments have arguably made of Colombia's "the most open system of judicial review" (Cepeda, 2005: 74) and have contributed to the legitimacy of the Constitutional Court from the outset (González, 2017).

On the other hand, the CCC has also implemented some strategies to further close the gap between the seemingly arcane world of legal and constitutional norms and the citizenry, contributing to boosting its openness. First, in salient and/or controversial issues, the court has taken to issuing press releases and to convening press conferences to announce and explain, in common language, its decisions. Although we know of no empirical studies on the use of such instances and their impact on the CCC's image,[4] it seems clear that its media exposure brings its rulings closer to the public.

Moreover, the court is widely open to third-party interventions through *amicus curiae* briefs. Any citizen, organization, or institution, even if it does not have a clear legal interest in the case, can file such a brief, which is considered by the justice charged with drafting the opinion. The court often also invites scholars, NGOs, trade guilds, or labor unions to submit an *amicus*. Arteaga-Iriarte and Rodríguez-Raga (2010) find that this openness has made of the CCC one of the courts that receives the highest number of *amicus* briefs in its abstract review cases. This mechanism, together with the practice of summoning public hearings in salient cases in which some of those who have filed *amicus* briefs and others are invited to present their arguments, conveys the idea that the court hears all parties and views related to the case, adding an image of neutrality to its openness.

Case Law and Legitimacy

Thus far we have detailed different mechanisms that have played a role in shaping the CCC's support over the past decades. That discussion is missing one potential source of legitimacy that is the focus of our attention: its case law and specifically how the court frames its arguments.

[4] See Staton (2006) for a theoretical argument linking the promotion of decisions to the media and judicial choice for the case of the Mexican Supreme Court.

The different cases and rulings that the CCC hears and makes may have different impacts on its public image. Each type of case can be analytically thought of as entailing a different incentive structure in terms of the costs and benefits they involve for the court's image. These costs and benefits are in turn a function of both the salience of the issues under review and the extent to which citizens approve of those decisions.

First, we identify those cases in which the CCC must arbiter horizontal conflicts. The CCC has played a central role in checking the power of the other branches. Not only does it routinely review acts passed by the legislature but it has also been involved in hotly contested legal and political battles that have impacted the very principle of separation of powers.[5] In fulfilling this role, the CCC has displayed an outstanding level of autonomy that is rare in Latin America and contrasts with the constitutional review role exerted by the old Supreme Court prior to 1991. More importantly, this autonomy, together with its accessibility, have allowed it to summon a certain level of prestige among legal scholars and practitioners in the nation and abroad (Merhof, 2015; Gardbaum, 2018; Uprimny, 2004),[6] and have contributed to the court building for itself a certain level of public legitimacy despite its short life (González, 2017).

Such instances involving a power dispute between branches, though central to the Colombian political system, are rather abstract and removed from the everyday life of the average Colombian, and therefore their impact on the public's support for the court may not be as clear and direct.

In contrast, a second type of cases, which involve the protection of citizen rights,[7] might carry either gains or losses to the court's legitimacy, depending on whether those rights are favored by a majority of the population or not. In fact, these cases – which may involve both abstract review of legislation and concrete review of *tutelas* – can be analytically classified in two groups depending on the extent to which they promote or hinder the court's legitimacy.

[5] Rodríguez-Raga and Virgüez-Ruiz (2019) argue that the court has been prudent but determined in arrogating itself with competencies that were not even stated in the constitution.

[6] Rodríguez-Raga (2011), however, has suggested that, such prestige notwithstanding, the court's behavior can be better described as *strategically prudent* in that its decisions tend to result from the anticipation of retribution by the other branches of government, especially the executive.

[7] Given the generous bill of rights included in the constitution and the CCC's extensive jurisprudence, the list of enforceable fundamental rights includes not only civil liberties and political rights, but also economic, social, and cultural rights.

On the one hand, the CCC has been highly activist in protecting social and economic rights and has ruled on issues that have contributed to shape social and economic policy – including the right to the *mínimo vital*,[8] healthcare, housing and mortgage policy, conditions of prison inmates, and living conditions of displaced populations (Cifuentes, 1995; Nunes, 2010; Rodríguez and Rodríguez, 2010; Uprimny, 2006; Yamin and Parra-Vera, 2009). In many of these cases the court has ordered the state and the government to provide goods and services, which has implied vast amounts of money in public expenditures (Uprimny, 2006). Those rulings, though criticized by economic elites and some scholars (Clavijo Vergara, 2001; Kalmanovitz, 2000), have benefited significant sectors of the population and hence have contributed to fostering the public's favor (Uprimny, 2003, 2006).

On the other hand, in enforcing civil liberties, minority rights, and issues regarding historically marginalized populations, the court has put itself in the middle of the so-called culture wars and has made controversial and even unpopular decisions, which may have negatively impacted its legitimacy. This was the case in 1994 when the CCC protected the right to carry and consume minimum doses of drugs[9] while the level of public's support for legalizing drug trafficking and consumption was and remains consistently low.[10] Also, despite the fact that at least until recently a majority of the population disapproved of same-sex marriage (Invamer, 2021: 122) and child adoption (Invamer, 2021: 130), the court has made several decisions aimed at protecting those rights since 2007 (Albarracín Caballero, 2011).[11] As we shall see, the issue of abortion, which the court legalized in three specific instances in 2006,[12] belongs to this group of cases in which the CCC might potentially jeopardize the public's good will.

Argumentation, Legitimacy, and the Issue of Abortion

In her note on the sociological concept of legitimacy with regard to constitutional courts in Latin America, Ruibal emphasizes that courts must find ways

[8] The court has defined the *mínimo vital* (literally, the vital minimum) as the portion of an individual's income devoted to "funding his/her basic needs such as food, housing, clothing, access to public utilities, recreation, healthcare," which are indispensable to effect the right to human dignity (see, among others, court decisions SU-995/1999 and T-678/2017).

[9] The original decision is C-221/1994. Other more recent rulings have mainly followed this precedent (see, for instance, decisions C-551/2003 and C-253/2019, plotted in Figure 7.1).

[10] At least since 2011, when Invamer started tracking this attitude, less than 30 percent favor such possibility (see Invamer, 2021: 135).

[11] Examples of these decisions are C-075/2007, C-683/2015, and SU-2014/2016, plotted in Figure 7.1.

[12] Decision C-335/2006 (plotted in Figure 7.1).

to "implement mechanisms that could convey to the public a sense of procedural fairness in decision-making processes" (Ruibal, 2010: 345). In addition to factors such as adhering to precedent, deliberative practices, and transparency in their judgments, Ruibal identifies the centrality of principled argumentation in order to attain such goal. Citing Fiss (1981), she argues that one of the main procedural rules aiming at enhancing courts' legitimacy is the "justification of decisions in universal terms or neutral principles" (Ruibal, 2010: 355).

With that in mind, we argue that, on top of the institutional and behavioral factors discussed earlier, the type of argument used in its decisions may also impact the way the public receives such rulings and, more generally, the legitimacy of the court. We hypothesize that arguments that better convey the idea that the decision is based on neutral principles are more likely to be related to higher levels of specific and diffuse support. Our experimental approach, described later in detail, contrasts four types of arguments: legalistic, scientific, majoritarian/public opinion-based, and religious. We suggest that arguments and decisions based on legal norms and precedent, as well as those grounded on scientific findings, better carry the idea of objectivity that can make an unpopular decision more palatable to the public. In contrast, resorting to public opinion polls or conjuring arguments based on religious doctrine and dogma might be less compelling, especially in highly controversial issues.

We test this hypothesis on one of those issues: abortion. In 2006 the court issued a decision decriminalizing the voluntary interruption of pregnancy if any of three circumstances occurs: (i) when continuing with the pregnancy is dangerous for the woman's life or health; (ii) when there is a serious malformation of the fetus that makes its life unfeasible; and (iii) when pregnancy is the result of rape, abusive or artificial insemination, unconsented transfer of fertilized ovum, or incest (decision C-355/2006).[13] Our experiment examines the responses of citizens to a simulated ruling in which the court goes further to totally decriminalize abortion.[14]

This has been a highly controversial issue in Latin America, especially in recent years as women's demands for the defense of their sexual and reproductive rights have clashed with conservative attitudes and

[13] Arteaga-Iriarte and Rodríguez-Raga (2010: 7) report that this case "attracted thousands of interventions including: children's letters and drawings (rejected by the Court); hundreds of preformatted briefs signed by citizens; briefs by biologists, lawyers, sociologists, physicians, physiologists and other professional experts; and NGOs, churches and public institutions briefs, among others." See also Jaramillo and Alfonso (2008).

[14] On February 21, 2022, almost four years after we conducted our study, the court issued a press release announcing a ruling on the total decriminalization of abortion up to the 24th week of pregnancy (Corte Constitucional, 2022).

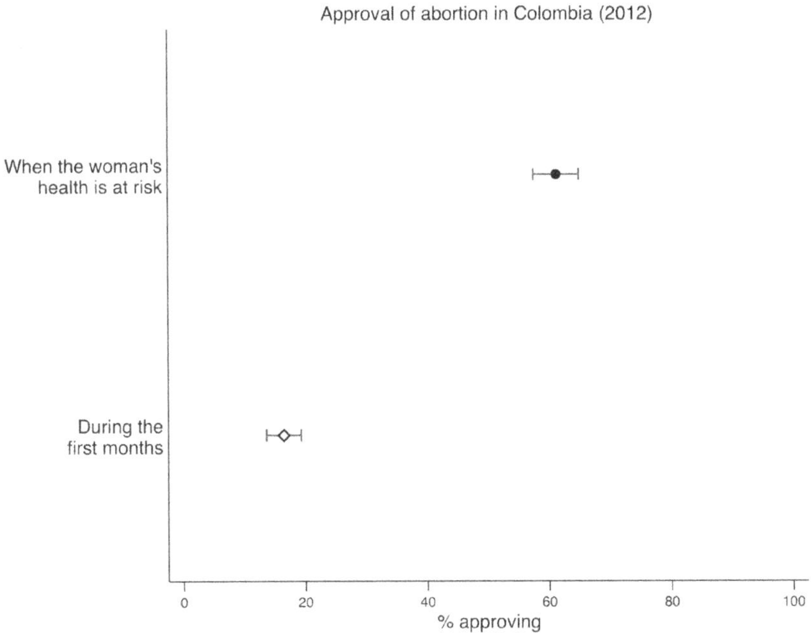

FIGURE 7.2. Support for abortion in Colombia (2012)

organized groups that oppose abortion. The region is characterized by a high level of religiosity,[15] and conservative political actors and groups and some factions of the Catholic and Evangelical churches have coalesced, taking advantage of these religious attitudes to advance an agenda against the defense of abortion and other fundamental rights.

Data from the 2018 wave of the AmericasBarometer shows that the level of citizen approval for the most frequently legal cause of abortion decriminalization – i.e. when the woman's health is at risk – is in most countries over 60 percent, with the highest rates in Uruguay and Chile. In the specific case of Colombia, these data indicate that approval of abortion when the woman's health is at risk was consistently around that level between 2012 and 2018. This condition is included in the CCC's decision of 2006. However, a sharp contrast appears when citizens are asked about their approval of abortion in the first months of pregnancy, with no other conditions. This difference is depicted in Figure 7.2, which shows

[15] According to the AmericasBarometer, in Colombia almost 70 percent of people report that religion is very important in their lives, which is consistent with the average of most of other countries in the region.

AmericasBarometer data for Colombia in 2012 (the only year in which questions for both situations were asked).

Abortion is accepted three times as often when there is risk to the woman's health – the legal status quo – as when this condition is absent. The latter is the fictional scenario we offer respondents in the experimental design described in the next section. This shows not only that this is an extremely controversial issue, but also that an actual court's intervention in this matter may encounter serious resistance in society, which, in turn, may hurt the court's stance in the public's eye. Our experiment addresses precisely this hypothetical situation.

THE EXPERIMENT: RESEARCH DESIGN

We conducted an experiment using a between-subjects vignette design that replicates – with modifications – the one used by Farganis (2012). It aims at isolating the effects of four types of arguments on the public's support for the court. The arguments chosen range from those that might convey a clearer and more compelling sense of fairness and neutrality to arguments that are likely to look more biased or at least less well-grounded in the public's eyes.

Since Farganis (2012) includes only three types of argumentation – legalistic, public opinion, and religious – one of the contributions of this chapter is to add the scientific type to the set of arguments tested. Studies in the social sciences have addressed the relationship between law and science around questions such as: Who are the experts and how do they build their legitimacy? How and to whom do they speak? How is a consensus on valid standards reached? Techno-scientific authority is increasingly present in different spaces, including legal-political decision areas, and it also tends to be very powerful. In fact, given their role as advisors, some scholars argue that scientists have positioned themselves as the fifth branch of government (Jasanoff, 1990).

The literature that addresses the issue of neutrality and objectivity of techno-scientific studies and their uses has been developed, mainly, in the United States and Europe on issues of transgenics and the effect of chemical substances on human health. In Latin America, empirical studies along these lines are scarce. In the specific case of the CCC, some scholars have analyzed the role of scientific experts in public hearings and *amici curiae* submissions, as well as their interaction with civil society organizations around controversial issues such as child adoption by same-sex couples (Moreno, 2014) and abortion (Maldonado Castañeda, 2014).

In sum, due to the fact that it is increasingly common for judicial decisions on controversial issues (in Colombia and elsewhere) to resort to scientific studies or perspectives, we aim at exploring to what extent the language of science in judicial decisions helps convey an image of neutrality or impartiality that is associated with higher levels of support and legitimacy.

We ran the experiment in May 2018 on a sample of over 200 legal-age students of the undergraduate political science program at Universidad de los Andes in Bogotá. One obviously important consideration in choosing this sample was ease of access. However, coming from an elite university, this sample is hardly representative of the Colombian adult population. This is why we should exert care in interpreting *absolute* levels of certain attitudes (e.g. support for the court or approval of abortion), which, coming from outliers in terms of education and/or socioeconomic status, might be inflated relative to the population as a whole.

While we are aware of these shortcomings, rather than making inferences on a larger population based on observational data, our aim is to contrast the four types of arguments and their impact on the opinions of respondents regarding the fictional decision and the court at large in an experimental setting and, hence, to focus on the *relative* value of those attitudes between the different treatment groups. In other words, the random assignment of individuals to treatments in our experimental design, though it does not fully overcome the representativeness issue, is a powerful tool to identify and isolate the effects of the argument types on the public's support for the court.

The universe of students in the political science undergraduate program was randomly divided into four groups of roughly the same size. Based on a list of all those students and their emails, each one was randomly assigned a number from one to four, corresponding to each of the treatments to be tested. Each treatment corresponds to one of the four types of argument described in detail in Table 7.1.

The questionnaire applied to respondents proceeds as follows:[16] First, all participants are asked for their sociodemographic information and their stance regarding ideology (left–right continuum), religiosity, trust in political institutions and the judiciary, approval of Santos's administration – the incumbent at the time of the survey – of former president Uribe, and Congress. Those are followed by questions related to

[16] The full questionnaires, as well as other supporting material, can be found at bit.ly/courting-legitimacy

TABLE 7.1. *Treatments: types of arguments in the court's decision*

Type of argument	Description
Legalistic	The decision is based on legal arguments: prevailing legal norms, the spirit of the constitution and the law, the rights of the people and the obligations of the state. Legal reasoning is given to support the decision.
Scientific	The decision is based on scientific arguments: studies and scientific research that have been advanced in the field, to biological and medical concepts, diseases, public health reports. Science is referred to as justification for the decision.
Public opinion/ majoritarian	The decision is based on public opinion arguments: studies and research advanced on the opinion of citizens, surveys, the opinion of the majority, the national consensus. It is justified based on empirical data about the citizens' opinions.
Religious	The decision is based on religious arguments: biblical passages, teachings of Jesus Christ, statements by the Pope. It is founded on Christian moral arguments.

three dimensions of ideological cleavages: support for same-sex marriage, support for state control of the economy, and support for the peace agreement signed in 2016 between Santos and the FARC guerrilla group.[17] At this stage of the questionnaire, we also include a question asking the extent to which respondents approve of the CCC's performance, which we use as a measure of the court's *specific* support (Gibson and Caldeira, 1992).

Then, each group is shown a different vignette related to a fictional note in a newspaper reporting on a supposedly recent court ruling announcing the total decriminalization of abortion. The vignettes include direct (fictitious) quotes from the court's president and from experts on the matter, reflecting the foundation of the decision (legalistic, scientific, public opinion, or religious) according to each treatment group.[18]

Finally, after reading the news, all respondents are required to answer the same questions related to whether or not they agree with the court decision

[17] The agreement with the FARC is arguably the most salient and polarizing issue in Colombia in the past few years.

[18] Great care was taken to capture the look and feel of an authentic online newspaper, including the layout, typeface, writing style, and other design features that increase believability. The vignettes are included in the online appendix available at bit.ly/courting-legitimacy

TABLE 7.2. *Items measuring loyalty to the court (diffuse support)*

Question	Direction showing loyalty
If the Constitutional Court started making a lot of decisions like the one you just read, then it might be better to do away with the court altogether	Disagree
If the Constitutional Court were to make a series of decisions like the one you just read, then Congress should reduce the court's power.	Disagree
If the Constitutional Court were to make more decisions like the one you just read, then the Constitution should be rewritten to reduce or eliminate the power of the court.	Disagree
If elected officials believe that the decision you just read would be bad for the country, then they should come up with their policies instead.	Disagree
If the Constitutional Court were to make a series of decisions like the one you just read, then people should still be willing to defend the court's power.	Agree
If a majority of Colombians oppose the decision you just read, then it should be ignored by the other branches of government.	Disagree

described in the vignette (no/yes), as a measure of what we term *immediate* support for the court's ruling. This is followed by a battery of questions seeking to measure the legitimacy that respondents confer to the court (*diffuse* support). This battery includes six items aimed at assessing the degree of respondents' loyalty, which are shown in Table 7.2 (along with a note on which answers are considered to be consistent with a loyal attitude towards the court).[19] We build an index of court loyalty based on these questions.[20]

We chose to focus on a case of abortion decriminalization to test the effect of different arguments for several reasons. Aside from its relevance to contemporary politics, abortion is the kind of controversial issue that is able to produce enough disagreement to allow us to measure attitudes towards the court and its ruling from both sides of the debate, which is a

[19] These are the same questions used in Farganis (2012).

[20] The index was built for all observations with valid answers to at least three of the six items. The index's validity was verified by a Cronbach's alpha of 0.71. Except for the sociodemographic questions and the binary one asking whether respondents agreed with the court decision, all answers to the items in the questionnaire were recoded on a 0–1 scale.

TABLE 7.3. *Sociodemographic information: descriptive statistics*

Treatment	Description	*N*	Age (mean)	Gender (% female)	Socioeconomic stratum (mean)	Semester (mean)
T1	Legalistic	55	20.56	61.8	4.29	6.02
T2	Scientific	60	20.88	50.0	4.42	6.45
T3	Public opinion	49	20.98	55.1	4.14	6.37
T4	Religious	46	20.91	45.7	4.35	6.33
	Total	210	20.83	53.3	4.30	6.29

requirement for this kind of experiment. Also, the case must be credible, a condition that was met given that, since its ruling of 2006, the Constitutional Court has issued various decisions on the subject. Therefore, it was plausible that this experimental setting was thought of as real by the respondents.[21] The selection of this issue, however, combined with the set of argument types we assigned to the treatment groups, may hinder such credibility. This is especially true regarding the fictional ruling legalizing abortion based on religious arguments for churches and religious organizations have typically and publicly opposed abortion. The interpretation of the findings related to this specific treatment must be done with care.

Also, the design of the experiment might raise a number of ethical issues because participants are presented a fictional and simulated decision on a highly sensitive and controversial issue as if it were real. In order to minimize the ethical risk, respondents were debriefed at the end of the questionnaire on the fact that the news piece was indeed untrue.[22]

Table 7.3 shows descriptive statistics for all sociodemographic items in the questionnaire, for each group/treatment. It suggests that the groups are roughly balanced in number and composition.

A similar balance is achieved regarding attitudes towards ideological issues (Table 7.4), with the possible exception of religiosity. In fact, respondents in the group assigned to the argument based on public

[21] Since 2019 the Court was again reviewing the issue of abortion, and there were speculations that it might rule its total legalization. On March 2, 2020, however, the CCC announced that it stood by its previous decisions (Berger, 2020).

[22] This was the only requirement of the IRB review of the experiment by the College of Social Sciences.

TABLE 7.4. *Issue attitudes: descriptive statistics*

Treatment	Description	Ideology	Religiousness	Support for same-sex marriage	Support for state-led economy	Support for the peace agreement
T1	Legalistic	0.39	0.28	0.95	0.34	0.84
T2	Scientific	0.41	0.27	0.91	0.34	0.81
T3	Public opinion	0.40	0.44	0.86	0.34	0.82
T4	Religious	0.44	0.35	0.90	0.33	0.79
	Total	0.41	0.33	0.91	0.34	0.82

opinion (T3) have on average a significantly higher level of religiosity. In the multivariate model we control for this factor.

Finally, we also have balanced treatment groups regarding the attitudes of respondents towards institutions and political figures, including our measure of specific support (court approval), as shown in Table 7.5.

FINDINGS: GAUGING SPECIFIC AND DIFFUSE SUPPORT FOR THE COURT

Assessing Differences between Treatment Groups

We measure the *immediate* support for the ruling by means of the dichotomous answer (yes/no) to the question *Do you agree with the Constitutional Court decision you have just read?* which is asked right after the vignette. We expect agreement to be present in a higher proportion for groups 1 and 2 (legalistic and scientific treatments, respectively) than for groups 3 and 4 (public opinion and religious treatments, respectively).

Table 7.6, which shows pairwise tests of differences between treatment groups of the proportion of respondents agreeing with the experimental decision, suggests that our expectations are empirically supported. We find that the level of agreement with the decision is higher for the group that read the vignette grounded on scientific arguments (86.7 percent) than for the group with legalistic arguments (78.2 percent), though the difference between these two groups does not reach statistical significance (p-value = 0.231). On the other hand, the two groups with the lowest agreement rates are those receiving public opinion (69.4 percent) and

TABLE 7.5. *Institutional attitudes: descriptive statistics*

Treat.	Description	Trust in institutions	Trust in judiciary	Govt. approval	Congress approval	Santos approval	Uribe approval	Court approval (specific support)
T1	Legalistic	0.44	0.34	0.52	0.35	0.47	0.22	0.62
T2	Scientific	0.43	0.36	0.51	0.37	0.56	0.24	0.55
T3	Public opinion	0.50	0.37	0.58	0.34	0.53	0.24	0.58
T4	Religious	0.47	0.41	0.60	0.35	0.52	0.28	0.60
	Total	0.46	0.37	0.55	0.35	0.52	0.24	0.59

TABLE 7.6. *Pairwise comparisons of levels of agreement with the court's decision*

Decision agreement						
Treatment	*N*	Proportion of "yes" answers	SE	Change	|z|	Two-tailed *p*-value
Legalistic	55	0.7818	0.0557			
Scientific	60	0.8667	0.0439	0.0848	1.199	0.231
Scientific	60	0.8667	0.0439			
Public opinion	49	0.6939	0.0658	−0.1728	2.199	0.028
Legalistic	55	0.7818	0.0557			
Public opinion	49	0.6939	0.0658	−0.0879	1.021	0.307
Public opinion	49	0.6939	0.0658			
Religious	46	0.6304	0.0712	−0.0634	0.654	0.513
Scientific	60	0.8667	0.0439			
Religious	46	0.6304	0.0712	−0.2362	2.839	0.005
Legalistic	55	0.7818	0.0557			
Religious	46	0.6304	0.0712	−0.1514	−1.675	0.094

religious (63.0 percent) treatments. In fact, the group that read a scientific argument agrees significantly more often with the decision than both the public opinion group (p-value = 0.028) and the religious one (p-value = 0.005). Moreover, the rate of agreement for the legalistic treatment is significantly higher (at the 10 percent level) than that for the religious group (p-value = 0.094).

These results suggest that the type of argumentation in court decisions matters with regard to immediate support. Decisions based on arguments showing more procedural fairness – that is, conveying a clearer sense of neutrality – are more accepted by citizens than those grounded on public opinion or religious beliefs.

Given that *specific* support – approval of the court's performance – is a measure taken before respondents were shown the vignettes, we do not expect to see any differences between treatment groups. In fact, we only find that, by chance, individuals assigned to the legalistic group have a mean approval that is significantly higher than those in the scientific group (at the 10 percent level of significance).

Regarding the relationship between the types of argumentation and *diffuse* support, however, the evidence is blurrier. In fact, we find no statistically significant differences between groups. Table 7.7 reports pairwise t-tests of loyalty mean differences between treatments. It shows that the level of loyalty to the court across groups is between 0.74 (religious) and 0.78 (legalistic).

In assessing the relationship between immediate and diffuse support, we find that within each treatment group loyalty to the court is higher for those who agree with the ruling than for those who disagree with it. Table 7.8 shows the differences in diffuse support between those who agree and disagree within each group. We see that these differences range from 12 percentage points (legalistic) to 28 percentage points (scientific). In all groups, the differences are statistically significant, which suggests a strong relationship between immediate and diffuse support regardless of the type of argumentation each group was exposed to.

Multivariate Analysis of Diffuse Support

We now move to exploring the relationship between specific and diffuse support for the court. We specify, first, a simple linear regression model (M1) linking the respondents' agreement with the ruling with their loyalty to the court. The results of this model, shown in the second column in

TABLE 7.7. *Pairwise comparisons of loyalty to the court*

Court loyalty						
Treatment	***N***	**Mean**	**SD**	**Change**	**|t|**	**Two-tailed *p*-value**
Legalistic	55	0.7797	0.1581			
Scientific	60	0.7488	0.1795	−0.0308	0.974	0.332
Scientific	60	0.7488	0.1795			
Public opinion	49	0.7468	0.1785	−0.0020	0.057	0.955
Legalistic	55	0.7797	0.1581			
Public opinion	49	0.7468	0.1785	−0.0328	0.994	0.323
Public opinion	49	0.7468	0.1785			
Religious	46	0.7417	0.1514	−0.0051	0.150	0.881
Scientific	60	0.7488	0.1795			
Religious	46	0.7417	0.1514	−0.0071	0.215	0.830
Legalistic	55	0.7797	0.1581			
Religious	46	0.7417	0.1514	−0.0379	1.224	0.224

TABLE 7.8. *Loyalty to the court by immediate support for each treatment group*

Treatment/agreement	N	Mean	SD	Change	t	Two-tailed *p*-value
Legalistic, agree	43	0.8062	0.1375			
Legalistic, disagree	12	0.6845	0.1948	−0.1217	−2.465	0.017
Scientific, agree	52	0.7866	0.1399			
Scientific, disagree	8	0.5030	0.2221	−0.2837	−4.907	0.000
Public opinion, agree	34	0.7934	0.1548			
Public opinion, disagree	15	0.6413	0.1884	−0.1521	−2.965	0.005
Religious, agree	29	0.7956	0.1195			
Religious, disagree	17	0.6499	0.1590	−0.1457	−3.528	0.001

Table A1 (in the online appendix),[23] confirm the relationship uncovered in Table 7.8; agreeing with the ruling that decriminalizes abortion is positively related to diffuse support.

We then estimate model M2, which adds the treatment variables as well as our measure of specific support – that is, approval for the CCC's performance (column 3 in Table A1[24]). As suggested in Table 7.7, the type of argument sustaining the ruling has no direct impact on the loyalty towards the court. Also, immediate support (agreeing with the specific decision) still has a significant impact on loyalty. On the other hand, when no other variables are included in the model, specific support appears to be significantly related to diffuse support. This means that the more citizens are satisfied with the court's performance, the more loyal they appear.

Does this relationship between court approval and court loyalty exist regardless of the treatment? In other words, besides the fact that the type of ruling argumentation seems not to be directly connected to the level of loyalty for the court, would it be plausible to find differences in the relationship between specific and diffuse support depending on how the CCC frames its decision on abortion? Model M3 in Table 7.9 explores this by adding interaction terms between the treatment factor variables and our indicator of specific support (which was measured before the treatment was applied).[25] The rationale for this specification therefore lies in the idea that the type of argument may be mediating the relationship between specific and diffuse support.

Figure 7.3 plots the mean marginal effect of court approval on loyalty for the different groups (along with their 90 percent confidence interval).[26] It shows that only for the group that received the scientific treatment is the effect of specific support on loyalty significant. In other words, a ruling based on scientific reasoning reinforces the link between specific and diffuse support.

[23] See bit.ly/courting-legitimacy [24] See bit.ly/courting-legitimacy

[25] This model is also included in Table A1; see bit.ly/courting-legitimacy

[26] Examining the coefficients of these interaction terms and their standard errors is insufficient to assess such mediation effect. In other words, one can reach invalid conclusions by observing the magnitudes and significances of the individual coefficients and of the multiplicative terms. It is therefore necessary to conduct an analysis of the marginal effects on loyalty of approval conditioned to the treatment groups (Kam and Franzese, 2007).

TABLE 7.9. *Multivariate model: loyalty to the court (diffuse support)*

Loyalty to the court (diffuse support)	M3
Agreement with the decision	0.151***
	(0.025)
Legalistic (base)	0.000
	(0.000)
Scientific	−0.102
	(0.083)
Public opinion	−0.006
	(0.081)
Religious	0.054
	(0.086)
Approval of the court (specific support)	0.127
	(0.102)
Legalistic × Approval	0.000
	(0.000)
Scientific × Approval	0.121
	(0.131)
Public opinion × Approval	−0.014
	(0.125)
Religious × Approval	−0.111
	(0.132)
Constant	0.583***
	(0.066)
Observations	210
Adjusted R-squared	0.202

Standard errors in parentheses
*** $p < 0.01$, ** $p < 0.05$, * $p < 0.1$

Finally, we estimate model M4 which includes a series of control variables that might impact diffuse support for the court.[27] These additional factors include ideology (from left to right), religiousness, support for same-sex marriage, support for more state intervention in the economy, and support for the peace agreement. We also included variables measuring approval of Congress, Santos, and Uribe, sociodemographic traits such as respondents' gender, age, and social stratum,[28] as well as the

[27] This model is shown in Table A1; see bit.ly/courting-legitimacy

[28] Social stratum is a rough measure of socioeconomic status based on a classification of households and neighborhoods determined by the state.

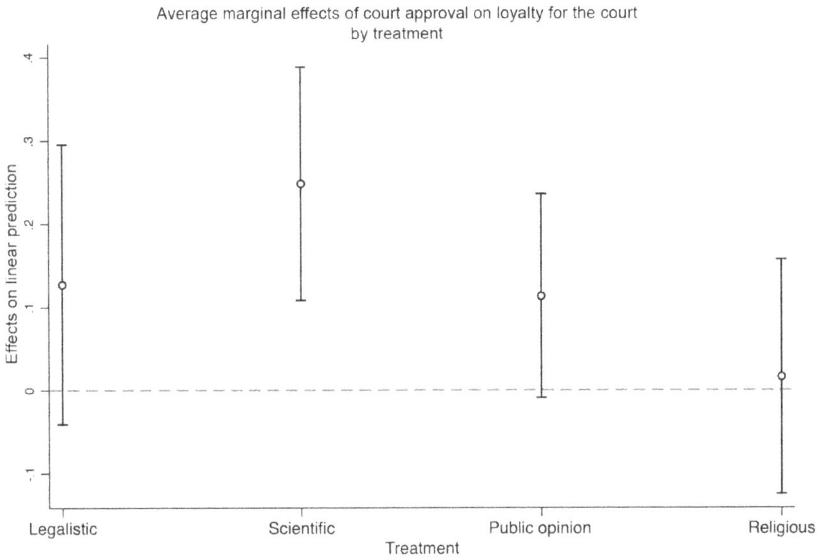

FIGURE 7.3. Marginal effect of specific support on diffuse support, by treatment

number of semesters they have been enrolled in their undergraduate programs. The correlation between immediate support for the ruling and loyalty, as well as the mediating effect of the treatment on the relationship between specific and diffuse support are all robust to the inclusion of these control variables. The impact of the level of approval of the court's performance on the public's loyalty towards it is conditioned by the type of argument provided in its ruling.

CONCLUSION

The Constitutional Court has played a relevant role in the Colombian context due to the social, political, and economic impact of its rulings. Despite recent corruption scandals in the judicial branch, the Constitutional Court has maintained a fair level of legitimacy. However, it is unclear which factors have contributed to the consolidation of such sustained legitimacy. This chapter aimed at filling this gap by conducting an experimental exploration of how citizens build this support. We suggest that the type of argument that the Constitutional Court uses to support a ruling is related to the extent to which citizens receive and appraise it, especially in highly controversial matters. In other words, not only the substance of the decision but also its framing may contribute to the public's immediate support for such decision.

Moreover, although the different types of argument do not seem directly related to the loyalty citizens may have for the court, the framing of those arguments does shape the relationship between specific support and diffuse support. In other words, we find that by wording and framing judicial rulings so that they convey a sense of principled reasoning and neutrality. The court helps translate specific support into diffuse support. Specifically, decisions based on scientific reasoning are more suitable to achieve that goal than other types of arguments, including those based on legal norms and precedent.

We are aware of the limitations of the present study due to the size of the sample and its representativeness in relation to the Colombian population. The random assignment of individual to groups in our experimental design, however, contributes to the identification of treatment effects. Also, the design and analysis we present here may be applied to larger, more representative samples to enhance the external validity of our findings.

Our choice to explore framing effects in the context of decriminalization of abortion entails some challenges which raise design issues and future research questions. First, because it is a highly sensitive issue that is deeply related to each person's innermost values, there might be confirmation bias in how respondents react to the hypothetical case they are asked to assess. In other words, people may already have an entrenched view regarding whether or not to accept abortion, and a judicial decision, no matter how it is argued, might not change their minds. In fact, we found no direct impact of the type of argument on legitimacy and even the indirect relationship we found might be caused by some underlying and unobserved factors.

Second, it would be worth attempting a study along the lines suggested in this chapter but with a fictional court decision that further bans the right to abortion. This alternative study, aside from overcoming the credibility issue regarding the religious argument, would allow us to have a more comprehensive understanding of the relationship between specific and diffuse support for the court.

Third, in the case of abortion it might be easy to distinguish what is the main argument that the court uses for its decriminalization. However, there are cases in which it may be hard to identify a unique type of argument. Again, the research agenda should include carrying out the experiment on other topics to check the robustness of the findings of the present exploration.

Finally, we think that there is an intrinsic difficulty in trying to capture in a snapshot what may be better understood as a dynamic process. Loyalty is something that the court arguably stockpiles over time. A longitudinal analysis might help supplement our findings in order to better understand the relationship between a court's specific and diffuse support.

Given these limitations, our findings could grow stronger as more scholars venture down this rich road of investigating the factors that explain to what extent and how citizens grant legitimacy to courts in general and to the CCC in particular, how diffuse and specific support are related, how they consolidate over time, and what it takes for courts to maintain them in order to preserve or strengthen the public esteem.

Legitimacy is crucial for the judiciary to be able to protect citizens' rights, especially in the case of minorities and traditionally disadvantaged populations. Without a reservoir of diffuse support, courts face strong disincentives to address controversial issues, especially as culture wars grow more acute and polarization around those issues is likely to be fueled and capitalized on by political parties and organizations. Despite courts' institutional vulnerabilities in Latin America, and despite the shortcomings of their jurisprudence and its enforcement, significant groups such as women, ethnic and gender minorities, and immigrants, among others, still rely on the judicial protection of their rights. As this chapter suggests, courts may find in the wording of their decisions a tactical weapon that might help them live up to that promise.

References

Albarracín Caballero, M. (2011). Social Movements and the Constitutional Court: Legal Recognition of the Rights of Same-Sex Couples in Colombia. *Sur-International Journal on Human Rights* 14, 7–32.

Arteaga-Iriarte, S. & Rodríguez-Raga, J. C. (2010). Interesting Friendships: Interest Groups and Amici Curiae Interventions before the Colombian Constitutional Court. Paper read at the Midwest Political Science Association annual Congress (Chicago, April 22–25).

Bartels, B. & Johnston, C. (2013). On the Ideological Foundations of Supreme Court Legitimacy in the American Public. *American Journal of Political Science*, 57(1), 184–99.

Berger, M. (2020). Colombia Was Close to Legalizing Abortion. Instead, a Top Court Kept Restrictions in Place. *Washington Post* (March 3). www.washingtonpost.com/world/2020/03/03/colombia-was-close-legalizing-abortion-instead-top-court-kept-restrictions-place/

Botero, S. (2020). Confianza, apoyo a la democracia y corrupción: una mirada a la Corte Constitucional en la opinión pública colombiana. *Latin American Law Review* 4, 25–47.

Bustamante, G. (2011). El origen y desarrollo de la acción de tutela en Colombia. *Semana* (June 9). www.semana.com/nacion/articulo/el-origen-desarrollo-accion-tutela-colombia/241093-3

Caldeira, G. & Gibson, J. L. (1992). The Etiology of Public Support for the Supreme Court. *American Journal of Political Science* 36(3), 635–64.

Cepeda, M. J. (2005). The Judicialization of Politics in Colombia: The Old and the New. In R. Sieder, L. Schjolden & A. Angell, eds., *The Judicialization of Politics in Latin America*. New York: Palgrave Macmillan, pp. 67–103.

Cifuentes, E. (1995). El constitucionalismo de la pobreza. *Dereito: Revista xuridica da Universidade de Santiago de Compostela* 4(2), 53–78.

Clavijo Vergara, S. (2001). Fallos y fallas económicas de las altas Cortes: El caso de Colombia, 1991–2000. *Revista Del Banco De La República* 74(882), 25–56.

Corte Constitucional (2022). Nota de prensa: Conducta del aborto solo será punible cuando se realice después de la vigésimo cuarta (24) semana de gestación y, en todo caso, este límite temporal no será applicable a los tres supuestos fijados en la Sentencia C-355 de 2006. www.corteconstitucional.gov.co/noticia.php?NOTA-DE-PRENSA—Conducta-del-aborto-solo-será-punible-cuando-se-realice-después-de-la-vigésimo-cuarta-(24)-semana-de-gestación-y,-en-todo-caso,-este-l%C3%ADmite-temporal-no-será-aplicable-a-los-tres-supuestos-fijados-en-la–Sentencia-C-355-de-2006-9225

Easton, D. (1965). *A Systems Analysis of Political Life*. New York: John Wiley.

Farganis, D. (2012). Do Reasons Matter? The Impact of Opinion Content on Supreme Court Legitimacy. *Political Research Quarterly* 65(1), 206–16.

Fiss, O. (1981). Objectivity and Interpretation. Stanford Law Review 34(4), 739–63.

Gardbaum, S. (2018). What Makes for More or Less Powerful Constitutional Courts? *Duke Journal of Comparative and International Law* 29(1), 1–40.

Gargarella, R. (1996). *La justicia frente al gobierno: Sobre el carácter contramayoritario del poder judicial*. Barcelona: Editorial Ariel.

Gibson, J. L. & Caldeira, G. (1992). Blacks and the United States Supreme Court: Models of Diffuse Support. *Journal of Politics* 54(4), 1120–45.

Gibson, J. L. & Nelson, M. (2014). The Legitimacy of the US Supreme Court: Conventional Wisdoms and Recent Challenges Thereto. *Annual Review of Law and Social Science* 10, 201–19.

(2015). Is the U.S. Supreme Court's Legitimacy Grounded in Performance Satisfaction and Ideology? *American Journal of Political Science* 59, 162–74.

Gibson, J. L., Caldeira, G. & Baird, V. (1998). On the Legitimacy of National High Courts. *American Political Science Review* 92(2), 343–58.

Ginsburg, T. (2008). The Global Spread of Constitutional Review. In K. E Whittington., R. D. Kelemen & G. Caldeira, eds., *The Oxford Handbook of Law and Politics*. Oxford: Oxford University Press, pp. 81–98.

González, D. A. (2017). The Colombia Constitutional Court: Building Legitimacy in its First Period. Unpublished paper. www.law.uchicago.edu/files/Session%20VI_Gonzalez.pdf

Hasen, R. L. (2013). End of the Dialogue: Political Polarization, the Supreme Court, and Congress. *Southern California Law Review* 86(2), 205–62.
Hirschl, R. (2004). *Toward Juristocracy: The Origins and Consequences of the New Constitutionalism*. Cambridge, MA: Harvard University Press.
(2008). The Judicialization of Politics. In K. E. Whittington, R. D. Kelemen & G. Caldeira, eds., *The Oxford Handbook of Law and Politics*. Oxford: Oxford University Press, pp. 119–41.
Invamer (2021). *Invamer Poll # 141*, August. https://img.lalr.co/cms/2021/09/02225313/Resultados-Invamer-Poll-144-3.pdf
Jaramillo, I. C. & Alfonso, T. (2008). *Mujeres, cortes y medios: La reforma judicial del aborto*. Bogotá: Siglo del Hombre Editores – Universidad de los Andes.
Jasanoff, S. (1990). *The Fifth Branch: Science Advisers as Policymakers*. Cambridge, MA: Harvard University Press.
Kalmanovitz, S. (2000). *Los efectos económicos de la Corte Constitucional*. Bogotá: Corporación Centro de Estudios Constitucionales, Plural.
Kam, C. D. & Franzese, R. J. (2007). *Modeling and Interpreting Interactive Hypotheses in Regression Analysis*. Ann Arbor: University of Michigan Press.
Linares, S. (2008). *La (i)legitimidad democrática del control judicial de las leyes*. Madrid: Marcial Pons, Ediciones Jurídicas y Sociales.
Maldonado Castañeda, O. J. (2014). Cortes, expertos y grupos de interés: movilización y localización del conocimiento experto en la sentencia C-355 de 2006. *Universitas Humanística* 77, 327–53.
Merhof, K. (2015). Building a Bridge between Reality and the Constitution: The Establishment and Development of the Colombian Constitutional Court. *International Journal of Constitutional Law* 13(3), 714–32.
Moreno, P. (2014). Producción de evidencia psicológica en el debate jurídico sobre adopción gay en Colombia. *Universitas Psychologica* 13(5), 1931–40.
Nunes, R. M. (2010). Ideational Origins of Progressive Judicial Activism: The Colombian Constitutional Court and the Right to Health. *Latin American Politics and Society* 52(3), 67–97.
Rivera, D., Plata, J. C. & Rodríguez-Raga, J. C. (2019). *Barómetro de las Américas 2018: Democracia e instituciones*. Bogotá: USAID-Universidad de los Andes.
Rodríguez, C. & Rodríguez, D. (2010). *Cortes y cambio social. Cómo la Corte Constitucional transformó el desplazamiento forzado en Colombia*. Bogotá: Dejusticia.
Rodríguez-Raga, J. C. (2011). Strategic Prudence in the Colombian Constitutional Court, 1992–2006. PhD dissertation, University of Pittsburgh. http://d-scholarship.pitt.edu/8953/
Rodríguez-Raga, J. C. & Virgüez-Ruiz, S. (2019). Strategically Prudent Judges and Power Expansion in the Colombian Constitutional Court. Unpublished manuscript.
Ruibal, A. (2010). The Sociological Concept of Judicial Legitimacy: Notes of Latin American Constitutional Courts. *Mexican Law Review* III(2), 343–56.
Scurich, N. (2018). Styles of Argumentation in Judicial Opinions (Legitimating Judicial Decisions). *Annual Review of Law and Social Science* 14, 205–18.

Sieder, R., Schjolden, L. & Angell, A., eds. (2005). *The Judicialization of Politics in Latin America*. New York: Palgrave Macmillan.

Simon, D. & Scurich, N. (2011). Lay Judgments of Judicial Decision Making. *Journal of Empirical Legal Studies* 8(4), 709–27.

Staton, J. (2006). Constitutional Review and the Selective Promotion of Case Results. *American Journal of Political Science* 50(1), 98–112.

Tate, C. N. & Vallinder, T. (1995). The Global Expansion of Judicial Power: The Judicialization of Politics. In C. N. Tate & T. Vallinder, eds., *The Global Expansion of Judicial Power*. New York: New York University Press, pp. 1–10.

Uprimny, R. (2003). Legitimidad y conveniencia del control constitucional a la economía. In G. Burgos, ed., *Independencia judicial en América Latina. ¿De quién? ¿Para qué? ¿Cómo?* Bogotá: ILSA

(2004). The Constitutional Court and Control of Presidential Extraordinary Powers in Colombia. In S. Gloppen, R. Gargarella & E. Skaar, eds., *Democratization and the Judiciary: The Accountability Function of Courts in New Democracies*. London: Frank Cass.

(2006). The Enforcement of Social Rights by the Colombian Constitutional Court: Cases and Debates. In R. Gargarella, P. Domingo & T. Roux, eds., *Courts and Social Transformation in New Democracies: An Institutional Voice for the Poor?* Burlington: Ashgate.

Yamin, A. E. & Parra-Vera, Ó. (2009). How Do Courts Set Health Policy? The Case of the Colombian Constitutional Court. *PLoS Medicine* 6(2), 147–50.

8

Family Ties and Nepotism in the Mexican Federal Judiciary

Julio Ríos-Figueroa

INTRODUCTION

Merit-based systems for hiring and promotion in public sector employment are foundational for effective, efficient, and legitimate public administration (e.g. Carpenter 2001; Brans and Hondeghem 1999; Grindle 2010; Pardo 2005; Longo 2004). Procedures that avoid the appearance of corruption, nepotism, and impropriety are especially important in law enforcement, dispute resolution, and the administration of justice. The selection and promotion process in the judiciary creates incentives that can impact the independence and performance of the courts. Although there are many such methods operating around the world, there is consensus on the importance of competitive, merit-based selection mechanisms and the reliance on formal training and qualifications in law (e.g. examinations, professional record). Judicial councils and appointments commissions are an increasingly common set of institutions governing selection: in 1985 only about 10 percent of the world's jurisdictions used judicial councils to select judges; by 2015 such bodies were involved in appointments in over 60 percent of jurisdictions (Garoupa and Ginsburg 2015, 110). Latin America is no exception; practically all countries in the region have adopted judicial councils (albeit with interesting design variations) as part of the waves of judicial reforms that created the institutional "superstructure" of judicialization (see the Introduction to this volume in Chapter 1). All too often, however, existing procedures fail to deliver results approaching this ideal. And while there has been considerable research on the causes and consequences of certain forms of corruption (bribery or diverting/appropriating public funds), there has been relatively little work that explicitly considers improper public employment of family members – nepotism.

Judicial councils were first created in Europe to increase judicial independence from the executive branch, which used to control the administration of human and material resources of the judiciary through the Ministry of Justice (Guarnieri and Pedezoli 2002). In Latin America, by contrast, supreme courts usually had power over budget management and judges' careers. Judicial councils were therefore created to combat patronage, patrimonialism, and nepotism within the judiciary (see Pozas-Loyo and Ríos-Figueroa 2011; Hammergren 2007). Mexico is a case in point. A judicial council was created at the end of 1994 with the explicit aim of establishing a merit-based system for the selection and promotion of judges at all levels of the federal judiciary. Before this year, the Mexican Supreme Court had the power to select and appoint lower court federal judges, and it also managed the budget of the judiciary. The judicial council in Mexico was thus created to take the administration of the human and material resources of the judiciary away from the Supreme Court. Whereas the judicial council has improved the Mexican judiciary in a number of ways, it is also true that there are still considerable challenges. This chapter focuses on one of them: the relatively high number of family ties and, potentially, nepotism.

The chapter takes advantage of a unique dataset to describe family relationships and nepotism in the Mexican Federal Judiciary.[1] Specifically, the chapter asks: to what extent are employees in the Mexican judiciary – both judges and lower level officials – connected by family ties? Do these family ties constitute nepotism? In other words, are these family connections used inappropriately to hire or to favor relatives in ways that would not have been possible absent the family connection? Behind these questions there is another, more general one, that connects this chapter with the main themes of the book: to what extent does the extensive presence of family ties and nepotism constitute a departure from the promises made in the judicial reform of 1994? Specifically, the reform of 1994 had two broad objectives: first, to strengthen the Supreme Court

[1] The data used in this chapter was collected by former judicial council member, Lic. Felipe Borrego Estrada, and his team of collaborators. The former councilor handed the data to an NGO, *Mexicanos Contra la Corrupción y la Impunidad* (MCCI – Mexicans against Corruption and Impunity), and that NGO asked the author of this chapter to analyze the data. The result was a report entitled *El deficit meritocrático: Nepotismo y redes familiares en el Poder Judicial de la Federación* (Ríos Figueroa 2018), on which the second and most of the third part of this chapter are based.

so that it could become a neutral arbiter of political conflicts and a guarantor of the rights established in the constitution; second, to create a professional judicial career in Mexico for all federal judges, removing the administration of the judiciary from the Supreme Court and transferring it to a judicial council.

Whereas the process for selecting judges instituted after 1994 is a considerable improvement on the informal hand-picking of federal judges by Supreme Court justices in the pre-1994 period (Pozas-Loyo and Ríos-Figueroa 2018), the pervasive presence of family relatives currently working in the federal judiciary can be considered a half-broken promise of the auspicious 1994 reform. In contrast to Basabe-Serrano's study of corruption in the Constitutional Court of Ecuador (see Chapter 9), I do not document individual cases of misuse of family ties within the judiciary. The chapter does, however, show that the poor implementation of the judicial career mandated in the reform of 1994 was facilitated by legal decisions taken by judges themselves. Inter alia, these rulings require merit examinations only for judges but not for other key positions in the judiciary, establish that calls for applications are open only to a limited pool of applicants, and afford wide discretion to judges to handpick the officials in their courtroom with minimal meritocratic requirements. A full-fledged explanation for this resistance to institutional change (Mahoney and Thelen 2010) is beyond the scope of this chapter, but in the conclusion I delineate the contours of a hypothesis: Broken promises are a result of the legacy of a long and peculiar authoritarian regime that allows for the persistence of norms of patrimonialism and patronage within the Mexican judiciary.

The other promise of the 1994 reform, namely strengthening the Supreme Court as both an arbiter of political conflicts and a protector of rights, has also produced mixed results. Specifically, whereas the court established itself as a considerably neutral arbiter, its role protecting rights has taken longer to take shape (e.g. Ansolabehere 2010; Suárez 2014). The mechanisms linking the poor implementation of the judicial career (and the extensive presence of family ties and nepotism) and the disappointment regarding the rights-protecting role of the Supreme Court is yet to be established. The chapters on Ecuador (Chapter 9) and Peru (Chapter 3) in this volume provide some clues as to where to look for this connection. Specifically, they imply that networks within the judiciary can either produce "judicial corruption" (Basabe-Serrano, Chapter 9) or undermine the zeal of individual judges motivated to defend rights (Baraybar and Gonzalez-Ocantos, Chapter 13). It is possible that extended family networks within the Mexican federal judiciary generate "judicial corruption" that harms rights, for instance, facilitating biased decisions in favor of mining companies against indigenous communities asking for their right to prior consultation. It is also possible that conservative family networks that span different courts discourage individual judges that harbor pro-rights attitudes, or reproduce formalistic attitudes towards the law through bias in the selection of court personnel and their socialization.[2]

CONCEPTUALIZING AND MEASURING NEPOTISM

What is nepotism? According to Transparency International (2019, 28), nepotism is a "form of favouritism based on acquaintances and familiar relationships whereby someone in an official position exploits his or her power and authority to provide a job or favour to a family member or friend, even though he or she may not be qualified or deserving." Similarly, Durante et al. (2011, 2) define nepotism as "the practice of favouring members of a network based on their family ties, independent of their actual qualifications." The *Encyclopedic Dictionary of Sociology* defines it as "favouritism and preferential treatment, that damages the principles of fair competency, in favour of relatives or friends by influential persons with access to public or private resources" (Hillmann 2001, 638). Gianfranco Pasquino, in the *Dictionary of Politics*, says that nepotism is "the concession of public jobs or contracts on the basis of family ties and not of merit" (Pasquino 2005, 377).

All of these definitions contain two elements: a family tie, and its instrumental and inappropriate use to obtain a position or a favor that would not be obtained without the connection. According to these definitions, nepotism is inherently corrupt when it takes place in public offices (understanding corruption as "the use of public resources for private gain," e.g. Rose-Ackerman 1999) and also arguably in a broader set of private practices (understanding corruption as a "dishonest or fraudulent conduct," *Oxford English Dictionary*). Empirical studies underscore this

[2] Of course, it is also possible that family ties within an organization such as the judiciary have positive effects. Family ties may be useful for increasing, not decreasing, the efficiency of an organization because the individuals are more willing to "go the extra mile" to help a relative (see Jaskiewicz et al. 2013). It is also possible that in contexts of institutional uncertainty or potential arbitrariness in external revisions, for example, family ties provide the loyalty and trust among the members of an organization necessary to make the organization work. These are hypotheses that warrant further empirical testing.

negative connotation, for instance, finding that in the US Congress the longer a legislator's time in office the higher the likelihood that some of their relatives will enter Congress (Dal Bó et al. 2009), or that the probability of finding a job or getting better payment and working conditions in the Italian public sector is higher for those persons whose father is also a public servant (Scoppa 2009; Gagliarducci and Manacorda 2016).[3]

Measuring nepotism is not an easy task (see Ríos-Figueroa and Soto Tamayo 2021). For starters, the two dimensions of the concept need to be identified and assessed: the family link *and* the instrumental and inappropriate use of it. Not all persons who have family ties within an institution are automatically culprits of nepotism. For instance, consider the case of a couple who meet at work and get married: there is a family link, but no inappropriate or instrumental use of it at least regarding entry to the institution. Establishing whether a family connection was inappropriately used is hard, but it is no less challenging to capture the family link itself. This is especially true for large groups and for blood relations that go beyond the first degree (e.g. father–son, brother–sister), not to mention legal relationships (e.g. husband–wife). Most studies capture nepotism indirectly, either using surveys or counting surnames, and do not distinguish between the two dimensions of the concept (i.e. the family tie and its misuse). When it comes to surveys, researchers essentially ask people in an organization how many colleagues have relatives working in the same organization (see Yasin et al. 2019; US Gov. 2016). An obvious concern is that people's perception of levels of nepotism in a specific institution might also reflect their attitudes toward management, or their own assessment of the value of helping relatives (Treisman 2007).

Counting surnames avoids this kind of perception bias. The basic idea is to count the occurrence of repeated surnames as a proxy for nepotistic relations (Allesina 2011). For instance, Durante et al. (2011) determined the presence of family networks by counting how many members in different Italian academic departments share the same surname, and then divided this number by the total number of members in each department.[4]

[3] Cruz et al. (2017) find that candidates running for public office with broader family and social networks are more likely to receive a higher vote share. They argue that this is because it is easier for politicians with less social distance to their constituents to exchange political favors such as access to clientelist goods, services, or vote-buying.

[4] Cruz et al. (2017) examine the joint occurrences of middle names and surnames for the candidates running for office in the Philippines in order to determine ties between families and calculate the network position of politician families.

Gagliarducci and Manacorda (2016) compare the coincidences of individuals' surnames in political office with individuals' surnames working for nongovernmental companies born in the same municipality. Grilli and Allesina (2017) count repeated surnames across academic departments in Italian universities, then compute the probability of observing a higher or equal number of shared surnames from what is expected at random, and finally divide the observed over the expected values. Finally, Sundell (2014) counts the number of person dyads in the entire Swedish federal administration, as well as the number of dyads sharing surnames within each agency, to calculate the probability that two randomly drawn persons that work in the same agency share the same surname.

The downside of counting surnames is that, on the one hand, sharing a surname does not necessarily imply a family relationship (Allesina 2011). By analyzing only shared surnames nothing can be said about family relationships between, for instance, spouses, nephews, and, in general, about in-laws (Durante et al. 2011). Counting surnames reveals the probability of having persons with family ties within an institution, but it says nothing about the possible misuse of those ties. That's why these measures require a standard of "normalcy" against which the observed probability of shared surnames is compared. One such standard is obtained by randomization methodologies (e.g. Gagliarducci and Manacorda 2016; Grilli and Allesina 2017) that themselves make strong assumptions about the data – for instance, that the distribution of surnames in the population is the same as the distribution of surnames in the institution under examination, or that the surnames from the sample are well represented across geography and socioeconomic groups.[5] In sum, indirect measures of nepotism (e.g. perceptions or counting surnames) are good attempts at capturing nepotism but they suffer from important limitations and cannot fully capture the concept.

In fact, it is worth asking whether it makes sense to think about measuring the concept of nepotism directly, in a single step. This is because measuring nepotism actually implies capturing the two dimensions of the concept. First, it is necessary to have evidence of the family ties among persons within an institution. Second, it is also necessary to ascertain whether at least one of the individuals in the family network obtained their position (or another privilege) *because* of those ties. It is hard to have a systematic prima facie single measure of the two parts

[5] Grilli and Allesina (2017) try to circumvent the distribution of surnames bias by applying different types of randomization.

implied in the concept of nepotism. However, it is possible to have direct measures of the first step, the family ties, and then either direct or proxy measures of the second step, the inappropriate use or abuse of the family relationship. This would be an improvement upon the measures based on counting surnames that indirectly capture both the first and second steps. Of course, after having a measure of the family ties, the stronger the connection between those ties and their misuse, the stronger the evidence of nepotism within an institution.

In the next two sections, I take advantage of a unique dataset that directly measures family ties within the Mexican federal judiciary, and I discuss some evidence of whether those ties constitute nepotism.

FAMILY TIES IN THE MEXICAN FEDERAL JUDICIARY

Some facts about the institutional organization of the Mexican federal judiciary and the judicial career of federal judges are important before introducing the data on family ties and nepotism. The federal judiciary has four layers: first instance trial courts (called district judgeships or *juzgados*), two layers of appellate courts (called unitary and collegiate *tribunals*), and the Supreme Court. Geographically, the federal judiciary is organized in circuits that host both layers of appellate courts (the *tribunales*), and also in judicial districts within the circuits that host the trial courts (the *juzgados*). A judicial council, in charge of administering the human and material resources of the judiciary, and an electoral jurisdiction (with trial courts and one appellate court) are also part of the federal judiciary. According to the 2019 justice census,[6] by the end of 2018 there were 32 circuits (each one coincident with a state), 267 collegiate appellate tribunals (composed of three magistrates each), 99 unitary appellate tribunals (composed of one magistrate each), and 438 district trial courts.[7] At the top is the Supreme Court that seats eleven justices. Next to the Supreme Court is the judicial council with seven councilors.

The judicial career in Mexico covers five positions: trial and appellate court judges, their respective law clerks, and the clerks' aides (actuaries). Merit examinations are required for district and circuit court judges, but not for other officials working in the judiciary whose job is relevant for

[6] Available at www.inegi.org.mx/programas/cnijf/2019/

[7] The criminal justice reform that started in 2008 and culminated in 2016 motivated the creation of so-called national criminal justice centers that deal with criminal cases under the accusatory system. By the end of 2018, there were forty-one of those centers.

the administration of justice. This includes other positions that are part of the judicial career, namely, clerks and actuaries, who are usually on track to becoming judges. Those positions (there are more than fifty, ranging from chauffeur to judge, including secretaries, technicians, administrators, and many others) are filled with different degrees of discretion by the district and circuit court judges in their respective courts. By the end of 2018 the Mexican federal judiciary employed about 55,000 persons out of whom about 1,500 were judges.

The data for this chapter was collected by a former member of the judicial council, Lic. Felipe Borrego, and his team of collaborators during the years 2015 and 2016. It is a unique dataset in which the observations are relationships between two individuals who were working in the federal judiciary at that time. Each row contains information regarding the exact workplace and the position of the first individual, called "the worker," and the same information on the second individual, called "the relative." In addition, the dataset records the specific type of family tie between the two individuals (e.g. brother, sister, son, father, spouse, cousin). The source of the data are judicial records that were accessed by the councilor and his team. The total number of observations in the dataset is $N = 6{,}284$ (1,107 if we restrict observations to those in which "the worker" is a judge). Notice that each relationship contains two persons, the "worker" and the "relative." Because some persons appear twice (once as a "worker" and once as a "relative") in the same relationship, when the unit of analysis is the relationship (the dyad) I exclude duplicates and the number of observations drops to 4,731 dyads.

The dataset has some limitations. Four of them are noteworthy. First, it does not systematically record all the possible family ties between individuals. For instance, suppose there is an entry specifying that person A is the brother of person B, and another entry specifying that person A is also the brother of person C. In these cases, the dataset may not include another entry specifying that person B is the brother of person C. Second, the information was collected by circuit. This means there is no systematic information of family ties between persons who work in different circuits. Third, the database does not contain information about the first circuit (Mexico City), the largest in the country, and it contains only partial information about the second circuit (State of Mexico), the second largest (the database does not contain information about the parts of the State of Mexico that are part of the metropolitan area of Mexico City). Finally, the database also does not contain information about people working at the Supreme Court (about a thousand, of whom eleven

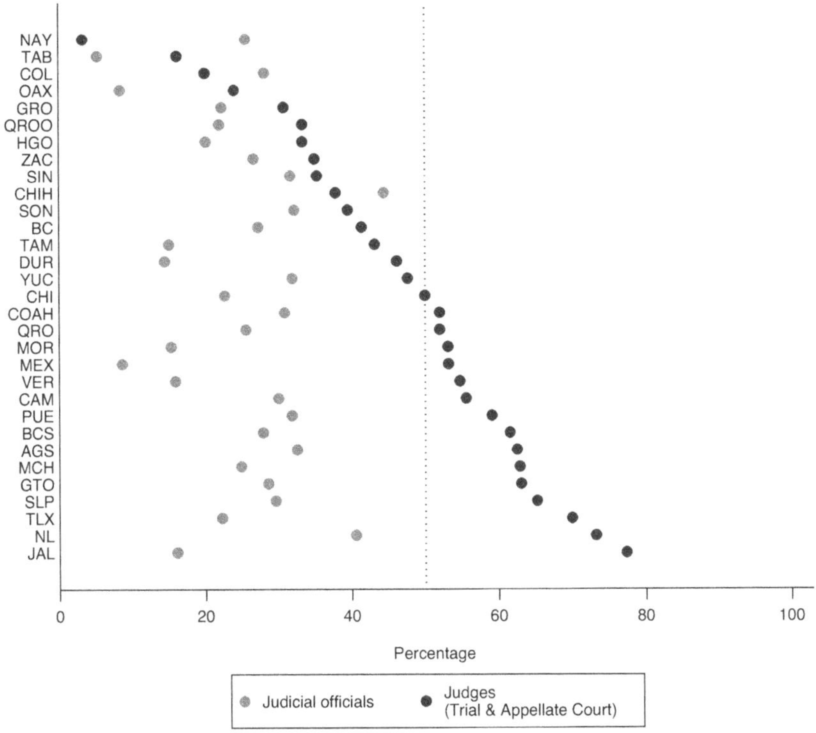

FIGURE 8.1. Judges and judicial officials with at least one relative per judicial circuit in the years 2015–2016

are the justices). In sum, though the dataset is highly valuable, it is also incomplete in important ways. The real extent of family ties in the judiciary is doubtless higher than reported here.

What is the extent of family ties in the Mexican Federal Judiciary? Figure 8.1 gives a sense of the magnitude of the phenomenon. The vertical axis lists each one of the judicial circuits. On the horizontal axis, the figure shows the percentage by circuit of both federal judges (black dots) and judicial officials (grey dots) with at least one family member also working in the same judicial circuit. The average is 51 percent for judges and 29 percent for judicial officials. There are circuits where the number of judges with at least one family member working in the same circuit is close to 80 percent (e.g. the two circuits at the bottom of the vertical axis: *Jalisco*, JAL, and *Nuevo León*, NL). How dense are these networks? In the case of federal judges, density ranges from one to eighteen family members working in the same circuit (the average is three family members per judge). Remember that this figure is based on 6,284 individuals working in the federal judiciary in 2015–2016.[8] Taking each relationship dyad as the unit of analysis (N = 4,731), 68 percent are consanguineous relationships and 32 percent are affinal relationships. Out of the consanguineous relationships, 49 percent are second grade (brothers/sisters, and grandparents–grandchildren), 34 percent are first grade (parents–children), and 18 percent are third grade (uncle/aunt–nephews). Out of the affinal relationships, 65 percent are first grade (married couples), and 21 percent are third grade (brother-/sister-in-law).

What positions are occupied by persons with family ties in the federal judiciary? To answer this question, I focus on the relatives of federal judges (trial and appellate court judges) because only those two positions are obtained by a three-part merit examination (a written exam on general knowledge, deciding a hypothetical case, and an interview). Other workers in the judiciary, including law clerks, actuaries, technicians, and so on are appointed by judges, who have different degrees of discretion to fill positions in their respective courts. I classified the more than fifty positions into six ordered categories depending on the level of meritocratic requirements and how well they are regulated. Level 1 includes positions obtained by a three-part merit examination and regulated with a high degree of detail. Level 2 includes positions obtained by competition but not as highly regulated as those in Level 1. Level 3 includes positions obtained by direct appointment by a collegial organ and regulated with a high degree of detail regarding entry requirements (usually including an online course, one examination, or an essay but without competition). Level 4 includes positions obtained by direct appointment by a single judge or administrator regulated with a high degree of detail regarding the entry requirements (usually including an online course, one examination, or an essay but without competition). Level 5 includes positions obtained by direct appointment by a single judge, and a high degree of detail regarding the entry requirements (but no meritocratic component such as an exam, course, or essay). Finally, Level 6 includes positions obtained by direct appointment by a single judge, and a low degree of regulatory detail regarding entry requirements.

[8] It is important to mention that whether the concentration of family members in the same circuit produces good or bad results is an open question that goes beyond the scope of this chapter. In order to test for the effects of nepotism, it is possible to exploit variation across circuits. There is also variation across types of court, especially if it can be shown, for instance, that civil federal courts work better than administrative federal courts and that these work better than criminal federal courts.

The data reveal that only 4 percent of the judges' relatives occupy positions in Level 1; a mere 0.35 percent in Level 2; 0 percent in Level 3; 37 percent in Level 4 (27 percent law clerks, and 10 percent actuaries who assist law clerks); and 58 percent in Levels 5 and 6 (of which the most common by far is the *oficial administrativo* – 43 percent – with the rest divided across the remaining forty-plus positions with less than 1 percent in each). In other words, 95 percent of judges' relatives occupy positions in Levels 4, 5, or 6. These positions are relatively easy to obtain if the person has the right connections. They are obtained by direct appointment by a single judge or administrator, and they require either mild proof of competence (such as an online course, one examination, or an essay but without competition) or none at all. The most common position occupied by judges' relatives (43 percent) is one called administrative official (*oficial administrativo*), a Level 5 position quite easy to obtain. While it pays a relatively low salary, it is a permanent position (*basificada*), thus giving the appointee a solid foothold within the federal judiciary.

Nepotism?

The percentage of judges in the Mexican Federal Judiciary that have at least one family member working in their own circuit ranges from 15 to 78 percent (the average is 51 percent) and the number of family members per judge ranges from one to eighteen. Is this high or low? The figures presented are most likely conservative estimates. The real number of family connections is undoubtedly higher because of the limitations of the dataset. Measurement issues aside, comparative data help put these numbers in perspective. A survey conducted across executive agencies in the United States in 2015 shows that in the Department of Justice people believe that 15 percent of officials have a family member working in the Department (US Gov. 2016, 27). In the Spanish *Tribunal de Cuentas* an investigation by the newspaper *El País* revealed that 14 percent of their employees have at least one family member working there (Hernández 2014). The number of judges with relatives in the Mexican federal judiciary is therefore considerably higher than those in the United States or Spain, especially if we look at some circuits where close to 80 percent of judges have at least one relative working in the same circuit.

Is there evidence that these family ties have been used inappropriately to get an undue favor or a position that would otherwise not have been obtained? In other words, is there evidence of systematic nepotism in the

Mexican federal judiciary? This is a hard question to answer conclusively because evidence of misuse of family ties is very hard to find. In what follows, I present some indirect and nonsystematic evidence that points towards the likely presence of nepotism in some circuits of the federal judiciary.

Merit Examinations

There are only two positions that are obtained through a three-part merit examination: trial and appellate court judgeships. Between 1995, when the merit examination was first implemented, and 2016, there were seventy-nine calls for applications published in the official newspaper (*Diario Oficial de la Federación*) to fill vacant positions in the federal judiciary (forty-one calls for trial court judgeships, and thirty-eight calls for appellate court judgeships; note that one call may cover several vacancies). Each year during this period there was at least one call, with an average of five calls per year (in 2009 there were nine). I read each one of the calls and found that in 87 percent of the calls, the set of eligible candidates was *restricted* to persons who were already working in the federal judiciary (for instance law clerks, actuaries, or *oficiales administrativos*). Only 13 percent of the calls were open to lawyers from anywhere in the country. Some calls were even more restricted. For instance, only law clerks for Supreme Court justices could participate in the competition. The last open call took place in 2010. Why is this relevant? While it is not evidence of nepotism, remember that judges' family members enter the judiciary in positions that do not require merit examinations. In light of this, the fact that 87 percent of the calls for judgeships are open only to persons already working in the judiciary becomes problematic: restricting the competition implies a bias in favor of judges' family members.

These aggregate numbers are not evidence of nepotism in specific cases, but they are nonetheless suggestive of the presence of the inappropriate use of the family ties to help relatives enter into the judiciary and then become judges. Most family members start working in the judiciary in positions that judges or high-level administrators can distribute fairly easily. Crucially, it is unlikely that rewarding a relative with one of these entry-level, low-paid jobs will sound alarm bells. After all, these are jobs that have little impact on judicial decision-making. In the longer term, however, these decisions can be highly consequential for the overall makeup of the bench, especially if judges or high-level administrators can also arbitrarily restrict who can apply for higher level positions. In other words, accessing one of these low-level positions provides the kind of work experience, connections, and, most importantly, requirements to apply for higher level positions, including those that are obtained only through a merit examination and are open only to those who are already part of the federal judiciary, i.e. trial and appellate court judgeships. As a result of these shenanigans, informal appointment practices at the lower levels indirectly undermine the goals of the reforms designed to improve the appointment process for higher level positions.

Endogamic and Exchange Relationships

It certainly does not look good when a judge appoints their relatives to positions in their own court, even though this is not prima facie evidence of misuse of the family tie. Another questionable practice, but one which can be more easily disguised, is when judges make exchange with other judges to appoint relatives: "I appoint your nephew, you appoint mine." In the database, there is evidence of both types of appointment practices. There is a total of 866 workplaces, the bulk of which (88 percent) are trial or appellate courts; the rest are administrative offices in judicial circuits. First, out of the total 4,731 family relationships in the database, 977 (21 percent) are *endogamic*, i.e. relationships where both relatives work in the same court. In some workplaces there is only one pair of relatives; in others there are more. In fact, there are four or more pairs of relatives in 50 percent of workplaces with endogamic hirings (the maximum number is twelve). Second, out of the total 4,731 family relationships, 991 (21 percent) are *exchanges*, i.e. relationships where two workplaces share family members. Some pairs of workplaces display only one exchange of relatives; others display two. There are at least four exchanges in 50 percent of the pairs of workplaces that share relatives. The maximum number of exchange relationships between any two workplaces is twelve (observed in two cases). Figure 8.2 shows the absolute number of *endogamic* (left panel) and *exchange* relationships (right panel) across judicial circuits.

I ranked judicial circuits based on the number of judges with relatives, the number of judicial officials with relatives, the number of exchange relationships, and the number of endogamic relationships. In order to calculate an overall nepotism ranking, I then added the ranking across categories and inverted the order (this is the total number in Table 8.1). The circuits with the lower overall score are those ranked higher in all categories and thus the ones where it is more likely to find nepotism. The ten circuits at the top of the list (Category 1 in Table 8.1) are the ones where it is more likely that the family ties may have actually been used

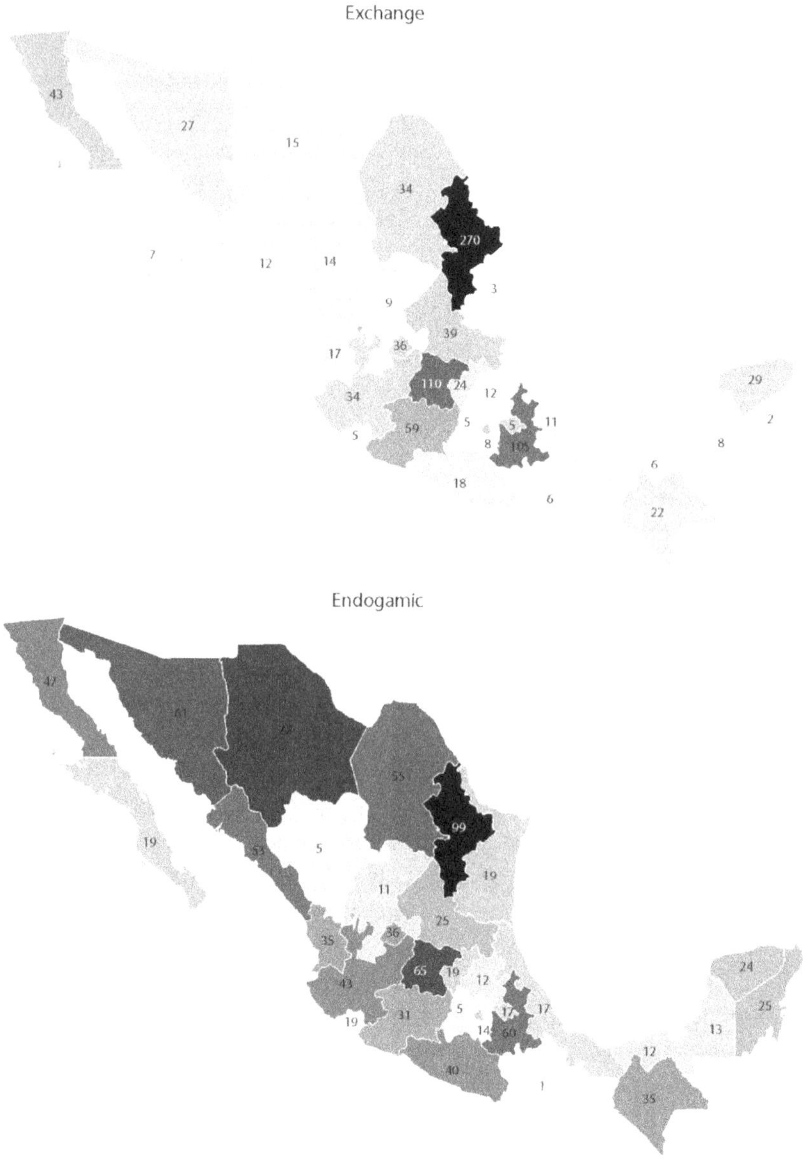

FIGURE 8.2. Endogamic and exchange relationships by judicial circuit

inappropriately and thus where it is more likely that there is nepotism. The ten circuits at the bottom of the list (Category 3 in Table 8.1) are the ones where it is less likely to find nepotism (at least according to available measures).

TABLE 8.1. *Judicial circuits and the likelihood of nepotism*

Category 1		Category 2		Category 3	
Circuit	*Total*	*Circuit*	*Total*	*Circuit*	*Total*
Nuevo León	5	Sinaloa	48	Morelos	81
Puebla	13	Aguascalientes	55	Durango	86
Guanajuato	13	Chiapas	57	BCS	94
Jalisco	23	Guerrero	60	Tlaxcala	95
BC	25	Querétaro	61	Quintana Roo	96
Coahuila	27	Yucatán	67	Colima	102
Michoacán	31	Nayarit	68	Zacatecas	102
Sonora	41	Veracruz	68	Tabasco	104
Chihuahua	43	México	79	Hidalgo	107
SLP	45	Tamaulipas	81	Campeche	107
				Oaxaca	113

One striking fact about the rankings reported in Table 8.1 is that, contrary to conventional wisdom, Category 1, where nepotism is most likely, includes judicial circuits in states that are more economically developed (e.g. Nuevo León, Puebla, Jalisco), and Category 3, where nepotism is most unlikely, includes judicial circuits in states that are relatively poor (e.g. Oaxaca, Campeche, Tabasco). This is puzzling because one would expect that where the private sector is smaller, there are fewer job opportunities outside the state, and therefore more nepotism in public institutions. It is beyond the scope of this chapter to provide and test an alternative account that explains this puzzle. One possibility that is worth exploring, however, is provided by Basabe-Serrano's chapter on Ecuador (Chapter 9). In richer states, litigation around the relatively large amount of commercial activity eventually reaches federal courts. Richer litigants imply the possibility of more and more lucrative bribes and side-benefits, making jobs in the local judiciary quite attractive. Furthermore, these jobs provide know-how and inside knowledge, as well as contacts with law firms and businessmen. These can eventually translate into opportunities for employment in, or joint ventures with, private sector actors.

Bias in Favor of Appellants with Relatives

Finally, decisions made by the judicial council in its daily management of the human resources of the judiciary can be appealed to the Supreme

Court (via an action called administrative review or *revisión administrativa*). Relevant decisions by the judicial council that can be appealed to the Supreme Court include disciplinary proceedings against judges or judicial officials. Similarly, the judicial council organizes and grades the merit examinations that candidates have to pass in order to become a judge. Once an applicant has passed the examination, the judicial council then decides the specific courtroom where the newly minted judge is going to work. This could be anywhere in the country. Both of these decisions (grades and appointment type/location), have a huge impact on someone's judicial career and can be appealed to the Supreme Court. Do family ties affect the way the Supreme Court handles these cases? If Supreme Court decisions are biased in favor of judicial "insiders," this would imply that the judicial council's oversight activities are likely being undermined. Such evidence would, in turn, further support the view that the promises of the 1994 reform are being broken. In particular, it would suggest that contrary to the spirit of the reform, the Supreme Court is still intervening in administrative decisions regarding the judicial career instead of fully concentrating on its jurisdictional role as political arbiter and rights defender.

The appeals data allows us to explore whether judges or judicial officials with family ties have an advantage when it comes to proceedings that can have a significant impact on their career prospects. In other words, are individuals with relatives in the federal judiciary shielded from adverse decisions at the Supreme Court? Figure 8.3 shows data on appeals filed in the Supreme Court between 1995 and 2016 to challenge decisions made by the judicial council. I distinguish between Supreme Court decisions in cases involving judges and officials without relatives in their own circuit, and those involving judges and officials with at least one relative. Each bar shows the average number of favorable decisions for each of the two groups. On average, the Supreme Court is twice as likely to grant the appeal to officials with family members in the judiciary than to officials without family ties. Again, this is not prima facie evidence of misuse of family relationships (nepotism) but is an indication that there might be some instances of such misuse that are worthy of further investigation. If family ties turn out to be mobilized to obtain favorable decisions – for instance, to obtain a transfer to one's most preferred judicial circuit – then the neutrality and efficiency of the judicial council would indeed be compromised by practices of nepotism.

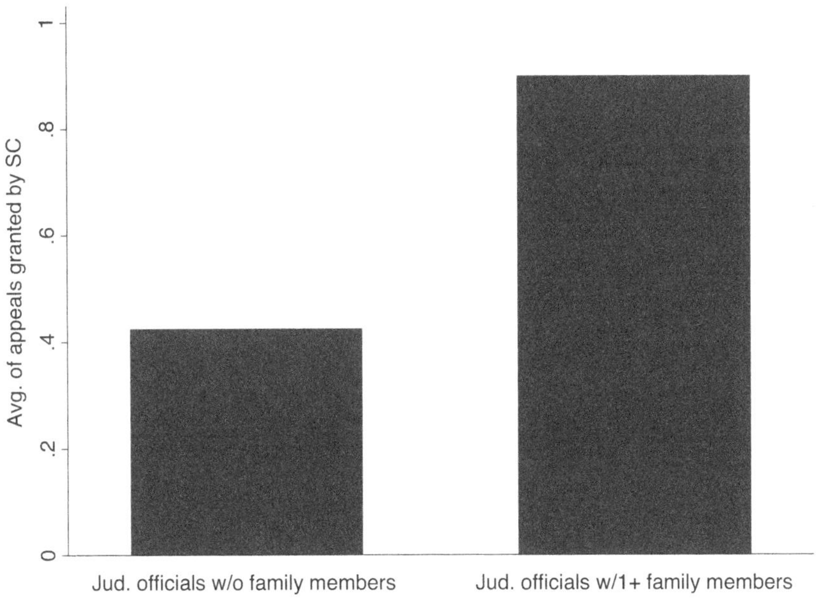

FIGURE 8.3. Supreme Court decisions on administrative review

CONCLUSION: AUTHORITARIAN LEGACIES AND BROKEN PROMISES

The sheer magnitude and pervasiveness of family relationships within the Mexican federal judiciary is astonishing. For those relationships to constitute nepotism we still need to find out whether they are indeed used or have been used inappropriately. In this sense, this chapter did not present specific stories of judicial corruption like those found in the chapters on Ecuador or Peru (Chapters 9 and 3). Whereas this chapter does not provide direct evidence of misuse, I described an institutional and legal ecosystem that effectively eviscerates meritocracy in the judiciary, and presents data that points to those judicial circuits in which misuse is more likely. In particular, the evidence seems to indicate that the promise to build a meritocratic judicial career enshrined in the 1994 judicial reform is yet to be fully met.

First, merit examinations are required for only two positions, district and circuit court judges, which represent only a small fraction of the relevant positions in the judicial career. The other positions are obtained by passing an easy online course, an aptitude test, or by direct appointment by the sitting judge. Moreover, competition for the two positions that do require merit examinations is artificially limited. Specifically, a large proportion (87 percent) of the calls to register for the merit exams are open only for individuals already working in the judiciary. The bulk of judges' relatives in the judiciary occupy precisely the positions that allow individuals to apply for those jobs, and which are allocated with a high degree of discretion by the judges themselves. While low in the ranking, entry-level positions enable judges' family members to amass the necessary experience to enter competitions for judgeships. Second, I presented evidence which suggests that the Supreme Court may actually consider the family connections of judicial personnel when reviewing administrative decisions made by the judicial council against those individuals. These administrative decisions are make or break moments in someone's judicial career, including decisions on whether someone is transferred to a courtroom that is far from their place of residence, or whether disciplinary measures applied by the judicial council stand or fall.

Informal practices that involve personal connections are part of the quotidian life of any organization or institution. However, sometimes these practices are systematic and determine the behavior of large groups of people within the institution or organization, to the point of becoming informal institutions. When these informal institutions run counter to what the formal institutions incentivize, the erosion of the latter is highly likely. Judicial reforms, such as the 1994 reform that created a meritocratic judicial career in Mexico, may be weakened by informal institutions that incentivize members of the judiciary to behave in ways that do not fully align with meritocratic standards. Thus, one way to explain the poor or disappointing performance of formal institutions is to identify the presence of informal institutions and to diagnose whether the incentives they pose on individuals complement or contradict those posed by formal institutions.

I believe that the culture of patronage and patrimonialism developed during the PRI's hegemonic party regime (1930–2000) goes a long way in explaining the persistence of nepotism despite ambitious reform efforts (Ríos-Figueroa and Sánchez-Talanquer 2021). This, in turn, points to the resilience of informal institutions and their power to subvert the promises of well-meaning formal institutional change. Specifically, the Mexican Constitution of 1917 granted the Supreme Court the power to appoint, oversee, and promote federal district and circuit court judges. However, for almost eight decades the organic laws of the judiciary did not detail how the justices should fulfill this duty, or offer any guidelines relative to the administration of judicial careers. To fill this void, Mexican justices tried different methods, and eventually one proposal – taking turns among justices to fill vacancies – took hold. Over time this became an informal institution known as the

"Gentlemen's Pact." As this patronage method of judicial selection consolidated, justices became the heads of networks known colloquially as their "sheep pens" (*corrales*) made up of themselves and their appointees further down the judicial hierarchy. The birth and development of the "Gentlemen's Pact" and of patronage networks was rocky and nonlinear but by the mid-1970s both were clearly established and effectively functioning throughout the federal judiciary (Pozas-Loyo and Ríos-Figueroa 2018).

The Judicial Council and a formally meritocratic judicial career were part of an institutional reform package implemented in 1994, aimed at stopping patronage by effectively taking away from the Supreme Court the power to appoint, oversee, and promote federal judges. In other words, the reform sought to put an end to the Gentlemen's Pact. Institutional changes have power-distributional consequences and thus a change in formal institutions is likely to trigger a response from the losers (Mahoney and Thelen 2010, 8). Moreover, because implementing new institutions is usually plagued with problems of interpretation and enforcement, spaces open up for losers to resist the new institution right after its enactment (Mahoney and Thelen 2010, 13). It is therefore not surprising that the Mexican Supreme Court resisted the creation of the Judicial Council. Supreme Court justices sought to control the selection of the majority of members in the council, and also lobbied to retain the power to review the council's decisions regarding the appointment and promotion of federal judges (Pozas-Loyo and Ríos-Figueroa 2011). This not only undermined the institutional autonomy of the council vis-à-vis the Supreme Court but also the integrity of the newly created system of meritocratic judicial selection. Supreme Court justices, judicial councilors, and also lower court judges thus managed to reproduce patterns of behavior that are similar to those of the patronage networks created under the authoritarian regime.[9]

[9] On December 14, 2020 the Mexican Congress approved a constitutional amendment reforming several aspects of the Mexican federal judiciary. The new judicial reform strengthens the Judicial Council as the organ that administers a fortified judicial career through a Judicial School in charge of the merit examinations to recruit judges and law clerks (as well as a center of continuing education for all members of the judiciary). The reform also directly addresses the problem of nepotism and corruption by, for instance, establishing a mandatory disclosure of the names of all relatives also working in the judiciary and, with this information, empowering the Judicial Council to enforce a policy that limits the number of relatives working in the same circuit. This reform generated controversy because it also further concentrates jurisdictional and administrative power in the Supreme Court and the Judicial Council, while keeping intact the influence of the court over the council, which may continue to threaten internal judicial independence (Ríos-Figueroa 2021).

To be sure, the authoritarian legacy hypothesis requires more systematic evidence of the links between past and present behavior (e.g. Simpser et al. 2019). Importantly, however, nepotism, patronage, and patrimonialism may constitute (in certain contexts and times) informal institutions that, in conjunction with formal institutions, determine the behavior of judges and judicial officials not only in Mexico but also in other Latin American judiciaries. For instance, the effectiveness of judicial councils shows interesting variation: whereas in some countries the council has protected internal judicial independence and fostered the professionalization of the judicial career, in other countries the judicial council has not been able to eradicate undue interferences on judicial selection and decision-making. Argentina may be an example of a well-functioning judicial council, especially during the period from 1998 to 2008 when the selection of lower court judges by the council produced quite good results: the meritocratic part of the judges' selection process (exam and initial evaluation of qualifications) was relatively more important for about 70 percent of the judges finally selected than for the other 30 percent for which political considerations were more important (Zayat 2009, 54–56). Peru would be an example of a dysfunctional council whose members participated in a network of judicial clientelism, "which involved Supreme Court judges, members of the National Judicial Council, provincial judges and prosecutors, and influential lawyers and politicians," working "behind the scenes to place friends and allies in key posts and micro-manage the outcome of court cases" (see Baraybar and Gonzalez-Ocantos, Chapter 13 in this volume). In order to account for this variation across the region, one potential and fruitful avenue would be to assess whether there was any preexisting informal institution affecting judges' selection and performance and, if there was one, to identify its type and evaluate the councils' performance taking this informal institution into account. The fact that supreme courts used to control the administration of the human and material resources of Latin American judiciaries before the creation of the judicial councils strengthens the case for exploring whether patronage, patrimonialism or nepotism consolidated into informal institutions and are actually compromising the effective performance of the councils.

References

Allesina, S. (2011). Measuring Nepotism through Shared Last Names: The Case of Italian Academia. *PLoS ONE* 6(8), 1–6.

Ansolabehere, K. (2010). More Power, More Rights? The Supreme Court and Society in Mexico. In J. Couso, A. Hunneus, and R. Sieder, eds., *Cultures of Legality: Judicialization and Political Activism in Latin America*. New York: Cambridge University Press, 78–111.

Brans, M., and A. Hondeghem (1999) *Bureaucratic Elites in Western Europe*. New York: Oxford University Press.

Carpenter, D. P. (2001). *The Forging of Bureaucratic Autonomy: Reputations, Networks, and Policy Innovation in Administrative Agencies, 1862–1928*. Princeton, NJ: Princeton University Press.

Cruz, C., J. Labonne, and P. Querubín (2017). Politician Family Networks and Electoral Outcomes: Evidence from the Philippines. *American Economic Review* 107(10), 3006–37.

Dal Bó, E., P. Dal Bó, and J. Snyder (2009). Political Dynasties. *Review of Economic Studies* 76(1), 115–42.

Durante, R., G. Labartino, and R. Perotti (2011). Academic Dynasties: Decentralization and Familism in the Italian Academia. National Bureau of Economic Research, Working Paper #17572.

Gagliarducci, S., and M. Manacorda (2016). Politics in the Family: Nepotism and the Hiring Decisions of Italian Firms. Institute for the Study of Labor (IZA), Discussion Paper Series # 9841.

Garoupa, N., and T. Ginsburg (2015). *Judicial Reputation: A Comparative Theory*. Chicago, IL: Chicago University Press.

Grilli, J., and S. Allesina (2017). Last Name Analysis of Mobility, Gender Imbalance, and Nepotism across Academic Systems. *Proceedings of the National Academy of Sciences* 114(29), 7600–05.

Grindle, M. S. (2010). *Jobs for the Boys: Patronage and the State in Comparative Perspective*. Cambridge, MA: Harvard University Press.

Guarnieri, C., and P. Pederzoli (2002). *The Power of Judges: A Comparative Study of Courts and Democracy*. New York: Oxford University Press.

Hammergren, L. (2007). *Envisioning Reform: Improving Judicial Performance in Latin America*. Philadelphia: University of Pennsylvania Press.

Hernández, J. A. (2014). Los lazos de parentesco en el Tribunal de Cuentas alcanzan a 100 empleados. *El País*. https://elpais.com/politica/2014/06/23/actualidad/1403548994_107851.html

Hillmann, K. H. (2001). Nepotism. *Diccionario enciclopédico de sociología*. Madrid: Herder, 636–39.

Jaskiewicz, P., K. Uhlenbruck, D. B. Balkin, and T. Reay (2013). Is Nepotism Good or Bad? Types of Nepotism and Implications for Knowledge Management. *Family Business Review* 26(2), 121–39.

Longo, F. (2004). *Mérito y flexibilidad: La gestión de las personas en las organizaciones del sector público*. Barcelona: Paidós.

Mahoney, J., and K. Thelen (2010). A Theory of Gradual Institutional Change. In J. Mahoney and K. Thelen, eds., *Explaining Institutional Change*. New York: Cambridge University Press, 1–37.

Pardo, M. C. (2005). *El Servicio Civil de Carrera Para un Mejor Desempeño de la Gestión Pública*. Ciudad de México: Cámara de Diputados / Auditoria Superior de la Federación.

Pasquino, G. (2005). Nepotismo. In N. Bobbio, N. Matteucci, and G. Pasquino, eds., *Diccionario de Política*. Buenos Aires: Siglo XXI.

Pozas-Loyo, A., and J. Ríos-Figueroa (2011). The Politics of Amendment Processes: Supreme Court Influence in the Design of Judicial Councils. *Texas Law Review* 89(7), 1807–33.

(2018). Anatomy of an Informal Institution: The "Gentlemen's Pact" and Judicial Selection in Mexico, 1917–1994. *International Political Science Review* 39(5), 647–61.

Ríos-Figueroa, J. (2018). *El Déficit Meritocrático: Nepotismo y Redes Familiares en el Poder Judicial de la Federación*. Ciudad de México: Mexicanos Contra la Corrupción y la Impunidad.

(2021). Mexico's Constitutional Reform: Threats to Judicial Independence from Within?, *ConstitutionNet*. https://constitutionnet.org/news/mexicos-constitutional-reforms-threats-judicial-independence-within

Ríos-Figueroa, J., and M. Sánchez-Talanquer (2021). Persistent Patronage Networks in the Mexican Federal Judiciary, 1917–2017. Unpublished manuscript.

Ríos-Figueroa, J., and L. Soto Tamayo (2021). Nepotism in the Judiciary: Concepts and Measures: Evidence from Mexico. Unpublished manuscript.

Rose-Ackerman, S. (1999). *Corruption and Government: Causes, Consequences, and Reform*. New York: Cambridge University Press.

Simpser, A., D. Slater, and J. Wittenberg (2019). Dead but Not Gone: Contemporary Legacies of Communism, Imperialism, and Authoritarianism. *Annual Review of Political Science* 21, 419–39.

Scoppa, V. (2009). Intergenerational Transfers of Public Sector Jobs: A Shred of Evidence on Nepotism. *Public Choice* 141(1/2), 167–88.

Suárez, A. A. (2014). *La protección de los derechos fundamentales en la novena época de la Suprema Corte de Justicia de la Nación*. México: Porrúa.

Sundell, A. (2014). Nepotism and Meritocracy. The Quality of Government Institute, Working Paper Series #16.

Transparency International (2019). *Anti-corruption Glossary*. Transparency International, www.transparency.org/glossary/term/nepotism

Treisman, D. (2007). What Have We Learned about the Causes of Corruption from Ten Years of Cross-National Empirical Research? *Annual Review of Political Science* (10), 211–44.

US Gov. (2016). *Preventing Nepotism in the Federal Civil Service. A Report to the President by the Congress of the United States*. Washington, DC: US Government.

Yasin, M., N. Tahir, M. Aslam, A. Bakhshd, S. Ullah, M. A. Imran, and M. T. Khaliq (2019). The Impact of Nepotism on Employment Status in Public Sector Institutions: An Evidence from Fresh Graduates of Pakistan. *Journal of Economic Impact* 1(1), 8–12.

Zayat, D. (2009). Between Merit and Politics: The Selection of Federal Judges in Argentina. MA dissertation. Stanford University.

9

Judicial Corruption

The Constitutional Court of Ecuador in Comparative Perspective

Santiago Basabe-Serrano

INTRODUCTION

Corruption is a decisive factor in preventing both the full realization of citizens' rights as well as the emergence of sustainable and vigorous economies.[1] In fact, a simple correlation analysis shows that there are no consolidated democratic regimes in which levels of corruption are worrying. Nor are there cases of economically developed countries that also present serious problems of corruption. It is therefore a public policy priority to understand the conditions that favour the emergence of corrupt practices.

One of the most interesting and understudied forms of corruption is that which unfolds inside judicial institutions. Studying judicial corruption is key not only because its presence weakens the mechanisms that serve to control political power, but also because it inhibits the protection and expansion of citizens' rights. This chapter contributes to one of the themes that guide this edited collection by illuminating the contrast between the high expectations generated by the construction of strong courts via ambitious reform efforts, and the reality of pervasive corruption within those same judicial institutions, especially where political power is concentrated. It does so by looking at the case of Ecuador, where a Constitutional Court with very broad formal powers granted by the 2008 Constitution was at one point in its history the site of corrupt exchanges between judges, lawyers and politicians. Crucially, such exchanges thrived when political power was concentrated: politicians

[1] Translated from Spanish by Ezequiel Gonzalez-Ocantos and Samuel Ritholtz.

demanded favourable decisions on specific issues and in exchange offered protection for judges seeking to engage in corrupt dealings with high-flying private litigants. Together with Rios-Figueroa's chapter on Mexico (Chapter 8), my analysis of the Ecuadorian Constitutional Court thus shows that in the absence of other conditions, the formal empowerment of judges does not automatically yield more transparent or public-spirited justice systems.

Studying corruption in the courts opens up space for a research agenda with repercussions beyond the academy. Unfortunately, progress in this direction is rather limited in the fields of political science and economics, which focus on the formal selective incentives that impact the behaviour of key actors, and therefore tend to ignore both the mechanisms through which judicial corruption occurs and the informal institutions that facilitate it. The same can be said for the bulk of legal scholarship on the topic, which is usually restricted to a prescriptive discussion of the role of the judge and the design of legal structures that more precisely define the actors and interactions that should be considered criminal.

In light of these shortcomings, this chapter contributes to the literature in two ways. First, I propose a definition of judicial corruption that is sufficiently parsimonious but at the same time capable of capturing different facets of the phenomenon in a broad universe of cases. In so doing, I distinguish between micro-, meso- and macro-level judicial corruption, identify the different interactions, negotiations, and payments that characterize the three types, and discuss the variables that best explain the presence of judicial corruption at each level. In the case of high courts, I argue that the concentration of political power fuels judicial corruption because it facilitates the formation of protection pacts between justices and politicians. Second, I rely on unprecedented access to judicial actors in Ecuador to unearth evidence of the informal interactions that constitute judicial corruption. In particular, I take as a case study the scandalous acts of judicial corruption that occurred in the Constitutional Court in the period 2009–2019.

JUDICIAL CORRUPTION: A DEFINITION

In order to study judicial corruption, it is important to first come up with a definition that is broad enough to include the large variety of illegal exchanges while avoiding laxity and platitudes (Hilbink and Ingram, 2019; Power and Taylor, 2011; Morris and Blake, 2010). With this in mind, I propose that judicial corruption involves any act carried out by a judge, prosecutor or judicial official who, by action or omission, alters the impartial direction or content of a decision or ruling in exchange for money or any other type of material or symbolic benefit, delivered by a person or corporate entity with a direct or indirect interest in the judicial process. In other words, judicial corruption exists only when damage to the administration of justice through an altered decision has actually been caused, and such action or omission occurs as a consequence of the delivery of resources of any kind. Both the attempt to alter the normal course of a judicial process and the mere promise of future payments do not in and of themselves constitute judicial corruption.

Two groups of actors engage in the actions necessary for judicial corruption to occur. The first group includes those who belong to the judicial field and whose participation is essential for an act of corruption to occur. In what follows, I discuss the concept as it applies to judges and officials (clerks) of first-level courts, courts of appeal or second instance courts, and supreme courts or courts of cassation. Included in this definition are also constitutional judges and constitutional court officials, as well as those in electoral courts and courts specialized in the resolution of agrarian conflicts or the implementation of transitional justice policies, which in some countries are not strictly speaking part of the judiciary. Included also are prosecutors and their assistants even if in some countries, such as Ecuador, the Public Prosecutor's Office is not part of the Judicial Branch. Independent of the decision-making arena, for the concept of judicial corruption to be applicable to a specific case, the participation of any of these actors is required.[2] Excluded from the concept of judicial corruption are those who, because of their expertise, are called upon to collaborate with their opinion during the proceedings: specifically, experts, judicial police personnel or those who contribute to the resolution of conflicts between individuals or between individuals and the state. Although the malicious handling of a professional expert's report or a police report may be criminal and would be part of a generic concept of corruption, the fact that these actors do not have a permanent link to the judicial branch removes them from the concept. Including these types of acts within the definition of judicial corruption could lead to conceptual stretching (see Gloppen, 2014).

The second group of actors involved in judicial corruption includes all those persons, natural or legal, who in interaction with any of the

[2] With regard to the differences between judicial and prosecutorial corruption, see Idowu and Ibidapo (2014); Ugochukwu (2011); Badel (2008).

aforementioned officials contribute to the exchange. This category includes lawyers, users of the judicial system and, in certain contexts, public officials as well as people who serve as intermediaries or who lobby between interested parties and judicial personnel. The range of actors in this category is therefore much broader and harder to specify. In short, while one of the subjects who interact to give rise to acts of judicial corruption must be part of the structure of the courts, the other can be any person whose intention it is to steer a judicial decision in one direction or another, in line with their interests.

What kinds of transactions between these two groups of actors constitute judicial corruption? I argue that for an act to be considered an instance of judicial corruption, it must consist of two phases. The first phase involves the delivery of money or any kind of benefit – material or symbolic – to the judge, prosecutor or clerk by a person interested in the outcome of a case.[3] In this sense, it is worth noting that the nepotistic networks described in Rios-Figueroa's chapter on Mexico (Chapter 8) are not necessarily instances of judicial corruption, because while highly deleterious for the correct functioning of the system, offers of employment in the judicial branch are not necessarily made conditional on future behaviour. The second phase of the transaction is related to the action or omission on the part of the judge, prosecutor or administrative official, through which the alteration of the judicial decision is materialized, in either its direction or content. Given the diversity of actors, interactions and types of payment covered by the concept of judicial corruption, the judicial decisions I refer to are not only those that end a legal process. They can also be resolutions on relevant aspects of a dispute, such as interlocutory appeals or other procedural resolutions that could have an impact on the course of the judicial process.

This characterization of the transactions that constitute judicial corruption has four important implications. The first is that if there is no delivery of money or goods (material or symbolic), an act does not constitute judicial corruption. For instance, when the judicial decision is altered under pressure from political or other actors, one can speak of a reduction in external judicial independence, but not of an act of judicial corruption. Similarly, the mere expectation of a future payment is not enough for an act to be considered part of the concept of judicial corruption. The second implication relates to the need for the judge, prosecutor

[3] For Gloppen (2014) "delivery" includes any form of inappropriate influence.

or clerk to actually change the direction or content of the judicial decision as a result of the delivery of money or other material or symbolic payments. If the judicial official does not comply, the attempt or act could be considered criminal but not a case of judicial corruption. A third implication relates to the actors involved – specifically those that offer money or other benefits in exchange for a modified court decision. Although this category of actors is broad, it does not include judges, prosecutors or court officials. If the exchange is between people who belong to the bureaucratic structure of the judiciary, it therefore does not fall within the concept of judicial corruption. In most cases where both parties are judicial officials, the exchange takes the form not of monetary benefits but of favours. Such behaviour is related to what is known in the literature as diminished internal judicial independence (Kapiszewski and Taylor, 2008). Finally, the concept does not specify which actor must initiate the exchange. Depending on whether it is the judge/prosecutor/judicial official who proposes the exchange or whether the initiative comes from the service user or some other intermediary, the criminal definition of the act may vary (Ayres, 1997). But while this may be a relevant distinction for criminal law purposes, it is irrelevant when it comes to constructing a concept of judicial corruption that is both parsimonious and empirically useful.

TYPES OF JUDICIAL CORRUPTION

Although the concept of judicial corruption applies to any decision-making space that involves the allocation of material or other resources in exchange for favourable judicial decisions, the modes through which this phenomenon occurs vary depending on the location of the court within the pyramid of the judicial branch. One way to differentiate the ways in which judicial corruption operates is therefore through a classification system based on the judicial hierarchy. We can distinguish between micro-level judicial corruption, which occurs within courts of first instance; meso-level judicial corruption, which corresponds to intermediate or appellate courts; and macro-level judicial corruption, which takes place in high courts, including supreme and constitutional courts or courts of cassation. The differences between the three types of judicial corruption include: (i) the type of actors involved in the interaction between the operators of justice and interested parties, (ii) the complexity of the negotiation, and (iii) the level of payments required to obtain a favourable decision.

In the case of micro-level judicial corruption, the interaction between the parties is direct (i.e., no mediators are usually required) and occurs on a daily basis. Unlike macro-level corruption, in these spaces corruption primarily involves clerks and other support staff, who are usually the ones in charge of altering the direction or content of judicial decisions. Moreover, the negotiation process between the parties tends to be less complex. In general, minor "favours" are requested during the judicial process and for this there are established fees (Mujica, 2011). Since decisions originating in this type of court are susceptible – in the vast majority of cases – to appeal, the possibility of reversing the decision in the next judicial instance reduces the costs incurred by those demanding fraudulent action from the judge, prosecutor or clerk. In other words, there are few guarantees that the investment will "pay off," so prices are lower.

Meso-level judicial corruption occurs in intermediate or appellate courts. In this type of judicial corruption there is greater intermediation between the judge, prosecutor or judicial officials and the interested party. Lawyers play a more relevant role as brokers between their clients and those in charge of altering the direction or content of the judicial decision. In addition, the terms of the negotiation tend to be more complex since in many cases this is the instance in which the final decision is made. This is both a function of the structure of the appeals process, which often limits the kind of decisions that can be litigated further, and also of the costs of pursuing a case beyond this instance. As a consequence of these dynamics, the monetary or symbolic value of the payments required tends to be higher.

Finally, macro-level judicial corruption occurs in higher courts, both those that act as courts of third instance and those that limit their action to resolving extraordinary appeals in cassation. By extension, this category also includes constitutional courts that are autonomous from the structure of the judicial branch and those courts of last instance for specific issues, such as the Bolivian Agri-Environmental Court. Because of the political nature of these courts, which arise from the type of mechanisms used for selecting and appointing judges, the interaction between the parties involved in judicial corruption is usually more sophisticated. The individual efforts of lawyers to gain access to judges or prosecutors are usually not enough; interested parties require more powerful connections, including links to political and economic actors. Sometimes, the links between those who alter the judicial decision and the final beneficiary are large and influential law firms, which combine legal expertise with proximity to the networks of political power and sociability in which judges and prosecutors are directly or indirectly involved. The terms of the negotiation are also more complex than in the other two types of judicial corruption, simply because of the material and jurisprudential implications, both direct and indirect, of altering the course of the judicial process. Moreover, since these are decision-making arenas where the dispute usually ends, the value of the payment required to alter the decision are much higher. As a result, only a very limited pool of interested parties can afford to engage in macro-level judicial corruption.

Having identified the different types of judicial corruption, in the next section I discuss the variables that scholars often cite to explain why the phenomenon is more or less pervasive at different levels of the judiciary. I complement this literature with a discussion of the role of power concentration in fuelling macro-level judicial corruption. I argue that when power is concentrated, judges can rely on politicians for protection, which in turn makes it safer and easier to engage in judicial corruption.

JUDICIAL CORRUPTION AND ITS CAUSES

So far, I have shown that the type of interactions, complexity of the negotiation processes and magnitude of the payments made to encourage judicial corruption vary depending on the location of the courts within the judicial branch. In this section, I argue that the variables which explain the pervasiveness of judicial corruption also depend on the type of court. Although judicial corruption is obviously a multi-causal phenomenon, some variables are likely to play a more important role at different levels of the judicial system. For analytical purposes, I present a taxonomy of possible explanations for judicial corruption, including those that emphasize economic, institutional, social and political factors.

Economic variables feature prominently in accounts of judicial corruption. This body of literature finds that judges with low salaries have a higher probability of being involved in corruption scandals (Badel, 2008; Barrett, 2005; Buscaglia and Dakolias, 1999; Rose-Ackerman, 2006; Wang, 2013). Along similar lines, research finds that the level of openness of the economy as well as GDP per capita also affect the degree of corruption that takes place inside the courts (Rose-Ackerman, 2006). However, there are also empirical findings that challenge this view and show the absence of a causal relationship between salaries and judicial corruption (Yang and Ehrichs, 2007). Similarly, Voigt (2007) reports that in the case of Singapore, an increase in salaries led to an increase in cases of judicial corruption.[4]

From an institutional perspective, one of the main explanations for judicial corruption has to do with the transaction costs – essentially time – generated by the number and complexity of the legal procedures required to obtain a (favourable) judicial decision (Buscaglia, 1997; North, 1993; Pepys, 2007; Rose-Ackerman, 2006; Voigt, 2007). In the face of a complex and cumbersome institutional design, there are greater incentives to seek prompt and efficient solutions through illegitimate payments or other forms of judicial corruption. An implication of this research is that the implementation of a more expeditious procedure should curb judicial corruption. This is precisely what scholars argue happened in Chile after a reform that streamlined the country's criminal procedure (Carbonell, 2008, 2007; Harasic, 2007). Other relevant institutional variables are the presence/absence of judicial organs of control, as well as overlap of jurisdictional and administrative prerogatives in the same organization, usually the Supreme Court (Buscaglia, 1997; Gloppen, 2014; Salazar and Ramos, 2007). Finally, the absence of selective incentives for honest judges, the presence of single-member courts or the permissiveness of judges and prosecutors regarding activities outside the administration of justice such as teaching are other possible institutional explanations for higher levels of judicial corruption (Pepys, 2007; Rose-Ackerman, 2007; Salazar and Ramos, 2007). However, the literature that emphasizes the importance of institutional design is yet to produce robust empirical evidence in support of the various hypotheses, or carefully theorize the causal mechanisms leading to corruption.

As for more sociological factors, a common argument in the literature is that the context in which judges, prosecutors or judicial officials work affects their propensity to engage in acts of judicial corruption. In this sense, scholars have indicated that citizen tolerance for this type of behaviour, also known as a culture of illegality, allows judicial corruption to thrive (Badel, 2008; Gloppen, 2014; Pepys, 2007). Furthermore, the presence of armed groups or other organized illegal actors favours the systematic presence of judicial corruption (Buscaglia and Dakolias, 1999). In both cases, however, it is difficult to establish whether there is indeed a causal link or whether it is in fact a circular relationship.

[4] Additionally, Voigt's (2007) work shows that the interaction of per capita GDP and the country's market openness explains only 46 per cent of judicial corruption in the sixty-three countries he studied.

Finally, among the variables of a political nature, the extent to which political power is concentrated or fragmented is a key factor favouring or discouraging judicial corruption. As the concentration of political power increases, the probability of judicial corruption increases. By contrast, a greater distribution of political power benefits good governance, promotes balance and internal checks in the courts, and thus reduces the occurrence of judicial corruption (Begovic et al., 2004; Montinola and Jackman, 2002; Ríos-Figueroa, 2012). Indeed, research on Latin America suggests that judicial corruption tends to be higher under dictatorship than under democracy (Basabe-Serrano, 2015a; Hammergren, 2007; Melgar Peña, 2007).[5]

As stated at the beginning of this section, the importance of different sets of explanatory factors likely varies across the judicial hierarchy. Following the same logic used to differentiate the mechanisms through which judicial corruption operates, I propose that the factors that affect judicial corruption are also micro-, meso- and macro-level in nature.

Due to the nature of recruitment in courts of first and second instance, these judicial bodies tend to be infused with a strong bureaucratic mindset, much like public employees in the executive branch. The variables that likely best explain judicial corruption are therefore those related to the incentives generated by often rigid and formalistic bureaucratic structures (Baum, 1997). For example, a fixed and uncompetitive salary could be one of the reasons why these officials engage in judicial corruption. At the institutional level, the weak sanctioning capacity of the administrative bodies designed to control the proper functioning of the judiciary, or the excessive burden of the highly formalistic procedures that must be followed prior to reaching a decision, could also be variables that favour the presence of judicial corruption in these courts (Basabe-Serrano, 2013).

In the case of supreme/constitutional courts and high-level prosecutors, the dynamics, interactions and actors involved in the recruitment process are usually political in nature. The variables that best explain judicial corruption are therefore also most likely related to political factors. In fact, while salaries or the complexity of existing procedures could determine the occurrence of judicial corruption at this level, they are not as decisive as in the case of lower courts. Supreme or constitutional judges are often among the best paid in the public administration, and have

[5] However, in an analysis of sixty-three countries, Voigt (2007) does not find a statistically significant relationship between judicial corruption and the fragmentation of political power, measured by the number of players with institutional veto power.

access to a broad range of perks and benefits which should in principle discourage corruption. With this in mind, I contend that judicial corruption in the highest courts is primarily related to the degree to which political power among the actors who participate in selecting and appointing judges and prosecutors is concentrated or fragmented. As the concentration of political power increases, the likelihood of judicial corruption in the highest courts of justice increases. Although acts of judicial corruption exist under conditions of power concentration and fragmentation, in cases of greater political power concentration the phenomenon is more likely to become endemic.

The link I propose between the concentration of political power and judicial corruption in high courts is as follows. Once a political actor has succeeded in accumulating a good deal of power, one of their first objectives is usually to try to control or influence supreme and/or constitutional courts. Their privileged position makes it easier for them not only to co-opt the arenas and actors that participate in the selection and appointment of judges and prosecutors but also to appoint judicial officials who are personally or ideologically close to their preferences. As a result, a relationship is established in which, out of fear, gratitude or political loyalty, judges and prosecutors respond favourably to requests by political actors in cases where their interests are at stake. Note that, given this level of acquiescence, there is usually no need for the political actor to provide additional economic incentives. This implies that while such dynamics trump judicial independence, they do not necessarily fall within my definition of judicial corruption. But the fact that judges adapt to the preferences of politicians buys them the ability to engage in judicial corruption vis-à-vis other actors without fear of punishment. This is because politicians compensate judicial docility by affording judges ample freedom to rule as they see fit in cases in which the political patron does not have specific interests. It is in these cases that judges practise judicial corruption, especially when disputes involve rich plaintiffs who can afford to pay handsome bribes. In short, I propose that the concentration of political power not only affects judicial independence, as others have noted in the literature on judicial politics, but also fosters an environment of impunity via the creation of tacit protection pacts in which judges and prosecutors are given carte blanche for the perpetration of corrupt acts.

Put differently, I argue that it is not the diminished independence of supreme and/or constitutional judges per se that facilitates acts of judicial corruption but rather the impunity that results from the concentration of political power. In analytical terms, what I propose is that, in scenarios of greater concentration of political power, supreme/constitutional judges are appointed by those who hold political power. In exchange for these positions, judges resolve cases in ways that favour those in power. Finally, and most importantly, this submissive attitude is rewarded by allowing, tolerating and overlooking acts of judicial corruption that occur in cases in which politicians do not have a direct interest. And, of course, by protecting the judges or prosecutors should the press or the opposition cry foul.

In Latin America there are several examples that illustrate the connection between the concentration of political power and judicial corruption. Some of the most striking include the Supreme Court of Paraguay after the return of democratic rule, as well as courts in Bolivia under Morales and Venezuela under Chavez and Maduro (Basabe-Serrano, 2015a; Gloppen, 2014; Sánchez-Uribarri, 2011). In the remainder of this chapter, I present yet another example in which the concentration of political power allowed macro-level judicial corruption to thrive: the case of the Constitutional Court of Ecuador under President Rafael Correa.

ECUADOR'S CONSTITUTIONAL COURT: AN EMBLEMATIC CASE OF JUDICIAL CORRUPTION

The Constitutional Court of Ecuador (CCE) is a good case study to illustrate my argument about the protection pacts that emerge when political power is concentrated, and their impact on macro-level judicial corruption. I rely on twenty in-depth interviews I conducted between February and July 2019 with constitutional lawyers and former officials of the CCE. I have at my disposal more than thirty hours of testimonies of people who were privy to the most egregious acts of judicial corruption that occurred during the administration of President Correa. Because of the nature of judicial corruption, interview data of this kind is extremely hard to collect. At the same time, it is usually only with this data that researchers can trace the processes that give rise to, and the transactions that characterize, judicial corruption. In fact, few studies of judicial corruption are based on such direct and reliable empirical evidence as that presented here. In order to elicit candid accounts of judicial corruption, I reassured my informants that their testimonies would remain strictly anonymous. In addition to the interviews, I also use information collected from the CCE's own archives, media reports and other relevant public documents related to the assets and professional and academic backgrounds of the judges of the CCE.

I concentrate on the period between 2008, when the CCE was created, and the dismissal of its penultimate cohort in August 2018. The CCE, which enjoys administrative and financial autonomy and is not part of the judiciary, consists of nine judges, elected for nine years and with partial renewals of three judges every three years. Nominations are made by the executive branch, the legislative branch and transparency and social control institutions.[6] Appointments, in turn, are the prerogative of a commission composed of two representatives from each of the aforementioned branches of government. In short, despite the fact that the constitution mandates a competitive public recruitment process with civil society oversight, those who nominate candidates are also those who choose the constitutional judges.

During the period analysed here, nineteen tenured judges distributed in three cohorts passed through the CCE. The first cohort was made up of judges who had been appointed to the Constitutional Court established under the 1998 Constitution, and who called themselves the "CCE for the transitional period" once the 2008 Constitution came into force. On 6 November 2012, the second cohort took office with six new judges and three who remained from the transitional court (Ruth Seni, Manuel Viteri and Patricio Pazmiño). In 2015 the first partial renewal took place (María del Carmen Maldonado, Antonio Gagliardo and Marcelo Jaramillo left the court), resulting in a third cohort.

In terms of accountability mechanisms, the 2008 Constitution included a number of provisions that make any kind of political and even judicial control over the CCE virtually impossible. Indeed, members of the CCE cannot be subject to impeachment or removal proceedings by the appointing authority. Criminal actions against CCE judges must be brought before the plenary of the National Court, and a vote of two-thirds of its twenty-one judges is required to declare CEE judges criminally liable. It is worth noting that this super-majority is required only in the case of CCE judges. By contrast, other public officials, such as the president or national legislators, are tried by a specialized criminal chamber of the National Court composed of only three judges. In other words, while the criminal responsibility of the executive or the legislature can be declared

[6] The 2008 Constitution created the Función de Transparencia y Control Social as a separate branch of government. It consists of the Council of Citizen Participation and Social Control, the Comptroller's Office, the Ombudsman's Office and the superintendencies for banks, companies, popular and solidarity economy, telecommunications, market power control, territorial ordering and the use and management of the land. Until recently, there was also a superintendency for information and communication.

with two votes (in the case of a split decision), for members of the CCE a minimum of fourteen votes is required. Both the impossibility of political prosecution and the need for a super-majority vote in the national court to declare the criminal responsibility of a member of the CCE were ratified through an interpretative resolution of Article 431 of the constitution in 2011.[7] Additionally, in the same resolution the CCE established that its members cannot be subject to pre-trial or trial actions in criminal matters due to the content of their opinions, resolutions or rulings. Finally, Ecuador's constitutional design establishes that in order for the removal of judges from the CCE to proceed (in the cases and circumstances established by law), a vote of two-thirds of its members is also required. In other words, in order for a CCE judge to be removed from the court, a vote of six members from that very organization is required.

If the absence of control mechanisms is one of the key institutional features of the CCE, another is its broad powers to prosecute and defend citizen rights and to limit and control political actors. In fact, along with its Colombian counterpart, the CCE is considered one of the most powerful in the region (Sotomayor, 2019; Brinks and Blass, 2018). The CCE not only has the capacity for *erga omnes* judicial review, but also the power to control states of emergency, sanction non-compliance of decisions, declare administrative acts unconstitutional and overturn decisions of courts of last resort for violations of constitutional rights, among others. In addition, the CCE may issue binding judgments with respect to writs of *habeas corpus* and *habeas data*.[8]

The broad powers of the CCE make it an attractive space for manipulation and control by political actors. In certain scenarios, when political power is distributed among several actors, one way this is done is through the famous "quota" system. Negotiations between political actors lead to a sort of tacit balance within the courts that favours mutual checks and balances between judges not only in terms of the direction of rulings but also in terms of corruption. By contrast, when a single actor enjoys sufficient political power to capture the CCE, the political dependence of judges increases, as do the spaces for corruption during judges' interactions with other users of the service.

[7] Constitutional Court Resolution No. 3, published in Official Registry No. 372 of 27 January 2011

[8] Article 436 of the Constitution of Ecuador describes the powers of the Constitutional Court.

In the case of Ecuador, the arrival of Rafael Correa to power in 2007 brought with it a new constitution in 2008 that dramatically increased the powers of the presidency. Additionally, in the 2009 presidential elections Correa won in the first round and his political party, Alianza País, obtained 47.58 per cent of the seats in the legislature. In the 2013 elections, Correa won again without the need for a run-off, and the size of his electoral base grew to 72.99 per cent. Such circumstances added to the popular support for the head of state, which fluctuated between 50 and 60 per cent, and an unprecedented economic bonanza anchored in high international oil prices laid the foundations for what could be called a case of imperial presidentialism (Basabe-Serrano, 2017).

In addition, the accumulation of political power in the hands of a single political actor inexorably led to the appointment of docile loyalists to the CCE. These were usually justices with no academic or professional training of note, and who, in the vast majority of cases, had previously held positions in the executive branch. A review of the judges' résumés reveals that prior to their arrival in the CCE, none of them had been lawyers with experience in constitutional matters, professors in areas related to that subject or part of the judicial branch. Although, in the previous Constitutional Court, judges with high professional and academic profiles were not in the majority, a group of them did meet minimum requirements that allowed them to guarantee high-quality decisions and high levels of independence.

The lack of professional or academic credentials not only made these judges grateful for having accessed positions of authority they would never have reached following a meticulous selection process, but also triggered absolute submission to the wishes of the executive in politically salient cases. In this respect, the legal secretary of the president, Alexis Mera, used to dictate the weekly schedule of decisions of the CCE, thus making sure the docket was aligned with the president's priorities or with the directives that every Saturday emerged from the so-called citizen contacts that President Correa organized around the country. As one of the interviewees points out:

> I can attest that Alexis Mera used to visit the Constitutional Court every week. He had a specific hour and a specific day. In fact, if you went at that time, that day, you would find Alexis Mera entering the office of Patricio Pazmiño, the president of the CCE. He had his list of cases. He would say "this case [should be decided] like this, this case like that". [Alexis Mera] didn't sign anything when he entered the building, unlike me and others who had to sign in. If you ask for the ledger, you're going to find everyone's signature but not his. He would go up with his security guards.

One former official also mentioned the direct interference of the national government in the decisions of the CCE:

> Alexis Mera used to go to the CCE. At least in the beginning he went practically every week. He would come in and say: "This case, this case, I want it like this." He would go straight to the president of the CCE and then to the office of the five judges who made up the majority. He would come in and say: "You have to solve such cases in this way." They said they were cases that came directly from the orders of Rafael Correa.

The cases in the hands of the CCE that were relevant for the government were thus decided by President Correa and communicated to the judges by Alexis Mera. In this type of exchange, there was no provision of resources by the executive. Instead, a decision in favour of the government was expected as a sign of subordination or gratitude to the person who had facilitated access to the court. One can therefore speak of interference in the independence of judges to decide free from pressure but not of judicial corruption. However, the submission of the CCE in cases in which the executive had an interest implicitly carried with it the guarantee of impunity when the judges decided to exchange favourable rulings for economic resources in other cases. As a result, in a context where the institutional design practically eliminated all forms of judicial and political control over the judges, and where the president's political power was almost absolute, judicial corruption was rampant.

Of the various prerogatives of the CCE, the one used frequently for the perpetration of acts of judicial corruption was the so-called extraordinary protection action (EPA). Through this prerogative, the CCE can annul or modify a ruling or final order in which the rights enshrined in the constitution have been violated by action or omission. The rules stipulating the conditions under which EPAs may be invoked are vague, minimally mandating that all prior ordinary and extraordinary remedies must be exhausted. While there are some additional criteria in the law, in general terms, accessing the CCE through an EPA is relatively straightforward. Since even cassation judgments issued by the chambers of the National Court can be overturned through an EPA, trial lawyers often refer to this writ as a "fourth instance". In fact, of the total number of writs presented to the CCE during the period under analysis, 75 per cent were EPAs.

In institutional terms, once an EPA is proposed, the first filter is the CCE's admissions chamber. There, three judges decide on the legal feasibility of the proposed action. If the application is accepted, the case is randomly assigned to one of the nine judges, who will be responsible for preparing a draft ruling that will finally be heard by the plenary of the CCE for a final decision. If, by contrast, the admissions chamber rejects the EPA, the possibility of appearing before the CCE ends. Consequently, the decision of the admissions chamber is key, and therein lies the first space for judicial corruption. In fact, it was in the admissions chamber that the first exchange of money would take place for a ruling that accepted or denied the EPA. On this subject, one of the informants explains:

> The famous admissions chamber became a kind of marketplace where everyone first negotiated whether to admit or not to admit cases, according to convenience. For example, if you have a tax issue and the amount you have to pay to the Internal Revenue Service is, say, \$5 million, then in order to get that case admitted they would first make sure that you paid for the whole process; that is, up to the judgment. But the real proof of love was the admission. If you are saving \$5 million in taxes then you have to pay \$1 million or 20 per cent. So, to admit the case you had to give \$200,000 first. By depositing that amount you were guaranteeing admission and also special treatment in the rest of the process. What was the special treatment? The special treatment was that the ruling could be drafted jointly with your lawyers.

Because of the hierarchy of the CCE, the negotiations were not carried out directly with the judges but through diverse and sophisticated channels of intermediation and negotiation. These channels included the judges' own advisors as well as legal firms created by former CCE officials. In general, the intermediaries took the initiative to contact litigants by telephone in order to offer their services both to obtain admission and for the subsequent stages until the final decision was reached. In this regard, another interviewee made the following point:

> The interaction or overlap [between litigants and CCE officials] is so important that some appointments were made from the inside out and then from the outside in. If one year you worked as a clerk in the court, the next year you were a legal assistant in a law firm. The revolving door was always like this [...] Then the judge's advisor could tell you to go to this law firm [...] "we are on good terms with that law firm" [...] Then you had to leave your lawyer and you had to change law firms [...] Judge XXXX, played a very important role because he had his own law firm, although all the charges were made in the name of his son.

When the interests at stake were more numerous, large law firms, especially in Quito and Guayaquil, were in charge of leading the negotiation between the judges of the CCE and the users of the service. In general, these firms not only had among their staff prestigious professionals, with expertise in constitutional matters, but also possessed privileged information about movements within the CCE. And officials of the CCE were at their service. A former official of the CCE explained:

> Large law firms have the following mechanism. They pay a person from the general secretariat every month to inform them about the process. They don't even to talk with the judge. That person has an extra salary because it is one thing to be the secretary general and have your salary and another thing to have another salary in addition to that. I knew of the case of a company that wanted to hire me to help them get information. They told me that a person from the general secretariat was charging them \$3,000 a month and that was too much. They were willing to pay me \$1,000 a month because they knew I had connections in there [at the CCE] and could get the same information at a lower cost. How about that?

While one way to obtain a decision from the CCE was to agree on the economic conditions for the whole process to be favourable, another option was to establish partial agreements: an amount to obtain admission; another to obtain a favourable draft sentence; and a third payment for the final decision by the plenary of the CCE. In this case, the total values could be higher since the intermediaries to the admission chamber were not necessarily those representing the presiding judge. This form of negotiation implied an additional agreement with the general secretariat, since that body, together with the presidency of the CCE, controlled which cases reached the agenda of the plenary. On the gatekeeping role of the general secretariat and the presidency of the CCE, one of the interviewees stated:

> The second filter was whether [the case] got to the court's daily schedule. This was totally controlled by the presidency as the rules of procedure indicated that the schedule of cases had to be drawn up by the president of the court, in theory, in chronological order. But the president of the court used to say: "This is a political case, we are not going to touch it. This is a private case, let's deal with it." How the schedule of cases was decided is a mystery because it was done by the president with the secretary who came with his checklist. The list included information on whether or not the disbursements had actually been made for each case.

Corruption in the CCE gradually became common practice.[9] Among seasoned lawyers it was common knowledge that corruption was especially rampant when it came to EPAs. For example, they knew that if money was not delivered, not only was a favourable decision unlikely, but the case could be shelved, either waiting for it to be placed on the agenda of the CC or for a ruling from the admissions chamber on whether or not

[9] Some interviewees pointed out that there were two or three judges of the "transitional court" who were not part of these acts of corruption. None of them was reappointed.

the action was admissible. The naturalization of corruption in the CCE reached such a point that if "help" was not accepted when a court intermediary communicated by telephone with a lawyer or client, the response was to automatically shelve the case. A lawyer explains:

> This is *vox populi*, everyone knows that to get a case admitted you used to have to pay. It only happened to me once. I had a very important case. Actually, I still have the case because since I didn't comply, it was never processed. I received a call from a person who identified himself with a name and surname that I did not know and who said he was extremely close to the president of the court. He told me: "I was in the judge's office on this case and I think you are right. I would like to be able to help you get it processed." So I asked him what the conditions were. He told me: "We would have to meet at the Marriot Hotel, I would tell you the room where we would meet. You'd have to go to your clients and obviously we'd discuss the terms there." So I said: "I don't do this kind of thing, but what I do in these cases is to communicate the offer to the clients so that if they wish they can get in touch with you." I talked to the clients, they refused, and I told the intermediary. He told me: "What a shame, then your case will not be processed." In fact, it's a case that hasn't been assigned to a judge in four or five years.

The large sums of money received by the judges of the CCE as a result of corruption not only bought them a standard of living inconsistent with their salaries, but also led to types of completely shameless behaviour, even in front of other CEE officials. Levels of impunity were such that it had an impact on every aspect of the life of the court. This impunity in turn guaranteed that they would be submissive to the government, which held almost absolute political power. One interviewee, who still has links to the CCE, explained:

> They were paid in cash. And you would see Judge XXXX with wads of cash, but I'm not talking about the judge having a hundred dollars in his pocket. No: you'd see him pulling a lot of bills out of the breast pocket of the suit. In every pocket he had wads of bills.

Another former CCE official recounted the following event:

> One day I was talking to the judge I was working with and the view from his office was towards El Arbolito Park. Suddenly, I tell the judge, "Look at that man." He was one of the secretaries of the court. This was about eleven o'clock in the morning. Together with him were two girls who worked here and they were carrying some bags. Then we see him reach into one of the bags and pull out a wad of bills. All the bags were full of bills and with those bills they went into the CCE.

Among the many cases of judicial corruption in the CCE that were subsequently revealed, one of the most emblematic involved a suit against the Cervecería Nacional (National Brewery) by a group of employees who claimed not to have received payment of their share of the profits for sixteen years. After several years of litigation, and while the case was being heard in the ordinary justice system in the city of Guayaquil, the CCE assumed jurisdiction over the legal process. This prerogative is similar to the *per saltum* in Argentina, and had never been used before in Ecuador. Given that more than $90 million in compensation for workers was at stake, observers became suspicious about this move. Later on, the plenary ruled to deny workers their right to compensation. But before the parties to the proceedings were notified of the ruling, Congressman Galo Lara claimed that one of the lawyers of the National Brewery had received $1 million.[10] What raised suspicions was that the lawyer had acquired his professional title only a few months before this happened. It was strange that a company of that size would not hire a more experienced professional.[11] Furthermore, the lawyer had been an advisor to the president of the CCE, Patricio Pazmiño, and was the brother of the secretary general of the court. Rumours therefore began to spread in various media outlets that the million dollars was intended as payment for a ruling in favour of the company.

The scandal that ensued was so great that immediately after the complaint was circulated, the plenary of the CEE decided to leave the ruling "without effect".[12] The implausible argument offered by the court was that, since the decision had not been formally notified to the plaintiffs, it had no legal value. Also in an effort to address the public outcry, the vice-president of the CCE immediately requested an investigation from the attorney general, while constitutional judge Alfonso Luz Yúnes publicly declared that he "requested that the plenary of the CCE proceed with the dismissal of the secretary of the court, Arturo Larrea Jijón", who was implicated in the scandal.[13] In spite of the societal pressure to investigate those involved, the attorney general, who had previously been a minister and the personal lawyer of President Correa, decided after a few months to close the investigation into the president of the CCE, citing lack of evidence.[14] Although the secretary general of the CCE did leave his post, the legal mechanism used was removal, which, unlike dismissal, allows

[10] "Cheque de Cervecería causa acusación a la Corte", *El Universo*, 5 February 2011.

[11] " Los Larrea tuvieron nexos con A. País", *El Comercio*, 20 February 2011.

[12] "La Corte deja sin efecto fallo de la Cervecería", *El Comercio*, 12 February 2011.

[13] "Caso de Cervecería regresó a los juzgados", *La Hora*, 12 February 2011 and " Corte Constitucional remueve a su secretario y asoma otro escándalo", *La Hora*, 4 March 2011.

[14] "Él no se mete con los alfiles del Presidente", *El Comercio*, 25 February 2012.

him to hold public office in the future.[15] The protection pact was on full display. The events following the scandal made it clear that the CCE relied on its political patrons for impunity.[16]

One of the first decisions of President Moreno, who succeeded Correa in May 2017 and quickly broke ranks with his predecessor, was to launch an ambitious institutional reform agenda.[17] This put an end to the protection pact. Moreno called a popular consultation, which initiated a process to review various bodies, among them the CCE. Specifically, a Transitional Citizen Participation Council proposed a thorough review of both the professional skills of CCE judges and their assets. In this context, corruption scandals were such a particular focus of attention that the Comptroller General's Office indicated there was mounting evidence against several CCE judges. One of my sources described the turmoil inside the court caused by the investigation:

> When the Transitional Participation Council came in at the end of 2018 to review the assets of the judges, they [members of the court] got scared and started bringing money to the office and ask for it to be deposited $5,000 at a time in different accounts. One of the court drivers told us this because it fell to him every day to go to the bank to make a deposit. He told us that the bills were as if they had just left the bank, and still had the wrapping with the delivery date. They were bills from 2013, 2015, 2016.

Once the members of Correa's CCE were dismissed, a merit-based competition was launched, led by a commission of experts. As a result of this recruitment process, on 5 February 2019 the National Assembly appointed nine new constitutional judges. The CCE now includes prestigious university professors and some practising lawyers. The new president, Hernán Salgado Pesántes, former president of the Inter-American Court of Human Rights and one of the most renowned jurists in the

[15] "Él no se mete con los alfiles del Presidente", *El Comercio*, 25 February 2012.

[16] The Cervecería Nacional case subsequently returned to the court of origin. A few months later, on 4 March 2011, the Provincial Court of Guayaquil ratified the decision of the first instance court, which sided with the workers. Cervecería Nacional reacted by requesting an EPA on 5 April of the same year. Unfortunately for the company, the case was delayed and could not be decided before the infamous "brewery court" was dismissed in August 2018 (see later). In fact, it was not until 2019 that a new CCE heard the case and issued a ruling favourable to the interests of the workers.

[17] A few months after his inauguration, President Moreno distanced himself from his predecessor. For example, Moreno turned against Vice-President Jorge Glas when the latter was criminally prosecuted and subsequently sentenced to six years in prison. Jorge Glas had previously served as vice-president under Correa and was a key player in preventing corruption scandals from escalating or leading to sanctions.

country, has initiated a restructuring plan that so far has managed to speed up the proceedings and restore public confidence in the CCE.

In sum, the case of Ecuador's CCE shows that in contexts where political power is concentrated, not only does judicial independence suffer, but also the spaces for judicial corruption tend to increase. The interview data presented here shows that as long as the government was satisfied with the resolution of politically salient cases, politicians were ready to provide protection for judges willing to pursue corruption in other cases involving wealthy private actors. Judicial corruption in the highest instance of constitutional justice in the country thus reached historic levels, with most decisions requiring the prior exchange of bribes.

CONCLUSION

This chapter proposed a definition of judicial corruption that is both parsimonious and heuristically productive. An act can be considered an instance of judicial corruption if there is a delivery of material or symbolic resources from a third party to a judge, prosecutor or judicial official in exchange for altering the direction or content of a judicial decision. This clearly defines the subjects that must be part of the interaction, the objective of the exchange and the actions necessary for judicial corruption to occur. Importantly, in an effort to distinguish judicial corruption from external and internal judicial independence, the definition excludes the conduct of judges, prosecutors or judicial officials that results from pressure exerted by political actors and judicial leaders. Although in all of these instances we observe changes to the natural course of the decision-making process, there are fundamental differences in the reasons that justice operators have for adapting their decisions to cater to the preferences of others. Finally, I argued that judicial corruption likely operates differently depending on the type of court under analysis. The actors and mechanisms of interaction, the complexity of the negotiations and the amount of resources that service users transfer in exchange for a decision vary depending on whether it is a court of first, second or third instance. For this reason, I distinguished between micro-, meso- and macro-level judicial corruption. The hierarchy of the court under study also determines which factors best explain the incidence of judicial corruption.

In this chapter I focused on the kind of judicial corruption that affects high courts, and pointed out that the key variable explaining whether corruption is merely episodic or endemic is the extent to which political power is concentrated or fragmented. When power is concentrated in a few hands, this not only limits judicial independence but also leads to an environment of impunity in which judges and prosecutors have the necessary protection for committing acts of judicial corruption. The Constitutional Court of Ecuador served as a case study to probe the dynamics of these protection pacts. Based on unique interview data, I presented an account of a court in which the exchange of money for decisions was practically the only way for users to access a favourable outcome.

The case of the CCE under Correa is striking because its corrupt behaviour differs markedly from that of prior constitutional courts in Ecuador. As I have shown elsewhere, the court created in 1998 was characterized by judges who guarded their professional prestige, and behaved with a high degree of independence and transparency in order to strengthen their legal careers after they left the court (Basabe-Serrano, 2011, 2012). These career or professional incentives, coupled with a high level of judicial instability and power dispersion, meant that the judges were less likely to engage in systematic corruption or benefit from protection pacts with politicians. By contrast, the judges of the "brewery court", as the corrupt CCE came to be known, were practically without exception lawyers with no expertise or credentials. They therefore had no reason to expect to embark on successful academic or professional careers after leaving the bench (in fact, none of them did). In this context, the cost of being known as corrupt was low in comparison to what they could gain economically from exorbitant bribes.

The discussion in this chapter sets the stage for a research agenda in the field of judicial corruption. On the one hand, it is essential to increase the number of comparative case studies because we still know perilously little about how judicial corruption works. Indeed, studies of the ways in which judicial corruption operates are still few and far between, and tend to focus on high courts (Llanos et al., 2016). In addition, research on the factors that encourage or discourage acts of judicial corruption is still in its infancy. Given that judicial corruption is not as pervasive in industrialized democracies, scholars should probably focus on developing democracies and authoritarian regimes to further develop and test theoretical propositions. Latin America offers excellent opportunities in this regard. While it is true that the harmful effects of judicial corruption on the consolidation of political institutions, economic growth, poverty reduction and levels of foreign investment are known (Gupta et al., 2002; Robertson and Watson, 2002; Selligson, 2002), studies in which corruption is the dependent variable are less common in the region. If the factors that affect the presence of judicial corruption or the dynamics that characterize these illegal exchanges are not well understood, it will be difficult to design public policies to curb the incidence of corruption in the courts. Perhaps this explains why the various waves of judicial reform in Latin America, at least in the area of corruption, have been unsuccessful and have not generated major positive results (Basabe-Serrano, 2015b; Hammergren, 2007; Inclán and Inclán, 2005; Oyanedel, 2019; Pásara, 2019; Sieder, 2003). Finally, we should also look into the ways in which judicial corruption restricts the capacity of the courts to control political power and also how its presence affects the protection and expansion of citizen rights. In this sense, while this chapter describes the presence of serious judicial pathologies, it has less to say about exactly how such "broken promises" undermine democracy.

References

Ayres, I. (1997). The Twin Faces of Judicial Corruption: Extortion and Bribery. *Denver University Law Review* 74 (4), 1231–53.

Badel, M. (2008). *La corrupción judicial en Colombia: Una aproximación al mapa de riesgos*. Bogotá: Corporación Transparencia por Colombia and Corporación excelencia en la justicia.

Barrett, K. (2005). Corrupted Courts: A Cross-National Perceptual Analysis of Judicial Corruption. Master's dissertation. Georgia State University.

Basabe-Serrano, S. (2011). *Jueces sin toga: políticas judiciales y toma de decisiones en el Tribunal Constitucional del Ecuador, 1999–2007*. Quito: FLACSO Ecuador.

(2012). Judges without Robes and Judicial Voting in Context of Institutional Instability: The Case of Ecuador's Constitutional Court. *Journal of Latin American Studies* 44 (1), 127–66.

(2013). Explicando la corrupción judicial en cortes intermedias e inferiores de Chile, Perú y Ecuador. *Perfiles Latinoamericanos* 42, 79–108.

(2015a). Informal Institutions and Judicial Independence in Paraguay, 1954–2011. *Law & Policy* 37 (4), 350–78.

(2015b). La reforma judicial en América Latina: avances, retrocesos y agenda de investigación. In Ministerio de la Presidencia de la República und Fundación PIEB, eds., *Reforma judicial en América Latina y el desafío de la revolución de la justicia en Bolivia*. La Paz: Ministerio de la Presidencia de Bolivia.

(2017). Las distintas caras del presidencialismo: debate conceptual y evidencia empírica en dieciocho países de América Latina. *Revista Española de Investigaciones Sociológicas* 157, 3–22.

Baum, L. (1997). *The Puzzle of Judicial Behavior*. Ann Arbor: University of Michigan Press.

Begovic, B., Mijatovic, B. & Hiber, D. (2004). *Corruption in Judiciary*. Belgrade: Center for Liberal Democratic Studies.

Brinks, D. & Blass, A. (2018). *The DNA of Constitutional Justice in Latin America: Politics, Governance and Judicial Design*. Cambridge: Cambridge University Press.

Buscaglia, E. (1997). Corruption and Judicial Reform in Latin America. *Policy Studies Journal* 17 (4), 273–95.

Buscaglia, E. & Dakolias, M. (1999). An Analysis of the Causes of the Corruption in the Judiciary. *World Bank*. Working Paper No. 20178.

Carbonell, M. (2007). Judicial Corruption and Impunity in Mexico. In Transparency International, ed., *Global Corruption Report 2007*. Cambridge: Cambridge University Press.

(2008). *El régimen constitucional de la transparencia*. Mexico City: Universidad Nacional Autónoma de México.

Gloppen, S. (2014). Courts, Corruption and Judicial Independence. In T. Soreide & A. Williams, eds., *Corruption, Grabbing and Development*. Cheltenham: Edward Elgar.

Gupta, S., Davoodi, H. & Alonso-Terme, R. (2002). Does Corruption Affect Income Inequality and Poverty? *Economics of Governance* 1 (3), 23–45.

Hammergren, L. (2007). Fighting Judicial Corruption: A Comparative Perspective from Latin America. In Transparency International, ed., *Global Corruption Report 2007*. Cambridge: Cambridge University Press.

Harasic, D. (2007). Chile's Partial Success. In Transparency International, ed., *Global Corruption Report 2007*. Cambridge: Cambridge University Press.

Hilbink, L. & Ingram, M. C. (2019). Courts and Rule of Law in Developing Countries. In W. R. Thompson, ed., *Oxford Research Encyclopedia of Politics*. Oxford: Oxford University Press.

Idowu, G. & Ibidapo, S. (2014). Perception of Judicial Corruption: Assessing Its Implications for Democratic Consolidation and Sustainable Development in Nigeria. *Journal of Sustainable Development in Africa* 2 (16), 67–80.

Inclán, S. & Inclán, M. (2005). Las reformas judiciales en América Latina y la rendición de cuentas del Estado. *Perfiles Latinoamericanos* 26 (2), 55–82.

Kapiszewski, D. & Taylor, M. M. (2008). Doing Courts Justice? Studying Judicial Politics in Latin America. *Perspectives on Politics* 6 (4), 741–67.

Llanos, M., Weber, C. T., Heyl, C. & Stroh, A. (2016). Informal Interference in the Judiciary in New Democracies: A Comparison of Six African and Latin American Cases. *Democratization* 23 (7), 1236–53.

Melgar Peña, C. (2007). Judicial Corruption and the Military Legacy in Guatemala. In Transparency International, ed., *Global Corruption Report 2007*. Cambridge: Cambridge University Press.

Montinola, G. R. & Jackman, R. W. (2002). Sources of Corruption: A Cross-Country Study. *British Journal of Political Science* 32 (1), 147–70.

Morris, S. D. & Blake, C. H. (2010). *Corruption and Politics in Latin America: National and Regional Dynamics*. Boulder, CO: Lynne Rienner.

Mujica, H. (2011). *Micro políticas de la corrupción: redes de corrupción y poder en el Palacio de Justicia*. Lima: Asamblea Nacional de Rectores.

North, D. (1993). *Instituciones, cambio institucional y crecimiento económico*. Mexico City: Fondo de Cultura Económica.

Oyanedel, J. C. (2019). *Assessing Judicial Reforms in Developing Countries*. London: Springer.

Pásara, L. (2019). La reforma judicial: balance y perspectivas reales de cambio. *Revista Argumentos* 13 (1), 18–23.

Pepys, M. N. (2007). Corruption within the Judiciary: Causes and Remedies. In Transparency International, ed., *Global Corruption Report 2007*. Cambridge: Cambridge University Press.

Power, T. J. & Taylor, M. M. (2011). *Corruption and Democracy in Brazil: The Struggle for Accountability*. Notre Dame, IN: Notre Dame University Press.

Ríos-Figueroa, J. (2012). Justice System Institutions and Corruption Controls: Evidence from Latin America. *Justice System Journal* 33 (2), 195–214.

Robertson, C. J. & Watson, A. A. (2002). Corruption and Change: The Impact of Foreign Direct Investment. *Strategic Management Journal* 25 (4), 385–96.

Rose-Ackerman, S., ed. (2006). *International Handbook on the Economics of Corruption*. Cheltenham: Edward Elgar.

Salazar, R. & Ramos, J. P. (2007). Increased Transparency Helps Curb Corruption in Costa Rica. In Transparency International, ed., *Global Corruption Report 2007*. Cambridge: Cambridge University Press.

Sánchez Uribarri, R. (2011). Courts between Democracy and Hybrid Authoritarianism: Evidence from the Venezuelan Supreme Court. *Law and Social Inquiry* 36 (4), 854–84.

Selligson, M. (2002). The Impact of Corruption on Regime Legitimacy: A Comparative Study of Four Latin American Countries. *Journal of Politics* 64 (2), 408–33.

Sieder, R. (2003). Renegociando la ley y el orden: reforma judicial y respuesta ciudadana en la Guatemala de posguerra. *América Latina Hoy* 35, 61–86.

Sotomayor, P. (2019). El poder constitucional en América Latina: hacia una tipología de las cortes constitucionales de la región. *Revista OPERA* 24 (1), 5–26.

Ugochukwu, B. (2011). The Pathology of Judicialization: Politics, Corruption and the Courts in Nigeria. *Law and Development Review* 4 (3), 58–87.

Voigt, S. (2007). When Are Judges Likely to Be Corrupt? In Transparency International, ed., *Global Corruption Report 2007*. Cambridge: Cambridge University Press.

Wang, Y. (2013). Court Funding and Judicial Corruption in China. *China Journal* 69, 43–63.

Yang, V. & Ehrichs, L. 2007. The Professionalism of Judges: Education, Salaries and Career Structure in Asia. In Transparency International, ed., *Global Corruption Report 2007*. Cambridge: Cambridge University Press.

10

Kickbacks, Crackdown, and Backlash

Legal Accountability in the Lava Jato Investigation

Luciano Da Ros and Matthew M. Taylor

INTRODUCTION

The Lava Jato corruption investigation offers an important case study of the evolution of legal accountability in consolidating democracies.[1] In its early years, Lava Jato offered hope that legal accountability was finally being achieved in Brazil, with a bevy of business leaders and even some political leaders finding themselves in an unprecedented position, behind bars. But the optimism this engendered among many Brazilians may have been misplaced, as the operation has now ground to an ignominious halt.

Legal accountability can be defined as the application of a punishment established in law for failing to comply with, or actively breaking, the behaviors stipulated in law (Da Ros 2014, 2019; Bovens 2007; Karklins 2005; Lindberg 2013). As such, it is considered "the most unambiguous type of accountability, as ... legal scrutiny will be based on detailed legal standards, prescribed by civil, penal or administrative statutes, or precedent" (Bovens 2007: 456). Although it is not limited to the judiciary, it is the form of accountability most clearly associated with the judicial system. Imposing legal accountability is a strategically complex process, especially in democracies attempting to overcome long legacies of the weak rule of law. The central challenge is that although the most idealized notions of judicial independence conceive of the legal system as somehow floating autonomously above broader political structures, in reality the

[1] The authors are grateful to Sandra Botero, Daniel Brinks, Ezequiel Gonzalez Ocantos, Maria Paula Bertran, Julio Ríos-Figueroa, and all the workshop participants for insightful comments.

ties between legal systems and the political arena mean that legal accountability cannot be understood in isolation from other patterns of horizontal and vertical accountability.

Legal accountability is especially unlikely so long as the parties that support horizontal controls are not accountable vertically, to the electorate. The Brazilian paradox is that political parties which might otherwise serve as powerful instruments of checks and balances are in fact unwilling to do so because they function largely as participants in coalitional presidentialism, a system whereby minority presidents build majority coalitions using a variety of tools that generate incentives for cooperation rather than confrontation (Chaisty et al. 2018: 14).

Cooperation between the branches of government, of course, can be very positive for governance and there are well-functioning coalitional presidential systems in a variety of countries. But the micro-institutions of the Brazilian coalitional presidential system effectively dilute checks and balances by aligning incentives and intricately intertwining the three branches of government. It is no surprise, as a consequence, that Lava Jato emerged in a trial court in remote Curitiba, rather than in the Supreme Federal Tribunal close to the political class in Brasília. It is also unsurprising that Lava Jato seemed to have bled out in Brasília, far from the relatively autonomous trial court.

This chapter builds from the concept of legal accountability to evaluate the Lava Jato investigations since 2014. The first section summarizes the investigation and the wrongdoing it revealed. The second looks at the imposition of legal accountability. The third turns to the backlash against the Lava Jato investigation, brought about by self-inflicted wounds, accommodation and realignment, and frontal reactions from the political system. The final section places this experience in a broader institutional context, evaluating the ties between imperfect legal accountability and broader legal–political structures.

KICKBACKS: THE LAVA JATO INVESTIGATIONS

Operação Lava Jato began as a criminal investigation into money laundering and grand corruption at state-controlled oil company Petrobras. It was launched in 2014 by a task force composed predominantly of members of the *Ministério Público Federal* prosecutorial body (MPF) and the federal police, with assistance from other agencies. The case was overseen by the *13ª Vara Federal*, one of two federal trial courts in the city of Curitiba specialized in money laundering. The court was led by federal judge Sérgio Moro from March 2014 until October 2018, when Moro resigned to become minister of justice; the court is led at this writing by Judge Luiz Antonio Bonat. Given its complexity and scale, Lava Jato cases were also tried in other courts, including the Supreme Court (*Supremo Tribunal Federal*, STF), the Superior Court (*Superior Tribunal de Justiça*, STJ), regional appeals courts, and trial courts in Rio de Janeiro, São Paulo, and Brasília.

Officially, the case began in March 2014, as the *Conselho de Controle de Atividades Financeiras* (COAF) financial intelligence unit tracked down money laundering at a gas station that, despite the investigation's name, does not possess a car wash (Fontoura 2019: 36). Investigators arrested Alberto Youssef, an illegal currency broker (*doleiro*), following an investigation that found evidence of links to Paulo Roberto Costa.[2] Costa, who served as Petrobras' director of supply, first admitted receiving improper gifts from Youssef when he was arrested three days later. However, Costa was released from prison by an STF decision, and recanted his confession in interviews and while testifying before Congress in June. The day after his congressional testimony, however, he was again jailed when evidence showed he held US$23 million in Swiss accounts. The federal police obtained footage of his two daughters and sons-in-law removing documents from his consultancy, and the *Ministério Público Federal* prosecuted the five of them for destroying evidence. Under pressure, Costa signed a plea bargain in August 2014.

Costa's plea detailed how political appointments within Petrobras were distributed, how a cartel of construction firms was built to win Petrobras contracts, the manner in which bribes were paid to political parties, and even how a congressional investigation into Petrobras was sidetracked in 2009 through bribes to influential congressmen. Costa's testimony implicated more than three dozen political figures, including ministers, governors, presidential candidates, party leaders from Lula and Rouseff's Workers' Party (PT) and its coalition allies, the Progressive Party (PP), and the Party of the Brazilian Democratic Movement (PMDB), a former president of the Brazilian Social Democratic Party

[2] The investigation had its origins in the *Mensalão* scandal (Michener and Pereira 2016). In 2009, the federal police began investigating accounts that the late congressman José Janene (PP) might have been using to launder money from that case. Janene died in 2010, but the investigation led the investigators to Alberto Youssef and his links to the PP. After placing Youssef under surveillance, investigators stumbled across evidence of ties between him and Costa (Rodrigues 2019).

(PSDB, which ostensibly opposed the PT); as well as two dozen different firms in the construction and shipping industries.

Costa's testimony showed the interconnection between politics, industry, and campaign finance. According to Costa, who had worked at Petrobras since 1977, directorates at the company were divided up between parties within the governing coalition. Costa noted that nobody at state-owned enterprises rose from a career to an appointed position without a political "godparent" (*padrinho*). His appointment and retention as a director from 2004 until 2012 were only possible because José Janene, the PP president, sponsored him.[3] As a Petrobras director, Costa had to provide money to the PP (and occasionally other parties), or else he might lose his job. Costa testified that payments to political parties were widespread across the Petrobras directorates, with the Services Directorate – headed at the time by Renato Duque – the largest source.

In an oil sector dominated by state-owned Petrobras, on the one hand, and highly concentrated private firms on the other, few firms had the technical capacity to take on the projects that Petrobras required, especially at the scale envisioned after the pre-salt oil discoveries in 2006. The small number of firms helps to explain the ease with which a cartel was formed around public contracts. Members of the cartel engaged in egregious price-fixing, holding meetings at their sectoral association, where they openly colluded to set prices for public contracts, establish bribe percentages, and determine which firms would win bids. There was no overt meddling in the bidding process: the cartel determined winners ahead of time, and the bidding process itself was therefore – strictly speaking – carried out within the formal limits of the law.[4]

In sum, Costa's testimony brought massive evidence of corrupt links between parties, private sector firms, state-controlled enterprises, and money launderers, links which may have been amplified in this period due to the euphoric spending on Petrobras' pre-salt discoveries. His allegations were confirmed by various other plea bargains and leniency agreements signed over the following years of investigation, corroborated by scheme participants' willingness to return over $3 billion dollars in ill-gotten gains. As a condition of their plea deals, Costa and another

[3] Fausto Macedo and Ricardo Brandt, "Lava Jato completa um ano com parte dos processos na etapa final," *O Estado de S. Paulo* (March 15, 2015).

[4] Termo de Colaboração no. 01, Paulo Roberto Costa. Superintendência Regional no Estado do Paraná, Policia Federal, August 29, 2014, p. 290, http://media.folha.uol.com.br/poder/2015/03/11/termo-de-colaboracao-001.pdf (accessed May 9, 2021).

Petrobras director returned nearly $124 million in bribes they had personally received. Giving further credence to the accusations, Petrobras wrote down US$16.8 billion in losses in April 2015 (relative to its 2014 financial results), equivalent to the company's total accumulated profit for nearly four years. Petrobras admitted that 12 percent of this write-down was directly related to corruption, while the rest was "impairment" from a variety of causes, including excess costs from over-priced goods that might also be corruption-related.[5]

The Lava Jato investigation quickly spread to other sectors of Brazil's state-controlled economy, including the energy sector, the Planning Ministry, the federal banks Caixa Econômica Federal and Banco do Brasil, and even some revisitation of wrongdoing in the postal service associated with the *Mensalão* scandal that began in 2005. As a result, investigations that started in Curitiba had ramifications in federal courts in other Brazilian states.[6] At the STF, which has original jurisdiction in cases involving sitting federal politicians, investigations began in March 2015, when Prosecutor General Rodrigo Janot presented a list of forty-eight members of Congress and the executive branch to be further investigated. In June 2016, Lava Jato arrived in the Rio de Janeiro trial courts following an investigation into the national nuclear program, and expanded quickly to the state's political elite. In 2017, Lava Jato arrived in São Paulo, primarily through investigations into the Rodoanel beltway, a top priority of the PSDB party that had governed the state since 1995, and was the leading opposition party to the PT presidents of the era.

The investigation also branched out internationally. In December 2016, the Odebrecht construction firm, its petrochemical subsidiary Braskem, and Brazilian, Swiss, and US authorities settled for $3.5 billion, the largest global corruption settlement in history at the time. Odebrecht admitted to paying $788 million in bribes in twelve countries – ten in Latin America and two in Africa – in exchange for $3.34 billion in ill-gotten benefits. Its methods included a shadow budget administered by a bribe payment department known as the "Division of Structured Operations." Payments were made through shell companies set up in offshore locations (US Department of Justice 2016). A variety of

[5] "Petrobras Takes $17 Billion Charge in Wake of Scandal, Promises 'Normality'," *Reuters* (April 22, 2015).

[6] The unusually broad jurisdiction of the Curitiba court required the tacit support of the STF. In 2014 justice Teori Zavascki halted Lava Jato on jurisdictional grounds, although he soon allowed it to proceed again, for reasons that remain unclear (Rodrigues 2019).

high-ranking officials abroad came under scrutiny. In Peru alone, as Baraybar and Gonzalez-Ocantos's chapter in this volume illustrates (Chapter 13), four former presidents were targeted by the resulting investigations.[7]

Compared to previous judicial efforts against high-level corruption in Brazil, Lava Jato was unprecedented. By its fifth birthday in March 2019, the investigation had reached its sixtieth phase, suggestively named "*Ad Infinitum.*" Costa's plea agreement was the first of 228 plea bargains signed in the trial courts; more than 180 other plea agreements are pending approval at the STF. Thirteen leniency agreements had been signed with businesses.[8] Plea bargaining and leniency agreements had already ensured the seizure or return of almost R$5 billion in assets. Nearly 200 individuals had been sentenced, including former president Luis Inácio Lula da Silva and former Chamber of Deputies president, Eduardo Cunha, as well as prominent executives. State political elites had also paid: in Rio de Janeiro, three former governors were arrested, as well as all the presidents of the state legislative assembly from 1995 to 2017, five out of the six senior members of the state audit court, and one former state prosecutor-general. At the STF, 241 investigations had been launched into high-ranking officials from fourteen different political parties, and 100 individuals had been charged by the prosecutor general (at the end of 2020, however, only six had been tried and three convicted at the high court).

Many Lava Jato cases are still pending. Yet, strictly from a sanctioning standpoint, Lava Jato initially succeeded where most previous investigations had failed. The complexity, scale, and number of elites implicated in Lava Jato were simply unprecedented. Previous investigations may have had similar potential, but were not able to dig as deep, go as far, and implicate so many powerful figures. Lava Jato gave hope to Brazilians who yearned for legal accountability.

CRACKDOWN: LEGAL ACCOUNTABILITY IN LAVA JATO

Why was the Lava Jato prosecution seemingly successful when others failed? There are many reasons why we should be careful about claiming Lava Jato was an unalloyed success. Not only are many Lava Jato cases still ongoing, but most politicians in the case may not go to trial for years.

[7] On Lava Jato abroad, see Gonzalez-Ocantos and Baraybar-Hidalgo (2019).

[8] Leniency agreements are roughly analogous to deferred prosecution agreements in the United States.

Former President Lula's imprisonment suggests that judicial treatment was unequal. Further, as the next section discusses, the leak of hacked Telegram messages to *The Intercept* suggests that Judge Sergio Moro and the chief prosecutor, Deltan Dallagnol, may have engaged in improper *ex parte* conversations, with Moro guiding the prosecutor on strategy and how to obtain evidence. Setting aside those important caveats temporarily, though, the relative effectiveness of Lava Jato was a consequence of improving capacity, legal and political strategy, and political context.

There is not space to fully detail all of the improvements in capacity among accountability agencies since the return to democracy. A quick list, however, should highlight new laws on money laundering, public sector corruption and organized crime; the generous resources and autonomy granted to the federal police, the MPF, the federal courts, and other oversight institutions; the creation of specialized anti-money laundering courts starting in 2003; and improvements in inter-institutional coordination among law enforcement agencies. Of the many ironies of the Lava Jato case, one of the greatest is that many accountability agencies were significantly strengthened under the PT governments from 2003 to 2016, and they came to Lava Jato ready to flex their newfound muscle, even if it meant challenging the very PT politicians who had helped to empower them. Two innovations were particularly critical. First, starting in 2003, the practice of appointing the prosecutor general from a list of three nominees elected by the association of career members of the MPF diminished the possibility that the prosecutor general would be passive, or worse, might act to protect political elites. Second, two new statutes changed the framework for fighting corruption. The 2013 Law of Criminal Organizations formalized the new technique of *colaboração premiada* (i.e., plea bargaining),[9] which has been used to an unprecedented extent in Lava Jato. It also established racketeering as a punishable offense, and made participation in a "criminal organization" a crime. Simultaneously, the 2013 Anti-Corruption Law clarified the civil and administrative penalties imposed on corporations for corruption.

Closer to the ground, the Curitiba task force had unusually broad experience with money laundering cases. As early as 2002, nearly 56 percent of all money laundering investigations in Brazil were headed by the Federal Police in Paraná, and its financial crimes unit was considered among the most skillful nationwide (Polícia Federal 2002, 127; Costa

[9] Talita Fernandes and Beatriz Bulla, "Lava Jato terá análise mas discreta no Supremo," *O Estado de S. Paulo* (January 31, 2015).

et al. 2016). Its specialization dates back at least to the 2003 Banestado scandal; four of the six prosecutors on the initial Lava Jato investigation worked together on Banestado (Dallagnol 2017: 69). They were responsible for the first plea bargain agreement signed, well before the 2013 law, with a *doleiro* who would come to prominence again a decade later, Alberto Youssef. A specialized anti-money laundering court was created in Curitiba in 2003, headed by Judge Sérgio Moro, one of the most experienced of a generation of young judges specialized in money laundering cases. Moro had analyzed the Mani Pulite anti-corruption operation in Italy, was the trial judge on both the *Banestado* and *Farol da Colina* investigations of money launderers, and had served as an auxiliary judge to the STF during the *Mensalão* trial.

As important as bureaucratic capacity was effective cooperation. Some of the key players had worked side by side on past investigations. Coordination between police, the revenue service, the central bank, and the prosecutorial service was unprecedented, and supported by the informal networks of trust between individual agents, as well as more formal bureaucratic ties. As the case progressed, the task force worked to streamline communications with Prosecutor General Rodrigo Janot, responsible for prosecuting sitting politicians. Unlike his predecessors in previous investigations, Janot played a supportive role, openly encouraging his colleagues in Curitiba. His decentralized management style, in turn, helped align interests between the bottom and top of the *Ministério Público Federal*. The team of thirteen senior prosecutors aiding Janot in Brasília was filled with corruption experts. Prosecutorial task forces were also created in other courts Lava Jato passed through, including the federal regional appellate court in the city of Porto Alegre, the Superior Court in Brasília, and trial courts in Rio de Janeiro and São Paulo. As of the end of 2019, a total of fifty-nine prosecutors – 5.1 percent of federal prosecutors nationwide – were participating in different task forces linked to Lava Jato. Meanwhile, the specialized money laundering court in Curitiba had its docket cleared of all other cases so that it could work exclusively on Lava Jato (Rodrigues 2019).

In addition, years of failure had taught Moro and prosecutors that cautious legal and political strategies were needed. To ensure that the high courts did not become a roadblock to effective accountability, both federal prosecutors and trial court judges progressed aggressively but carefully. The aggressiveness of their approach included a high number of indictments and convictions, the widespread and unprecedented use of instruments such as search warrants, *conduções coercitivas* (similar to bench warrants), pretrial detentions, and plea bargaining agreements. Moro's willingness to convict in instances in which there was not a clear quid pro quo between corrupt actors may have been partly a result of his specialization in money laundering, which made him aware of the difficulty of finding direct evidence of bribery. The legal instrument that enabled convictions even without a direct quid pro quo is referred to in Portuguese as *teoria do domínio do fato* (a term with parallels to the concept of "willful blindness" in the US legal system) and it made its first appearance in Brazil during the *Mensalão* trial (Michener and Pereira 2016; see also Mota Prado and Rodriguez Machado's chapter in this volume, Chapter 11).

Together, these tactics contributed to a domino effect among defendants (Moro 2004). The investigation moved through phases organized to incrementally target specific groups of conspirators. The fast pace of the investigations, which produced an increasing sense of unease among politicians, was particularly visible in 2015 and 2016, when thirty phases of the operation took place – one phase every twenty-four days – each with numerous arrests, warrants, and depositions, which in turn led to new plea bargains, investigations, and indictments, all amply covered by the news media.

This assertiveness, however, had to be tempered to avoid problems that had waylaid past investigations. Both prosecutors and the trial court tried to avoid controversial tactics that might lead the high courts to overturn decisions. No defendants were handcuffed by the federal police when they were arrested during Lava Jato, complying with a decision made by the STF in the wake of the *Satiagraha* case of 2008. When Moro attempted to speed up some cases by having witnesses and defendants notified by phone, prosecutors warned him that the STJ might regard this as a violation. Similarly, there was a legal debate associated with the new use of plea bargains: how to address the fact that some defendants were preventively detained on the basis of plea bargain agreements that were protected by judicial secrecy provisions. Prosecutors recognized that if they did not provide defendants with the content of the plea bargains, they would be accused – as they were – of using plea bargains merely to decree preventive detention. So they agreed to provide the plea bargains to defendants' lawyers.

Another important tactical innovation was the navigation of tricky rules on the original jurisdiction of the STF in all criminal cases involving sitting federal politicians. Particularly in the first phases of Lava Jato, Judge Moro was very careful to keep any mention of sitting politicians out of his courtroom, to ensure that his judgments could not be overturned on jurisdictional grounds.[10] Although it pursued a variety of influential *doleiros* and businessmen, the Lava Jato task force in Curitiba initially limited its forays against political elites to non-sitting politicians and party bureaucrats. This caution paid off. Although some justices did express concern about tactics, the Fourth Regional Federal appeals court (TRF4), the STJ, and the STF initially upheld most trial court decisions. Nearly all of the habeas corpus requests that reached the STJ in the crucial first year of the investigation were declined.[11] Likewise, the STF justices tasked with overseeing Lava Jato largely upheld trial court decisions.

Still, Lava Jato could not circumvent the STF forever. Indeed, if the investigation was to realize its full potential, it would have to reach sitting politicians and, consequently, work its way through the STF. At least initially, the STF did not hinder Lava Jato, and even indirectly encouraged it in its early years, reaching two decisions that contributed directly to the prosecutors' success. First, in May 2015 the STF resolved a longstanding debate over the legality of prosecutors' role in criminal investigations – a responsibility the federal police had long argued was theirs alone – in favor of prosecutors. Then, in 2016, the court altered an understanding about post-conviction imprisonment that it had held since the mid-2000s. Until this decision, it was impossible to jail a convicted defendant until every last one of their appeals had been exhausted. In practice, the slow pace of the courts meant that even in the most egregious cases, imprisonment of wealthy elites with access to good lawyers was rare. With the STF decision, however, it now became possible to jail convicted criminals once their first appeal failed. The Curitiba court was under the appellate jurisdiction of the TRF4, which upheld most of the penalties imposed by Moro – and at times even increased them.[12] Together, the STF's decision on jail upon failed appeal and the affirming decisions offered by the TRF4 meant that defendants now faced a real risk of prison time, which may have altered their calculus about whether or not to sign plea agreements.

10 Pedro Canário, "Procuradores da 'lava jato' estão preocupados com nulidades processuais," *Consultor Jurídico* (December 6, 2014).

11 "Em 2014, casos do STJ foram da Copa do Mundo à operação 'Lava Jato'," *Consultor Jurídico* (December 14, 2014).

12 "'Lava jato' não precisa seguir regras de casos comuns, decide TRF-4," *Consultor Jurídico* (September 23, 2016).

Similarly, decisions by the STF had a direct effect. When Senator Delcídio Amaral (PT) was recorded offering to help Petrobras' services director, Nestor Cerveró, escape Brazil in return for his silence, the STF immediately ordered Amaral's arrest for obstruction of justice. This was the first time a sitting senator had been removed from office and preventively jailed since re-democratization. Less grandiose decisions were also important. When Janot submitted the names of forty-eight sitting politicians for investigation by the STF in March 2015, Justice Zavascki decided to make the records of the investigations public – against previous practice – and thereby provided enormous visibility to the case. The so-called "Janot list" included the names of some of the most influential members of Congress, including the sitting speakers of both the House and the Senate, as well as long-time leaders of various political parties, such as Senators Romero Jucá (PMDB), Gleisi Hoffman (PT), Fernando Collor (PTB), Ciro Nogueira (PP), and Antônio Anastasia (PSDB), among others.

Lava Jato's success was also a consequence of prosecutors' political tactics. The fast pace with which Lava Jato proceeded, increasingly involving numerous important political figures, drew immense public attention and support. Judge Moro's actions were supported by over 60 percent of the population polled in early 2016 (Oliveira 2019), and massive public demonstrations between 2015 and 2016 made this explicit. Lava Jato also attracted enormous media coverage, starting especially in November 2014, immediately following the reelection of Dilma Rousseff (Feres Jr. et al. 2018: 210). Coverage of Lava Jato was also both more intense and less critical of prosecutors than in previous scandals (Marona and Barbosa 2018: 137). Public support and media coverage were useful in at least two ways: putting pressure on the STF and raising the costs of curtailing the investigation.

For prosecutors, the intended appointment of former president Lula as chief of staff to President Rousseff in early 2016 threatened just such a curtailment. The episode is recounted in greater detail in Chapter 11 of this volume. For now, suffice it to note that Moro's decision to release wiretapped conversations between Lula and Rousseff was effective in protecting the Lava Jato task force, as well as enormously controversial. But it was representative of the hardball tactics that Moro and prosecutors felt necessary to protect themselves from pushback.

Lava Jato's political strategy went well beyond playing defense: prosecutors lobbied to enact new criminal justice reforms, such as the "10 Measures against Corruption," officially launched in early March 2015.

Prosecutors openly campaigned to collect the 1.5 million signatures needed for the package to be submitted to Congress under the public initiative process.[13] After approximately one year of intense campaigning, prosecutors had enough support to submit the package to Congress as a bill in March 2016. The Lava Jato task force's reliance on public and media support, and its campaign for legislative reform, suggests that it felt the need to cultivate a receptive public, fed up with recurring corruption scandals.

The third factor that contributed to Lava Jato's initial success was the political context within which it took place. This context defined the options available to political actors. Indeed, it may be impossible to analytically detach the political context from Lava Jato itself. As the investigations gained traction and publicity, they shaped the very political context within which they developed. Political instability created an environment in which Lava Jato faced fewer constraints and could evolve without significant opposition.

There was already intense anti-corruption fervor before Lava Jato, motivated in part by the STF's unprecedented Mensalão trial. Simultaneously, what began as a campaign against bus fare hikes in a few cities grew into a generalized wave of mass protests throughout the country in July 2013. Protestors expressed dissatisfaction with public services and inefficient government spending, with corruption soon becoming a central rallying cry. Public fervor intensified during the presidential elections of 2014, which took place just as Lava Jato got underway. Although the details of what would become Lava Jato's key arguments remained hazy, the combination of public malaise, economic decline, fiscal profligacy, and early evidence of wrongdoing by the incumbent Workers' Party meant that Rousseff's reelection became quite uncertain. She squeaked through in October by the narrowest margin since reelection was instituted in 1998.

Rousseff's new governing strategy seemed engineered to further undermine her coalition. Upon her second inauguration, she promptly threw out her campaign promises of policy continuity and instead installed a fiscal hawk in the Finance Ministry, with a mandate to dramatically reduce the fiscal deficit by the end of 2015. She stimulated the formation of a new party, the Social Democratic Party (PSD), which directly competed with her coalition allies in the PMDB. In the February elections to

[13] Under the 1988 Constitution, a "popular initiative" can be placed on the legislative agenda if it has the support of 1 percent of the electorate.

lead the Chamber of Deputies, Rousseff insisted on a candidate from the PT rather than supporting a coalition ally from the PMDB. The result was a revolt, and the election of the PMDB's Eduardo Cunha as chamber president. Rousseff had thus alienated both the PT, via fiscal reform, and a large portion of her coalition in Congress, by competing with the PMDB. As Lava Jato progressed and implicated members of the governing coalition, these missteps proved fatal. The extent to which these decisions mattered was highlighted by the release of Janot's list of politicians under investigation in March 2015. On the list were various coalition allies, including the presidents of both the Chamber and the Senate, who were both members of the PMDB alongside the vice-president, Michel Temer.

Rousseff was unable, and perhaps even unwilling, to quash Lava Jato outright, even though doing so might have pleased her coalition allies (Da Ros and Ingram 2018). Instead, to the consternation of many of her allies, Rousseff expressed support for the investigations, asking the police to "proceed with candor and impartiality in the investigations."[14] During her first term, in part as a response to protestors, Rousseff had pushed the anti-corruption law through Congress. In September 2015, she reappointed Janot against congressional opposition. Yet Rousseff received little credit from the public for her anti-corruption moves because she continued to defend the PT against mounting evidence of wrongdoing. She was also in an impossible position when she claimed to have had no knowledge of what would become the Lava Jato case, given that she was head of the Petrobras board and the minister of mines and energy as the scheme was unfolding. Critics were unsparing, noting that she must have been either incompetent or complicit in Petrobras' undoing.

The collapse of the Rousseff administration was already largely foreordained by the end of 2015. What should have been Rousseff's four-year second term was a political soap opera, with too many twists and turns to describe here. The critical point for our purposes is that this political turmoil presented an unlikely window of opportunity for the Lava Jato team. An extremely fragile presidency was not able to interfere with the workings of the federal police. Broad public mobilizations provided explicit support to the task force, raising the costs of any attempt to curtail the investigations. The collapse of the governing coalition led to a race between politicians for mutually destructive accountability: for example,

[14] "Operação Lava Jato aumenta número de mandados de prisão para 49," *Consultor Jurídico* (November 15, 2014).

the PT threw its weight against Eduardo Cunha, who was thus expelled from the Chamber and subject to jailing by the trial court; in response, Cunha and his allies did all they could to undermine the Rousseff administration and drive her impeachment forward. In this shifting political landscape, with a population that was pointing to "corruption" as the country's most pressing problem (Oliveira 2019), there was plenty of room for the investigations to proceed. This cycle of instability was in turn fueled by Lava Jato: the heat and fire of investigations contributed enormously to the government's difficulty in reassembling a governing coalition.

BACKLASH: NEUTERING LEGAL ACCOUNTABILITY

By 2016, the pendulum had begun to swing back against the Lava Jato investigation, impelled by self-inflicted wounds, the realignment of political coalitions in a context of public exhaustion, and frontal reactions in defense of coalitional politics.

Prosecutors' and judges' adoption of a political–legal strategy to tackle corruption in some ways carried the seeds of its own ruin. Political outreach may have enabled some early successes, by keeping an intense media focus on the investigations, by putting public pressure on the high courts, and by drawing attention to politicians' self-serving actions. But over the long haul it engendered a backlash, leading to allegations of prosecutorial bias. Key legal actors also overstepped their bounds, in ways that gave credence to the allegation, common to anti-corruption campaigns, that reformers are fighting abuse with another form of abuse (Merriner 2004).

Two controversies are discussed in greater detail in the next chapter, by Mota Prado and Rodriguez Machado. First, the unsavory relation between detention and plea bargains. While prosecutors noted that only one in six pleas were signed while the defendant was in detention, more than half of all pleading witnesses had spent time in prison before their deal was signed (Fontoura 2019: 51). This was particularly controversial because the plea bargain was new to Brazilian law. Second, the novel practice of judicial transparency helped generate public support, but the selective release of information was controversial and may have overstepped the bounds of legality.

A third controversy came out of the Prosecutor General's Office. A cloud fell over the 2017 leniency agreement signed by meatpacking giant J&F when it was discovered that a senior aide to Janot had been hired by defense lawyers, and may even have fed them information about prosecutorial strategy.[15] Although J&F's owners reached a plea bargain with Lava Jato, providing incriminating tapes of conversations with President Michel Temer and Senator Aécio Neves, the deal was suspect. This controversy enabled Temer to appoint a new prosecutor general who was seen as less supportive of Lava Jato than the frontrunner for the post.

Lava Jato's conviction of Lula was also a double-edged sword. Lava Jato unveiled illegal practices that took place during his administration and established that no one is above the law. But the legitimacy of the prosecution was undermined by avoidable mistakes. Lead prosecutor Deltan Dallagnol gave a vacuous presentation on Lula's guilt, which brought immediate internet ridicule. Nor was the case a certainty: the relatively indirect evidence used, much of it obtained through plea bargains, did not change many minds. The political–legal strategy of the Lava Jato authorities was also matched by defense lawyers, whose narrative of "lawfare" helped to cast a shadow over the proceedings, and led 35 percent of the population to agree with pollsters that former president Lula had been treated worse than other defendants (Oliveira 2019).

Judge Moro's decision to resign from the bench and join the administration of President Bolsonaro in 2019 only reinforced this narrative, especially because Moro did so only a few months after removing former president Lula from electoral contention.[16] Moro's resignation was harmful to Lava Jato in a variety of ways. It removed a skillful judge who had assertively but carefully moved the case forward. It hurt perceptions of judicial impartiality. As Shapiro (1981) famously argued, courts are triads only until the moment a judge renders a decision; after that, the loser inevitably sees it as a 2–1 dynamic. Because the judiciary justifies its performance and existence through procedure, rather than through results, judicial form and appearance of impartiality are vital to reinforce its authority and legitimacy. Moro's star dimmed as a result of perceived politicization, as well as the repeated ignominies he suffered at Bolsonaro's hands.

The *Intercept*'s release in 2019 of *ex parte* conversations between Moro and Dallagnol, apparently hacked from prosecutors' phones, were

[15] Karin Salomão, "Além da Lava Jato: as investigações que envolvem JBS e J&F," *Revista Exame* (May 18, 2017); Renan Truffi, "CPI da JBS conclui que PGR orientou gravações," *O Estado de S.Paulo* (December 7, 2017).

[16] Because he was convicted both in Moro's trial court and subsequently in appeals court, Lula was subject to the Clean Slate Law, which prevents those convicted on appeal from running for elected office.

a further blow to Lava Jato's image. The messages showed that judge and prosecutor were in regular communication about the case: above all, judge and prosecutor seemed to be trying to find the most effective strategies for overcoming roadblocks in the high court. The extent to which these conversations were permissible, under either Brazilian law or international practice, are a subject of bitter debate. While the conversations did not suggest manipulation of the evidence, they nonetheless cast an enduring pall over the impartiality of the investigations, reinforced both by the defense's public relations strategy and Moro's decision to join the Bolsonaro administration.

A second cause of the pendulum's swing against Lava Jato was realignment in the face of economic and political crises. These crises began to boil in 2014 and, as the years passed, Brazilians adopted a variety of survival strategies to deal with cascades of frequently catastrophic news. Many citizens disengaged from public life, including from political discussions with family; street protests slowed and shifted direction; a "pox on all their houses" mentality grew with regard to political parties; and the hope and even enthusiasm that initially greeted Lava Jato were replaced by realism and even cynicism.

Waning public attention sapped energy from the anti-corruption agenda and enabled a political realignment in Brasília. The Bolsonaro administration played a double game, nominating Moro and claiming to be tough on corruption, even as it sought to protect the president and his family against a variety of scandals. Congress was also eager to move away from the corruption agenda. The high court became active in this realignment, keeping Bolsonaro and his family above the law, while also becoming less assertive against sitting politicians. As of late 2020, more than 100 sitting politicians remained under investigation, and very few cases had actually been tried, resulting in the conviction of only one sitting politician. The high court's slow pace has enabled politics to return to a semblance of the *status quo ante*, almost as though Lava Jato had never taken place at all. Even at the trial court the fast pace that characterized Lava Jato in its initial years slowed noticeably. Judge Bonat, who replaced Moro at the Curitiba trial court, took almost one full year to render his first decision in cases pertaining to the investigation (Fontoura 2019).[17]

Realignment at the STF also led to a more lenient stance. Justices revisited a decision that had allowed prison after conviction on appeal,

[17] Nathan Lopes, "'Novo Moro' muda ritmo e demora um ano para dar sentença na Lava Jato," *UOL* (March 6, 2020).

meaning that defendants could only be jailed after all appeals had been exhausted. The STF stripped federal trial courts of jurisdiction over illegal campaign finance, transferring these cases to the much weaker electoral courts. The STF eventually cleared Lula of all charges on procedural grounds. One consequence of the STF's decisions is a significant discrepancy between the treatment of politicians in the STF and defendants in the trial courts: levels of impunity are low for civil servants; middling for businesspeople; and high for politicians. The relative invulnerability of the political class has profound implications for the country's ability to reach a new anticorruption equilibrium.

Not coincidentally, a third cause of the pendulum's swing has been the reaction from politicians. Lava Jato was an icy shock to the political system, and in its early years, many politicians appeared paralyzed by the legal onslaught. Rousseff's political morass meant that her administration was too distracted to slow its progress, the STF's anti-corruption epiphany during the *Mensalão* trial provided legal cover, and public mobilization ensured that blundering congressional efforts to slow accountability were thwarted. But in part because of public exhaustion, and the self-inflicted wounds noted earlier, anti-corruption efforts increasingly became vulnerable to attacks from politicians across the spectrum.

These efforts at self-protection are almost too numerous to list. Congress began working to neuter Lava Jato during the Rousseff administration. A congressional committee of inquiry (CPI) into Petrobras was concluded in December 2014, determining that no one should be reported for criminal investigation into alleged corruption at the company. Although the committee later amended its report to suggest that fifty-two individuals be investigated, none were sitting politicians. A second CPI was created in the subsequent legislature, in 2015, but similarly concluded without implicating sitting politicians (Limongi 2017).

Congress was also active in stalling legislative reforms to fight corruption. It put a chokehold on the "10 Measures against Corruption," championed by Lava Jato prosecutors. The bill was disfigured by amendments in the lower house, and the Senate did not attempt to resurrect it. As justice minister, Moro attempted a bill of his own, but it was significantly diluted, in ways that may actually complicate future prosecutions.

Congress has on occasion been even more aggressive in working to ease pressure on defendants in corruption cases. One constitutional amendment proposal in 2013 sought to limit the investigatory powers of prosecutors, meaning that only police would be allowed to investigate crimes, to the detriment of other agencies. The proposal was overwhelmingly defeated, not least because the vote coincided with the gargantuan street protests of 2013. Nonetheless, the proposal continues to resurface from time to time. Similarly, discussion around a provisional measure governing leniency agreements (MP 703) in 2015 seemed designed to sow confusion. The underlying issue has not been completely resolved: which agencies have the ability to sign leniency agreements? Without consensus on that issue, defendants may be able to engage in elaborate machinations to game the system. An amnesty on the repatriation of capital was approved in 2016, allowing funds to be brought back to Brazil without explanation, provided the recipient paid taxes (Taylor 2018). An abuse-of-authority bill was approved in mid-2019.[18] Eminent scholars such as Rogério Arantes defend the bill, arguing that it was made necessary by the excesses of Lava Jato (Arantes 2019). Yet as Transparency International points out, the bill provides unethical actors with a powerful tool to cow prosecutors and judges.[19]

The executive branch was also active against Lava Jato. The Rousseff administration was too weak to neuter Lava Jato, although its justice ministers did attempt to curtail investigators. The Temer coalition was much more brazen, as exemplified in a wiretap of Senator Romero Jucá, a Temer ally who was recorded before the impeachment telling the corrupt head of a state-owned company, "we need to staunch the bleeding" (Limongi 2017). The Temer administration demonstrated clear intent to neuter Lava Jato, appointing loyalists to head accountability agencies, changing key personnel, transferring police investigators out of Curitiba,[20] failing to renew task forces, diminishing the power of the Comptroller General's Office, and offering pardons, among many others. Under Bolsonaro, similarly, efforts to better control the financial intelligence unit COAF and the federal police continued apace. Justice Minister Moro, meanwhile, repeatedly threatened to resign in the face of interference in the federal police; when Bolsonaro fired the director of the federal police in April 2020, Moro finally stepped down.

[18] Anne Warth and Daniel Weterman, "Bolsonaro deu aval para a derrubada de vetos da Lei de Abuso de Autoridade," *O Estado de S.Paulo* (September 26, 2019).

[19] Bruno Brandão and Guilherme France, "Threats against Anti-Corruption Framework in Brazil Multiply," *Voices for Transparency on Medium* (September 23, 2019).

[20] "Ex-coordenadora da Lava Jato é transferida para a PF em SC," *RBS* (February 25, 2017); Estelita Carazzai, "Polícia Federal encerra grupo exclusivo da Lava Jato em Curitiba," *Folha de S. Paulo* (July 6, 2017); "Desmonte de força tarefa da Polícia Federal compromete Lava Jato," *Jornal da USP* (July 7, 2017).

The high courts also became a part of this pushback, for motives that may range from deeply held legal convictions to sympathy for the defendants to pure politics. Gradually, the court moved back to the timid stance toward politicians that had marked it until 2013. The STF came under intense pressure as the political elite pressed the court for relief, and some justices began to draw attention to Lava Jato's excesses, especially after the death of Justice Teori Zavacki in 2017. Self-preservation was a consideration. The court, for instance, was humiliated when it determined the imprisonment of Senator Renan Calheiros, but he simply refused to go to jail. As a result, when the court had to decide whether or not to imprison Aécio Neves, it argued that the court needed congressional permission to do so.[21] Politicians have not so subtly threatened the court. The number of impeachment requests of STF justices submitted to Congress reached an all-time high following Lava Jato (Bogéa and Da Ros 2020). Other pressures are even more overt: Bolsonaro's son famously argued that all you need to shut down the court is a "private and a corporal" and others suggested a "Lava Toga" operation to investigate the judiciary.

Partly in consequence of these pressures, the gap between the performance of the Curitiba trial court and the high court in Brasília has been enormous. The STF took 1,183 days until it convicted a single sitting politician in Lava Jato; over the same period, the *13ª Vara Federal* in Curitiba convicted 132 individuals.[22] This difference means that remaining a sitting politician with access to the original jurisdiction of the high court is a key perk, and pressure to preserve these benefits is strong.

A RETURN TO THE BACKSLAPPING OF PRE-LAVA JATO COALITIONAL PRESIDENTIALISM?

The challenges of legal accountability in Brazil's broader accountability landscape are significant. The overlapping roles of elected officials as members of both the legislative branch and the executive coalition dent incentives to press forward on investigations of problematic practices or wrongdoing. Checks and balances are neutered. The overlap between

21 "Delcídio Amaral e Aécio Neves: por que um foi preso e o outro não?" *GaúchaZH* (September 29, 2017).

22 Edson Sardinha, "STF levou 1.183 dias até primeira condenação na Lava Jato. Moro condenou 132 no período," *Congresso em Foco* (May 30, 2018).

executive and legislative roles spreads horizontally, across oversight agencies like the Federal Accounting Tribunal (Tribunal de Contas da União, TCU) and within executive bodies such as state-owned enterprises, where the coalition's political appointees have influence. The unseemly intermingling also appears to spread into the high courts, the STF and STJ, albeit less through direct partisan control of court seats than through an overall pact of elite protection: it is hard to say that a particular justice's party affiliation is X or Y, but it is possible to argue that justices are almost always "creatures" of Brasília, with close ties to leading political figures in the executive and legislative branches, and acute survival instincts.

What is unique about Brazil in this regard? After all, many countries have coalitional political systems and do not suffer from high-level corruption and collusive politics. The simple answer seems to be that horizontal accountability is not complemented by vertical accountability. There is little reward or incentive for the politician who bucks the coalition in an effort to make checks and balances function: such a move would likely reduce support from party leaders, lessen the flow of campaign contributions, and probably also threaten budget allocations to their home district, all of which are needed for electoral success. Since the return to democracy, there have been few cases of legislators who were active anti-corruption campaigners. While some politicians have a reputation for personal integrity (e.g., Eduardo Suplicy, Miro Teixeira), few have made a name as active reformers or enforcers, because there are few incentives for doing so. Furthermore, the already weak vertical links between voters and the party system have been weakened in recent years by declining trust in parties, a sharp drop-off in partisan identification, and increasing fragmentation.[23] Centrist parties do not want to be too critical of any administration because they all eventually become a part of it. The same is true for the opposition: it may not target centrist parties in the governing coalition because opposition members may eventually join those centrist parties or may need those parties' support. The situation is even more fraught once we factor in federalism and subnational coalitions. Overall, there are few incentives to expose wrongdoing by the administration, the opposition, or coalition partners.

[23] The relationship between horizontal and vertical accountability institutions has been complex. As Hagopian (2016, 127) notes, "the bonds of vertical accountability were more tenuous than they appeared" and as stronger horizontal accountability institutions uncovered corruption, they "paradoxically eroded the bonds of vertical accountability."

This may have much to do with the incentives to live and let live. On the legislative side, the open-list proportional representational system in large districts, the corresponding importance of campaign funds in the hands of a few concentrated donors and of name recognition to electoral victory, and the electoral gains of being part of the presidential coalition provide legislators with few incentives to support accountability functions. Even opposition members have few incentives to press for effective accountability: as the anemic role of the PSDB and its one-time presidential candidate Aécio Neves showed in the Lava Jato case, this may be due in part to their own dirty laundry, their dependence on the same campaign benefactors that illicitly finance incumbents, and the potential gains from appointments and influence in the federal government.

Similarly, the executive branch profits little from checking wrongdoing in the legislative sphere. While a particularly egregious case of individual wrongdoing (e.g., Deputy Hildebrando Pascoal, convicted of running a death squad) may elicit a response, nothing is to be gained from fighting the broader coalition required to govern. While improvements in accountability have come about in recent decades as a consequence of the perception that everyone stood to gain from better controls on fiscal profligacy, these improvements have not brought with them legal accountability. An implicit deal has been reached to curb the worst fiscal excesses, but without challenging the modus operandi of the political system. It is probably less surprising than it should be that politicians who were long reputed to be mercenary have survived and even prospered (e.g., Paulo Maluf, Eduardo Cunha, Eliseu Rezende, and Geddel Vieira Lima).

It is not altogether surprising that in responding to these incentives, presidents appoint justices and oversight officials who are attuned to the realities and "exigencies" of politics. This means that these officials are often willing to bend over backward to provide the benefit of the doubt to political elites, to curb the "abuses" committed by police or prosecutors, and otherwise shield the system from effective legal accountability. The rise and decline of Lava Jato casts enormous doubts over the continuity of a promising process of incremental change that had built up the Brazilian "web" of accountability institutions from 1985 to the beginning of Lava Jato in 2014. At the end of the day, it would not be terribly surprising if, in the face of the incentive structures imposed by the broader political system, the civil servants in oversight bodies such as the federal prosecutorial service, the federal police and the accounting tribunals were to conclude that the costs of challenging the system are simply too great to be worthwhile.

The slow erosion of Lava Jato speaks to many of the themes of this volume. Even as recently as a decade ago, many scholars expressed optimism that newly empowered courts might serve as a check on long-festering patterns of elite collusion, corruption, and impunity. Yet for all the advances brought by Lava Jato, the accountability promise of the courts remains unfulfilled. Ironically, Lava Jato demonstrates the pervasive power of elite self-protection, even under democracy. Only a small subset of the judicial branch – some prosecutors and a few courts – has acted in ways that demonstrate true independence from the political system. The editors of this volume describe a "clash between the judicial and political establishments" in Latin America; Lava Jato suggests the clash has been more of an unequal uphill struggle between maverick judges and prosecutors and the joint political–judicial protection racket at the top of the hill. Efforts to overcome longstanding patterns of collusion between political elites have been neutered by the high courts. Informal dealings between the high courts and political elites hollow out the meaning of the judicial independence granted by the post-authoritarian 1988 Constitution. Too often, the only clash between the branches has been a clash over institutional prerogatives – which branch has the power to conduct which policies and what budget and salary provisions each will receive. The language of democracy, the protection of civil rights in particular, is frequently used to protect elites in ways that undermine the very meaning of that democracy. It is not the case that Brazil's courts are incapable of establishing legal accountability: the law is strictly enforced on the least privileged of citizens. Indeed, one of the most horrific ironies of Lava Jato's heyday has been the recurring complaint about preventive detention, which is a cruel reality for two of every five prisoners in the regular jail system, but in practice is seen as somehow too harsh for Brazil's corrupt elites.

References

Arantes, R. B. (2019). Coluna: Lei de Abuso de Autoridade: equilibrando o jogo. *Revista Época*, September 2.

Bogéa, D. & Da Ros, L. (2020). Limitando Supremas Cortes: Perspectivas Analíticas sobre *Court Curbing* e Pedidos de ar Impeachment de Ministros do Supremo Tribunal Federal. Paper presented at the 12th Meeting of the Brazilian Political Science Association.

Bovens, M. (2007). Analyzing and Assessing Accountability: A Conceptual Framework. *European Law Journal* 13(4), 447–68.

Chaisty, P., Cheeseman, N. & Power, T. J. (2018). *Coalitional Presidentialism in Comparative Perspective: Minority Presidents in Multiparty Systems*. Oxford: Oxford University Press.

Costa, A. M. T., Machado, B. A. & Zackseski, C. (2016). *A Investigação e a Persecução Penal da Corrupção e dos Delitos Econômicos: Uma Pesquisa Empírica no Sistema de Justiça Federal*. Brasília: ESMPU.

Da Ros, L. (2014). Mayors in the Dock: Judicial Responses to Local Corruption in Brazil. PhD dissertation, University of Illinois at Chicago.

(2019). Accountability legal e corrupção. *Revista da CGU* 11(20), 1251–75.

Da Ros, L. & Ingram, M. C. (2018). Law, Courts, and Judicial Politics. In B. Ames, ed., *Routledge Handbook of Brazilian Politics*. New York: Routledge, pp. 339–57.

Da Ros, L. & Taylor, M. M. (2022). *Brazilian Politics on Trial: Corruption and Reform under Democracy*. Boulder, CO: Lynne Rienner Publishers.

Dallagnol, D. (2017). *A Luta contra a Corrupção: A Lava Jato e o futuro de um país marcado pela impunidade*. São Paulo: Primeira Pessoa.

Feres Jr., J., Barbabela E. & Banchini, N. (2018). A Lava Jato e a Midia. In F. Kerche & J. Feres Jr., eds., *Operação Lava Jato e a Democracia Brasileira*. São Paulo: Contra Corrente, pp. 199–228.

Fontoura, L. Z. (2019). A justiça de Curitiba em números: uma análise quantitativa das sentenças proferidas pela Operação Lava Jato no Paraná (2014–2018). MA dissertation, Universidade Federal do Rio Grande do Sul.

Gonzalez-Ocantos, E. & Baraybar-Hidalgo, V. (2019). Lava Jato beyond Borders: The Uneven Performance of Anti-Corruption Judicial Efforts in Latin America. *Taiwan Journal of Democracy* 15(1), 63–89.

Hagopian, F. (2016). Brazil's Accountability Paradox. *Journal of Democracy* 27 (3), 119–28.

Karklins, R. (2005). *The System Made Me Do It: Corruption in Post-Communist Societies*. Armonk, NY: M. E. Sharpe.

Limongi, F. (2017). Impedindo Dilma. *Novos Estudos Cebrap*, special issue on "Dinâmicas da Crise," June, 5–13.

Lindberg, S. I. (2013). Mapping Accountability: Core Concepts and Subtypes. *International Review of Administrative Sciences* 79(2), 202–26.

Marona, M. C. & Barbosa, L. V. Q. (2018). Protagonismo judicial no Brasil: de que estamos falando? In M. C. Marona & A. Del Río, eds., *Justiça no Brasil: às margens da democracia*. Belo Horizonte: Arraes, pp. 133–55.

Merriner, J. L. (2004). *Grafters and Goo-Goos: Corruption and Reform in Chicago*. Carbondale: Southern Illinois University Press.

Michener, G. & Pereira, C. (2016). A Great Leap Forward for Democracy and the Rule of Law? Brazil's Mensalão Trial. *Journal of Latin American Studies* 48 (3), 477–507.

Moro, S. F. (2004). Considerações sobre a Operação Mani Pulite. *Revista Centro de Estudos Judiciários* 26, 56–62.

Oliveira, A. (2019). *Qual foi a influência da Lava Jato no comportamento do eleitor? Do lulismo ao bolsonarismo*. Curitiba: CRV.

Polícia Federal (2002). *Relatório Anual*. Brasília: Ministério da Justiça.

Rodrigues, F. A. (2019). Operação Lava Jato: Aprendizado Institucional e Ação Estratégica na Justiça Federal. MA dissertation, Universidade de São Paulo.

Shapiro, M. (1981). *Courts: A Comparative and Political Analysis*. Chicago, IL: University of Chicago Press.

Taylor, M. M. (2018). A corrupção e as reformas anticorrupção no Brasil: um longo caminho. In M. Seligman & F. Mello, eds., *Lobby Desvendado: Democracia, Políticas Públicas e Corrupção no Brasil Contemporâneo*. Rio de Janeiro: Record, pp. 97–127.

US Department of Justice (2016). Odebrecht and Braskem Plead Guilty and Agree to Pay at Least $3.5 Billion in Global Penalties to Resolve Largest Foreign Bribery Case in History, December 21, www.justice.gov/opa/pr/odebrecht-and-braskem-plead-guilty-and-agree-pay-least-35-billion-global-penalties-resolve

11

Turning Corruption Trials into Political Tools in the Name of Transparency

The Lava Jato Case

Mariana Mota Prado and Marta Rodriguez Machado

INTRODUCTION

Brazil's Lava Jato was a massive anti-corruption investigation publicly launched in 2014.[1] According to the investigation, executives from the country's state-run oil company, Petrobras, received bribes to award contracts to corporations at inflated prices. These executives were in turn appointed by politicians, who received bribes and campaign donations from both Petrobras executives and the companies they benefited. The scope of the corruption revealed is unprecedented: illegal payments received between 2004 and 2012 ammounted to hundreds of millions (if not billions) of dollars, with Brazil's largest construction companies implicated. The investigation's results were also shocking: as of 2021, there had been 294 criminal lawsuits with 1,710 individuals prosecuted and sentences totalling over 2,249 years; corporations involved in the scheme had paid 28.4 billion reais in fines and restitution (around USD5.7 billion);[2] and at least 50 politicians had been investigated, including the speakers of both the House of Representatives and Senate. Lava Jato seemed to be a turning point in anti-corruption enforcement in Brazil.

The operation has drawn criticism for bending rules in order to fight corruption (Prado & Machado, 2022). This includes criminal justice

[1] We are deeply grateful for the research assistance of Eduardo Cornelius and Matheus de Barros and to the participants of the FGV-Columbia Workshop, 2019.

[2] The most up-to-date figures available vary by city or court. Updated in 2021: Curitiba, Rio de Janeiro, the Superior Court of Justice, and the STF. Updated in 2020: São Paulo. Updated in 2019: Federal Court of the 2nd Region. See www.mpf.mp.br/grandes-casos/lava-jato/resultados

actors' aggressive strategy to increase transparency. The Public Prosecutor's Office created a user-friendly website with numbers, decisions, and reports on the case.[3] Lava Jato's leading prosecutor, Deltan Dallagnol, gave regular press conferences to announce his main findings and publicize the investigation's next steps (Dallagnol, 2017). Along the same lines, the case's lower court judge, Sergio Moro, made his decisions electronically available and often used accessible language, rather than the complicated technical terms and obtuse constructions that make most judicial decisions in Brazil inaccessible to the lay person. Moro and the appellate court used livestreaming for judicial hearings, drawing large audiences for many of the questionings conducted in the Lava Jato case. These actors argued that such measures were not only necessary to enhance effectiveness but were also required to raise public awareness of the case and to prevent interference by vested interests. However, in some instances, under the guise of transparency, judge Sergio Moro seems to have engaged in – sometimes blatant, sometimes subtle – violations of due process and the rule of law.

In line with other contributions to this edited volume (see Chapter 13), this chapter shows how judges and prosecutors who worked in corruption trials resorted to innovative strategies in an attempt to bypass what they perceived to be an ineffective legal system.[4] More specifically, we discuss three instances in which Sergio Moro acted in ways that did not seem to strictly follow Brazilian law. The first was his order to forcibly bring former President Lula in for questioning when Lula was a suspect in the investigation. The second was Moro's decision to publicize the audio recording of a wiretap of former President Lula's cell phone. The third was releasing to the public, in the middle of an electoral campaign, the plea bargain agreement of a former minister accusing Lula of corruption. Moro's transparency actions in Lula's case, alongside the fact that he eventually convicted Lula, raised suspicion. Lula was the front-runner in the 2018 presidential elections; after Moro's sentence was confirmed by an appeals court Lula became ineligible.[5] This gave his contender, Jair Bolsonaro, a great advantage. The fact that Moro would become President Bolsonaro's justice minister raised further suspicion that Moro

[3] Ministério Público Federal [Public Prosecutor's Office] (Braz), "Caso Lava Jato e". www.mpf.mp.br/grandescasos/lava-jato.

[4] For a discussion of the Brazilian system's deficiencies, see Taylor and Buranelli (2007).

[5] The Brazilian "Clean Slate Law" (Complementary Law no. 135 (Braz.), 4 June 2010) prohibits anyone convicted by an appeal court of certain crimes (including corruption, money laundering and abuse of power) from running for office for eight years.

had been driven by political motives. The suspicion was further increased as a series of media stories revealed leaked messages between Moro and prosecutors, suggesting that they had coordinated efforts to convict Lula. Eventually, in 2021, the Brazilian Supreme Court decided Moro was biased against Lula, annulling his sentences.

These three events show Lava Jato's creative use of legal tools and media mobilization, which could have contributed to the operation's impact. However, these strategies may have caused significant harm. We thus analyse the costs of such strategies and the risk of having an anti-corruption regime that embraces principles of transparency without accounting for the possibility that actors in the criminal justice system may be driven by political motives.

LAVA JATO'S TRANSPARENCY: FROM GOOD PRINCIPLES TO QUESTIONABLE DECISIONS

Coercive Questioning with Media Coverage

We start our analysis with the "coercive questioning" of former President Lula. Under Brazilian law, during an investigation, the police can call in the accused, witnesses, experts, or victims for questioning. If that person does not respond to the request, the Brazilian Code of Criminal Procedure[6] allows the judge to instruct the police to forcibly bring them in for questioning, hence the name coercive questioning. Lava Jato operations have extensively resorted to this tool: from 2014 to 2017, there were 222 coercive questionings.[7]

Despite being legal since 1941, coercive questioning has always been controversial. Considering that the accused has the right to remain silent, many jurists argue that coercive questioning of suspects or the accused is unconstitutional (Amaral, 2018; Lopes Jr., 2005, pp. 236–37). In 2011, however, the Supreme Court ruled not only that coercive questioning was constitutional but also that the police could use it without previous judicial authorization,[8] based on the fact that the constitution entrusts the police with investigative powers (article 144, § 4°). This ruling was

[6] Decree-law no. 3,689 (Braz), 3 Oct. 1941.

[7] Ministério Público Federal [Public Prosecutor's Office] (Braz), "Caso Lava Jato e". www.mpf.mp.br/grandescasos/lava-jato

[8] Supremo Tribunal Federal [Supreme Court] (Braz), "Habeas Corpus 107.644/SP", 6 Sept. 2011.

heavily criticized, as many jurists believe that such power should be reserved for the courts (Akutsu, 2013; Malan, 2015).

Coercive questioning came under the spotlight with Lava Jato, a case in which this measure was used not only with high frequency but also in an unexpected manner. Many of the investigated brought in for questioning were caught by surprise, never having received a formal request as required by the Code of Criminal Procedure.[9] Scenes of the accused being escorted by police to questioning received extensive media coverage. Former President Lula's coercive questioning in March 2016 was the most notorious and controversial episode. First, there was no formal request for questioning, making it illegal to resort to a coercive measure. Second, the police's "surprise" visit to Lula's house was closely covered by the media, which captured the entire scene in photos and videos that were immediately made available to the public. Many lawyers have accused the Lava Jato taskforce of seeking publicity and trying to damage Lula's image (Casara, 2015, p. 130), all in violation of privacy and due process rules.[10]

The Public Prosecutor's Office published a justification shortly afterwards, arguing that the measure is less draconian than temporary detention and aims at ensuring the safety of the accused while creating adequate conditions for evidence collection and questioning.[11] To justify its argument, the office cited the aforementioned 2011 Supreme Court decision allowing the use of coercive questioning without prior judicial authorization.[12] However, the office failed to mention that the Supreme Court had never authorized coercive questioning to be used in the absence of a previous formal request.

In December 2017, one Supreme Court Justice (Mendes) issued an injunction forbidding any authority from coercive questioning of suspects or the accused. This was in response to two cases brought to the court: in 2015, the Workers Party (Lula's party) had requested that the court

[9] Decree-law no. 3,689 (Braz), 3 Oct. 1941.

[10] Carta Capital, "Moro não fundamentou a decisão de condução coercitiva do Ex-Presidente", 10 March 2016; Consultor Jurídico, "Condução de Lula para depor foi ilegal e espetacularizada, dizem advogados", 4 March 2016.

[11] Ministério Público Federal [Public Prosecutor's Office] (Braz), "Nota de esclarecimento da força-tarefa Lava Jato do MPF em Curitiba", 5 March 2016.

[12] Supremo Tribunal Federal [Supreme Court] (Braz), "Habeas Corpus 107.644/SP", 6 Sept. 2011.

declare coercive questioning unconstitutional,[13] and in 2017 the same request was made by the National Bar Association.[14] They both argued that coercive questioning violated the right to freedom of movement, protected by the 1988 Constitution. Justice Mendes argued that it violated not only freedom of movement but also the presumption of innocence.[15] He did, however, stipulate that any information previously obtained as a result of coercive questioning of suspects or the accused would still be admissible in criminal trials. In 2019, the Supreme Court issued a final decision in both cases, determining that coercive questioning of suspects or the accused violates the constitution.[16] In the same year, Congress passed a bill criminalizing the illegal ordering of coercive questioning (Law no. 13,869[17]).

Publicizing Evidence and Privileged Information

On 16 March 2016, Judge Moro decided to publicize the audio recording of a wiretap of former President Lula's cell phone. The timing was delicate: Lula was going to become a minister in President Dilma Rousseff's cabinet the following day. This appointment would have granted him "special jurisdiction", moving cases against him (until then handled by Moro) to the Supreme Court. According to Moro, the recording, a conversation between Rousseff and Lula, suggested that the reason for the appointment was to grant protection to the former president.

Moro's decision triggered strong criticism. While courts can authorize wiretapping for purposes of criminal investigations, the Brazilian legal system does not authorize publicizing the content of the recordings. Judge Moro was fully aware of this and justified his decision with the following statement:

> As I have decided in all cases pertaining to the Lava Jato investigation, in cases of crime against the public administration, the public interest and the constitutional provisions about transparency in judicial processes (Federal Constitution,[18]

[13] Supremo Tribunal Federal [Supreme Court] (Braz), "Arguição de Descumprimento de Preceito Fundamental 395/DF", 9 Oct. 2019.

[14] Supremo Tribunal Federal [Supreme Court] (Braz), "Arguição de Descumprimento de Preceito Fundamental 444", 19 Dec. 2017.

[15] Ibid.

[16] Ibid.; Supremo Tribunal Federal [Supreme Court] (Braz), "Arguição de Descumprimento de Preceito Fundamental 395/DF", 9 Oct. 2019.

[17] Law no. 13,869 (Braz), 5 Sept. 2019.

[18] Federal Constitution [Constituição da República Federativa do Brasil de 1988] (Braz), 5 Oct. 1988.

article 5, LX and article 93, IX) prohibit the secrecy of judicial cases' files. This decision will not only allow the accused to defend themselves but will also allow for a healthy level of public scrutiny over the acts of the executive branch and the judiciary. Democracy in a free society requires the governed to know what their leaders do, even when they try to hide in shaded paths.)[19]

To back his ruling, Judge Moro cited a Supreme Court decision which, similarly, went against the *law* in the name of *justice*. In such a case, the court had ordered the preventive arrest of a senator, Delcídio do Amaral, even though the Brazilian Constitution granted full immunity to congressional representatives. To justify waiving this constitutional protection, the court argued that, without the arrest, Amaral could impede ongoing investigations in which he was a suspect. For the Supreme Court, the alleged risk of obstruction of justice justified bending the law. According to Moro, the same flexible interpretation of constitutional provisions should apply to Lula's case, as there was also a risk of obstruction of justice.[20]

From a legal perspective, there was an additional complication. Judge Moro had authorized the wiretapping of former President Lula, starting on 17 February 2016. On 16 March 2016, the day the recordings were eventually released, he decided to interrupt the recording. On 16 March 2016, at 11:13 am, Judge Moro wrote an order to the police and the telephone company to stop recording. The order was communicated to the police half an hour later and to the telephone company shortly thereafter. However, the recording was not immediately interrupted and, as a result, accidentally captured the conversation between President Rousseff and former President Lula. Nevertheless, Moro decided to make all the recordings public, even though they could not be used as evidence in court. As violating the privacy of telephone conversations is sanctioned with two to four years of imprisonment in Brazil (Law no. 9,296, article 10[21]), some jurists have argued that Moro should be held criminally liable.[22] While the conversation between Lula and Rousseff received the most attention, conversations between Lula and other authorities were also included in the recording. As some of

[19] Justiça Federal do Paraná [Paraná Federal Court] (Braz), "Pedido de Quebra de Sigilo n. 5006205-98.2016.4.04.7000/PR", 16 March 2016 (authors' translation).

[20] Justiça Federal do Paraná [Paraná Federal Court] (Braz), "Pedido de Quebra de Sigilo n. 5006205-98.2016.4.04.7000/PR", 16 March 2016.

[21] Law no. 9,296 (Braz), 24 July 1996.

[22] "Moro vs. Lula: esse crime chamado Justiça", *Justificando*, 22 July 2017; "O escândalo do levantamento do sigilo das interceptações telefônicas", *Justificando*, 15 Jan. 2018.

the authorities involved in these conversations had "special jurisdiction", some jurists argued that Moro should have sent the recording to the Supreme Court.[23]

One day after releasing the recording, Judge Moro rebutted the criticism in a public document added to the criminal file. He acknowledged that he did not notice that the relevant conversation had happened after he had ordered the police to stop the recording. But he dismissed it as irrelevant since the recording had been previously authorized.[24] Moro also argued that Lula was a regular citizen, and the fact that he was having conversations with people with "special jurisdiction" did not change his status. In Moro's view, the recording accidentally captured conversations with people outside the jurisdiction of the court, but the focus was Lula. Moro further claimed that even the "supreme ruler of the Republic" does not have the right to privacy over their communications if they are collected accidentally, as decided by the American Supreme Court in *U.S. v. Nixon*.[25]

In June 2016, the Brazilian Supreme Court declared Moro's decision illegal.[26] According to Justice Teori Zavascki, the fact that the recordings involved officials with "special jurisdiction" did indeed require the lower court to send the recordings to the Supreme Court. Moreover, the Supreme Court declared that Moro's decision had violated the constitution, and the law, which expressly forbids any publicity of information recorded in wiretapping and requires a court to destroy any recordings that are not relevant for criminal investigations. Justice Zavascki demanded an explanation from Moro. In response, a few days later, Moro sent his respectful apologies to the court.[27]

Despite its illegality, the conversation between Lula and Rousseff generated reactions inside and outside the judiciary. A Supreme Court injunction, issued by Justice Mendes on 18 March 2016, prevented Lula

[23] "Vazamento de Moro contra Dilma e Lula Rende Prêmio Jornalístico a GloboNews", *Jornal GGN*, 22 June 2017; "Sergio Moro Divulgou Grampos Ilegais de Autoridades com Prerrogativa de Foro", *Consultor Jurídico*, 16 March 2016; "O escândalo do levantamento do sigilo das interceptações telefônicas", *Justificando*, 15 Jan. 2018.

[24] "Moro reconhece erro em grampo de Dilma e Lula, mas mantém divulgação", *Consultor Jurídico*, 17 March 2016.

[25] Justiça Federal do Paraná [Paraná Federal Court] (Braz), "Despacho/Decisão em Pedido de Quebra de Sigilo de Dados", no. 5006205–98.2016.4.04.7000", 3 March 2016.

[26] Supremo Tribunal Federal [Supreme Court] (Braz), "Reclamação 23457/DF", 13 June 2016.

[27] "Por que os Áudios de Lula Viraram um dos Episódios Mais Controversos da Lava Jato", *Nexo Jornal*, 19 July 2016.

from being inaugurated. This decision departed from a long tradition of the Brazilian Supreme Court of not interfering with discretionary acts of the executive branch. According to Mendes, the leaked conversation indicated that the appointment was intended to obstruct the investigation.[28] While some have argued that the injunction was driven by a concern with legality (i.e., the illegality of Moro's decision should not exempt the current and former president from complying with the law), others have claimed that once the recordings became public, the Supreme Court felt pressured by public opinion to halt Lula's nomination.[29]

In addition to the legal dimensions, there were also important political consequences associated with this episode. The recording was widely publicized by media outlets.[30] At the time, public opinion was highly polarized, with a significant segment of Brazilian society opposing the Workers' Party. After the recordings were released, there were popular protests against the Workers' Party government in fifteen cities around the country, fuelling popular opposition to President Rousseff, who was facing impeachment.[31] In this delicate context, there is a question about timing. The publicity had significant political consequences. And despite the fact that the act was declared illegal by a higher court, it was hard – if not impossible – to undo its political effects.

The political dimensions of this episode became more evident after 2019, when The Intercept Brasil – the Brazilian arm of the non-profit investigative news agency – published a series of cell phone messages between Moro and Dallagnol.[32] The messages revealed not only a questionable level of coordination between judge and prosecutor,[33] but also suggested that political goals had driven some of these actors' decisions in the case. In one of the conversations, Moro expressed concerns about prosecutors' investigations of former President Fernando Henrique Cardoso. Dallagnol stated that the investigation was an attempt to

[28] "Gilmar Mendes suspende nomeação de Lula como ministro da Casa Civil", *O Globo*, 18 March 2016.

[29] Ibid.

[30] "Vazamento de Moro contra Dilma e Lula Rende Prêmio Jornalístico a GloboNews", *Jornal GGN*, 22 June 2017.

[31] "Áudio com diálogo de Lula e Dilma leva milhares de manifestantes às ruas", *El País*, 19 March 2016.

[32] "Leia os Diálogos de Sergio Moro e Deltan Dallagnol que Embasaram a Reportagem do Intercept", *The Intercept Brasil*, 6 Dec. 2019.

[33] While Brazilian law gives judges a more active role in seeking evidence, they are not allowed to collude with prosecutors.

"signal impartiality", to which Moro replied: "it jeopardizes someone whose support is important".[34]

The Intercept revelations (nicknamed *Vaza Jato*, or Car Leak) also showed that only a portion of the wiretapping recording discussed in the previous section had been publicized.[35] Non-publicized portions of the recording revealed that there was a lot of political pressure for Lula to take the job. This pressure came from the parties that formed the government's coalition, as they were concerned about the relationship between Congress and the presidency.[36] For example, Lula and then vice president Michel Temer discussed the fact that the government needed to better articulate the relationship between the executive and legislative branches, suggesting that there was a legitimate political reason for Lula to accept the nomination.[37] In other conversations, Lula expressed fear that his nomination would be perceived as a strategy to evade the Lava Jato investigations and that this could be held against him. In summary, if Moro had publicized all the recorded conversations, it would not have seemed so clear that the nomination was simply designed to protect Lula. This reinforces the hypothesis that Moro was more concerned with the political rather than legal outcome when he made the conversations public.

The Intercept Brasil also revealed that the prosecutors were fully aware of the political implications of the decision to release the audio recordings. Lava Jato's prosecutors expressed concern over the legality of Moro's decision, including whether they, too, might be subject to disciplinary action. One prosecutor suggested that if Moro was sanctioned, they should collectively resign in protest.[38] Dallagnol, in turn, tried to calm down those who believed that Moro's decision was illegal by arguing that this was only relevant for jurists: In the political sphere, the illegality was a minor, irrelevant detail. Dallagnol stated that there was no reason for

[34] "Moro repreendeu Deltan sobre investigação contra FHC: 'melindra alguém cujo apoio é importante'", *The Intercept Brasil*, 29 Aug. 2019 (authors' translation).

[35] The Intercept Brasil and Folha de S. Paulo had access to the notes from the federal police agents who monitored Lula, with summaries of twenty-two conversations. See "Conversas de Lula mantidas sob sigilo pela Lava Jato enfraquecem tese de Moro", *Folha de São Paulo*, 8 Sept 2019.

[36] "Confira resumos de conversas grampeadas de Lula com Temer e aliados", *Folha de São Paulo*, 8 Sept. 2019.

[37] "Confira resumos de conversas grampeadas de Lula com Temer e aliados", *Folha de São Paulo*, 8 Sept. 2019.

[38] "Leia Diálogos da Lava Jato sobre Escutas Telefônicas do ex-presidente Lula", *Folha de São Paulo*, 8 Sept. 2019.

concern, as "things were still favourable to them". In response, one of the prosecutors who believed that Moro's decision to publicize the recording was illegal stated: "I agree. This will have to be dealt with from a legal perspective. However, the [political] damage is done. And it is significant."[39]

Disclosing Confessions during the 2018 Elections

The third episode involved Moro's decision to publicize the plea bargain agreement of Antonio Palocci, a former minister in Lula's cabinet and chief of staff in Rousseff's, that could affect the 2018 elections. Palocci was convicted for corruption and money laundering and sentenced to twelve years in prison. He tried to negotiate a plea bargain with the Lava Jato prosecutors, but they concluded that there was no basis for an agreement. Palocci then turned to the federal police and reached an agreement with them in April 2018.[40] While the agreement with the police displeased the Public Prosecutors' Office,[41] the Brazilian Supreme Court considered it legal.

On 1 October 2018, six days before the first round of the Brazilian presidential elections, Moro, acting on his own initiative, i.e., without receiving a request from any of the parties, decided to add Palocci's plea bargain to Lula's case files, hence making them public.[42] As in the previous episode, the timing was extremely sensitive: the Workers' Party presidential candidate, Fernando Haddad, was rising in the polls. To justify his decision, Moro argued that this would help Lula's defence. However, Palocci's plea agreement contained politically sensitive information that could harm the Workers' Party. According to Palocci, 90 per cent of the executive decrees enacted during Lula's and Rousseff's presidencies involved bribes. He also stated that most of the campaign contributions the Workers' Party had received from companies came from corruption schemes. Perhaps the most sensitive piece of information was Palocci's assertion that Lula had known about the corruption scheme

39 Ibid. (authors' translation).

40 In Brazil, it is possible to obtain a plea bargain deal after being convicted (Law no. 12,850 (Braz), 2 Aug. 2013).

41 "Sergio Moro entra na campanha eleitoral ao suspender sigilo de parte da delação de Palocci", *Época*, 8 May 2018.

42 Justiça Federal do Paraná [Paraná Federal Court] (Braz), "Despacho/Decisão na Ação Penal no. 5063130-17.2016.4.04.7000/PR", 1 Oct. 2018.

involving Petrobras since at least 2007. Lula's direct involvement in the scheme, however, has never been proved.

In the same decision in which Moro decided to publicize Palocci's plea bargain, he also rejected a request made by Lula's lawyers to suspend the case during the elections. They were concerned about the political exploitation of the case. According to Moro, there was no need to suspend the case because there were no hearings scheduled, and the case would only involve written submissions during the campaign period. Yet, in a previous decision, Moro had suspended Lula's hearings because Lula "[had] transformed them into political events".[43] Moro added that "holding hearings during elections could create risks for the hearing, as well as for Lula's supporters and opponents".[44]

Moro's decision to publicize Palocci's plea bargain was heavily criticized. Lula's lawyer, Cristiano Zanin, argued that "there was a clear intent to generate a political impact on Lula and his political allies".[45] A representative of the Brazilian Association of Jurists for Democracy stated that "this decision clearly tries to influence the electoral outcome, I have no doubt about it. Why now? Why not two weeks ago, or two weeks ahead?"[46]

When the National Justice Council (CNJ) demanded an explanation, Moro responded he had no intention of influencing the 2018 elections. He stated:

> [I]f I had any intention to influence the elections, I would have released the video with the testimony, which was much more impactful than the written version of the statements and would be more broadly exploited by the televised press or on the Internet ... I cannot stop my work simply because there is an election in progress ... Publicity and transparency are fundamental to the judiciary, and a judge cannot be the guardian of the dark political secrets of actors accused of

[43] In the original: "Lula da Silva que tem transformado as datas de seus interrogatórios em eventos partidários." Justiça Federal do Paraná [Paraná Federal Court] (Braz), "Despacho/Decisão na Ação Penal no. 5063130-17.2016.4.04.7000/PR", 1 Oct. 2018 (authors' translation).

[44] In the original: "Realizar o interrogatório dele durante o período eleitoral poderia gerar riscos ao ato e até mesmo à integridade de seus apoiadores ou oponentes políticos." Justiça Federal do Paraná [Paraná Federal Court] (Braz), "Despacho/Decisão na Ação Penal no. 5063130-17.2016.4.04.7000/PR", 1 Oct. 2018 (authors' translation).

[45] In the original: "nítido objetivo de tentar causar efeitos políticos para Lula e seus aliados." "Divulgação da delação de Palocci foi decisão 'eleitoral' de Moro, dizem juristas", *Brasil de Fato*, 1 Oct. 2018.

[46] Ibid.

corruption. To delay the release of the testimony until after the elections would be as inappropriate as its publicity before it.[47]

The disclosure of Palocci's plea bargain had significant political consequences. First, the content of the agreement received great publicity. On 1 October 2018, the main Brazilian television news programme (*Jornal Nacional*) dedicated nine minutes to cover the released agreement,[48] which also appeared in the headlines of Brazil's major newspapers. Palocci's plea agreement "became a weapon against Haddad [the Workers' Party's presidential candidate]".[49] For example, Geraldo Alckmin, who was the presidential candidate for the Brazilian Social Democracy Party (PSDB), used images of Palocci next to Lula and Rousseff, indicating that Palocci said Lula knew about the Petrobras corruption scheme. The advertisement also suggested that Lula and Rousseff's 2010 and 2014 campaigns had received illegal contributions. Alckmin's campaign advertisement's narrator would say: "Scandal! It is now proven what Brazil already knew. Lula knew everything about the Petrobras corruption scheme. If the Workers' Party returns [to power], corruption will continue."[50] Bolsonaro, then one of the presidential candidates, congratulated Palocci on the plea bargain and stated that the revelations made by Palocci would change the result of the elections.[51] In line with Bolsonaro's prediction, at least one newspaper projected that it "should have an impact in the first round of the elections".[52]

[47] Original: "caso fosse intenção deste Juízo influenciar nas eleições teria divulgado a gravação em vídeo do depoimento, muito mais contundente do que as declarações escritas e que seria muito mais amplamente aproveitada para divulgação na imprensa televisiva ou na rede mundial de computadores ... o Juízo não pode interromper os seus trabalhos apenas porque há uma eleição em curso ... Publicidade e transparência são fundamentais para a ação da Justiça e não deve o juiz atuar como guardião de segredos sombrios de agentes políticos suspeitos de corrupção. Retardar a publicidade do depoimento para depois das eleições poderia ser considerado tão inapropriado como a sua divulgação no período anterior." Conselho Nacional de Justiça [National Justice Council] (Braz), "Reclamação Disciplinar no. 0008908-46.2018.2.00.0000", 10 Feb. 2018, pp. 3–4. (authors' translation)

[48] "Moro achava fraca delação de Palocci que divulgou às vésperas de eleição, sugerem mensagens", *Folha de São Paulo*, 27 Aug. 2019.

[49] "Delação de Palocci vira arma contra Haddad", *ISTOÉ*, 3 Oct. 2019.

[50] Original: "Escândalo. Comprovado o que o Brasil tinha certeza. Lula sabia de tudo sobre a corrupção na Petrobras. Se o PT voltar, a corrupção vai continuar." "Delação de Palocci vira arma contra Haddad", *ISTOÉ*, 3 Oct. 2019.

[51] "Bolsonaro parabeniza Palocci e diz que delação deve mudar eleição", *UOL Notícias*, 4 Oct. 2018.

[52] "Delação de Palocci vira arma contra Haddad", *Estado de São Paulo*, 3 Oct. 2018.

Moro's disclosure of Palocci's plea agreement reinforces the hypothesis that the judge was politically motivated. Lava Jato's prosecutors had decided that Palocci's testimony contained no evidence against Lula. The prosecutors had said so publicly, but The Intercept's revelations provided more details about the lack of robustness in the testimony. After analysing cell phone messages exchanged among Lava Jato prosecutors and the five versions of documents presented by Palocci to these prosecutors, The Intercept concluded that:

> [I]n 18 of the 53 documents appended, there was no reference to any evidence. In at least nine other cases, Palocci pointed to existing trials and to plea bargaining documents by other accused ... as evidence that he was telling the truth. In many cases, the evidence provided did not seem enough to corroborate Palocci's testimony. For instance, the former minister says that he went to Safra Bank to collect cash on behalf of Lula on five occasions, but his only evidence were documents showing the places he had been in the city in those days.[53]

The blatant lack of evidence, combined with the timing of the release (near voting day), makes it plausible that the disclosure was a political strategy, disguised as a regular exercise of judicial discretion.

LAVA JATO'S STRATEGIES AND BRAZILIAN LAW

This section provides an overview of existing regulations on judges' interactions with the media and politics, showing that the three episodes described characterize varying degrees of violation of existing norms and represent the paradoxical cultures of legality that prevail in Latin America.

Existing Regulations

There are three categories of rules governing judges and prosecutors' behaviour in Brazil: (1) constitutional provisions on due process, impartiality, and publicity and transparency in criminal trials; (2) a statutory

[53] Original: "Em 18 dos 53 anexos, não há nenhuma referência a provas. Em pelo menos outros 9 casos, Palocci apontou processos em andamento na justiça e depoimentos de outros delatores ... como garantias de que estava falando a verdade. Em vários casos, as provas pareciam insuficientes para comprovar os relatos de Palocci. O ex-ministro diz que foi até o banco Safra recolher dinheiro em espécie para Lula em cinco ocasiões, mas só apresentou como prova registros de seus deslocamentos pela cidade nos dias em que afirmou ter feito as entregas." "Moro achava fraca delação de Palocci que divulgou às vésperas de eleição, sugerem mensagens", *Folha de São Paulo*, 27 Aug. 2019.

prohibition from engaging in partisan politics; and (3) regulations on these actors' interactions with the media (via interviews, or commentary on existing cases).

To ensure judicial impartiality and independence, the constitution prohibits ad hoc courts, establishes organizational rules for the judiciary, and determines that the law should define how cases are to be assigned to judges (article 95). The constitution also ensures that judges can only be fired via a judicial process and that their salaries cannot be reduced (article 95). In addition, the constitution prohibits judges from engaging in another profession (teaching excepted), or political activities, and from receiving gifts from public or private entities (article 95, sole paragraph, items I to V).

As a rule, criminal proceedings in Brazil should be public, but judges, prosecutors, and the police have wide discretion to waive this rule. The Brazilian Constitution stipulates that all judicial proceedings must be public and that the law can only limit publicity when it violates privacy or the public interest (article 5°, LX; article 93, IX). The Code of Criminal Procedure also requires all judicial proceedings to be public, secrecy being authorized only under special circumstances.[54] The code allows judges to restrict public access to hearings and court sessions only if publicity may cause "a scandal, serious inconvenience, or risk disturbing the social order" (article 792, § 1). The code also allows judges to restrict third-party access to case files to protect victims (article 201, § 6). Investigations are also public as a rule, but the police and prosecutors have wide discretion to conduct investigations in secrecy "if necessary for determining the facts or if required by society's interest" (Code of Criminal Procedure, article 20).[55] However, as a general rule, lawyers should be allowed to access their clients' files (Lopes Jr., 2020). The publicity of plea negotiations has different rules. Prosecutors and the police can hear a plea bargain testimony in secrecy, but the agreement must become public when formalized (Law no. 12,850/13, article 4, II, §7 and article 7, §3[56]). In contrast, wiretapping recordings in the course of judicial investigations must be kept secret (Law no. 9,296/96, articles 8 and 9[57]). In summary, in Brazil, the transparency of criminal trials is seen as an

54 Decree-law no. 3,689 (Braz), 3 Oct. 1941.

55 Ibid. See also Conselho Nacional do Ministério Público [National Council of the Public Prosecutor's Office] (Braz), "Resolução n. 181/2017", 7 Aug 2017.

56 Law no. 12,850 (Braz), 2 Aug. 2013.

57 Law no. 9,296 (Braz), 24 July 1996.

integral component of the rule of law, but the law provides judges with great discretion to resort to secrecy.

While transparency may serve as a mechanism to keep the judiciary accountable, there is no regulation on how the media can report these cases, except for crimes against one's honour. Brazil's military dictatorship (1964–1985) enacted a statute regulating the media (Law no. 5,250/67) that was struck down as unconstitutional in 2009[58] and is yet to be replaced. Unconstrained media reporting of judicial proceedings is often a source of concern, considering that the media can generate social uprising and moral panics (Critcher, 2003; Moore, 2013), undermining the right to a fair trial (see Roberts et al., 2002).

In contrast, judges' and prosecutors' interactions with politics and the media is well regulated in Brazil. Both the constitution[59] and the Judicial Code of Ethics[60] (*Código da Magistratura*) forbid judges to participate in any activity related to party politics (Federal Constitution article 95; Judicial Code of Ethics, article 7). Judges are also prohibited from expressing opinions about pending cases or criticizing judicial decisions when not in court (Judicial Code of Ethics, article 12; Complementary Law no. 35/79, article 36[61]). Judges must also avoid any self-promotional or self-aggrandizing behaviour (Judicial Code of Ethics, article 13). Recently the National Justice Council (CNJ) enacted regulations on judicial behaviour on social media.[62]

During the Lava Jato investigations, the Brazilian Congress revived debates on a 2007 Bill criminalizing abuse of power, including abusive use of media and social media during investigations and trials. Enacted in 2019, the new law attempts to balance transparency and presumption of innocence. The law also criminalizes the release of audios that cannot be used as evidence (Law no. 13,869/19, article 28[63]). For some, this provision were perceived to be an attempt to contain Judge Moro and as a political backlash against Lava Jato.[64] Yet the new statute only sanctions

[58] Supremo Tribunal Federal [Supreme Court] (Braz), "Reclamação 23457/DF", 13 June 2016.

[59] Federal Constitution [Constituição da República Federativa do Brasil de 1988] (Braz), 5 Oct. 1988.

[60] Judicial Code of Ethics [Código de Ética da Magistratura] (Braz), 26 Aug. 2008.

[61] Complementary Law no. 35 (Braz), 14 March 1979.

[62] Conselho Nacional de Justiça [National Justice Council] (Braz), "Resolução n. 305/2019", 17 Dec 2019.

[63] Law no. 13,869 (Braz), 5 Sept. 2019.

[64] "Entenda a Lei de Abuso de Autoridade: Proposta que prevê punição a juízes e membros do Ministério Público é vista como reação da classe política a operações como a Lava Jato", *Estado de São Paulo*, 3 Jan. 2020; "Lei do abuso de autoridade: conheça três casos

with imprisonment the most extreme behaviour, which was already forbidden; other types of discretionary decisions by judges and prosecutors remain unregulated.

Currently, most of Brazil's institutional arrangements seem to operate under the assumption that law and politics are parallel but independent accountability systems. Under this conception, lawsuits supposedly run their course according to the rule of law and due process. To the extent that legal proceedings influence public opinion or may affect the ballot box, the implicit assumption is that they do so in a neutral fashion – evidence is presented, facts are determined, decisions made, and these are duly reported by the media, allowing voters to make informed decisions. The current regulatory structure does not acknowledge that there is a risk that legal actors are able to influence public opinion and political processes by releasing information, timing decisions to minimize or maximize electoral impact, or other strategic uses of their discretion. Yet, as we have shown, prosecutors and judges may actively and strategically select what, when, and how information is publicized, and these decisions may be motivated by political purposes.

Problems with the Current System: The Lack of Judicial Accountability

The three episodes described reveal three different problems with control of judicial behaviour in Brazil. Moro was never held accountable for ordering Lula's coercive questioning, releasing Lula's phone conversations, or disclosing Palocci's plea agreement. The following paragraphs discuss how the Brazilian accountability system is inadequate to deal with these varying degrees of legal violations, and general difficulties in regulating judicial behaviour.

That Moro was not held accountable for Lula's coercive questioning shows a lack of effective sanctioning for legal violations. Coercive questioning is allowed only after the accused's failure to attend a hearing. Lava Jato's prosecutors and judges did develop a legal argument to justify using coercive questioning without issuing a formal request in advance. They argued that this was an "autonomous injunction" (*medida cautelar autônoma*), which, while not listed in the Code of Criminal Procedure,[65] is legal since judges have a "general power" to issue injunctions. When

da Lava Jato nos quais investigadores e juízes poderiam ser punidos", *BBC News Brasil*, 17 Aug. 2019.

[65] Decree-law no. 3,689 (Braz), 3 Oct. 1941.

coercive questioning of suspects or the accused was challenged before the Brazilian Supreme Court, the prosecutor general argued that "it is a tool to guarantee the efficacy (and overcome obstacles) in the production of evidence in criminal cases".[66] While Moro was never sanctioned for violating the law, the Supreme Court's declaration of the entire practice (even if preceded by an initial request for questioning) as unconstitutional seems to be an attempt to prevent its abusive use.

Moro's unpunished leak of Lula's wiretapping is another example of the lack of effective sanctioning for violations of existing norms. Moro's claim that his action was necessary to protect the "public interest" may satisfy the layperson, but, as argued, it is not a solid legal justification. The conduct could have been punished by internal mechanisms of accountability within the judicial branch. However, Moro was not sanctioned.

Finally, attaching Palocci's plea agreement to Lula's case file and making it public is not a clear legal violation. In fact, plea-bargaining agreements must be made public once formalized, and judges have the discretion to bring external documents to cases. However, the timing of the release makes Moro's behaviour extremely problematic. Even though there is no law regulating when judges can make information public, one could argue that the timing of Moro's decision violates rules of forbearance, i.e., informal norms that govern public officials' behaviour. These violations take place when actions, while respecting the letter of the law, clearly violate its spirit (Levitsky & Ziblatt, 2019).

These three problems reveal structural deficiencies within the Brazilian accountability system. The 1988 Constitution accorded the judiciary – and other legal actors – substantial power and responsibility. To fulfil its role, the Brazilian judiciary enjoys great independence (Ballard, 1999; Castro, 1997). To counterbalance this freedom, in 2004 the National Justice Council (CNJ) was created to assure transparency and accountability in the judiciary. Rather than the usual reason for instituting judicial councils – protecting the judiciary's independence – the CNJ was created to discipline judges' behaviour and perform other accountability functions (Franco & Cunha, 2013). However, although the CNJ has the power to impose disciplinary sanctions against judges who violate professional duties, it has seldom done so. There are numerous examples of judges publicly behaving improperly with little to no consequence

[66] Ministério Público Federal [Public Prosecutor's Office] (Braz), "Manifestação na Arguição de Descumprimento de Preceito Fundamental 395/DF", 6 Feb. 2017.

(Savarese, 2014). Even Supreme Court justices have shown deplorable behaviour, which has not only gone unpunished but is frequently unremarked (Arguelhes & Hartmann, 2017).

In this context of lax enforcement, it is no surprise that Lava Jato judges and prosecutors have not been punished. Although Moro has faced fifty-five disciplinary proceedings at the CNJ, based on complaints presented by lawyers, professional associations, and political parties, all have been archived or dismissed. As of June 2019, thirty-four had been dismissed, including an administrative process to investigate Moro's decision to release the wiretapping of the conversation between Lula and Rousseff.[67] Some cases, held *in camera*, have been dismissed without any public justification, as in the complaint against Lula's coercive questioning. All other cases have been archived since Moro left the bench.[68] Recently a political party (PDT) made a formal complaint to CNJ to investigate the facts uncovered by The Intercept, but the council dismissed the request, arguing that Moro is no longer a judge.[69]

The Intercept messages suggest that Lava Jato's prosecutors were not only aware of this environment of impunity, but one of the prosecutors suggested that there was a low risk of disciplinary action because of the strong popular support for Lava Jato. This comment may be interpreted as yet another example of the conflicting cultures of legality that prevail in Latin America (Couso et al., 2010, p. 5). While the law is regarded as a promising tool to solve complex problems in the region – a phenomenon labelled "fetishization of the law" (Comaroff & Comaroff, 2006), it is also blatantly disregarded (Mendez et al., 1999), creating spheres of lawlessness. The classic example is police violence in Latin America, where rampant police killings often go unpunished. These are perpetrated by state law enforcement agents, who try to obtain "results" by not

[67] "STF Anula Grampo entre Lula e Dilma e Envia para Sergio Moro Investigações contra Ex-presidente", *Veja*, 13 June 2016; "Invicto no CNJ, Moro teve arquivados 34 processos por suspeita de infração", *Folha de São Paulo*, 13 June 2019. We have resorted to a newspaper report after failed attempts to obtain information about all cases directly from the CNJ database.

[68] As of March 2022, the CNJ website indicated that there were thirty-one cases against Moro and all had been archived. There is no public information available about cases held *in camera*.

[69] Conselho Nacional de Justiça [National Justice Council] (Braz), "Pedido de Providências n. 0004190-69.2019.2.00.0000", Brasília, DF, 11 June 2019.

abiding by due process or respecting individual rights. While these killings are illegal, they are strongly supported by the population, which sees them as a strategy to fight crime (Brinks, 2006, pp. 201–26). Lava Jato demonstrates that the disregard for rules also takes place inside the courts, i.e., by those in charge of interpreting the law.

But even if the three episodes described had been punished, pieces of information would still have been conveyed to the public, generating consequences that could not have been prevented or mitigated. Once the video of Lula being escorted by the police reached TV screens, once the leaked wiretapping was reproduced by the media, and once Palocci's plea agreement was publicized, the political damage was done. Even if disciplinary sanctions were imposed or compensatory damages awarded, the political impact was irreversible. There is no way of restoring the previous status quo. Thus, the transparency of trials and interactions between legal actors and the media should be treated as sensitive issues. Lava Jato's political impact show the complexity of controlling the non-judicial consequences that the justice system produces.

Forbearance rules may make actors refrain from engaging in unwarranted behaviour (Brinks, 2003, pp. 1–19; Helmke & Levitsky, 2006, p. 101). However, Lava Jato shows that when courts themselves decide to disregard these informal rules, it is hard to discipline them. This raises interesting questions about when these informal rules are effective in disciplining judicial actors, and why in certain cases they fail. In other words, informal rules can be associated with institutional weaknesses (Brinks et al., 2019) but they may also contribute to institutional robustness. Specifically, these rules seem to play an important role in preserving the rule of law. Numerous studies show the negative effects of informal norms (corruption, clientelism, patrimonialism) on judicial behaviour, but very few analyse their positive effects.

Moreover, if one assumes that legal actors, especially judges, can behave as political actors, there may be a direct connection between written and unwritten rules governing judicial behaviour and safeguards to democracy. The three episodes discussed in this chapter have deeply affected Brazil's political landscape. This suggests that such rules should not be analysed in isolation (e.g., rules governing party politics are distinct from those applicable to judicial actors, but can interact in complex ways). As the judiciary becomes an active player in the political game – as is often the case in corruption trials – formal and informal rules for the judiciary may become critical to democracy.

CONCLUSION

Like many countries, Brazil has a long history of impunity for corruption (Taylor & Buranelli, 2007). In these countries, it is common for citizens to regard judicial actors who try to sanction those involved in corruption as heroes, and for the Bar and the Bench to cultivate this image (Della Porta, 2001). In a system plagued by corruption, these judges are seen as lone rangers against "the system". Often portrayed as beacons of morality and respect, they may find public support, even pressure, to run for office. This happened in Brazil with Justice Barbosa of the Brazilian Supreme Court during the *mensalão* case,[70] and it was not surprising that it happened again with Moro.[71] Indeed, at the time of this writing (May 2022), Moro is running for a congressional seat in the 2022 federal elections.

As outlined in this volume's introduction, many scholars have emphasized the benefits of highly popular judicial institutions. Their key assumption is that, as the "least dangerous branch", the judiciary needs to amass public legitimacy to be effective and prevail in inter-branch struggles (Forero-Alba and Rodríguez-Raga, Chapter 7 in this volume). In this context, courts' mobilization of public opinion could be laudable. Interestingly, this was the argument used by Lava Jato actors to justify their innovative transparency measures. The argument carries some currency in the Brazilian context: the federal police have sought publicity for their "operations", successfully galvanizing the public (Arantes, 2011). This was also the argument that Moro supporters have used to defend him: he was trying to achieve justice despite the obstacles imposed by a system that has always protected the corrupt classes ruling Brazil.

On the other hand, Moro's critics accuse him of having political aspirations from the beginning and launching a crusade against the Workers' Party.[72] Regardless of Moro's political aspirations and ideological intentions, critics claim that his actions created a judicial

[70] "Corruption Trial Makes Black Brazilian Judge a Hero", *Reuters*, 1 Nov. 2012.

[71] "He's the 'Hero' Judge Who Oversaw Brazil's Vast Car Wash Corruption Probe. Now He's Facing His Own Scandal", *Washington Post*, 17 June 2019.

[72] "Moro vs. Lula: esse crime chamado Justiça", *Justificando*, 22 July 2017. According to The Intercept Brasil, Moro and the Lava Jato task force also attempted to interfere in Venezuelan politics. Leaked messages show that Moro suggested to Dallagnol a plea agreement accusing the Venezuelan president, Nicolás Maduro, of receiving bribes. In other conversations, prosecutors reportedly discussed strategies to make the agreement public without being held accountable for doing so. "Lava Jato tramou vazamento de delação para interferir na política da Venezuela após sugestão de Sergio Moro", *The Intercept Brasil*, 7 July 2019.

dictatorship in Brazil.[73] When the Supreme Court decided Moro was biased against Lula, Minister Gilmar Mendes listed the three episodes explored in this chapter as evidence of Moro's bias, along with his appointment as Bolsonaro's minister and the personal messages leaked by The Intercept.[74] It is hard to determine if Moro had political aspirations all along or simply took the opportunity that presented itself when Bolsonaro took office. Regardless of Moro's motivation, as Da Ros and Taylor argue in this volume (Chapter 10), he engaged in a political battle beyond his role as a judge. Ironically, in April 2020, Moro left Bolsonaro's government, accusing the president of illegally interfering with the federal police's work, in an attempt to curtail a corruption investigation of his family members. When he announced his departure, Moro stated that the previous Workers' Party government had many failures but always respected the federal police's autonomy.

As we have shown, transparency and publicity in criminal law work is a double-edged sword. On the one hand, strategies such as holding press conferences and televising judicial hearings fall squarely within the purview of what is authorized by Brazilian law and can be interpreted as attempts to seek trust and public support. On the other hand, the three episodes we have explored deviate from existing rules and informal norms of behaviour. Transparency and trust in the judicial system are often touted as positive, but they can also venture into dangerous territory. Popular opinions about criminal law seldom coincide with the most basic rule of law principles. A clear example is the widespread support for "mano dura" policies in Latin America, where police violence is accepted and welcomed because of a popular belief that criminals are not entitled to rights ("*Bandido bom é bandido morto*") (Caldeira, 2000). The Lava Jato discursive strategy tapped into these feelings, opening the door for abuses. Thus, it is important to distinguish between public support that enhances judicial legitimacy and strengthens the judiciary versus public support that fosters judicial populism.

In summary, there are significant tensions that arise when courts try to influence public opinion. Restraining the judiciary from doing so would go a long way to prevent it from becoming a political actor and violating separation of powers principles. Yet regulating how legal actors interact

[73] "O escândalo do levantamento do sigilo das interceptações telefônicas", *Justificando*, 15 Jan. 2018.

[74] Supremo Tribunal Federal [Supreme Court] (Braz), "Habeas Corpus 164.493/PR", 23 March 2021.

with the media and public opinion requires a complex balance between private rights and public interest. A well-designed and strictly enforced system for legal actors (judges and prosecutors) is not enough if the complex interactions between these rules and the political system are not accounted for. While transparency should not be abandoned, further research should investigate how legal reform can prevent abuses that impact the rule of law, and how the criminal justice system may undermine democracy.

References

Akutsu, J. R. C. (2013). Condução coercitiva e a necessária reserva de jurisdição. *Boletim Do IBCCRIM* 252, 13–14.

Amaral, T. B. do. (2018). A inconstitucionalidade da condução coercitiva. *Boletim Do IBCCRIM* 1, 2–3.

Arantes, R. B. (2011). The Federal Police and the Ministério Público. In T. J. Power & M. M. Taylor, eds., *Corruption and Democracy in Brazil: The Struggle for Accountability*. Notre Dame, IN: University of Notre Dame Press, pp. 184–217.

Arguelhes, D. W., & Hartmann, I. A. (2017). Timing Control without Docket Control: How Individual Justices Shape the Brazilian Supreme Court's Agenda. *Journal of Law and Courts* 5(1), 105–40.

Ballard, M. J. (1999). The Clash between Local Courts and Global Economics: The Politics of Judicial Reform in Brazil. *Berkeley Journal of International Law* 17, 230–76.

Brinks, D. M. (2003). Informal Institutions and the Rule of Law: The Judicial Response to State Killings in Buenos Aires and São Paulo in the 1990s. *Comparative Politics* 36(1), 1–19.

(2006). The Rule of (Non) Law: Prosecuting Police Killings in Brazil and Argentina. In S. Levitsky & G. Helmke, eds., *Informal Institutions and Democracy: Lessons from Latin America*. Baltimore, MD: Johns Hopkins University Press, pp. 201–26.

Brinks, D. M., Levitsky, S., & Murillo, M. V. (2019). *Understanding Institutional Weakness: Power and Design in Latin American Institutions*. Cambridge: Cambridge University Press.

Caldeira, T. P. R. (2000). *Cidade de muros: crime, segregação e cidadania em São Paulo*. Translated by Frank de Oliveira and Henrique Monteiro. São Paulo: Editora 34; EDUSP.

Casara, R. (2015). *Processo Penal do Espetáculo: Ensaios sobre o Poder Penal, a dogmática e o autoritarismo na sociedade brasileira*. Florianópolis: Empório do Direito.

Castro, M. F. de. (1997). The Courts, Law, and Democracy in Brazil. *International Social Science Journal* 49(152), 241–52.

Comaroff, J., & Comaroff, J. L., eds. (2006). *Law and Disorder in the Postcolony*. Chicago, IL: University of Chicago Press.

Couso, J., Huneeus, A., & Sieder, R., eds. (2010). *Cultures of Legality: Judicialization and Political Activism in Latin America*. Cambridge: Cambridge University Press.

Critcher, C. (2003). *Moral Panics and the Media*. Buckingham, PA: Open University Press.

Dallagnol, D. (2017). *A luta contra a corrupção: A Lava Jato e o futuro de um país marcado pela impunidade*. Rio de Janeiro: Sextante.

Della Porta, D. (2001). A Judges' Revolution? Political Corruption and the Judiciary in Italy. *European Journal of Political Research* 39(1), 1–21.

Franco, I. C. da S. de, & Cunha, L. G. (2013). O CNJ e os discursos do Direito e Desenvolvimento. *Revista Direito GV* 9(2), 515–34.

Helmke, G., & Levitsky, S., eds. (2006). *Informal Institutions and Democracy: Lessons from Latin America*. Baltimore, MD: Johns Hopkins University Press.

Levitsky, S., & Ziblatt, D. (2019). *How Democracies Die*. New York: Broadway Books.

Lopes Jr., A. (2005). *Introdução crítica ao Processo Penal: Fundamentos da Instrumentalidade Garantista*. 3rd ed. Rio de Janeiro: Lumen Juris.

(2020). *Direito Processual Penal*. 17th ed. Sao Paulo: Saraiva.

Malan, D. (2015). Condução coercitiva do acusado (ou investigado) no processo penal. *Boletim Do IBCCRIM* 266, 2–4.

Mendez, J. E., O'Donnell, G. A., & Pinheiro, P. S., eds. (1999). *(Un)Rule of Law and the Underprivileged In Latin America*. Notre Dame, IN: University of Notre Dame Press.

Moore, S. (2013). The Cautionary Tale: A New Paradigm for Studying Media Coverage of Crime. In J. Petley, C. Critcher, J. Hughes, & A. Rohloff, eds., *Moral Panics in the Contemporary World*. London: Bloomsbury Academic, pp. 33–50.

Prado, M. M., & Machado, M. (2022). Using Criminal Law to Fight Corruption: The Potential, Risks and Limitations of Operation Car Wash (Lava Jato). *American Journal of Comparative Law*.

Roberts, J. V., Stalans, L. J., Indermaur, D., & Hough, M. (2002). *Penal Populism and Public Opinion: Lessons from Five Countries*. Oxford: Oxford University Press.

Savarese, M. (2014, 13 November). You Can't Say a Judge Is not God in Brazil (According to Judges Themselves). https://abrazilianoperatinginthisarea.wordpress.com/2014/11/13/you-cant-say-a-judge-is-not-god-in-brazil-according-to-judges-themselves/

Taylor, M. M., & Buranelli, V. C. (2007). Ending up in Pizza: Accountability as a Problem of Institutional Arrangement in Brazil. *Latin American Politics and Society* 49(1), 59–87.

12

Fighting Corruption, Dismantling Democracy

Antagonism, Communication, and the Political Use of Lava Jato in Brazil

João Guilherme Bastos dos Santos and Esther Solano Gallego

INTRODUCTION

In this chapter we investigate affinities between *Bolsonarismo* (i.e. groups supporting Jair Bolsonaro's government and ideas) and *Lavajatismo* (groups supporting the Lava Jato investigation) both online and offline from 2015 to 2019. Our analysis shows the links between the denial of rights, the push for accountability through the courts, and far-right discourse, combining two original data sources. First, we conducted semi-structured interviews with members of the so-called *verde e amarelos* ("green and yellow", which are the colours of the Brazilian flag) during mass anti-corruption demonstrations in 2015 and 2017. Participants at these rallies were characterized by the use of the Brazilian yellow jersey as a symbol of nationalism, "anti-communism", and anti-corruption. Second, we present the results from a lexical analysis of 13,800 posts on Facebook pages supporting Lava Jato, posted between April 2016 and February 2019. This period included former President Dilma Rousseff's impeachment, former President Luiz Inácio "Lula" Da Silva's imprisonment, and Jair Bolsonaro's rise to power. It is worth mentioning that the *verde e amarelos* strongly supported the impeachment of Rousseff in 2015, the Lava Jato Operation, and Bolsonaro's candidacy in 2018.

In line with regional trends, the judicialization of politics in Brazil (Arantes, 2005) is characterized by an increasing number of groups trying to solve political conflicts through the courts. Beyond the expansion of minority rights, it fostered a conservative backlash that simultaneously attacks the Federal Supreme Court's (Supremo Tribunal Federal, STF) role in defending the constitution and gives strong political support for actors promising solutions to address the delays introduced by respecting due process during corruption investigations. In this context, conservative voices hail judges and prosecutors that promise solutions to courts' inability to promptly answer to corruption. In particular, they portray actors willing to enforce criminal accountability at any cost – for either "ordinary criminals" or corrupt politicians – as courageous patriots despite their disdain for due process or human rights.[1] This backlash movement built a bridge between far-right politicians, anti-corruption demonstrators, and judicial actors. In this context, selective judicial decisions against parties at crucial political junctures have raised concerns regarding the possibility that the judicialization of politics (and corruption) may morph into politicized justice.

Given that the law relies on symbolic practices to sustain its legitimacy (Couso, Huneeus & Sieder, 2010: 4), it is essential to understand the role that is played by these ideas, discourses, and informal practices in the relationship between justice and politics in an age of judicialization. Interviews and statements by prosecutors involved in Lava Jato shed light on the specific *political grammar* they have developed, one which values a super-majoritarian model and concentration of power to deal with the "existential threats" posed by mainstream political parties to society (Sá e Silva, 2020). This grammar is not dissimilar to the analogies and arguments used by Brazilian far-right activists, and echoes some of the words of its most well-known contemporary representative: Jair M. Bolsonaro. By amassing enough support through their anti-corruption rhetoric, prosecutors and judges can thus pave the way to an illiberal version of democracy – which Moro's nomination as justice and public security minister under Bolsonaro seems to confirm.

We focus on how Lava Jato's specific brand of "punitivism" (a punishment-centred conception of justice) reinforced Bolsonaro's far-right discourse, boosting penal populism and anti-politics. At the heart

[1] These narratives juxtaposing due process and criminal accountability have produced strong divisions even among Brazilian magistrates themselves, with some falling into the "garantista" camp ("guarantors", focused on guaranteeing the right to a fair trial) and others in the "punitivist" camp ("punishers", focused on ensuring punishments at all cost). The Ministério Público Pró-Sociedade (Pro-Society Prosecution Services), a group of prosecutors who favour "moral and religious values", "the family", and "gun licences for good citizens", as well as the Ministério Público Democrático (Democratic Prosecution Services) and groups like the Prerogativas (Prerogatives), which defend due process, are important actors in this debate.

of this discursive affinity is the view that efficient accountability measures and full respect for due process are incompatible. Both narratives ultimately prioritize punishing "the enemy" over respect for the constitutional limits that ought to protect fundamental rights. This popular demand for punishment stems in part from the perception that the judiciary tends to perform poorly, especially when it comes to corruption cases. As Arantes (2005: 250) puts it:

> [M]uch public debate has also focused on the poor performance of the judiciary. This debate has concentrated on a number of features: first, the excessive slowness of procedures, which means that it can take many years to reach a final judgement ... [W]henever corruption scandals in government or common crimes shocking to public opinion occur, the justice system is harshly criticized for its inability to respond promptly to tackle impunity.

The growing strength of these conservative forces in Brazil is marked by constant attacks against the expansion of fundamental rights through the courts, accusing the STF of protecting corrupt politicians on due process grounds; participating in a pro-human rights communist plot; and disseminating gay propaganda. In the period analysed here, this rhetoric was part of a conservative backlash in response to STF decisions, including those regarding gay marriage (Pimentel, 2017) and those that revoke the arrest of politicians when such arrests are solely based on a second-instance conviction. It was intensified in 2021, when even STF ministers previously seen as allies of Lava Jato ruled that Sergio Moro did not act impartially during proceedings against Lula, and reinstated the former president's political rights.

LAVAJATISMO: ANTI-POLITICS AND PUNITIVISM

In the Introduction we referred to Lava Jato's communicative dimension. The interviews and public speeches made by Lava Jato prosecutors during the course of the investigation were widely publicized inside and outside Brazil – working as an external source of legitimacy. In an interview with a conservative newspaper in 2017, prosecutor Deltan Dallagnol stated that the Brazilian system is too protective of due process rights and "takes the side of defendants at the expense of victims and society" (Sá e Silva, 2020: 18–19). Later on, the same newspaper published an editorial entitled "The Danger of Authoritarian Law".[2] The editorial criticized

[2] "O perigo do direito autoritário", *O Estado de São Paulo* (6 February 2017).

his description of due process as if defendants' rights were necessarily in tension with society's interests. Under this conception of fairness, due process rights are not a safeguard against arbitrariness, but simply an obstacle to reaching a guilty verdict. Prosecutors often expressed these views using a variety of colourful analogies – for instance, claiming that they were fighting a "cancer" in the national body politic. Obviously, a cancer is never a legitimate adversary; it must be extinguished for the system to survive. Both the idea of authoritarian law and the "cancer" metaphor are relevant for understanding the convergence between Lavajatismo and Bolsonarismo, discussed in the following sections.

How did this conception of justice come about? Starting in March 2014, the so-called Lava Jato Operation profoundly changed Brazilian politics and public perceptions of corruption. During its first five years, it issued 227 bench warrants, 155 temporary arrest warrants, 150 preventive imprisonments, and 426 indictments – generating a constant stream of media coverage. Investigators uncovered a huge corruption scheme involving Brazil's state-owned oil company, Petrobrás, and large Brazilian construction companies, notably Odebrecht. The bribery and money-laundering scheme included political parties, politicians, and businessmen. The "innovative tools" used in the operation to identify and punish corruption crimes were made available by the promulgation of laws 12.850/13 (Criminal Organization Law) and 12.846/13 (Anti-Corruption Law) during Dilma Rousseff's (PT) first presidential term.

Among supporters of Lava Jato, judge Sergio Moro is the most acclaimed figure. Moro was the first-instance judge in charge of overseeing the case against former President da Silva and became President Bolsonaro's minister of justice and public security in 2019. The imprisonment of Lula – then leading most opinion polls against Bolsonaro – months before the 2018 presidential election is the most controversial decision in Moro's career. Another important figure is Deltan Dallagnol, the coordinator of the Lava Jato Curitiba taskforce in the Federal Public Prosecutor's Office (MPF).[3] Reports accusing the investigators of leaking sensitive information obtained through pleas and wiretaps during key moments of the electoral cycle and Dilma's impeachment process, and specifically targeting the Workers' Party (PT), raised concerns about political bias and lack of impartiality (see Chapter 11).

[3] "Após cinco anos de operação, Lava Jato mantém foco em 'núcleo politico'", *O Estado de São Paul* (9 March 2019).

More recently, a series of reports by Glenn Greenwald from *The Intercept*, in partnership with major Brazilian newspapers, brought Lava Jato to the centre of a national debate. *The Intercept* published Telegram messages in which Sergio Moro gave advice to Dallagnol in violation of procedural rules; received sensitive information and forwarded it to the prosecutors without making an official record; and asked the prosecutors to leak information to the press in order to mobilize public opinion during Lula's trial. The reports also show that Dallagnol planned to leak information to the media to pressure suspects into signing confessions implicating other people; was paid to give a speech to a company under investigation; and worried about the possibility of a PT victory in the 2018 presidential election.[4] One of the most controversial statements made by Dallagnol in response to other prosecutors' concerns about Moro's behaviour was that "laws are filigree [superficial detail, or, literally, tiny ornamental details made with fragile metal threads] in this larger, political context"[5] (Sá e Silva, 2020).

The Intercept's exposé revealed that judges and prosecutors took public opinion very seriously. They developed public relations tactics that relied on controversial prosecutorial strategies aiming to shore up support for the investigation. In particular, there was a clear attempt to brand Lava Jato as a highly punitivist anti-corruption movement, willing to do whatever it takes to enforce criminal accountability. Even before *The Intercept*'s intervention, Dallagnol himself admitted this rather unorthodox aspect of the prosecutorial strategy, with social communication being a fundamental element for the performance of the taskforce, each phase of the operation being widely publicized, fostering support of public opinion to "neutralize the attacks" that come from outside the judicial system (Dallagnol, 2017: 125).

This is part of what Dallagnol described as a *pulse strategy*, which included, for example, a quick succession of high-profile search and seizure measures to ensure that public opinion maintained an interest in the investigation, saw concrete results, including high levels of public support (Dallagnol, 2017: 90). These attempts to keep corruption revelations at the forefront of public debate relate to what Pérez-Liñán calls the *political economy of popular outrage*, in which investigators sought to channel corruption-induced popular anger against high-level politicians

4 "Secret Brazil Archive", *The Intercept* (19 August 2019).

5 "Como Barroso, Fachin e Fux blindaram a Lava Jato no STF", *The Intercept* (6 October 2019).

fostering impeachment processes in Latin America (Pérez-Liñán, 2010). In addition to carefully timed searches, Lava Jato used other tools, most notably the so-called *delação premiada*, which is similar to plea bargains in the United States. Between March 2014 and March 2019, the investigators made 183 agreements of this kind, and used some of them strategically to influence public opinion. For example, testimony obtained through one of these plea bargains, but not yet validated by the Superior Court, was leaked during the 2014 presidential campaign. This controversial move triggered a debate among lawyers about possible biases in prosecutorial selectivity (Singer, 2018: 244). The same happened during the 2018 presidential election when, less than a week before the first round, Sergio Moro released a statement from a former Workers' Party minister – this testimony had been rejected by the Federal Prosecutor's Office more than six months before due to lack of supporting evidence.

This communications strategy was amplified by a strong online social media component designed to fuel public debate. In fact, dozens of unofficial Facebook pages supporting Lava Jato have been set up since 2014. While obviously not representative of the population as a whole, these pages provide an unparalleled window into the popular discourse of political activists around the operation, their appropriation of images and phrases produced by its coverage, their vocabularies, and the networks of meaning behind Lava Jato. In subsequent sections, we will explore these online discourses in greater depth, showing how the analogies and arguments used have a strong affinity with Bolsonaro's radical discourse.

BOLSONARISMO

Several aspects of Bolsonaro's discourse are perfectly in line with Lavajatismo. Central to Bolsonaro's discourse is the idea of an internal threat, which justified the 1964 military dictatorship as well as the adoption of radical measures in the present. A key component of the discourses constructed by the military to justify the persecution and torture of political opponents was the portrayal of the nation-state as a body, and of internal rivals as "threats" to its health and survival: "Brazil's General Golbery Couto e Silva, an anti-communist ... suggested that the nation-state's body politic might not only face threats from outside but might also have to deal with 'cancerous cells' internally, such as a communist groups or regional independence movements" (Herod, 2011: 188–89).

Golbery played a central role in promoting the "internal war" and "anti-communist rhetoric", and in the development of the dictatorship's military "information systems" (Figueiredo, 2005: 95–105). From his perspective, the idea of opponents as "threats" to the nation is attractive because it leaves no space for due process, and any attempt to protect opponents can be portrayed as an attempt to jeopardize the "health" of the entire nation. The similarity with Dallagnol's analogy of corruption as a cancer is hard to miss, and will be explored in greater detail later on. For now, it is important to recall the interactions among the courts, state bureaucracies, and military elites that sustained the *authoritarian legality* characterizing military dictatorships in Brazil, Chile, and Argentina during the twentieth century (Pereira, 2010). It provided a formal legal justification for both coups and human rights abuses and the last Brazilian dictatorship invested heavily in these judicial façades to achieve legitimacy. It constrained the Supreme Court's sphere of action without closing it down – for example, changing the number of magistrates to ensure that the military had a loyal majority.

Not surprisingly, during Jair Bolsonaro's first year in office, one of his major allies (federal deputy Bia Kicis) proposed a constitutional amendment to change the compulsory retirement age of Supreme Court judges, trying to ensure the appointment of four new judges during Bolsonaro's first term. The congressman is a retired prosecutor who justified this with reference to "popular dissatisfaction" with "Supreme Court activism"[6] – confirming the backlash mentioned in the Introduction. The proposal echoes what happened during the 1964 dictatorship, when the military forced the retirement of three judges and two others resigned in solidarity. The regime also suspended the possibility of the Supreme Court granting *habeas corpus* in cases of crimes "against national security" through Institutional Act No. 5 (AI-5), and increased the number of magistrates through Institutional Act No. 2 in the year following the coup, enabling the regime to expand the number of justices from eleven to sixteen. In 2020, Bolsonaro's supporters called for a new AI-5 to "clean up" Congress and the Supreme Court.[7]

Given the limited electoral traction of this "dictatorship nostalgia", Bolsonaro's campaign forged an alliance with diverse groups and their so-called warrantors, leaders who could compensate for Bolsonaro's initial unpopularity. These included church ministers, ultra-liberal economists,

6 "Deputada que propõe revogar 'PEC da bengala' quer Supremo mais 'liberal e conservador'", *O Estado de São Paulo* (9 March 2019).

7 "Brazilian President's Son Suggests Using Dictatorship-Era Tactics on Leftist Foes", *The Guardian* (1 November 2019).

policemen's groups, and the *verde e amarelos*, the latter being anti-corruption groups strongly identified with Lava Jato and in favour of Dilma Rousseff's impeachment. The punitivist rhetoric of Lava Jato supporters was therefore part of Bolsonarismo from the beginning and exists quite comfortably alongside the "internal threat" discourse inherited from the dictatorship.

Sergio Moro's decision to accept a position in Bolsonaro's cabinet as justice and public security minister seems to confirm this proximity. In fact, Moro's pet project during his time as minister is indicative of how both streams of discourses eventually merged. The so-called anti-crime package tried to enshrine in law, and legitimize, some of the most controversial tools and tactics used during Lava Jato. It thus catered to the demand for more severe punishment of corrupt politicians, but also addressed Bolsonaro's tough on crime agenda in several ways: by reducing the liability of the military and security officers in operations ordered by the presidency to guarantee law and order; banning the flagrant imprisonment of security officers, and establishing that the Attorney General's Office should act in favour of military and security agents in related inquiries; and shielding policemen from homicide charges when they act under "fear, surprise, or strong emotion". In response to criticisms of this draconian reform package, Moro stated that "this is not authoritarian; this is not fascism. It is the rule of law".[8]

Interestingly, the package conveniently ignored a major public security issue: the rise of the "*milícias*" (paramilitary groups led by former public security agents). Militias pose a huge threat to public order and have surpassed drug lords in terms of territorial control in Rio de Janeiro. Historically, Bolsonaro did not see the *milícias* as a problem; instead, he portrayed them as an ally in the war against "internal threats". Summarized with the slogan "human rights are for righteous humans", the defence of the military police's violent illegal actions in favelas is a crucial component of Rio de Janeiro's right-wing discourse. Among defenders of the legacy of the 1964 dictatorship, it is common to consider critics of the violation of human rights in favelas as "communists" opposed to "good citizens", "honourable military policemen", and "patriots". In 2014, various Facebook pages associated with this violent police culture, e.g. Faca na Caveira ("Knife in the Skull", a reference to the Special Operations Battalion emblem), aggressively supported

[8] "'Não é fascismo, é rule of law': os 6 pontos centrais da coletiva de Moro", *Exame* (4 February 2019).

Bolsonaro's candidacy in online fora (Santos & Cunha, 2014). In 2008, the Rio de Janeiro State Assembly approved a Parliamentary Inquiry Committee (CPI) on *milícias* proposed by deputy Marcelo Freixo after a group of journalists from *O Dia* newspaper were kidnapped and brutally tortured by the militia of Batan, West Zone. The investigation resulted in a document indicting 226 people: 67 military policemen, 2 militaries from the army, 5 militaries from other organs, 3 military firefighters, 2 penitentiary agents, 8 civil police officers, one Rio de Janeiro state deputy, and 130 civilians.

Milícias are now a sensitive topic again, particularly the one led by Adriano da Nóbrega, killed in February 2020: previously rewarded and praised by Bolsonaro's family as a hero, his *milícia* is accused of murdering leftist councilwoman Marielle Franco.[9] Flávio Bolsonaro (the president's son) is accused of employing Adriano's relatives to divert wages in an embezzlement scheme (so-called *rachadinha*). President Bolsonaro's interference with the federal police during the investigation into these allegations led to Moro's exit from government in April 2020.[10]

DISCURSIVE AFFINITIES BETWEEN BOLSONARISMO AND LAVAJATISMO

Discourses supporting both the Lava Jato and Bolsonaro share features that make it easy for them to blend into one when convenient. As stated in the previous sections, the idea that recognizing the rights of a specific group is somehow opposed to society's interests (therefore considering people under investigation as social outcasts even before trial) is a common feature of far-right discourse in Brazil. The same thinking seems to justify the need for "exceptional measures" against specific political parties and politicians: they are fighting a "cancer", and need to be careful with "infected cells" able to spread it.

Particularly relevant is the fact that, beyond these medical analogies, both Bolsonaro's militarist supporters and Lava Jato enthusiasts initially equated one political party, namely the PT, with these "cancerous cells". The former associate the PT's role in opposing the dictatorship,

9 "Police Kill Militia Man Linked to Bolsonaro's Son", *Folha de S. Paulo* (10 February 2020).

10 "Brazil's Star Justice Minister Sergio Moro Resigns in Blow to Jair Bolsonaro", *The Guardian* (24 April 2020).

distributing "gay kits", and denouncing the violation of human rights as part of a "communist plot"; the latter associate the PT with corrupt schemes designed to gain support from other parties in Congress. The party came to personify diverse far-right groups' own enemies, always framing themselves as victims facing imminent threats. For the religious fundamentalists, the PT was involved in "gay propaganda" corrupting children, and for ultra-liberals it was expanding the state to a point of "no return" that would "kill" the economy.

These narratives are constituted through antagonism based on five elements: (1) an imminent threat (corruption and/or communism), (2) embodied by a specific person or group (the PT and/or human rights activists), which is (3) supported by an unpopular elite (complacent superior courts and/or international communist organizations), and (4) can be fought through the concentration of power in – and massive popular support for – a "hero" (Moro and/or Bolsonaro). Popular participation is essential to put pressure on the institutions, and therefore (5) people must pay attention to communication channels recommended by the leader (the conservative press and/or alternative online social networks). Disagreement with these propositions is interpreted as support for the immoral enemies (or for the "diseases" threatening the nation). The discourses equate "heroes" (Moro and/or Bolsonaro) to "moral righteousness" (patriotism and/or the fight against corruption), making it immoral to criticize or disagree with them and their methods. Even far-right critics of Bolsonaro's policies are immediately considered "communists" and attacked on social media. Similarly, journalists who are well-known critics of the PT, but who voice concerns about some of the strategies of the Lava Jato operation, are accused of being "Free Lula campaigners".

This affinity between Bolsonarismo and Lavajatismo is facilitated by the fact that the same analogies can be used to target various groups: the PT, the Supreme Court, human rights defenders, and traditional institutions, among others. Political parties, for example, are figures of hate. In this regard, depicting political parties as criminal organizations, as Lava Jato has done, puts other actors, such as military personnel, in a privileged moral position compared to politicians. This contrast is exploited by Bolsonaro, who embraces an anti-politics rhetoric and anchors his power in the imaginary around institutions such as the army. Similarly, the STF is equally criticized by Lava Jato members and attacked by Bolsonaro supporters. Constitutional limits imposed by the STF are considered interferences in the will of the majority. Dictatorship supporters also tend to portray the Brazilian Constitution, which the STF is mandated to uphold, as a document made by communists. In 2019 the court came to the centre of the Lava Jato debate when a decision revoked Lula's imprisonment until all appeal options had been exhausted, and again in 2021 when the STF recognized that Moro had acted partially in his proceedings against Lula. It is therefore not surprising that Bolsonaro's second year in office was marked by attacks against STF ministers, including demonstrations asking for the closure of the court, in which people threw tomatoes at posters of ministers' faces and asked for a military intervention. The same demonstrations portrayed Moro as a hero, sometimes wearing a Superman suit.

When it came to *The Intercept*'s exposé, some supporters justified Moro's questionable behaviour by claiming that "the crimes under investigation are more serious than irregularities in the investigation". This line of argument follows the highly controversial logic of Moro's effort to justify the leak of wiretaps of conversations between Rousseff and Lula. The release was considered unconstitutional by the STF, and minister Teori Zavaski stated that Moro acted "without any of the safeguards required by law".[11] During an event organized by *Veja* magazine on 27 March 2017, Moro stated that he does not regret disclosing the conversation, arguing that critics aim to "confuse public opinion". Instead of discussing possible crimes, these critics "attack people responsible for the process, for the accusation, for the judgement". Moreover, "the problem is not the disclosure itself, but the content of the recorded dialogue". Pointing out violations of due process is therefore interpreted as an attack on the judges, just as pointing out human rights violations by security forces are interpreted as an attack against "the police".

Prosecutor Deltan Dallagnol reacted in a similar fashion when STF minister Dias Toffoli harshly criticized Lava Jato for its lack of planning to avoid a negative impact on the economy (estimated in R$180 billion)[12] and transparency. According to Dallagnol, blaming Lava Jato for these economic losses is irresponsible: "the criminals are the ones responsible.

[11] "Decisão de Moro sobre telefonemas de Lula foi inconstitucional, decide Teori", *Consultor Jurídico* (22 March 2016).

[12] By simultaneously involving major infrastructure and oil companies without proper sectoral protection measures, the Lava Jato operation's impact led to accumulated losses of R$180 billion and the direct dismissal of 60 per cent of employees from the firms under investigation (Warde, 2018: 54–61). The taskforce estimates it can recover approximately R$15 billion spent on corruption. See "Toffoli diz que Lava Jato 'destruiu empresas' e MP é pouco transparente", *O Estado de São Paulo* (9 March 2019).

Lava Jato just applied the law."[13] Dallagnol also received a warning from the National Public Prosecution Council for commenting on an STF decision, stating that the court "sends a strong message of leniency in favour of corruption". Reacting to the warning he received, Dallagnol blamed judicial elites and the "system of justice that doesn't work against the powerful".[14]

Both due process and democratic rights are tacitly portrayed as excuses to avoid punishment, and the assumption is that only elites' support for "the enemy" can explain the defence of these constitutional guarantees. Differing from agonistic relations in which you recognize the legitimacy of your adversaries' rights, the alleged threat implies enemies that must be banned or eliminated, leaving no space for legitimate disagreement. The antagonistic relationship thus provides justification for exceptional measures in which due process is an obstacle for salvation through punishment/accountability and must be disregarded. The idea that the STF is part of a system unable to do "justice", or of a powerful plot that relies on due process as an excuse for not punishing "communist criminals", fits quite well with Bolsonaro supporters' populist discourse. In fact, they selectively appropriate statements made by Lava Jato taskforce members.

To understand how right-wing, "anti-corruption", and anti-PT discourses blend into one, we now proceed to discuss how these discourses developed during online campaigns and street demonstrations.

NETWORKING AGAINST THE ENEMY: HOW LAVAJATISMO AND BOLSONARISMO BLEND ONLINE

Lavajatismo and Bolsonarismo converge on the need to "clean up" the country's political system through popular support for exceptional measures. This "majority" expresses itself mainly through online social networks and protest, attacking actors perceived as opponents of the anti-corruption operation. As shown in the next sections, activists in street demonstrations echo the discourse found in these online fora, blending both streams of popular opinion into a single radical discourse.

For example, during the 2018 presidential campaign, there was an intense circulation of images on pro-Bolsonaro WhatsApp groups with

[13] "Deltan responde a Toffoli: 'dizer que a lava jato quebrou empresas é uma irresponsabilidade'", *Época* (16 December 2019).

[14] "Conselho do MP pune Deltan Dallagnol com advertência por fala sobre ministros do STF", *GI* (26 November 2019).

slogans such as "Whoever is afraid of Moro dies of fear of Mourão [retired army general and Bolsonaro's running mate]"; "the army is the guarantor of Lava Jato"; "Not voting for #Bolsonaro17 is betraying Sérgio Moro"; and "If Moro already does this damage, imagine Mourão" (the suffix "ão" is superlative in Brazilian Portuguese, making the surname Mourão sound like "a big Moro"). This language points to an imaginary in which Lava Jato and the army walk side by side against an enemy that includes the PT, its "allies" in the Supreme Court, and other "democratic façades". Previous work has identified the use of a similar rhetoric against the Electoral Court in WhatsApp groups (Santos & Freitas, 2019).

Facebook pages dedicated to Lava Jato also became a vehicle for far-right mobilization. In other words, Lavajatismo gradually blended into radical Bolsonarismo. This was facilitated by the discursive affinities described in the previous sections. The analysis of the anti-corruption social network pages supporting Jair Bolsonaro points to the confluence of at least two different ideas: the fight against a corrupt political class and the fight against "ordinary criminals" with a militaristic, anti-human rights and anti-communist bias; and the defence of "the family", with a moralistic and religious tone. In other words, Lavajatismo and anti-corruption rhetoric became a front for the promotion of other causes.

To better understand how Lavajatismo was used to mobilize the population through online social networks, it is useful to analyse diverse Facebook pages discussing the fight against corruption, spreading and interpreting the media content that resulted from Lava Jato's "pulse strategy". Part of it involved people related to the taskforce. For instance, during the 2014 presidential campaign, the coordinator of the federal police taskforce for Lava Jato and other police officers (i.e. *delegados*) used their personal Facebook pages to insult and campaign against the PT, Lula, and Dilma (Singer, 2018: 242). But the most active part of this mobilization happened in unofficial pages dedicated to the operation, Moro, and Dallagnol, continuously producing and interpreting events.

Fabio de Sá e Silva's (2020: 13) analysis of interviews and statements by Lava Jato members reveals that the discursive dimension of the operation can be understood "as a lawyer-led social process, in which a stock of meanings or a political grammar was intensely produced among Brazilian lawyers and disseminated to the Brazilian populace" (Sá e Silva, 2020: 13). Like any political grammar, these discourses involve patterns of association among words and their respective meanings. Different perspectives produce diverse ways of speaking and connecting words, specific vocabularies, and pointing out different ways of organizing ideas around a specific word/object. It is possible to recognize the organization and structuring of a specific vocabulary by looking for co-occurrences of words registered through relational metrics. It indicates the existence of specific lexical worlds (i.e. political vocabularies).

We selected thirty-two different Facebook pages dedicated to supporting Lava Jato and used Facebook API 3.1 to retrieve 13,854 posts and related comments from 25 April 2016 to 3 February 2019. Our first step was to identify and differentiate the diverse vocabularies found on these posts (i.e. identify word patterns to characterize specific groups of pages, or differentiate some groups from others). We used the R program's Multidimensional Text Analysis package (IRaMuTeQ is its French acronym) to apply the descending hierarchical clustering or Reinert method. After exploring the co-occurrences of words characterizing some lexical patterns, we could use the keywords and themes found to assist our qualitative analysis of these texts. We identified four main vocabularies.

The first vocabulary (class 1) is dominated by the theme of opposition and antagonism, denouncing politicians' lack of morals, the incompetence of political parties, the lack of truth in media reporting, among others. The vocabulary thus creates a political unity against the enemy and the political system that sustains it. The use of the word "Não" (No) is the most pervasive connection, including combinations such as "no party", "no politics", "no government", "no more", "is not", "not moral", "not truth", and "don't believe". The opposition to diverse elements of the "system" seems to be a key factor integrating discourses, confirming the role of antagonism. A second vocabulary (class 2) is clearly centred around the word "corruption" and its relation to "measures", "fighting", "transparency", and "impunity", among others. It is also marked by hashtags supporting measures against corruption. An initiative led by Dallagnol to change Brazilian laws based on "ten measures against corruption" is frequently present. This campaign collected more than 2 million signatures from supporting citizens and was debated in Congress:

> The "ten measures" meant to ensure the fast and harsh punishment of corrupt individuals and the recovery of assets derived from corruption. Yet this invariably meant giving a lot more power to Brazilian prosecutors and judges in all criminal cases. The proposed changes included, for instance, limitations on the legal scope of habeas corpus petitions, stipulations on an "abuse" in the "right to appeal", "integrity tests" with simulations of corrupt offers to detect, and remove, potentially corrupt state officials, and an expansion in the scope of pretrial detention.
>
> (Sá e Silva, 2020: 18)

The proposal was embraced by the far right and one of its defenders in Congress was deputy Eduardo Bolsonaro, son of Jair Bolsonaro.

The third vocabulary (class 3) is dominated by juridical jargon, including words such as "public ministries", "Supreme Court", "federal instances", "case", "crime", "decision", "prison", "judge", "investigation", and "prosecutor", among others. It involves technical terms and deals with topics related to corruption without necessarily conveying antagonism. Despite the presence of words such as "crime" and "prison", the word "militias" does not appear as a relevant topic, not being clearly connected to corruption – repeating the omission found in Moro's "anti-crime package". Finally, a fourth vocabulary (class 4) contains words and expressions related to online campaigns and "calls to action", including links to newspapers, blogs, information about politicians, the Supreme Court, and online campaigns/petitions. It is associated with links to websites, social network sites such as Facebook, and the use of the Internet to press public policy in what concerns measures against corruption, mobilization of support through demonstrations, and information sharing.

The four vocabularies identified by the lexical analysis reflect the different constitutive elements of the punitivist, anti-political discourse of the Lava Jato taskforce, which eventually blended with Bolsonarismo. The behaviour of these online fora, however, varied through time. Throughout 2015, expressions of support for the impeachment of Dilma Rousseff recurrently appeared on these pages. Criticisms of Lula and Dilma cover three main themes: (1) they are the most corrupt politicians in Brazil and the PT is the most corrupt party; (2) the PT is the only party responsible for the economic crisis, inflation, "abusive" interest rates, and unemployment; and (3) they are organizing an international Bolivarian crusade for the establishment of communism in Latin America. These discourses suggest not just that the PT is essentially corrupt, but that it is the source of all corruption in the country, sometimes in direct contrast to incorruptible military officers. In this narrative, Lula is the leader of a criminal organization and, together with former President Dilma Rousseff, they led the country to the current moral, economic, and political crisis. At the same time, Sergio Moro appears as someone with the "mission" of "cleaning" up corruption in Brazil. He is the representative of the "good"; his messianic task is to save Brazil from "politicians". In this sense, images of Lula's arrest represent the most desired symbolic achievement of this moral anti-corruption struggle.

Despite references to "the system", corruption is not analysed in its structural dimension, but rather as a problem of individual moral failure that affects members of a single group, namely, "the politicians". If this group were banished, the problem would be solved, and therefore the law must change to make it easier to do just that, dismantling democracy in the process, if necessary. The perception of corruption focuses on public agents (not the private business paying for preferential treatment). This legitimizes the need for the retrenchment of the state – a key concern among Bolsonaro's liberal supporters – because "politicians are corrupt" and "the state is necessarily corrupt and ineffective". It is interesting to note that the army does not receive the same treatment and is considered an example of efficiency.

In 2017 a new component of the anti-corruption discourse appears. After the impeachment, and as Lava Jato spread beyond Curitiba, the operation included prosecutors from other states and targeted politicians outside the PT. More and more posts on these pages came up with the idea that corruption is a "cancer" that affects the party system as a whole. Once it was clear that the problem of corruption goes beyond the PT, the discourse changed to encompass the presence of "corrupt agents" or "infected cells" in Congress and high courts. These narratives depict all traditional parties (PT, the Brazilian social democratic party, or PSDB, and the party of the Brazilian democratic movement, or PMDB, whose founding members are also criticized by the far right because they fought against the dictatorship) as corrupt machines through which elites obtain personal benefits. Therefore, the scope of banishments needed to clean up "our" political system must be expanded, bringing connections between this sanitizing rhetoric and the rhetoric used by apologists of the military dictatorship. As discussed earlier, the dictatorship was also justified in terms of the need to extirpate cancerous cells from the body politic, often concluding that Brazil should open the door to "alternative" and "moral" parties – including the PSL, which Bolsonaro and far-right digital "anti-corruption" influencers used as a platform to run for office.

In this second period, the idea of parties as criminal organizations gains traction and encompasses most parties and branches of government. The ministers of the Supreme Court are repeatedly portrayed as colluding with corrupt actors. These posts even ask for the impeachment of ministers – mainly those seen as an obstacle to Lava Jato or Bolsonaro's proposals – to "clean up the judiciary". Likewise, during the 2018 election, the Supreme Electoral Court (TSE) was vehemently attacked using hashtags such as #vergonhaTSE ("shameTSE"). Bolsonaro himself raised suspicions about the election supervised by the TSE and the validity of the vote count.

Finally, the communication strategy not only attacks the judges, but is also associated with the hope that the military can "clean up" democracy from traditional political parties, working as a "non-political" guarantor of the will of the "majority". The idea that "the army is the guarantor of Lava Jato" challenges the legitimacy of institutions such as the STF, which often points out the operation's irregularities. Following the idea that any systemic disfunction is "criminals' fault", the only guarantee evoked is that of harsh punishment (if necessary, through military intervention) against those opposing the "majority". The idea of military intervention as compatible with Lava Jato is, of course, extremely problematic.

To further understand how the blend between Lavajatismo and Bolsonarismo took shape during in-person *verde e amarelo* anti-corruption demonstrations, and identify ideas already present in the pro-impeachment protests of 2015, we now turn to findings from interviews with demonstrators.

"AGAINST THEM ALL": ANTI-PARTISANSHIP WHEN LAVAJATISMO TAKES TO THE STREETS

The ideas and online discourses shown in the previous section were appropriated by street demonstrators in different ways, showing how the separation between Bolsonarismo and Lavajatismo can be subtle in the wider population. Moro and Bolsonaro were both portrayed as heroes on inflatables and banners carried by activists using the national football team yellow jersey and defining themselves as "patriots": the so-called *verde e amarelo* demonstrators.

To understand demonstrators' support for Lava Jato, and its relation to the rise of Bolsonaro and other far-right political actors, we conducted a series of interviews during anti-government demonstrations in 2015 and 2017. We asked questions regarding participants' opinions on corruption, due process, political parties, and a series of events involving Lava Jato. Our aim here is to show that elements of Lavajatismo and Bolsonarismo appear in the way this group of ordinary citizens talks about politics and justifies its support for Bolsonaro.

Their discourses during the interviews were noticeably clear: "corrupt politicians are not subjects of law", "corrupt politicians deserve punishment", "they ought to be put in jail and any other argument is just drama", among others. When figures like Dallagnol state that corrupt people must be considered as "drug dealers" (Sá e Silva, 2020) or "as a murderer" it brings to political discourse a popular right-wing motto justifying the non-recognition of rights: "human rights are for righteous humans". If we can deny rights to drug dealers, we could do the same with politicians. Support for Sérgio Moro's original anti-crime package further bridges these discourses.

Take for example the following extracts from conversations between one of us and selected protesters:

SOLANO: And what do you think about Lula's bench arrest warrant? Do you think this violates his rights?

DEMONSTRATOR 1: What rights? The guy is the biggest thief in this country and still wants rights? Now a corrupt politician is a source for drama. He is a prisoner. Rights, what rights?

SOLANO: What do you think of the role of the press in the coverage of Lava Jato?

DEMONSTRATOR 2: I think things have to go even further in the press. We have a right to know. Oh, if it weren't for the press they would have smothered everything. No, no, it has to be in the National Journal [TV news programme].

SOLANO: And the leaks, do you agree?

DEMONSTRATOR 2: Yes! They must really leak. You see, if it wasn't for that, they'd hide, we wouldn't know, and they wouldn't go to jail.

SOLANO: Do you think the Lava Jato Operation violates the rights of the politicians under investigation?

DEMONSTRATOR 3: What rights? It has nothing to do with that! The guy wants rights, so he better not steal. They are all the same. PT, PSDB. Power is power. They do not care about us. It's all corrupt, dirty, everything.

This portion of the public sees a fight between the moral forces of good and evil dividing Brazil into two organized groups. The Manichean narrative reached its maximum expression during Lula's testimony at Moro's court in Curitiba on 10 May 2017. It is important to note the strong symbolic dimension of this event: in fact, several magazines presented "Lula versus Moro" as a boxing or wrestling match on their front pages. It is therefore not surprising that the "judge who fights against corruption" appears in the collective imagination as a saviour, a messianic figure with the task of "cleaning Brazil" from the "cancer" of corruption. In the interviews conducted during the demonstrations of 16 August 2015, this heroic-messianic narrative was a common denominator. In fact, during the march there was a big inflatable of Moro depicted as Superman, a figure of the Judge-Hero, the Judge-Messiah:

DEMONSTRATOR 4: Judge Moro has a mission, to clean Brazil because the cancer of Brazil is the corrupt politicians.

DEMONSTRATOR 5: I believe he is our saviour. If it were not for him nothing would have happened. It is the duty of all Brazilians to support Lava Jato. He is going to clean up Brazil. He is the man we were waiting for.

DEMONSTRATOR 6: If it were not for him, we would be lost. He's a hero.

The idea of God acting through certain humans to produce change, which Dallagnol, a devout Evangelical, endorses (Sá e Silva, 2020), encourages this messianic interpretation. It also helps bridge Lavajatismo with the discourse espoused by religious leaders involved in conservative politics, a key constituency for Bolsonaro. When these messianic figures accuse a politician, it is not hard to understand why their "enemies" are portrayed as "evil".

Finally, when asked about their vote in 2018, many of the interviewed answered along the following lines:

DEMONSTRATOR 7: Oh, I think Bolsonaro is different and can change all that. We believe in him. We have faith in him, hope, he is not the same. I will vote for him.

Corruption is at the heart of this argument. Not only are professional politicians considered corrupt, but politics itself is dirty. The state bureaucracy and the entire system of political representation triggers negative emotions such as shame and rejection. Moro then appears characterized as a hero, a saviour, someone who "has a task", "is an envoy", and "will clean Brazil" from corrupt politicians who, from a moralistic and dualistic point of view, represent evil, the enemy to be exterminated, "a cancer". In the testimonies, the concept of "cleaning up" appears much more than the concept of "doing justice": a messianic and punishment-based notion of justice that increases the collective feeling that politics and political parties are despicable and heinous.

One of the issues that most consistently appears in the interviews with Lava Jato supporters voting for Bolsonaro is that he represents "someone different", an outsider capable of facing a totally corrupted political class. The word "hope" or "change" linked to the figure of Bolsonaro appeared in all of them. He is seen as authentic and honest, an anti-mainstream figure, capable of capturing the protest vote, frustration, and anger against the traditional political system. Traditional parties are perceived as equally dirty and concerned only with their own privileges. It is the binary conception of the old (i.e. traditional politics) versus the new (i.e. outsiders), and the new is a category of enormous political impact – despite Bolsonaro's decades as a congressman. Political novelty appears as a value in itself.

In retrospect, it is clear that during the pro-impeachment demonstrations throughout 2015, social Bolsonarismo was already latent among this portion of the public. At a 16 August 2015 demonstration against the PT on Paulista Avenue in São Paulo, 96 per cent of demonstrators said they were not satisfied with the political system, 73 per cent said they did not trust political parties, and 70 per cent did not trust politicians. When asked the reason why, the answer was unanimous among the demonstrators: the system and the parties are all corrupt. Groups such as Vem pra Rua (Come to the Streets) have captured this anti-political sentiment in the slogan "*Faxinageral*" (General cleaning). Though anti-PT sentiments are the most evident common denominator among these groups, the idea that corruption is spreading throughout all parties, and therefore the party system is not reliable, is indeed present. When asked about who inspired most trust, Bolsonaro's name came first: 19.4 per cent trusted him very much. In that same demonstration, only 11 per cent said they trusted the PSDB (the party for which most of the people demonstrating had voted in the 2014 election), and 1 per cent trusted the PMDB (party of then vice-president Michel Temer); 56 per cent agreed with the statement "someone outside the political game would solve the crisis"; 64 per cent said that "an honest judge" would; and 88 per cent had confidence in an "honest politician".[15]

At that time, the construction of Bolsonaro and Moro as honest outsiders who could serve as "saviours of the nation" was already brewing. The solution would come from outside the system. Mara Telles and her research team studied this anti-PT phenomenon at the pro-impeachment demonstration on 12 March 2015 in Belo Horizonte (Telles, 2017). The demonstrators similarly expressed their indignation at corruption (36 per cent), but also their dissatisfaction with politics (18 per cent). Along with corruption, the theme that most connected the demonstrations was anti-PT feelings: 91 per cent said that the PT did great harm

[15] For the full results of this survey of 571 demonstrators, see "Um protesto contra todo o sistema político?", *El País* (14 April 2015).

and 82 per cent gave a score of 0 to the PT government. The most often repeated sentence among demonstrators interviewed by Telles was that the "PT was the most corrupt party in the history of Brazilian democracy".

Over the years (2014–2016), anti-PTismo evolved to become a strong identity. During Bolsonaro's 2018 campaign, a broader narrative widened the cast of enemies: the link among anti-PT, anti-communism, and anti-leftist sentiments. These antagonisms work by amplifying the notion of an existential threat related to "the enemy" (not just a party, but an international communist plot), strengthening the ties among different groups and justifying the need for exceptional measures.

The idea that some people are not entitled to rights because it would be an obstacle for justice recurred. Statements denying rights to politicians convey an understanding of justice not as a process through which a person could be proved guilty or innocent, but one involving people considered guilty by default. This is precisely where Bolsonarismo and Lavajatismo meet.

CONCLUSION

This chapter has analysed how Lava Jato's punishment-centred discourse recreated key analogies constitutive of Brazilian far-right vocabularies. At the heart of this process is the use of the dictatorship's infamous biological analogy: their enemies are a "cancer", an internal threat, that must be expunged from the national body politic. This threat justifies exceptional measures against people working as "infected cells", whose full recognition as subjects of rights would work against the "greater good" of society. Our empirical sections showed how Lavajatismo and Bolsonarismo blended into one, in both social media spaces supporting Lava Jato and anti-corruption street demonstrations. The ideas expressed by Lava Jato supporters, treating political parties as criminal organizations, considering superior courts' full respect for due process as an affront to "the nation's struggle against the powerful", and linking Lava Jato to God's plan to change Brazilian politics, all set up clear bridges to the political grammar of Bolsonarismo.

The evidence presented here also confirms that antagonism plays a key role in the political and strategic use of "corruption" (and the vocabularies related to it). Differing from simple activism against ethical deviance, it moves towards discourses centred around the denial of political actors' legitimacy and due process. The identification of enemies is particularly compatible with the construction of political identities through antagonism (Mouffe, 2000), removing the possibility of legitimate defence for opponents, who are labelled as "corrupt", "public enemies", or a "cancer". This is a rhetoric clearly attuned to Bolsonaro's discourse, denouncing communism and urging for family values against "evil politicians". This scenario is particularly conducive to strengthening emotional attachments to a group by fostering hostility towards those outside it (McDermott, 2011).

An important point to note is the gradual expansion of the list of "enemies": from anti-PT and anti-human rights activists to anti-partisan and (among strong supporters of Bolsonaro) purportedly anti-democratic institutions such as the Supreme Court and the Congress. The idea that "we should clean the Supreme Court the same way we did with the Workers' Party" summarizes this discursive transition. It shows the danger of mobilizing people to put pressure on institutions, asking for a departure from due process. The same logic could be used to move towards illiberal versions of democracy, marked by selective accountability and concentration of power. Demonstrators seem to consider the perceived enemy of their enemies as necessarily a friend, positively valuing actors that position themselves against parties, courts, and democratic institutions. This logic resembles that leading to growing support for Rio de Janeiro-based militias, particularly before 2006. Back then, a group fighting violence by dislodging drug lords won the sympathy of part of the population, the latter being legitimately worried about a public security crisis. Here again, the enemy of their enemy was considered a friend without any consideration for the broader implications of this association. When different militias threatened and murdered journalists, politicians, judges, police officers, and civilians, it became clear that the mutual hostility between two criminal groups could never be considered as a sign of the legitimacy of one of them.

In the narratives analysed here, to be labelled corrupt one does not need a formal trial. To worry about due process is therefore to create a dangerous and unnecessary obstacle. The perceived needs and desires of the "majority" become the centre of the criminal process and the fundamental rights of the accused are treated as expendable, in what is sometimes called "criminal process for show":

> The typical values of the liberal-inspired criminal jurisdiction ("truth" and "freedom") are abandoned and replaced by a plot that bets on imprisonment and suffering imposed on the investigated and accused as a way to keep the attention

> and please the public; this makes procedural activity more and more limited to confirming the accusatory hypothesis ... The law, then, becomes subordinated to the logic of media-mercantile hyperculture.
>
> (Casara, 2017: 160–61)

As with any spectacle, it oversimplifies reality to fit the narratives. Among Lava Jato supporters, a moralistic and punitive script prevails, one that presents the dynamics of the criminal process as a fight of good against evil. Even when following formal procedures – as authoritarian legality does – this conception of justice potentially jeopardizes democracy and consolidates an anti-political discursive environment that weakens the institutional order, leaving the door open for anti-system political "heroes". In this context, selectively fighting corruption can be used as an excuse by actors willing to dismantle democratic processes. This is perhaps the darkest side of the judicialization of politics in Latin America.

References

Arantes, R. B. (2005). Constitutionalism, the Expansion of Justice and the Judicialization of Politics in Brazil. In R. Sieder, A. Schjolden, and A. Angell, eds., *The Judicialization of Politics in Latin America*. London: Palgrave.

Casara, R. (2017). *Post-democratic- State: Neobscurantism and Management of the Undesirables*. Rio de Janeiro: Brazilian Civilization.

Couso, J., Huneeus, A., and Sieder, R. (2010). *Cultures of Legality: Judicialization and Political Activism in Latin America*. Cambridge: Cambridge University Press.

Dallagnol, D. (2017). *A luta contra a corrupção: A Lava Jato e o futuro de um país marcado pela impunidade*. Rio de Janeiro, Primeira Pessoa.

Figueiredo, L. (2005). *Ministério do Silêncio: a história do serviço secreto brasileiro de Washington Luís a Lula (1927–2005)*. Rio de Janeiro: Record.

Herod, A. (2011). *Scale*. Abingdon: Routledge.

Mcdermott, R. (2011). Emotional Manipulation of Political Identity. In W. L. Cheminant and J. Parrish, eds., *Manipulating Democracy: Democratic Theory, Political Psychology, and Mass Media*. London: Routledge.

Mouffe, C. (2000). *The Democratic Paradox*. London: Verso.

Pereira, A. W. (2010). *Ditadura e Repressão – o autoritarismo e o Estado de Direito no Brasil, no Chile e na Argentina*. São Paulo: Paz e Terra.

Pérez-Liñán, A. (2010). *Presidential Impeachment and the New Political Instability in Latin America*. Cambridge: Cambridge University Press.

Pimentel, M. B. (2017). Backlash às decisões do Supremo Tribunal Federal sobre união homoafetiva. *Revista de Informação Legislativa: RIL* 54(214), 189–202.

Reinert, M. (1990). Alceste, uneméthodologied'analyse des donnéestextuelles et une application: Aurelia de Gerard de Nerval. *Bulletin de MethodologieSociologique* 26, 24–54.
Sá e silva, F. (2020). From Car Wash to Bolsonaro: Law and Lawyers in Brazil's Illiberal Turn (2014–18), *Journal of Law and Society* 47(1), 90–110.
Santos, J. G. B., and Cunha, V. C. C. (2014). "Bandido bom é bandido morto": A função da retórica da intransigência na construção da identidade política do deputado Jair Bolsonaro no Facebook. Paper presented at the Congresso Brasileiro de comunicação e marketing político, São Bernardo do Campo, UMESP.
Santos, J. G. B., and Freitas, M. (2019). *WhatsApp, política móvil y desinformación: ¿cómo se dio a viralización de las noticias falsas en las elecciones brasileñas?* Buenos Aires: Centro de Estudios en Libertad de Expresión y Acceso a la Información (CELE), Universidad de Palermo.
Singer, A. (2018). *O Lulismo em crise: um quebra-cabeça do período Dilma (2011–2016)*. São Paulo: Companhia das Letras.
Telles, M. (2017). Corruption, Democratic Legitimacy and Protests: The Right's Boomin National Politics? *National Interest* 30, 97–126.
Warde, W. (2018). *O espetáculo da corrupção: Como um sistema corrupto e o modo de combatê-lo estão destruindo o país*. Rio de Janeiro: Leya.

APPENDIX

The Facebook data analysed in this chapter was obtained through Data API 3.1, following these steps. First, we retrieved all page ID's related to "Lava Jato" and excluded those not related to the operation. Second, we used page ID's to retrieve posts, images, and comments related to these posts. The outcome was a SQL dataset of 13,854 textual posts and comments posted between 25 April 2016 and 3 February 2019. The data was converted into a textual corpus, isolating messages and dates into aggregate textual data (impersonal), including co-occurrence of words and the proportion of the combinations identified in our corpus. The data was analysed through topic modelling and natural language processing, mainly through the R programming language LDA package and also using IRaMuTeQ as an interface to test the results of the ALCESTE/ Reinert method. IRaMuTeQ software is an interface that uses R language packages to execute lexical analysis of our retrieved posts and comments, guided by the approach developed by Reinert (1990) and labelled ALCESTE (Analyse Lexicale par Context d'un Ensemble de Segments de Texte). This approach uses the co-occurrence of words to identify diverse "vocabularies" (i.e. classes) inside a given text and their interrelations. It is useful to reveal patterns of relationships, degrees of proximity, or separation among these clusters of interconnected words or "classes", which we can represent through dendrograms (similar to genealogical trees).

13

Prosecutorial Agency, Backlash and Resistance in the Peruvian Chapter of Lava Jato

Viviana Baraybar and Ezequiel Gonzalez-Ocantos

INTRODUCTION

Brazil's *Operação Lava Jato* quickly evolved into a much larger investigation that revealed a transnational bribery scheme. The turning point for the internationalization of Lava Jato came in December 2016, when Odebrecht, the Brazilian construction company at the heart of the case, struck an agreement with the authorities of the United States. It emerged that Odebrecht had offered bribes to public officials in a variety of countries, and financed electoral campaigns in exchange for preferential treatment in the allocation of construction projects. According to US Department of Justice documentation, between 2001 and 2016, Odebrecht "paid approximately $788 million in bribes in association with more than 100 projects in 12 countries, including Angola, Argentina, Brazil, Colombia, Dominican Republic, Ecuador, Guatemala, Mexico, Mozambique, Panama, Peru and Venezuela" (US Department of Justice 2016: 7).

Given the source and tenor of the allegations, judges and prosecutors in various Latin American countries had little room to ignore the news and were forced to open local chapters of Lava Jato. The political repercussions across the continent have been far-reaching. In fact, several national chapters of Lava Jato directly or indirectly contributed to the downfall of sitting presidents, or to the indictment, arrest and conviction of former presidents and their closest aides (Gonzalez-Ocantos and Baraybar 2019). In this chapter, we present a detailed analysis of how the investigation unfolded in Peru. With the exception of Brazil, Peru stands out as the case where investigators have been able to stretch the tentacles of Lava Jato the most. Initially, the Peruvian chapter of Lava Jato focused primarily on officials responsible for accepting bribes during bids for three major infrastructure projects. But the investigation quickly expanded its remit. A special prosecutorial taskforce established that Odebrecht had also bribed officials to secure additional projects, and engaged in the illegal financing of electoral campaigns, including a referendum in Lima and various presidential races. To date, the investigation has uncovered evidence against every single elected president since the return of democracy in 2001, as well as some of the most powerful political figures in the country. In the process, it contributed to President Kuczynski's (2016–2018) downfall in 2018, the shut-down of Congress in 2019, and the impeachment of yet another president in 2020 (President Vizcarra).

Peru presents another opportunity to study some of the most interesting and overlooked tensions at the heart of the judicialization of politics in Latin America, one of the key goals of this volume. First, in line with the other chapters on Lava Jato, we show that when courts and prosecutors are willing to exercise their accountability functions effectively, they often test the limits of the rule of law. The successful prosecution of grand corruption requires the presence of judicial actors with enough determination to take on powerful political and economic interests. But these investigations present a series of challenges related to how to secure evidence in notoriously hostile and information-poor environments. Overcoming these challenges without jeopardizing the integrity of the inquiry is no small feat because the tools that prosecutors and judges must rely on, including plea bargains, pre-trial detentions, the redefinition of traditional evidentiary standards and public relations strategies, are controversial, to say the least. In other words, the tensions between, on the one hand, prosecutorial effectiveness, and on the other, respect for due process and lawful punishment, are difficult to resolve. This chapter digs deep into the micro-dynamics of Peru's Lava Jato to discuss the nature of these challenges and how judicial actors, especially prosecutors, dealt with them.

Second, like other chapters in this edited collection, ours addresses the phenomenon of backlash. Politicians are rarely passive bystanders during anti-corruption investigations. They don't just let prosecutors collapse their governments, sully their reputations or demolish their electoral chances. Quite the contrary: politicians who are the target of zealous judges and prosecutors tend to respond not only by defending themselves in court, but also by deploying ruthless tactics to delegitimize, remove or block the investigative effort. We explain what triggered political backlash in the Peruvian case, discuss how it conditioned the behavior of prosecutors, and identify the reasons why, so far, investigators were able to mitigate the impact of backlash. In so doing, our case study also converses with the chapters on judicial corruption in Mexico (Rios-Figueroa, Chapter 8) and Ecuador (Basabe Serrano, Chapter 9). One of the most interesting features of the Peruvian experience with Lava Jato is that investigators not only had to deal with an obstructive political class, but also with networks of judicial clientelism commanded by senior judges and prosecutors, who also happened to be loyal allies of some of those implicated in the scandal. As a result, backlash came within and from outside judicial institutions. We look at how prosecutors defied these bureaucratic pathologies and protected the inquiry from their superiors.

Finally, our case study shares with Da Ros and Taylor's chapter on Brazil (Chapter 10) the narrower goal of trying to understand the conditions that lead to the success or failure of massive anti-corruption investigations. To do so we present a careful reconstruction of the ongoing prosecutorial effort in Peru, relying on primary sources such as news reports, official documents and confidential interviews with some of the main protagonists. The narrative highlights the role of interactions between judicial actors, and between them and political/economic players, in determining prosecutorial outcomes along the way. Without downplaying the impact of institutional (or superstructural, to use the editors' terminology) factors, such as, for example, the adequacy of the legislation governing the prosecution of corruption, the relative power of the elites under investigation or the make-up and autonomy of the judicial branch and prosecution services, we focus on the role of prosecutorial agency. We show that contingent choices by prosecutors often determined whether enough evidence came to light, thus widening windows of opportunity for ambitious investigative efforts in a hostile environment, or whether external attacks could be diffused.

AGENCY IN ANTI-CORRUPTION INVESTIGATIONS

Scholars of corruption prosecutions tend to assume that what happens in the courtroom is the direct product of dynamics external to the judicial process. For some, it is the will of political leaders that propels anti-corruption probes forward (Rotberg 2017). This is particularly true in dictatorships, where autocrats use judicial rituals to legitimize the side-lining of opponents and signal regime strength (Pei 2018; Shen-Bayh 2018). In democracies, corruption investigations may also be politically orchestrated. Maravall (2003) famously describes the use of the "rule of law as a political weapon" in Spain, where the right politicized and judicialized corruption in order to make electoral gains. Similarly, Popova and Post's (2018) work on Eastern Europe argues that prosecutions consist mostly of legal proceedings purposefully targeted against weak rivals rather than genuine accountability efforts. Finally, Helmke et al. (2019) show that former Latin American presidents are more likely to end up in jail if their successors are anti-establishment outsiders who are not afraid to politicize corruption, or if irregular exits from office severely damage the electoral competitiveness of outgoing presidents and their parties (see also Conaghan 2012).

These explanations provide useful insights into the macro-political conditions that favor anti-corruption crackdowns but ignore the process of investigating and punishing corruption through the courts. As a result, they have less to say about the capabilities that enable anti-corruption agents, namely judges and prosecutors, to translate opportunity into outcomes. While it is certainly true that judicial actors do not act in a political vacuum, and likely evaluate the permissiveness of the political environment vis-à-vis the prosecution of certain leaders, there is no reason to assume (a) that they are perfect agents of politicians seeking to weaponize or stop prosecutions for political gain; (b) that judicial behavior, with or without intention, has no independent impact on the outcome of prosecutions, both in contexts where powerful politicians welcome convictions and where elites have a preference for impunity; or (c) that judges and prosecutors are always helpless in the face of backlash. In other words, to understand why investigations against corrupt politicians gain momentum, particularly why they become crusades of historic proportions, we also need to take the role of prosecutorial and judicial agency seriously.

A few studies of the Mani Pulite operation in Italy point in this direction. Scholars have assigned great explanatory power to judges' acumen, courage, creativity and prior experience with cases of macro-criminality. For example, Della Porta and Vanucci (2007: 845) see the roots of the Italian "judicial revolution" of the 1990s in prior changes to the judiciary's institutional identity: "In the 1970s and 1980s, especially in the struggle against terrorism, mafias and corruption, a new generation of judges began to exercise a 'substitutive function' with respect to a weak and divided political class, thus increasing its own *espirit de corps*."

Similarly, Sberna and Vanucci (2013: 582) explain that "Italian judges started to perceive themselves as charged by a civic mission of responsibility towards society and community." This new judicial role conception, coupled with smart decisions taken at the start of the investigation, largely explain the success of Mani Pulite: "As soon as the first politicians and entrepreneurs in jail – deliberately put by the Milanese judges into a prisoner's dilemma-like situation – started to collaborate with judges, the whole mechanism was set in motion. The amount of information gathered by the prosecutors on illegal activities of political actors grew exponentially, with a domino effect" (Sberna and Vanucci 2013: 576).

One key lesson from the Italian case is therefore that prosecutorial success in grand corruption cases calls for the presence of assertive judicial actors with a very specific set of skills and values. In particular, in order to exploit opportunity structures that favor anti-corruption crusades, or manufacture momentum when the anti-corruption cause is politically inexpedient, judicial actors must not only be ready to take on the establishment and accept the possibility of backlash; they must also be willing and able to embrace creative ways to secure the flow of high-quality information. The latter point is especially important. Corruption crimes leave behind very opaque evidence trails. The mechanisms used to camouflage and launder the proceeds of corruption are indeed extremely convoluted (Klinkhammer 2013; Martini 2015). Crimes tend to be transnational in nature and involve the use of figureheads in multiple countries, secret offshore accounts in financial havens and intricate asset ownership structures. Uncovering these schemes requires highly technical financial investigations and often makes legal assistance between jurisdictions imperative. Complicating things further, corrupt elites have the uncanny ability to adapt in the face of prosecutorial risk (Della Porta and Vanucci 2007). Passive, reactive or highly bureaucratic judicial role conceptions are likely to repress investigative zeal and encourage a reliance on routine tactics that are not fit for purpose. By contrast, judges and prosecutors who are prepared to go beyond their comfort zones, and act in unconventional ways, are more likely to uncover "smoking-guns." Importantly, this high-quality information is likely to generate new information and enhance momentum because it can alter the strategic calculus of key witnesses contemplating whether or not to confess or sign a plea bargain agreement. It may also provide political cover for committed investigators, who now have the perfect pretext not to abandon their lines of inquiry even when "invited" to do so by powerful elites, or the necessary push for reluctant ones, who now have fewer excuses to turn a blind eye.

On a practical level, prosecutorial progress tends to be a function of the extent to which investigators are willing and able to rely on three crucial investigative tools, namely pretrial detentions, plea bargain agreements and international cooperation, and how they navigate the complications and tensions that inevitably arise from the use of these tactics.

First, judges and prosecutors must decide whether and how to use pretrial detentions. Grand corruption cases target defendants who are well connected and might therefore end up distorting the investigative process at various stages (Bertossa 2003). Pretrial detentions are useful precisely because they help neutralize the firepower of such actors. In addition, pretrial detentions sometimes enable investigators to extract confessions. But despite these benefits, not all judicial actors are likely to feel comfortable with the use of pretrial detentions, especially if they adhere to liberal conceptions of criminal law.[1] Legal preferences aside, the benefits of pretrial detentions are highly conditional on the extent to which they are used with caution, as they can quickly turn into accusations of political "revanchism" or lack of respect for due process. In other words, if not used or explained carefully, pretrial detentions can backfire, damaging the integrity of the investigation and jeopardizing the viability of the case in the appellate stages. This is particularly true when the tool is used strategically, because critics may convincingly cry foul, arguing that judges and prosecutors are biased against certain individuals or groups.

Second, investigators must consider the use of plea bargains. First-hand accounts of anti-corruption investigations almost always make the case that balancing carrots and sticks is the only way of obtaining incriminatory evidence. As Sergio Moro points out, it is very difficult to proceed without the collaboration of those involved. Milanese prosecutors relied heavily on this tool because they soon concluded that "corruption involves someone who pays and someone who gets paid; if both shut up, we won't ever find out." According to Moro, getting a criminal to confess in exchange for benefits "is in fact collaborating with the law and with the application of the laws of a country" (Moro 2004: 58). But the use of carrots is not as uncontroversial as he makes it sound. Legal preferences also play a role. Judicial actors may simply refuse to consider plea bargains as a matter of principle because they regard them as incompatible with their mission to punish the guilty, not reward them.

[1] In Latin America, the term used is "garantismo."

Complicating things further, in some legal cultures the very notion of prosecutorial selectivity is an alien one and therefore hardly a routine, "go to" tactic (Langer 2004). Professional dilemmas aside, these moves need to be planned and executed with great care. Trading immunity for information can be unpopular, and lead to the charge that investigators are abdicating their role or simply biased. In fact, plea bargains often provide the perfect ammunition for those who wish to cast doubt on the impartiality and effectiveness of the investigators.

Third, investigators need to nurture relations with foreign companies, banks and judicial institutions that possess critical information. Judges and prosecutors are not always well-versed in these practices, which involve venturing into the worlds of international relations and penal cooperation. Crucially, in order to build and maintain these new associations, investigators must do more than just issue formal information requests. Unfortunately, domestic judicial authorities cannot directly compel foreign banks or prosecution services to hand over the evidence. Instead, investigators must work hard behind the scenes to establish bonds of trust that make comprehensive cooperation possible, as this informal approach is the best way to secure productive exchanges rather than limited formalistic responses. In addition to certain personality traits or the willingness to travel abroad, cooperation also requires a great deal of creativity in the interpretation of domestic law and international anti-corruption conventions in order to make the evidence that results from these efforts admissible in court. Any mistake while navigating these unchartered waters can prove fatal, as it may alienate crucial information sources or trigger byzantine admissibility battles. Finally, when it comes to cooperation agreements with the companies responsible for bribing politicians, prosecutors must be willing to offer penal, economic and commercial benefits in exchange for information. These could range from granting immunity to top executives to lifting commercial sanctions that could cripple company finances. Deals of these sorts present similar professional dilemmas and strategic risks to those associated with pretrial detentions and plea bargains with defendants. In Latin America they are particularly experimental because the relevant legislation is very recent.

In sum, securing the evidence needed to punish corrupt politicians depends on the presence of investigators willing to learn fast and innovate, take risks and step outside their comfort zones. This condition is especially hard to meet in very hierarchical judiciaries or prosecution services, where careers are tightly controlled from above, and those in charge are either opposed to prosecutions or favor a highly formalistic and cautious approach.[2] In these environments, the rational bureaucratic response is to avoid crossing the anti-corruption Rubicon and stay put. But even if judges and prosecutors enjoy considerable internal independence, as they do in Brazil or Peru as a result of superstructural reforms implemented in the 1990s and 2000s (Gonzalez-Ocantos et al. 2021), or suddenly muster the courage to defy bureaucratic inertia and assume professional risks, success is far from guaranteed. Pursuing an aggressive prosecutorial strategy that relies heavily on the strategic use of pretrial detentions, plea bargains and transnational cooperation channels to overcome evidentiary lacunae requires great skill. This is because corrupt elites will most certainly try to politicize or undermine the prestige of the investigation by questioning the use of these tactics. To secure some degree of insulation and protect the integrity of the investigation, judges and prosecutors must therefore combine courage with doses of pragmatism, savviness and moderation.

In what follows, we trace how Peruvian prosecutors navigated these challenges between 2016 and 2019. The narrative reveals that securing high-quality information hinged on their willingness to privilege an aggressive prosecutorial style over a more traditional one, especially when it came to designing a strategy of international cooperation vis-à-vis Odebrecht. We also discuss the compromises required by this aggressive approach, and how those compromises made prosecutors vulnerable to backlash.

THE PERUVIAN CHAPTER OF LAVA JATO

Within days of the December 2016 revelations, the Peruvian chapter of Lava Jato began in earnest, with a focus on bribes paid to secure three major infrastructure projects: a segment of the Inter-Oceanic Highway built during Alejandro Toledo's administration (2001–2006); an electric trainline built during Alan García's administration (2006–2011); and a coastal infrastructure project sponsored by the regional government of El Callao. The investigative effort soon expanded to include an inquiry into an illegal campaign financing scheme, which targeted, among others, former president Ollanta Humala (2011–2016) and his wife, Nadine Heredia; opposition leader and several times presidential candidate, Keiko Fujimori; and former Lima mayors, Susana Villarán and Luis Castañeda.

[2] For a discussion of internal judicial independence, see Ríos-Figueroa (2019).

The scandal erupted six months into President Kuczynski's administration. With the Fujimorista opposition in total control of Congress (73 out of 130 seats), inter-branch relations were tense from the start (Léon 2019; Sifuentes 2019). Keiko Fujimori had been defeated in the second round of the presidential race by a razor-thin margin and quickly turned her legislative prowess into an obstructionist force. At first, the Lava Jato inquiry seemed to be centered on some of Fujimori's favorite figures of hate, especially former presidents Alejandro Toledo and Ollanta Humala. Fujimoristas naturally saw the scandal as an opportunity to further discredit them. Given that Kuczynski had served under Toledo, it was also a great opportunity to try to implicate the president. For example, with help from former president García's party (Alianza Popular Revolucionaria Americana, APRA), Fujimoristas launched a congressional investigation. During these proceedings, Fujimoristas and Apristas went to great lengths to safeguard their respective leaders, ensuring the scandal maintained its initial narrow focus (Roca 2019). While the specter of the Lava Jato inquiry did eventually come to haunt Kuczynski, precipitating his resignation in March 2018, the investigation also ended up implicating Fujimori and García. When this happened, Fujimoristas enlisted key allies in the judiciary and prosecution services to orchestrate a backlash. Interestingly, however, these efforts failed and backfired because, as we shall see, in September 2019 they led to the dissolution of Congress, Fujimori's main institutional stronghold.

Several actors enmeshed in this severe inter-branch conflict tried to weaponize the anti-corruption crusade. Unfortunately for them, though, they were never able perfectly to control the prosecutors in charge of the case. As a result, Lava Jato quickly expanded beyond its original remit, implicating politicians both in and out of power. In so doing, judicial actors served to exacerbate the political crisis still further. To understand why the inquiry stretched its tentacles, and why prosecutors were able to withstand backlash, we need to pay attention to prosecutorial agency. Central to this process was an innovative and controversial investigative strategy, which included a frenzy of pretrial detentions and intense negotiations with the main bribe-payer, Odebrecht.

Pretrial Detentions

By December 2017, just a year into the investigation, the team of prosecutors in charge of the case had identified sixty-four bank accounts and fifty offshore companies used in the bribery scheme, reviewed more than

2,000 suspicious wire transfers, and conducted searches at fifty different addresses.[3] Throughout, they adopted an aggressive approach to pretrial detentions. In fact, between December 2016 and July 2019 judges agreed to order at least fifty-one jail terms. During interviews, sources close to the investigation mentioned that these requests were strategically planned in part because prosecutors were well aware of the controversial nature of such measures. It was of course entirely possible that, while vital for neutralizing powerful defendants and extracting confessions, some judges could consider the requests excessive, risky or politically inexpedient. To circumvent such obstacles, our sources tell us that it was common for the prosecutors to time the requests in order to make sure they landed on the desks of sympathetic judges.

Regardless of the veracity of these claims, the prosecutors certainly found an echo in the courts. For example, personalities such as Miguel Navarro Portugal, deputy communications minister under García; César Alvarez, former governor of Ancash; and Keiko Fujimori, leader of the opposition, served time in pretrial detention. Ollanta Humala and Nadine Heredia also spent time in jail between July 2017 and April 2018. Furthermore, in February 2017, national and international arrest warrants were issued against Alejandro Toledo. At the time of writing, Toledo awaits a final decision on an extradition request after being apprehended in California in July 2019. The former governor of Callao, Félix Moreno, was similarly handed a pretrial detention order, but is currently a fugitive. Finally, former presidents Alan García and Pedro Pablo Kuczynski were initially banned from leaving the country. Kuczynski was eventually placed in preliminary pretrial detention in April 2019 after he asked for permission to travel abroad, and was later put under house arrest. Most tragically, when a preliminary pretrial detention order was issued against García that same month, he committed suicide.

In some cases, pretrial detentions made a difference. For example, after the authorities captured businessman Gil Shavit in April 2017, prosecutors traded immunity for information. This agreement was instrumental in determining that Odebrecht had paid US$4 million in bribes to Callao governor Félix Moreno. Similarly, in December 2017 prosecutors placed the top executives of Peruvian construction conglomerate Graña & Montero in pretrial detention for eighteen months. They were suspected

[3] Figures released by the Prosecution Services. See www.mpfn.gob.pe/equipo_especial/logros/ (accessed April 19, 2019).

of facilitating bribe payments in the Inter-Oceanic Highway case. While the detentions were cut short in March 2018, the decision to "turn the heat" on Graña & Montero forced a restructuring of the company's management team. The new chief executives were eager to mitigate the damage inflicted on their reputation and, one year later, agreed to sign a cooperation agreement with the prosecutors. And when prosecutors threatened the former executives with another stint in jail for their alleged participation in the Metro de Lima case, they quickly agreed to a plea deal. Finally, Susana Villarán, former mayor of Lima, was accused of receiving money from Odebrecht to fund a 2013 recall referendum campaign and her 2014 reelection bid, and was placed in pretrial detention in May 2019. This move persuaded a witness to sign a plea bargain agreement in which they corroborated the charges. Days later, Villarán confessed to the crimes despite having denied the charges during a congressional hearing.

These victories notwithstanding, the use of pretrial detentions has not been without controversies or costs. For example, the prosecutors placed Keiko Fujimori in pretrial detention in October 2018 because they suspected she was working behind the scenes to obstruct the investigative effort. But the decision to put her in jail for thirty-six months without a conviction, the maximum allowed by law, became the subject of a byzantine legal battle that put prosecutors on the defensive. In fact, this battle risked undermining the effectiveness of pretrial detentions as both the Supreme Court and the Constitutional Court subsequently handed down rulings limiting the conditions under which it is legitimate to resort to this tool. In one of those decisions, for example, the Supreme Court reduced the length of Fujimori's detention from thirty-six to eighteen months. Contributing to the onslaught, Fujimoristas in Congress orchestrated a move to undermine the prosecutors' claim that the money Keiko received from Odebrecht to fund her presidential bid could be classified as "money laundering." Specifically, they passed a law in August 2019 creating the lesser crime of "illegal financing of electoral campaigns." On the basis of this change, judges could eventually apply the principle of retroactivity of the most favorable criminal law, thus forcing the prosecutors to abandon the money laundering classification. This classification allows for longer investigations, longer pretrial detentions and tougher sentences.

The fallout from García's suicide was similarly problematic. The tragedy led to accusations of overzealousness and recklessness against the prosecutors. Echoing these criticisms, Apristas and Fujimoristas in Congress tabled bills to reform the rules governing pretrial detentions.

A few observers argue that the prosecutors suddenly sensed that tolerance for their aggressive strategy was declining and responded by lowering the rate of pretrial detention requests. There is indeed some indication that at least in high-profile cases prosecutors opted for placing defendants under house arrest or simply issued international travel bans. For example, some sources speculate that had García not committed suicide, former mayor of Lima, Luis Castañeda, would have been handed a pretrial detention in 2019 rather than simply an international travel ban. Furthermore, in light of these criticisms, judges also became warier of agreeing to pretrial detentions: between April and June 2019, the courts rejected at least six requests.

Deal or No Deal?

The difficulties in striking a fine balance between an aggressive investigative approach that leads to quick results and maintains momentum and a more cautious one that minimizes the fallout from using controversial prosecutorial strategies, can also be seen in the use of plea bargains.[4] Plea bargains have been the main (and most effective) tool in the arsenal of Peruvian prosecutors since December 2016. They allowed the investigators to generate the evidence needed to expand the remit of the inquiry beyond the three large infrastructure projects, and justify some of the most controversial pretrial detentions. Interestingly, however, the use of this tool was fraught with difficulties. First, unlike pretrial detentions, offers of immunity in exchange for information were not universally endorsed by prosecutors, opening internal rifts and generating inconsistencies in the overall strategy. At times this caused mistrust among key informants and led to the interruption of information flows. Second, negotiating cooperation agreements with companies such as Odebrecht was unprecedented, and required adapting negotiating tactics. Prosecutors also had to coordinate with government lawyers (*procuradores*), whose primary role was rather different: to impose fines on the company. Excesses on this front would not help the prosecutors ensure the company's cooperation. And even after agreeing a common strategy with government lawyers, any benefits prosecutors exchanged in order to

[4] According to article 474 of the Code of Criminal Procedures, prosecutors are permitted to strike plea bargain agreements in cases of macro-criminality, including illicit associations, terrorism, money laundering, cyber-crime, crimes against humanity and human trafficking.

lock in corporate cooperation would have to be defended from those eager to accuse the investigation of bias in favor of foreign business interests.

In December 2016, the chief prosecutor created a taskforce to investigate the Odebrecht scandal. Led by Hamilton Castro, these prosecutors trained their eyes on the bribery scheme mounted to secure major infrastructure projects. A second group of prosecutors commanded by Rafael Vela was tasked with pursuing the inquiry into Odebrecht's campaign contributions. When it came to negotiations with Odebrecht, the two teams adopted very different approaches.[5] As early as January 2017, the company expressed willingness to collaborate in exchange for immunity for executives implicated in the scandal. Odebrecht was also after a deal that would allow it to resume operations in Peru and continue contracting with the state. Vela's team welcomed this overture. He and Alonso Peña Cabrera, head of the international cooperation division of the prosecution services, quickly negotiated a plea bargain agreement with Jorge Barata, former head of Odebrecht in Peru, and two other Brazilian executives, including Marcelo Odebrecht. In the deal signed on June 8, 2017, Peruvian prosecutors agreed to refrain from bringing charges against them. This was an important concession not only because it generated goodwill among key witnesses, but also because Brazilian judicial authorities refused to release relevant case files if this risked opening the door to the possibility of double jeopardy.[6] The agreement permitted access, among other things, to the official video of the confession that Marcelo Odebrecht made in Curitiba in May 2017. It also made it possible to further interrogate Odebrecht in November 2017, and thus obtain new evidence about illegal donations to Keiko Fujimori's and Ollanta Humala's presidential campaigns. These accusations were corroborated by Barata in February 2018, who also confessed donations to other politicians, including Toledo, Kuczynski, García and Villarán. In other words, this initial plea bargain agreement was instrumental in allowing Vela and his associates to make quick progress on their side of the investigation.

By contrast, Castro proved more reluctant to grant immunity to those willing to help. This was a major problem for everyone involved. First, it hampered progress on the more significant line of inquiry. Second,

[5] Gustavo Gorriti, "Entre el Silencio y la Confesión," *IDL-Reporteros* (February 22, 2018).
[6] Gustavo Gorriti, "Quieres la Información? Firma Primero," *IDL-Reporteros* (June 12, 2017).

because Castro's cases involved bribes that cost the state millions in overpriced infrastructure projects, he held the keys to the broader agreement the company was after, i.e., a reduction in damages and an end to the ban on bidding for future government contracts. Without these benefits, Odebrecht executives had few incentives to continue cooperating with Vela's team.

Castro's relationship with Odebrecht was very tense from the start. Despite signing a preliminary agreement in January 2017, in which the company promised to assist the work being done in the *Inter-Oceanic Highway* and *Metro de Lima* cases, Castro opened a formal investigation against Odebrecht. Castro also refused to entertain the possibility of closing a preexisting investigation into Odebrecht's participation in a case not included in the original agreement, in exchange for additional cooperation. More importantly, while Barata's cooperation had enabled some of the most high-profile pretrial detentions ordered by members of his team, Castro never offered Barata full immunity from prosecution and asset embargoes.[7] Castro's decision to spend several months testing Barata's good intentions with numerous requests for additional information eroded trust, limited the flow of evidence and stalled the negotiations. At one point, Castro concluded that Barata had withheld information from his team, so he decided to open a formal investigation against the star witness and asked a court to freeze Barata's assets. The potential implications of this decision were huge, as it violated the terms of existing cooperation agreements, and therefore jeopardized the admissibility of the testimonies and evidence that Barata and other collaborators had provided thus far to Vela's team. The relationship reached breaking point in July 2018, when Odebrecht decided to stop talking to Peruvian prosecutors.

As a result of these contrasting prosecutorial approaches, the two streams of the Lava Jato inquiry moved at very different paces. This illustrates the importance of securing confessions in order to make progress in grand corruption cases. Factors such as the legal framework governing plea bargain negotiations, or the formal independence of the prosecution service, obviously cannot explain such contrasting approaches between similarly situated prosecutors. The observed variation across teams is likely a function of a host of other factors, including professional role conceptions and personality traits. In this sense, most of

[7] Gustavo Gorriti, "Hablaste, te fregaste," *IDL-Reporteros* (June 14, 2018).

our interviewees, including journalists with privileged access as well as prosecutors involved in the inquiry, described Castro as a "traditional" prosecutor, with a structured and conservative style. Plea bargains with a company were simply unprecedented. Castro was therefore extremely cautious and tried to make sure he extracted as much information as possible before agreeing to any deal. And even if this high informational threshold was ever met, Castro never seemed persuaded of the value and appropriateness of offering exceptional monetary benefits on top of immunity from prosecution. For example, he showed little interest in coordinating strategies with the *procuradores* tasked with estimating the fines. Partly as a result of this lack of coordination, throughout this period the *procuradores* pursued a maximalist strategy, at one point asking for S./3,000 million in reparations, which clearly undermined the chances of the prosecutors reaching a deal. Odebrecht was not in a position to pay such an exorbitant amount. If it ever agreed to do so, the outcome would most certainly be bankruptcy, a situation that would have also doomed any prospect of obtaining additional information.

By contrast, Vela and his team were anything but "traditional," and showed greater willingness to take risks. For instance, their decision to classify the crimes under investigation as instances of money laundering reveals quite daring and creative personalities. Under existing Peruvian law, accepting campaign contributions of this kind could easily be characterized as an administrative offense. Instead, they sought to prove that various Peruvian political parties were essentially criminal organizations designed to launder money from corruption. This approach made strategic sense because investigations for money laundering can last longer and pretrial detentions can be extended up to thirty-six months. When it came to the issue of immunity, they were similarly open to risk-taking. In their view, without a deal with the company there would be no information, and without information, no case against the politicians. If a deal meant being accused of "rewarding" a corrupt company, so be it. Furthermore, in contrast to Castro, Vela was prepared to accept that the company had no incentive to provide access to all the evidence it had about corruption in Peru, so at some point his team would have to stop asking for more information, agree to grant generous criminal and commercial benefits, and trust that in the future Odebrecht would be more forthcoming. In line with this pragmatism, Vela's team was also willing to invest time in establishing a personal relationship with Brazilian prosecutors via messaging apps, emails and trips to Brazil, and thus improve their predisposition to share evidence. Castro, by contrast, was more reticent to engage in informal transnational adventures.

Deal!

Two events improved the prospects of a deal with Odebrecht. First, a team of provincial prosecutors stumbled upon incontrovertible evidence of influence peddling by members of the judiciary while investigating a drug-trafficking organization based in the port city of Callao. They had strong reasons to believe that a network of judicial clientelism, which involved Supreme Court judges, members of the National Judicial Council, provincial judges and prosecutors, and influential lawyers and politicians, worked behind the scenes to place friends and allies in key posts and micromanage the outcome of court cases. Reporters obtained information about this separate investigation, and published a series of high-impact exposes starting in July 7, 2018, just a few days after Odebrecht withdrew from the negotiating table in the Lava Jato case.[8] The revelations, which came to be referred to as the *Cuellos Blancos del Puerto* (White Collars of the Port) scandal, sent shockwaves across the judiciary. In an effort to change the narrative by showing the system's commitment to fighting corruption, Chief Prosecutor Pedro Chavarry removed Hamilton Castro as the head of the Lava Jato taskforce, and appointed Vela. As a result of this decision, both streams of the inquiry would now benefit from Vela's pragmatism and greater coordination. Cuellos Blancos had an additional positive externality for Lava Jato. The senior law enforcement actors involved in the scandal were also those who had been trying to contain the probe from the start. This is because of their connections to some defendants, especially Keiko Fujimori. Fujimoristas in Congress adamantly tried to shield these judges and prosecutors from impeachment or resignation, but this was not possible in all cases. And with their political links now exposed, those who did manage to stay in post would in the future find it much harder to disguise obstructionist shenanigans in technical legalese.

Second, in March 2018 the government promulgated Law 30-373, which created a formula to calculate fines for companies implicated in corruption cases. This replaced a more subjective set of criteria outlined in the Civil Code. With the construction sector paralyzed, Lava Jato was

[8] "Corte y corrupción," *IDL Reporteros & Justicia Viva* (July 7, 2018).

severely damaging the economy. Payments along the supply chain were at a standstill and companies had trouble securing loans to fund operations as banks feared that existing and future corruption allegations would cripple their finances. The government therefore hoped that the new objective criteria to estimate fines would avoid excessive penalties, bring certainty to balance sheets, and reassure the banks. The law also had the potential to provide a clear focal point for negotiations between the company and the *procuradores*, which until now had been marred by massive disagreements over the amount that was due in damages.

Determined to get a deal, Vela abandoned Castro's policy to conduct separate plea bargain negotiations with individual executives and the company. The decision to bring all negotiations under the same umbrella had one key objective: speed up the process of corroborating the information and establishing the credibility of the witnesses. Without this, no judge would approve the final deal. Crucially, while the company could supply hard evidence of the illicit payments, only the individual executives could provide the necessary context to fully grasp the dynamics of the bribery scheme and assign individual criminal responsibility. For example, the executives were the only ones who could reconstruct the sequence of informal meetings or decipher the pseudonyms used in the company's parallel accounting system to identify each client. It therefore made sense to unify both sets of negotiations and corroboration exercises.

As negotiations resumed, Vela also inaugurated a new chapter in the relationship between the Lava Jato taskforce and the *procuradores*. By law, any deal on the criminal front had to be accompanied by a deal on the civil front (i.e., the fine). It was therefore essential to coordinate efforts between government branches, something that had been missing under Castro. The prosecutors agreed that the *procuradores* would be solely responsible for negotiating the fine and the payment scheme. While the law allowed the prosecutors to take over this aspect of the process, the job was simply too complex, and Vela recognized that his team lacked the necessary time or technical expertise. In addition, because the *procuradores* were now strictly constrained by law in what they could demand from the company, in terms of both a maximum and a minimum amount, they were in a better position to negotiate a fine that would be high enough to insulate the deal from criticism, and low enough to avoid crippling the company. And given that the prosecutors' main goal was to extract information, not money, their threats to the company regarding the lowest fine they were prepared to offer would be less credible. The *procuradores*, for their part, came to terms with the idea that negotiating the fine in the context of a plea deal with the prosecutors was the best way to make sure the company paid. With the new formula in place, the *procuradores* needed the information obtained by the prosecutors to estimate damages. Cooperation was therefore essential. This confluence of interests made it possible to agree on a joint strategy.

The *produradores* established damages for S./ 610 million and refused to budge. The company protested, turning to Vela. But in line with the strategy agreed beforehand, Vela and his team refused to get involved with the financial negotiations. Vela thus forced the company to sort things out with the *procuradores*, and only then come back to negotiate immunity from prosecution and an end to the ban on the company's ability to do business with the state. Odebrecht finally agreed to pay S./ 610 million. While much lower than the amounts floated in previous months, it was still a debilitating figure. In order to make sure the company could pay, the *procuradores* accepted a proposal for a flexible payment plan and removed an asset embargo hanging over the company. The prosecutors then agreed to offer full immunity from prosecution and to lift the aforementioned ban. They also agreed to a dynamic deal, whereby the benefits wouldn't be automatically suspended should the investigators discover new crimes. In doing so, Vela accepted that the company would not disclose everything at once. Finally, Odebrecht agreed to give information about the corruption scheme mounted to secure four major infrastructure projects (the Vía Evitamiento in Cusco, the Costa Verde in El Callao, the Inter-Oceanic Highway and the Metro de Lima), and to surrender the information saved in the My Web Day and Drousys servers, which included (among other things) information about the payments made through the infamous Division of Structured Operations.[9]

Backlash

Because the company had to establish credibility and reliability, the flow of information accelerated as the final negotiations progressed. With new evidence in hand, in October 2018 a prosecutor filed the aforementioned pretrial detention request against Keiko Fujimori and conducted an unprecedented search in her party's headquarters. This was a daring move: Fujimori's party still controlled Congress and was well-known

[9] This was the division set-up to manage relations with politicians and government officials across Latin America.

for having allies in the upper echelons of the judiciary and prosecution services. The *Cuellos Blancos* scandal had revealed that much. The pretrial detention, coupled with the imminence of a deal, put the establishment on high alert, and a fierce backlash ensued. On December 31, 2018, Chief Prosecutor Pedro Chavarry dismissed Vela and one of his lieutenants, Prosecutor Pérez, accusing them of mishandling the relationship with Odebrecht. When Chavarry promoted Vela back in July as a gesture, in an attempt to weather the storm unleashed by *Cuellos Blancos*, he expected to be able to control the new team. In particular, Chavarry, whose links to the network of judicial clientelism eventually came to light, hoped the investigation would not move too far away from its initial focus and implicate Fujimori. In so doing, he fatally underestimated the prosecutors' commitment to the case and their willingness to pursue all lines of inquiry.

What followed was an impressive display of media savviness on the part of the embattled prosecutors. By going public, Vela and Pérez managed to engineer mass support for what until that day had been a relatively obscure prosecutorial taskforce, and also secured the backing of important political personalities. This public support became particularly visible on January 2, 2019 (three days after they were fired). A huge group of protesters marched to the headquarters of the prosecution services to demand Chavarry's resignation. This unprecedented display of support for judicial actors was reinforced by the *Junta de Fiscales Supremos* (Board of Supreme Prosecutors), which immediately asked for Chavarry's resignation. These developments forced Chavarry to reinstate Vela and Pérez. He resigned a few days later. Far from being a function of systemic political support for the investigation, the survival of the Lava Jato team, and the continuing momentum behind the case, were thus the result of daring prosecutorial defensive efforts.

A reinvigorated Lava Jato taskforce sealed the deal with Odebrecht on February 15, 2019 at the Peruvian consulate in São Paulo. Immediately after, Jorge Barata confirmed that Odebrecht had supported former President García's campaign, corroborated the existence of a cartel in the construction sector, proved that Odebrecht had bribed Toledo to secure the Inter-Oceanic Highway project, and showed that former Lima mayor Susana Villarán knew of Odebrecht's contributions to her campaigns. In other words, no one was spared. The prosecutors thus confirmed that they had been right to see the deal as the main pillar of the investigative strategy.

Their problems, however, did not end there. While big chunks of the network of judicial corruption revealed by *Cuellos Blancos* were dismantled surprisingly fast, key members still survived as senior prosecutors and Supreme Court justices, and were prepared to go to great lengths to protect some of the defendants. Had it not been for timely media exposés detailing the links between these individuals, the *Cuellos Blancos* network and Fujimorismo, it is possible that in July 2019 the Supreme Court would have endorsed the request of a senior prosecutor, himself involved in *Cuellos Blancos*, asking for Keiko Fujimori's release from pretrial detention. Such a move would most certainly have torpedoed efforts to deepen the campaign finances stream of the Lava Jato inquiry, and with it the most productive pillar of the entire investigation.[10] With the Supreme Court option now out of bounds, Fujimoristas trained their eyes on the Constitutional Court, which had to decide on a *habeas corpus* request filed by Fujimori's lawyers. Their goal was to establish a precedent against pretrial detentions and the classification of the Lava Jato crimes as instances of "money laundering." To do so, in September 2019 Fujimorista members of parliament tried to manipulate the appointment of new Constitutional Court justices. But like previous attacks against judicial institutions, the move failed. In fact, it triggered a full-blown inter-branch conflict with the executive, which ended with the dissolution of Congress, Fujimori's only remaining institutional stronghold.

These developments suggest that the judicialization of corruption often leads to extreme attempts to politicize the judiciary, but that overt and unscrupulous forms of backlash against the courts can backfire. Not all the avenues chosen to fight back against the Lava Jato taskforce, however, were equally clumsy or ineffective. Discursively, at least, opponents of the investigation have consistently embraced fairness and "rule of law" arguments to discredit the prosecutors. First, critics framed the deal with Odebrecht as a capitulation to foreign business interests. The focus was almost invariably on the fine, which they deemed too low. For example, according to Luz Salgado, a member of the Fujimorista parliamentary group, "[the prosecutors] don't know how the debts are going to be paid, [...] what I see is mostly a concern for the interests of the company instead of our own." Her colleague Rosa Bartra agreed: the prosecution

[10] One Supreme Court justice mentioned in the *Cuellos Blancos* wiretaps had to recuse himself from the case, which delayed the proceedings. The senior prosecutor who advised the court to release her was also implicated in the scandal.

is "giving everything to a criminal organization that has perverted our system." Second, shortly after the courts had reviewed and approved the deal, reporters revealed that the Drousys server contained records of bribes that the company had failed to confess. This was an excellent opportunity to depict the prosecutors as naïve at best or biased in favor of the company at worst. While the law didn't leave prosecutors with much wiggle room to impose a higher fine, and thus insulate the deal from the first line of attack, their negotiating strategy did open the door for the second line of attack when they agreed to a deal that would not punish the company for lying or withholding information. Their calculation, of course, was that this would at least ensure that the cases included in the original agreement could be prosecuted swiftly.

Partisan objections against plea bargains and pretrial detentions were also picked up by independent journalists and lawyers. Going forward, as the investigation struggles to deal with the complications brought about by the Covid-19 pandemic (e.g., most defendants were released from prison on health grounds), as well as with the fallout of the controversial deal and Lava Jato's role in the impeachment of President Vizcarra in 2020,[11] efforts to discredit the investigation will continue and perhaps become more effective. These developments underscore the risks of a prosecutorial strategy that is reliant on daring and occasionally questionable decisions. If the prosecutors can't show results fast enough, key actors, including the mass public, may quickly start to lose faith in the taskforce. They may begin to wonder whether the price paid for the company's secrets was the right one, and whether protracted pretrial detentions and other controversial tactics are actually being used to conduct more effective inquiries or to simulate effectiveness, all at the expense of the rule of law.

CONCLUSION

At the time of writing, Peru's Lava Jato is still ongoing and the taskforce is beginning to send the main cases to trial, including the one against Keiko Fujimori. As society awaits a resolution to the drama, the political

[11] The opposition succeeded in impeaching Vizcarra after a source leaked to the press that the Lava Jato taskforce was finalizing a plea deal that would show the president had accepted bribes when he was governor of Moquegua. Several opinion leaders accused the prosecutors of "playing politics" or "playing dirty" instead of pursuing justice. See Luis Pásara, "Los fiscales han jugado sucio," *La Mula* (November 17, 2020).

establishment will continue in a state of utter disarray. The wounds inflicted by the most ambitious and consequential anti-corruption probe in history won't heal fast.

The judicialization of corruption in Peru pitted a small group of committed prosecutors against a large portion of the country's political class. The Lava Jato taskforce also had to respond to obstructionist maneuvers orchestrated by high-ranking members of the judicial and prosecutorial establishments. A key takeaway from this story is that prosecutorial agency should be taken seriously when trying to understand why the inquiry gained momentum, often against all odds. It does not all come down to the preferences of key political actors or the balance of power between government and opposition. The choices prosecutors made along the way, especially their willingness and capacity to innovate and abandon bureaucratic comfort zones, had an impact on the kind of evidence that came to light and how much they could expand the scope of the investigation. Prosecutors who were well-intentioned but reticent to rely on pretrial detentions, strike plea bargains or court foreign actors would not have achieved as much. And as in any story that emphasizes agency, contingency played a central role. For example, given the complexity of the negotiations with Odebrecht, it is not hard to come up with a long list of things that could have gone terribly wrong (e.g., failure to coordinate with the *procuradores*; failure to triangulate information from different plea deals to corroborate confessions; etc.). Similarly, had the *Cuellos Blancos* network not been exposed, the Lava Jato taskforce would have probably faced more effective opposition from within the judiciary and the prosecution services.

Not everything, of course, comes down to agency. Three aspects of the institutional and political environment emerge as particularly important to understand why this innovative and ambitious prosecutorial strategy was possible. In other words, superstructural reforms of the kind reviewed in this book's Introduction do play a role in reinforcing the ability of judicial actors to exercise accountability functions. First, like many other Latin American countries, from the late 1970s Peru introduced a series of important independence-enhancing reforms to the prosecution services.[12] In 1979, for example the Ministerio Público became autonomous from the executive. As a result, the chief prosecutor exercises a high degree of control over criminal prosecution policies. A key

[12] The process was similar to the one that Da Ros and Taylor describe in Chapter 10. For a more general account of prosecutorial reforms in Latin America, see Michel (2018).

prerogative in this regard is the ability to create special taskforces that specialize in the investigation of certain crimes. A Lava Jato taskforce could therefore be created relatively quickly. Crucially, the investigation benefited from the appointment of prosecutors with experience in teams tasked with investigating various forms of macro-criminality. These teams had been set up during a process of organizational strengthening that started in the aftermath of the democratic transition, at a time when the Peruvian state was trying to reckon with Fujimori's legacy of corruption, human rights violations and judicial capture (Dargent 2005, 2009; Gonzalez-Ocantos et al. forthcoming). It is still worth remembering, however, that Chief Prosecutor Chavarry made use of this same prerogative to try to get rid of committed investigators in December 2018. The skills and commitment displayed by Vela and his team are hence still important to understand why, once appointed, the taskforce was able to survive and perform its accountability functions. In other words, superstructural change alone is insufficient to enhance the accountability potential of judicial institutions.

Second, several key legislative changes equipped the prosecutors with better tools to investigate corruption. For example, the Code of Criminal Procedures was reformed in the 2000s, marking a transition to the accusatorial model, which strengthens prosecutorial power (Langer 2004; Michel 2018). The new code also allows for plea bargain agreements in cases of macro-criminality, including criminal conspiracies, terrorism, money laundering, cyber-crime, crimes against humanity and human trafficking. More recently, Law 30-373, passed in March 2018, further regulated corporate plea bargains and made it easier to strike leniency agreements with companies. But here again prosecutorial agency also played a role: had it not been for the speed at which the investigation had progressed up to that point, and the damage this inflicted on the construction sector, the government would not have felt the pressure to facilitate corporate cooperation via changes in the law and thus save the economy from paralysis. Vela's dexterity and zeal was also critical when it came to negotiating the actual deal, which was by all accounts unprecedented.

Third, the longstanding weakness of Peruvian political parties also helped the prosecutors (Levitsky and Cameron 2003; Munoz 2019). Politicians such as former presidents Toledo and Humala or former Lima mayor Susana Villarán had few political resources to defend themselves. Those who found themselves in a better position because of their leverage in the legislature, i.e. Fujimori and García, or because they controlled the presidency, i.e. Kuczynski, did not fare much better. Fujimoristas and Apristas first tried to capitalize on the investigation to discredit Toledo and Humala, and further weaken President Kuczynski. Later on, when the prosecutors trained their eyes on Fujimori and García, their parties relied on Congress and connections in the upper echelons of the judicial and prosecutorial establishments to obstruct the inquiry. These tactics, however, proved too clumsy, and led, for example, to the dissolution of Congress in 2019 and Fujimori's loss of her main institutional asset in the elections called to replace the defunct legislature in 2020. The underlying feebleness of all political organizations in the country likely facilitated this poor strategic planning and exacerbated political tensions, leading politicians to destroy each other in the process. Prosecutors were simply smart enough to take advantage of a situation they unintentionally helped create.

As we saw, however, the kind of innovation that allowed prosecutors to remain standing in a context in which everyone else suffered severe political defeats was not without costs for the political system. This suggests that judicial actors that enjoy more power and are highly committed to their accountability mission may not always benefit democracy. Where some see unwavering determination to fight corruption, others see serious affronts to the rule of law, especially in the way defendants are treated, as well as risks for the stability and openness of democratic competition. This raises uncomfortable questions about the real implications and value of horizontal accountability efforts via the decisive judicialization of grand corruption. This is especially so in light of the political devastation that the Lava Jato investigation produced in a short period of time, contributing to the downfall of two presidents, unworkable interbranch relations, and greater political fragmentation and party weakness.[13]

Furthermore, the inevitability of backlash, and the continued presence of rogue actors in senior judicial and prosecutorial roles despite ambitious institutional reforms mean that anti-corruption prosecutors can easily fall prey to politicization. This obviously risks undermining the prestige of the system of horizontal accountability, and limits the reach of punitive outcomes in the medium to long term. Vela and his team may be unique personalities in the Peruvian judicial system. While the *Cuellos Blancos* case did help remove some figures with the power to block or stop the

[13] For example, the 2020 parliamentary elections resulted in the rise of hitherto marginal far-right parties and extremely high levels of fragmentation.

inquiry on appeal, it is still unclear whether the case will lead to convictions. And even if we leave aside judicial corruption, trial-level judges and prosecutors may eventually question the admissibility or quality of evidence obtained through unusual channels, and find issue with the way defendants were treated in the investigative phase. These are all problems born out of the aggressive and creative investigative strategy the taskforce deemed necessary in order to succeed. Going forward, the absence of clear results will most likely multiply the voices against the investigation and raise questions about whether zeal and unorthodoxy were actually worth it.

References

Bertossa, B. (2003). Difficulties Encountered by the Judiciary: A Summary of Key Issues. In Asian Development Bank, ed., *Effective Prosecution of Corruption*. Manila: Asian Development Bank, pp. 9–12.

Conaghan, C. M. (2012). Prosecuting Presidents: The Politics within Ecuador's Corruption Cases. *Journal of Latin American Studies* 44(4), 649–78.

Dargent, E. (2005). Juzgando a los Señores: Reflexiones sobre el Proceso Anticorrupción en el Perú. In F. Portocarrero, ed., *El Pacto Infame: la Persistencia de la Corrupción en el Perú*. Lima: Red para el Estudio de las Ciencias Sociales en el Perú (IEP, PUCP, UP).

(2009). Determinants of Judicial Independence: Lessons from Three "Cases" of Constitutional Courts in Peru (1982–2007). *Journal of Latin American Studies* 41(2), 251–78.

Della-Porta, D. & Vannucci, A. (2007). Corruption and Anti-Corruption: The Political Defeat of "Clean Hands" in Italy. *West European Politics* 30(4), 830–53.

Gonzalez-Ocantos, E. & Baraybar, V. (2019). Lava Jato beyond Borders: The Uneven Performance Anti-Corruption Judicial Efforts in Latin America. *Taiwan Journal of Democracy* 15(1), 63–89.

Gonzalez-Ocantos, E. Muñoz Chirinos, P., Pavao, N. & Baraybar, V. (forthcoming) The Criminalization of Corruption in Latin America: Prosecutors, and Voters during Lava Jato. New York: Cambridge University Press.

Helmke, G., Jeong, Y., Kim, J. & Ozturk, S. (2019). Upending Impunity: Explaining Post-Tenure Presidential Prosecutions in Latin America. Unpublished manuscript.

Klinkhammer, J. (2013). On the Dark Side of the Code: Organizational Challenges to an Effective Anti-Corruption Strategy. *Crime, Law and Social Change*, 60, 191–208.

Langer, M. (2004). From Legal Transplant to Legal Translations: The Globalization of Plea Bargaining and the Americanization Thesis in Criminal Procedure. *Harvard International Law Journal* 45(1), 1–64.

León, R. (2019). *Vizcarra: Retrato de un poder en construcción*. Lima: Debate.

Levitsky, S. & Cameron, M. A. (2003). Democracy without Parties? Political Parties and Regime Change in Fujimori's Peru. *Latin American Politics and Society* 45(3), 1–33.

Maravall, J. (2003). The Rule of Law as a Political Weapon. In J. Maravall & A. Przeworski, eds., *Democracy and the Rule of Law*. Cambridge: Cambridge University Press.

Martini, M. (2015). *Fighting Grand Corruption*. New York: Transparency International.

Michel, V. (2018). *Prosecutorial Accountability and Victims' Rights in Latin America*. Cambridge: Cambridge University Press.

Moro, S. (2004). Considerações sobre a operação Mani Pulite. *Revista CEJ* 8(26), 6–62.

Muñoz, P. (2019). *Buying Audiences: Clientelism and Electoral Campaigns When Parties are Weak*. Cambridge: Cambridge University Press.

Pei, M. (2018). How Not to Fight Corruption: Lessons from China. *Daedalus* 147 (3), 216–30.

Popova, M. & Post, V. (2018). Prosecuting High-Level Corruption in Eastern Europe. *Communist and Post-Communist Studies* 51(3), 231–44.

Ríos-Figueroa, J. (2019). Judicial Independence in Judicial Hierarchies: Civil Law Systems. In L. Demetrius & S. Sterett, eds., *Research Handbook on Law and Courts*. London: Elgar Publishing, Chapter 7.

Roca, D. (2019). *Lava Jato en el Congreso, la corrupción en el Perú*. Lima: Revuelta.

Rotberg, R. (2017). *The Corruption Cure*. Princeton, NJ: Princeton University Press.

Sberna, S. & Vannucci, A. (2013). It's the Politics Stupid! The Politicization of Anti-Corruption in Italy. *Crime, Law and Social Change* 60(5), 565–93.

Shen-Bayh, F. (2018). Strategies of Repression: Judicial and Extrajudicial Methods of Autocratic Survival. *World Politics* 70(3), 321–57.

Sifuentes, M. (2019). *K.O. PPK: Caída pública y vida secreta de Pedro Pablo Kuczynski*. Lima: Planeta.

US Department of Justice. (2016). *Odebrecht Plea Agreement*. New York: US Department of Justice.

Index

CPSIA information can be obtained
at www.ICGtesting.com
Printed in the USA
LVHW100309200922
728806LV00003B/104